# ACCA

## Paper F5

## Performance management

Complete Text

ACCA
Approved Publisher

KAPLAN

PUBLISHING

## British library cataloguing-in-publication data

A catalogue record for this book is available from the British Library.

Published by:
Kaplan Publishing
Unit 2 The Business Centre
Molly Millars Lane
Wokingham
Berkshire
RG41 2QZ

ISBN 978-1-84710-237-9

© FTC Kaplan Limited, 2007

Printed and bound in Great Britain by William Clowes Ltd, Beccles, Suffolk

Acknowledgements

We are grateful to the Association of Chartered Certified Accountants and the Chartered Institute of Management Accountants for permission to reproduce past examination questions. The answers have been prepared by Kaplan Publishing.

# Contents

KAPLAN PUBLISHING

# How to use these materials

These Kaplan Publishing learning materials have been carefully designed to make your learning experience as easy as possible and to give you the best chances of success in your examinations.

The product range contains a number of features to help you in the study process. They include:

1   Detailed study guide and syllabus objectives
2   Description of the examination
3   Study skills and revision guidance
4   Complete text or essential text
5   Question practice

**The sections on the study guide, the syllabus objectives, the examination and study skills should all be read before you commence your studies. They are designed to familiarise you with the nature and content of the examination and give you tips on how best to approach your learning.**

**The complete text or essential text** comprises the main learning materials and gives guidance as to the importance of topics and where other related resources can be found. Each chapter includes:

- The learning objectives contained in each chapter, which have been carefully mapped to the examining body's own syllabus learning objectives or outcomes. You should use these to check you have a clear understanding of all the topics on which you might be assessed in the examination.

- The chapter diagram provides a visual reference for the content in the chapter, giving an overview of the topics and how they link together.

- The content for each topic area commences with a brief explanation or definition to put the topic into context before covering the topic in detail. You should follow your studying of the content with a review of the illustration/s. These are worked examples which will help you to understand better how to apply the content for the topic.

- Test your understanding sections provide an opportunity to assess your understanding of the key topics by applying what you have learned to short questions. Answers can be found at the back of each chapter.

- Summary diagrams complete each chapter to show the important links between topics and the overall content of the paper. These diagrams should be used to check that you have covered and understood the core topics before moving on.

- Question practice is provided at the back of each text.

To help you find your way through the material you will find useful icons throughout each chapter:

| Definition | | Key definitions that you will need to learn from the core content. |
|---|---|---|
| Key exam points | | Identifies topics that are key to success and are often examined. |
| Tricky topic | | When reviewing these areas care should be taken and all illustrations and test your understanding exercises should be completed to ensure that the topic is understood. |
| Expandable text | | Expandable text provides you with additional information about a topic area and may help you gain a better understanding of the core content. Essential text users can access this additional content on-line (read it where you need further guidance or skip over when you are happy with a topic). |
| Illustration | e.g | Worked examples help you understand the core content better. |
| Test your understanding | | Exercises for you to complete to ensure that you have understood the topics just learned. |

KAPLAN PUBLISHING

## On-line subscribers

Our on-line resources are designed to increase the flexibility of your learning materials and provide you with immediate feedback on how your studies are progressing.

If you are subscribed to our on-line resources you will find:

1   On-line referenceware: reproduces your Complete or Essential Text on-line, giving you anytime, anywhere access.

2   On-line testing: provides you with additional on-line objective testing so you can practice what you have learned further.

3   On-line performance management: immediate access to your on-line testing results. Review your performance by key topics and chart your achievement through the course relative to your peer group.

Ask your local customer services staff if you are not already a subscriber and wish to join.

# Paper introduction

## Paper background

The aim of ACCA Paper F5, **Performance Management**, is to develop knowledge and skills in the application of management accounting techniques to quantitative and qualitative information, for planning, decision making, performance evaluation and control.

## Objectives of the syllabus

- Explain, apply and evaluate cost accounting techniques.

- Select and appropriately apply decision-making techniques to evaluate business choices and promote efficient and effective use of scarce business resources, appreciating the risks and uncertainty inherent in business and resolving those risks.

- Apply budgeting techniques and evaluate alternative methods of budgeting, planning and control.

- Use standard costing systems to measure and control business performance and to identify remedial action.

- Assess the performance of a business from both a financial and non-financial viewpoint, appreciating the problems of controlling divisionalised businesses and the importance of allowing for external aspects.

## Core areas of the syllabus

- Specialist cost and management accounting techniques.

- Decision-making techniques.

- Budgeting.

- Standard costing and variances analysis.

- Performance measurement and control.

# Syllabus objectives

We have reproduced the ACCA's syllabus below, showing where the objectives are explored within this book. Within the chapters, we have broken down the extensive information found in the syllabus into easily digestible and relevant sections, called **Content Objectives**. These correspond to the objectives at the beginning of each chapter.

| Syllabus learning objective | Chapter reference |
|---|---|

**A  SPECIALIST COST AND MANAGEMENT ACCOUNTING TECHNIQUES**

**1  Activity based costing**

(a)  Identify appropriate cost drivers under ABC.[1]  1
(b)  Calculate costs per driver and per unit using ABC.[2]  1
(c)  Compare ABC and traditional methods of overhead absorption based on production units, labour hours or machine hours.[2]  1
(d)  Explain the implications of switching to ABC for pricing, sales strategy, performance management and decision making.[2]  1

**2  Target costing**

(a)  Derive a target cost in manufacturing and service industries.[2]  1
(b)  Explain the difficulties of using target costing in service industries.[2]  1
(c)  Explain the implications of using target costing on pricing, cost control and performance management.[2]  1
(d)  Suggest how a target cost gap might be closed.[2]  1

**3  Life-cycle costing**

(a)  Identify the costs involved at different stages of the lifecycle.[2]  1
(b)  Explain the implications of lifecycle costing on pricing, performance management and decision making.[2]  1

**4  Back-flush accounting**

(a)  Describe the process of back-flush accounting and contrast with traditional process accounting.[2]  1
(b)  Explain the implications of back-flush accounting on performance management and the control of a manufacturing process.[2]  1
(c)  Identify the benefits of the introduction of back-flush accounting.[2]  1
(d)  Evaluate the decision to switch to back-flush accounting from traditional process control.[3]  1

**4    Quantitative analysis in budgeting**

(a)  Analyse fixed and variable cost elements from total cost data (high/low and regression).[2]                        8

(b)  Explain the use of forecasting techniques. (Techniques: time series, simple average growth models and estimates based on judgement and experience.) Predict a future value from provided time series analysis data using both additive and proportional data.[2]          8

(c)  Estimate the learning effect and apply the learning curve to a budgetary problem. This includes calculations on steady states.[2]                        8

(d)  Discuss the reservations with the learning curve.[2]     8

(e)  Apply expected values and explain the problems and benefits.[2]

(f)  Explain the benefits and dangers inherent in using spreadsheets in budgeting.[1]

**5    Behavioural aspects of budgeting**

(a)  Identify the factors which influence behaviour.[2]       6

(b)  Discuss the issues surrounding setting the difficulty level for a budget.[2]                        6

(c)  Explain the benefits and difficulties of the participation of employees in the negotiation of targets.[2]        6

**D    STANDARD COSTING AND VARIANCES ANALYSIS**

**1    Budgeting and standard costing**

(a)  Explain the use of standard costs.[2]               9

(b)  Outline the methods used to derive standard costs and discuss the different types of costs possible.[2]         9

(c)  Explain the importance of flexing budgets in performance management.[2]                  9

(d)  Prepare budgets and standards that allow for waste and idle time.[2]                        9

(e)  Explain and apply the principle of controllability in the performance management system.[2]             9

(f)  Prepare a flexed budget and comment on its usefulness.[2]                        9

**2    Basic variances and operating statements**

(a)  Calculate, identify the cause of and interpret basic variances:[1]                        9

(i)   sales price and volume

(ii)  materials total, price and usage

(iii) labour total, rate and efficiency

(iv) variable overhead total, expenditure and efficiency

(v)  fixed overhead total, expenditure and, where appropriate, volume, capacity and efficiency.

The superscript numbers in square brackets indicate the intellectual depth at which the subject area could be assessed within the examination. Level 1 (knowledge and comprehension) broadly equates with the Knowledge module, Level 2 (application and analysis) with the Skills module and Level 3 (synthesis and evaluation) to the Professional level. However, lower level skills can continue to be assessed as you progress through each module and level.

# The examination

## Examination format

Paper F5, Performance management, seeks to examine candidates' understanding of how to manage the performance of a business.

The paper builds on the knowledge acquired in Paper F2, Management accounting, and prepares those candidates who will decide to go on to study Paper P5, Advanced performance management, at the Professional level.

There will be calculation and discursive elements to the paper. Generally the paper will seek to draw questions from as many of the syllabus sections as possible:

|  | Number of marks |
|---|---|
| Four 25-mark questions | 100 |

Total time allowed: 3 hours with 15 minutes reading time

## Paper-based examination tips

Spend the fifteen minutes of reading time **reading the paper** and planning your answers. During the reading time you may annotate the question paper but not write in the answer booklet. In particular you should use this time to ensure that you understand the requirements, highlighting key verbs, consider which parts of the syllabus are relevant and plan key calculations.

**Divide the time** you spend on questions in proportion to the marks on offer. One suggestion **for this examination** is to allocate 1 and 4/5 minutes to each mark available, so a 10-mark question should be completed in approximately 18 minutes.

Spend the last **five minutes** reading through your answers and **making any additions or corrections.**

If you **get completely stuck** with a question, leave space in your answer book and **return to it later**.

If you do not understand what a question is asking, state your assumptions. Even if you do not answer in precisely the way the examiner hoped, you should be given some credit, if your assumptions are reasonable.

You should do everything you can to make things easy for the marker. The marker will find it easier to identify the points you have made if your answers are legible.

**Case studies:** Most questions will be based on specific scenarios. To construct a good answer first identify the areas in which there are problems, outline the main principles/theories you are going to use to answer the question, and then apply the principles/theories to the case. It is essential that you taylor your comments to the scenario given.

**Essay questions:** Some questions may contain short essay-style requirements. Your answer should have a clear structure. It should contain a brief introduction, a main section and a conclusion. Be concise. It is better to write a little about a lot of different points than a great deal about one or two points.

**Computations:** It is essential to include all your workings in your answers. Many computational questions require the use of a standard format. Be sure you know these formats thoroughly before the exam and use the layouts that you see in the answers given in this book and in model answers.

**Reports, memos and other documents**: some questions ask you to present your answer in the form of a report or a memo or other document. So use the correct format - there could be easy marks to gain here.

## Study skills and revision guidance

This section aims to give guidance on how to study for your ACCA exams and to give ideas on how to improve your existing study techniques.

### Preparing to study

### Set your objectives

Before starting to study decide what you want to achieve – the type of pass you wish to obtain. This will decide the level of commitment and time you need to dedicate to your studies.

### Devise a study plan

Determine which times of the week you will study.

Split these times into sessions of at least one hour for study of new material. Any shorter periods could be used for revision or practice.

Put the times you plan to study onto a study plan for the weeks from now until the exam and set yourself targets for each period of study – in your sessions make sure you cover the course, course assignments and revision.

If you are studying for more than one paper at a time, try to vary your subjects as this can help you to keep interested and see subjects as part of wider knowledge.

When working through your course, compare your progress with your plan and, if necessary, re-plan your work (perhaps including extra sessions) or, if you are ahead, do some extra revision/practice questions.

## Effective studying

### Active reading

You are not expected to learn the text by rote, rather, you must understand what you are reading and be able to use it to pass the exam and develop good practice. A good technique to use is SQ3Rs – Survey, Question, Read, Recall, Review:

1   **Survey** the chapter – look at the headings and read the introduction, summary and objectives, so as to get an overview of what the chapter deals with.

2   **Question** – whilst undertaking the survey, ask yourself the questions that you hope the chapter will answer for you.

3   **Read** through the chapter thoroughly, answering the questions and making sure you can meet the objectives. Attempt the exercises and activities in the text, and work through all the examples.

4   **Recall** – at the end of each section and at the end of the chapter, try to recall the main ideas of the section/chapter without referring to the text. This is best done after a short break of a couple of minutes after the reading stage.

5   **Review** – check that your recall notes are correct.

You may also find it helpful to re-read the chapter to try to see the topic(s) it deals with as a whole.

### Note-taking
Taking notes is a useful way of learning, but do not simply copy out the text. The notes must:

*   be in your own words
*   be concise
*   cover the key points
*   be well-organised
*   be modified as you study further chapters in this text or in related ones.

Trying to summarise a chapter without referring to the text can be a useful way of determining which areas you know and which you don't.

**Three ways of taking notes:**

**Summarise the key points of a chapter.**

**Make linear notes** – a list of headings, divided up with subheadings listing the key points. If you use linear notes, you can use different colours to highlight key points and keep topic areas together. Use plenty of space to make your notes easy to use.

**Try a diagrammatic form** – the most common of which is a mind-map. To make a mind-map, put the main heading in the centre of the paper and put a circle around it. Then draw short lines radiating from this to the main sub-headings, which again have circles around them. Then continue the process from the sub-headings to sub-sub-headings, advantages, disadvantages, etc.

**Highlighting and underlining**
You may find it useful to underline or highlight key points in your study text – but do be selective. You may also wish to make notes in the margins.

**Revision**
The best approach to revision is to revise the course as you work through it. Also try to leave four to six weeks before the exam for final revision. Make sure you cover the whole syllabus and pay special attention to those areas where your knowledge is weak. Here are some recommendations:

**Read through the text and your notes again** and condense your notes into key phrases. It may help to put key revision points onto index cards to look at when you have a few minutes to spare.

**Review any assignments** you have completed and look at where you lost marks -put more work into those areas where you were weak.

**Practise exam standard questions** under timed conditions. If you are short of time, list the points that you would cover in your answer and then read the model answer, but do try to complete at least a few questions under exam conditions.

Also **practise producing answer plans** and comparing them to the model answer.

If you are stuck on a topic find somebody (a tutor) to explain it to you.

**Read good newspapers and professional journals**, especially ACCA's **Student Accountant** – this can give you an advantage in the exam.

Ensure you **know the structure of the examination** – how many questions and of what type you will be expected to answer. During your revision attempt all the different styles of questions you may be asked.

## Further reading

You can find further reading and technical articles under the student section of ACCA's website.

## Formulae sheet

### Learning curve

$$Y = ax^b$$

Where  y = average cost per batch
a = cost of first batch
x = total number of batches produced
b = learning factor (log LR/log 2)
LR = the learning rate as a decimal

### Regression analysis

$$y = a + bx$$

$$b = \frac{n\sum xy - \sum x \sum y}{n\sum x^2 - (\sum x)^2}$$

$$a = \frac{\sum y}{n} - \frac{b\sum x}{n}$$

$$r = \frac{n\sum xy - \sum x \sum y}{\sqrt{(n\sum x^2 - (\sum x)^2)(n\sum y^2 - (\sum y)^2)}}$$

### Demand curve

$$P = a - bQ$$

$$b = \frac{\text{change in price}}{\text{change in quantity}}$$

a = price when Q = 0

KAPLAN PUBLISHING

# Advanced costing methods

## Chapter learning objectives

Upon completion of this chapter you will be able to:

- explain what is meant by the term cost driver

- identify appropriate cost drivers under activity-based costing (ABC)

- calculate costs per driver and per unit using (ABC)

- compare ABC and traditional methods of overhead absorption based on production units, labour hours or machine hours

- explain the implications of switching to ABC on pricing, performance management and decision making

- explain what is meant by the term 'target cost' in both manufacturing and service industries

- derive a target cost in both manufacturing and service industries

- explain the difficulties of using target costing in service industries

- explain the implications of using target costing on pricing, cost control and performance management

- describe the target cost gap

- suggest how a target cost gap might be closed

- explain what is meant by the term 'life-cycle costing' in a manufacturing industry

- identify the costs involved at different stages of the life-cycle

- explain the implications of life-cycle costing on pricing, performance management and decision making

- describe the process of back-flush accounting and contrast with traditional process accounting

- explain, for a manufacturing business, the implications of back-flush accounting on performance management

- evaluate the decision to switch to back-flush accounting from traditional process control for a manufacturing business

- explain throughput accounting and the throughput accounting ratio (TPAR), and calculate and interpret, a TPAR

- suggest how a TPAR could be improved

- apply throughput accounting to a given multi-product decision-making problem.

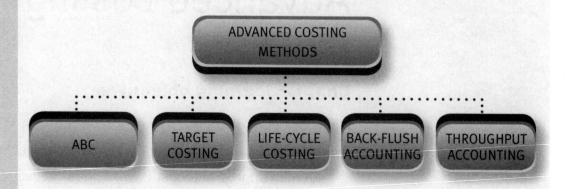

# 1 Activity based costing

## 1.1 Introduction – absorption costing

In F2 we saw how to determine a cost per unit for a product. Key issues of relevance here are the following:

- Firms have the choice of two basic costing methods – marginal costing and absorption costing.

- Under absorption costing it is necessary to absorb overheads into units of production using a suitable basis.

- The main basis of absorption used in F2 questions is direct labour hours. This involves calculating an overhead absorption rate (OAR) for each production department as follows:

$$\text{OAR} = \frac{\text{total budgeted department overheads}}{\text{budgeted department direct labour hours}}$$

- To enable this, all overheads must first be allocated/apportioned/ reapportioned into production departments, again using a suitable basis (e.g. rent on the basis of floor area).

Overhead expenses incurred/budgeted

**Step 1:** Overheads allocated or apportioned to cost centres using suitable bases

Cost centres (usually departments)

**Step 2:** Service centre costs reapportioned to production centres

**Step 3:** Overheads absorbed into units of production using an OAR (usually on the basis of direct labour hours)

Output

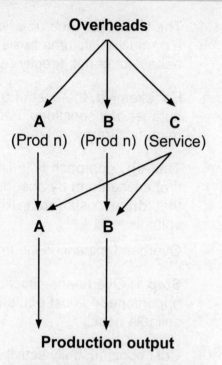

**Overheads**

A        B        C
(Prod n)  (Prod n)  (Service)

A        B

**Production output**

| **Expandable text** |
| --- |

The assumption underlying the traditional method of costing is that overhead expenditure is connected to the volume of production activity.

- This assumption was probably valid many years ago, when production systems were based on labour-intensive or machine-intensive mass production of fairly standard items. Overhead costs were also fairly small relative to direct materials and direct labour costs; therefore any inaccuracy in the charging of overheads to products costs was not significant.

- The assumption is not valid in a complex manufacturing environment, where production is based on smaller customised batches of products, indirect costs are high in relation to direct costs, and a high proportion of overhead activities – such as production scheduling, order handling and quality control – are not related to production volume.

- For similar reasons, traditional absorption costing is not well-suited to the costing of many services.

## 1.2 ABC and cost drivers

ABC is an alternative approach to the traditional method of absorption costing outlined above.

The traditional method of overhead absorption effectively absorbs on a production volume basis and may be misleading for costs where the behaviour is not directly related to production volume.

For example, the cost of quality control may be driven more by the number of inspections made rather than the overall volume of units manufactured.

The ABC approach is to link overhead costs to the products or services that cause them by absorbing overhead costs on the basis of **activities** that '**drive**' costs (**cost drivers**) rather than on the basis of production volume.

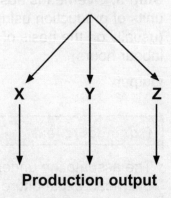

Overhead expenses incurred

**Step 1:** Overheads allocated or apportioned to cost pools using suitable bases

Cost pools (usually activities)

**Step 2:** Overheads absorbed into units of production using cost drivers

- A **cost pool** is an activity that consumes resources and for which overhead costs are identified and allocated. For each cost pool, there should be a cost driver.
- A cost driver is a unit of activity that consumes resources. An alternative definition of a cost driver is a factor influencing the level of cost.

**Expandable text**

The concepts or assumptions underlying ABC are:

- In the long run, all overhead costs are variable. Some overheads are variable in the short run. However, overhead costs do not necessarily vary with production volume or service level.

- Activities consume resources.

- The consumption of resources drives cost.

Products incur overhead costs because of the activities that go into providing the products or services, and these activities are not necessarily related to the volumes of the product that are manufactured. Direct labour hours and machine hours are not the drivers of cost in many modern business environments.

> Understanding the relationship between overhead costs, activities and products (or services) is essential for managing overhead costs and product or service profitability.
>
> Absorption of overheads into unit costs on a volume basis may be misleading, particularly in a modern manufacturing environment where overhead costs are influenced by the diversity and complexity of output rather than volume.

## Illustration 1 – ABC

A company manufactures two products, X and Y. The company uses absorption costing and fixed production costs are absorbed into production costs on a direct labour hour basis.

The budgeted information for the next financial year is as follows:

|  | Product X | Product Y | Total |
|---|---|---|---|
| Production and sales | 2,000 units | 5,000 units |  |
| Direct labour hours per unit | 3 | 2 |  |
| Budgeted direct labour hours | 6,000 | 10,000 | 16,000 |
|  |  |  |  |
| Fixed production costs |  |  | $48,000 |
| Absorption rate per direct labour hour |  |  | $3 |
| Fixed overheads absorbed | $18,000 | $30,000 |  |

**Using ABC**

A review of the incidence of costs has established that the number of setups is the driver of the fixed production costs. Using ABC the fixed production costs would be allocated as follows:

|  | | | |
|---|---|---|---|
| No. of setups per 1,000 units | 8 | 1.6 |  |
| Budgeted setups | 16 | 8 | 24 |
| Cost per setup |  |  | $2,000 |
| Fixed overheads allocated | $32,000 | $16,000 |  |

This difference in costing could have significant implications for pricing, especially if a cost-based approach is used for profit calculation. These, and other implications are discussed in more detail below.

Activity-based costing could provide much more meaningful information about product costs and profits when:

- indirect costs are high relative to direct costs

- products or services are complex

- products or services are tailored to customer specifications

- some products are sold in large numbers and others in small numbers.

### 1.3 Identifying appropriate cost drivers under ABC

Under ABC costs are driven by activities and not production volume.

Typical overheads which are NOT driven by production include the following:

- Setup costs – driven by the number of manufacturing setups.

- Order processing costs – driven by the number of orders.

- Packing department costs – driven by the number of packing orders.

- Engineering department costs – driven by the number of production orders.

- Air conditioning maintenance - number of air conditioning units

### Test your understanding 1

**Identify for a hospital x-ray department possible cost drivers for the following activities:**

- equipment preparation

- patient preparation

- patient aftercare

- film processing

- film reporting.

### Test your understanding 2

Country Travels offers four standard holiday tours, to the north, south, east and west of the country in which it operates. It wants to establish the costs and profitability for each customer on each of the four tours, and thinks that a useful estimate of cost can be obtained using ABC techniques.

The costs of the business have been grouped into the following categories:

| Category | Comments |
| --- | --- |
| • Bookings and invoicing | |
| • Printed materials and maps | |
| • Hotel accommodation and meals | |
| • Cost of tour guides | Tour guides are hired by the day. Tours to each of the different areas vary in length, between 2 days and 7 days. |
| • Entrance costs to tourist sites and centres | |
| • Vehicle hire charges, including drivers | The company pays a bus company a fixed rate for each tour. |
| • Customer services | Experience has shown that customers are twice as likely to complain or raise queries if they are on tours to the north or the east than if they are on tours to the south or the west. |
| • General administration costs | |

**Suggest how a full cost for each customer of the company might be established.**

## 1.4 Calculating costs per driver and per unit using ABC

There are five basic steps in establishing and applying a system of ABC:

**Step 1** Identify activities that consume resources and incur overhead costs.

**Step 2** Allocate overhead costs to the activities that incur them. In this way, each identified activity becomes a cost pool for overhead costs. It is important that overhead costs should be directly allocated to a cost pool. There should not be any arbitrary apportionment of overhead costs.

**Step 3** Determine the cost driver for each activity or cost pool.

Step 4 Collect data about actual activity for the cost driver in each cost pool.

Step 5 Calculate the overhead cost of products or services. This is done by calculating an overhead cost per unit of the cost driver (a cost per unit of activity). Overhead costs are then charged to products or services on the basis of activities used for each product or service.

## Illustration 2 – ABC

A business has identified that the processing of customer orders consumes large amounts of overhead cost. In its ABC system, order handling is therefore a cost pool activity. The cost driver for the activity is the number of orders processed.

The total costs for the activity are $60,000.

| Product | Number of orders | Total number of units ordered |
|---|---|---|
| A | 5 | 5,000 |
| B | 12 | 4,000 |
| C | 4 | 10,000 |
| D | 9 | 21,000 |
| | 30 | 40,000 |

The cost of order processing is $60,000/30 orders = $2,000 per order.

Overhead costs will therefore be charged to products as follows:

| Product | Number of orders | Cost $ |
|---|---|---|
| A | 5 | 10,000 |
| B | 12 | 24,000 |
| C | 4 | 8,000 |
| D | 9 | 18,000 |
| | 30 | 60,000 |

## Test your understanding 3

A company manufactures two products, P and Q. Monthly data relating to production and sales are as follows.

| | Product P | Product Q |
|---|---|---|
| Direct material cost per unit | $15 | $20 |
| Direct labour hours per unit | 1 hour | 2 hours |
| Direct labour cost per unit | $20 | $40 |
| Sales demand | 100 units | 950 units |

Production overheads are $200,000 each month and are absorbed on a direct labour hour basis. The OAR is $100 per direct labour hour.

The management accountant has produced a report on the potential value of ABC as a preferred alternative to the traditional absorption costing system, and has found that there are five main areas of activity that can be said to consume overhead costs. The management accountant has gathered the following monthly information:

| Activity | Total cost $ | Cost driver | Total number | Product P | Product Q |
|---|---|---|---|---|---|
| Setting up | 20,000 | Number of setups | 4 | 1 | 3 |
| Machining | 80,000 | Machine hours | 2,000 | 100 | 1,900 |
| Order handling | 20,000 | Number of orders | 4 | 1 | 3 |
| Quality control | 20,000 | Number of inspections | 5 | 1 | 4 |
| Engineering | 60,000 | Engineering hours | 1,000 | 500 | 500 |
| | 200,000 | | | | |

**Calculate the costs, in total and per unit, for Product P and Product Q, using ABC.**

## 1.5 Comparing costs per driver and per unit using traditional methods and ABC

Traditional absorption costing charges overhead costs to products (or services) in an arbitrary way.

The assumption that overhead expenditure is related to direct labour hours or machine hours in the production departments is no longer realistic **for the vast majority of companies**.

This will lead to very different values of overheads absorbed per unit.

### Illustration 3 – ABC

A manufacturing business produces two products, X and Y. The products are manufactured in batches. The batches differ slightly, in that different designs are used for each product, and each batch is for one particular design of a product.

Production data for a given period are as follows:

| | Product X | Product Y |
|---|---|---|
| Number of units produced | 2,000 | 6,000 |
| Production time | 1,000 hours | 1,500 hours |
| Number of batches | 5 | 3 |

Overhead costs relating to setting up the machinery for each batch run and getting the raw materials ready totalled $40,000.

This information suggests three different ways of apportioning costs:

| Basis / driver | Unit | Production hours | Batches |
|---|---|---|---|
| Driver volume | 8,000 | 2,500 | 8 |
| OAR | $5 per unit | $16 per hour | $5,000 per batch |
| Overheads to X | 2,000×5 = **$10,000** | 1,000×16 = **$16,000** | 5×5,000 = **$25,000** |
| Overheads to Y | 6,000×5 = **$30,000** | 1,500×16 = **$24,000** | 3×5,000 = **$15,000** |

The selection of the cost driver can therefore make a significant difference.

## Test your understanding 4

Cabal makes and sells two products, Plus and Doubleplus. The direct costs of production are $12 for one unit of Plus and $24 per unit of Doubleplus.

Information relating to annual production and sales is as follows:

| | Plus | Doubleplus |
|---|---|---|
| Annual production and sales | 24,000 units | 24,000 units |
| Direct labour hours per unit | 1.0 | 1.5 |
| Number of orders | 10 | 140 |
| Number of batches | 12 | 240 |
| Number of setups per batch | 1 | 3 |
| Special parts per unit | 1 | 4 |

Information relating to production overhead costs is as follows:

| | Cost driver | Annual cost $ |
|---|---|---|
| Setup costs | Number of setups | 73,200 |
| Special parts handling | Number of special parts | 60,000 |
| Other materials handling | Number of batches | 63,000 |
| Order handling | Number of orders | 19,800 |
| Other overheads | - | 216,000 |
| | | 432,000 |

Other overhead costs do not have an identifiable cost driver, and in an ABC system, these overheads would be recovered on a direct labour hours basis.

> (a) Calculate the production cost per unit of Plus and of Doubleplus if the company uses traditional absorption costing and the overheads are recovered on a direct labour hours basis.
>
> (b) Calculate the production cost per unit of Plus and of Doubleplus if the company uses ABC.

## 1.6  Advantages and disadvantages of ABC

ABC has a number of advantages:

- It provides much better insight into what drives overhead costs.

- ABC recognises that overhead costs are not all related to production and sales volume.

- In many businesses, overhead costs are a significant proportion of total costs, and management needs to understand the drivers of overhead costs in order to manage the business properly. Overhead costs can be controlled by managing cost drivers.

- It can be applied to derive realistic costs in a complex business environment.

- ABC can be applied to all overhead costs, not just production overheads.

- ABC can be used just as easily in service costing as in product costing.

Criticisms of ABC:

- It is impossible to allocate all overhead costs to specific activities.

- ABC costs are based on assumptions and simplifications. The choice of both activities and cost drivers might be inappropriate.

- ABC can be more complex to explain to the stakeholders of the costing exercise.

- The benefits obtained from ABC might not justify the costs.

## 1.7  The implications of switching to ABC

The use of ABC has potentially significant commercial implications:

- Pricing can be based on more realistic cost data.

  - The traditional method of absorption of overheads into unit costs on a volume basis may be misleading, with the result that product costs can, potentially, be materially under/over-stated.

  - Thus, where cost plus pricing is in use, products that have been materially under-costed may be priced at levels that generate a loss whilst products that have been materially over-costed may be priced at levels that are uncompetitive.

- Sales strategy can be more soundly based.

    - More realistic product costs as a result of the use of ABC may enable sales staff to:

        - target customers that appeared unprofitable using absorption costing but may be profitable under ABC

        - stop targeting customers or market segments that are now shown to offer low or negative sales margins.

    - Front line sales staff will be able to negotiate prices with greater confidence

    - ABC can be used to review the profitability of products and services with a view to focusing the efforts of sales staff upon those products and services which offer the highest sales margins.

- Performance management and decision making can be improved

    - Research, production and sales effort can be directed towards those products and services which ABC has identified as offering the highest sales margins.

    - ABC can influence decisions as to which:

        - new products/services to develop

        - existing products/services to curtail or drop

        - products/services should be promoted

        - overhead costs to target.

**Expandable text**

Possible applications for management of ABC information:

- Product costs and product profitability are measured more realistically.

- It identifies ways of reducing overhead costs in the longer-term. This is because ABC shows the nature of resource-consuming activities, the costs incurred by each activity and the cost drivers for those activities.

- It identifies activities and costs that do not add value. If an activity does not contribute to the final product or service, the driver of the non-value-adding cost can be identified and eliminated.

**KAPLAN PUBLISHING**

- It can be used to analyse the profitability of individual customers or categories of customer, as well as the profitability of products or services.

- If products or jobs are priced on a cost-plus basis, ABC can help management to make sensible pricing decisions.

- ABC can be used as a basis for budgeting and longer-term forward planning of overhead costs.

### Test your understanding 5

A manufacturing business makes a product in two models, model M1 and model M2. Details of the two products are as follows.

|  | Model M1 | Model M2 |
|---|---|---|
| Annual sales | 8,000 units | 8,000 units |
| Number of sales orders | 60 | 250 |
| Sales price per unit | $54 | $73 |
| Direct material cost per unit | $11 | $21 |
| Direct labour hours per unit | 2.0 hours | 2.5 hours |
| Direct labour rate per hour | $8 | $8 |
| Special parts per unit | 2 | 8 |
| Production batch size | 2,000 units | 100 units |
| Setups per batch | 1 | 3 |
| Issues of material for each batch | 1 | 1 |

| Overhead analysis | $ | Cost driver |
|---|---|---|
| Setup costs | 97,600 | Number of setups |
| Material handling costs | 42,000 | Number of batches |
| Special part handling costs | 50,000 | Number of special parts |
| Customer invoicing costs | 31,000 | Number of sales orders |
| Other overheads | 108,000 | Direct labour hours |
|  | 328,600 |  |

A customer has indicated an interest in placing a large order for either model M1 or M2, and the sales manager wishes to try to sell the higher-priced model M2.

(a) **Calculate the profit per unit for each model, using ABC.**

(b) **Using the information above indicate what advice you would give to the sales manager on the basis of the information provided by your ABC analysis.**

## 2 Targeting costs

### 2.1 Definition of target costing

**Target cost**

A target cost is a cost estimate derived by subtracting a desired profit margin from a competitive market price.

In effect it the opposite of conventional 'cost plus pricing' and is sometimes referred to as 'price minus costing'.

It may be used in both manufacturing and service industries.

The main theme behind target costing is thus not finding what a new product does cost but what it should or needs to cost. The firm can then focus on which costs can be reduced and which can not to see whether such a target cost is achievable. Obviously cost reductions must be seen in the context of quality concerns as well. This will involve product comparisons with the competitors used to set the competitive market price in the first place.

| Illustration 4 – Targeting costs |
| --- |

Real world users:

- Sony
- Toyota
- Swiss watchmakers – Swatch.

| Test your understanding 6 |
| --- |

**Briefly identify the implications for a profit-orientated organisation if it chooses to use cost plus pricing.**

### 2.2 Deriving a target cost

**Steps**

1  Estimate a selling price for a new product that will enable a firm to capture a required share of the market.

2  Reduce this figure by the firm's required level of profit. This could take into account the return required on any new investment and on working capital requirements or could involve a target margin on sales.

3  Produce a target cost figure for product designers to meet.

4  Reduce costs to provide a product that meets that target cost.

## Illustration 5 – Targeting costs

Katy Inc, a toy manufacturer, is about to launch a new type of bicycle on which it requires a Return on Investment of 30%.

Buildings and equipment needed for production are to cost $5,000,000.

Expected sales levels are 40,000 toys pa at a selling price of $67.50 per item Costs are currently estimated to be $32 per unit.

**Required:**

What is the target cost for annual production?

**Solution**

|  | Working | $ |
|---|---|---|
| Revenue | (67.50 × 40,000) | 2,700,000 |
| Target costs | (balancing figure) | (1,200,000) |
|  |  | ————— |
| Target return | (30% × 5,000,000) | 1,500,000 |
|  |  | ————— |

Target cost = $30 per item giving a target cost gap of $2 per unit. The firm would then analyse its budgeted costs to see whether/how costs savings can be made.

## Test your understanding 7

LMN Ltd makes and sells two products, X and Y. Both products are manufactured through two consecutive processes – assembly and finishing. Raw material is input at the commencement of the assembly process. An ABC approach is used in the absorption of product specific conversion costs.

The following estimated information is available for the period ending 31 December 20X5:

|  | Product X | Product Y |
|---|---|---|
| Production/sales (units) | 12,000 | 7,200 |
| Selling price per unit | $75 | $90 |
| Direct material cost per unit | $20 | $20 |
| ABC variable conversion cost per unit |  |  |
|    -   assembly | $20 | $28 |
|    -   finishing | $12 | $24 |
| Product-specific fixed costs | $170,000 | $90,000 |
| Company fixed costs |  | $50,000 |

LMN Ltd uses a minimum contribution/sales (C/S) ratio target of 25% when assessing the viability of a product. In addition, management wish to achieve an overall net profit margin of 12% on sales in this period in order to meet return on capital targets.

**Explain how target costing may be used in achieving the required returns and suggest specific areas of investigation.**

## 2.3 The difficulties of using target costing in service industries

Target costing was introduced by major Japanese manufacturers for use in a manufacturing environment where:

- a new product was to be designed to meet the target cost

- a substantial part of the production cost consisted of bought-in materials.

This environment facilitates use of a target cost approach since:

- Professional design teams can alter the design specification of a new product until it matches their cost requirements.

- Very large manufacturers such as Sony and Toyota are able to exert considerable pressure on (usually much smaller) suppliers to reduce their prices.

Service industries (e.g. banking, insurance, travel) provide a less favourable environment for the use of target costing:

- It is much more difficult to make service comparisons than product comparisons, making it harder to determine a market driven price in the first place.

- The introduction of new products and services in service industries usually occurs far less frequently than in a manufacturing environment (e.g. Sony and Toyota introduce new models on a regular basis) and, in consequence, the equivalent of manufacturing design teams are rarely found in service industries.

- Bought in materials are usually of modest significance so there is little scope for exerting pressure on external suppliers.

- The major cost of any new product or service is salaries and unless lower cost delivery mechanisms (e.g. the internet) or radically different ways of working can be exploited there is limited scope for substantial cost reduction.

**Illustration 6 – Targeting costs**

A major bank and provider of credit cards wished to reduce the time taken to process credit card application forms and issue a credit card. The staff responsible for processing applications and issuing new cards were asked to suggest how the period (of 14 days) could be reduced.

The staff were unable to identify any significant time savings. The senior executive responsible for the area decided to pursue a version of target costing and instructed his staff that new cards were to be issued within 24 hours of an application being received and it was their responsibility to identify how this could be achieved.

The imposition of this target forced a new approach to the problem and radical new ways of processing and approving applications were identified and implemented with the result that the 24-hour target was met.

## 2.4 The implications of using target costing on pricing, cost control and performance management

**Pricing**
- Target costing forces product/service designers to 'think outside the box' and identify new and imaginative ways in which costs can be reduced in order to meet the target cost.

- This approach can result in substantial cost savings being identified, thereby enabling prices to be set at levels that are very competitive but still generate a profit. A policy of penetration pricing can then be pursued with a view to substantial market share being captured.

- Target costing is usually considered superior to cost plus pricing as it considers the demand for a product or service. As long as the estimates for demand at the target price are accurate and costs are controlled then an organisation will achieve its required return on investment.

**Cost control and performance management**
- Target costing has a potentially major positive impact on cost control since it seeks to change the accounting mindset from one of recording costs to one of reducing costs in order that the cost target can be met.

- The requirement to meet a target cost can generate new ideas and new ways of working which in turn can generate substantial cost savings and facilitate a more proactive approach to cost control.

- Performance management is also potentially enhanced since

the setting of a target cost requires a business to identify how costs can be managed down to the target cost level. This may involve product/service redesign and new ways of working (e.g. outsourcing, greater use of the internet etc.).

A key performance target for many banks is to reduce staff costs as a percentage of total bank costs.

The launch of first telephone banking and then internet banking for personal customers (both services enabling bank customers to access their bank accounts, transfer funds and pay bills on a 24-hour basis) has enabled the banks to vary the level of bank staff involvement in the provision of these services and to provide a relatively cost-effective service.

**Test your understanding 8**

Target costing is best understood as finding:

(a) **What a new product or service actually costs.**

(b) **The cost of a new product or service of target competitors.**

(c) **What a new product or service should cost.**

## 2.5 Closing the target cost gap

Target cost gap = Estimated product cost – Target cost

It is the difference between what an organisation thinks it can currently make a product for, and what it needs to make it for, in order to make a required profit.

Alternative product designs should be examined for potential areas of cost reduction that will not compromise the quality of the products.

Questions that a manufacturer may ask in order to close the gap include:

- Can any materials be eliminated, e.g. cut down on packing materials?

- Can a cheaper material be substituted without affecting quality?

- Can labour savings be made, for example, by using lower skilled workers?

- Can productivity be improved, for example, by improving motivation?

- What production volume is needed to achieve economies of scale?

- Could cost savings be made by reviewing the supply chain?

- Can part-assembled components be bought in to save on assembly time?

- Can the incidence of the cost drivers be reduced?

- Is there some degree of overlap between the product-related fixed costs that could be eliminated by combining service departments or resources?

A key aspect of this is to understand which features of the product are essential to customer perceived quality and which are not. This process is known as 'value analysis'. Attention should be focused more on reducing the costs of features perceived by the customer not to add less value.

## Expandable text

Value analysis, otherwise known as 'cost engineering' and 'value engineering', is a technique in which a firm's products, and maybe those of its competitors, are subjected to a critical and systematic examination by a small group of specialists. They can be representing various functions such as design, production, sales and finance.

Value analysis asks of a product the following questions:

- Does the use of the product contribute value?

- Is its cost proportionate to its usefulness?

- Does it need all of its features?

- Is there anything better for the intended use?

- Can a usable part be made better at lower cost?

- Can a standard product be found which will be equally usable?

- Is it made on appropriate tooling, considering the quantities used?

- Do material, labour, overheads and profit constitute total cost?

- Will another dependable supplier provide it for less cost?

- Is anyone buying it for less than its stated price?

The strategic implications can be measured in terms of a component's relative cost versus its relative performance. There are four different situations:

1   If a component is both more expensive than and inferior to that of a competitor, a strategic problem requiring change might be necessary. It could be, however, that the component is such a small item in terms of both cost and impact on the customer that it should be ignored.

2   If the component is competitively superior, a value analysis, where a component's value to the customer is quantified, may suggest a price increase or promotion campaign.

3   If a component is less expensive than but inferior to that of a competitor, a value analysis might suggest either de-emphasising that part or upgrading the relative rating.

4   If a component is less expensive than and superior to that of a competitor, a value analysis might suggest that component is emphasised, perhaps playing a key role in promotion and positioning strategies.

A cost advantage may be obtained in many ways, e.g. economies of scale, the experience curve, product design innovations and the use of 'no-frills' product offering. Each provides a different way of competing on the basis of cost advantage.

### Test your understanding 9

The Swiss watchmaker Swatch reportedly used target costing in order to produce relatively low cost watches in a country with one of the world's highest hourly labour wage rates.

**Suggest ways in which Swatch may have reduced their unit costs for each watch.**

## 3   Life-cycle costing

### 3.1   Definition of life-cycle costing

Many goods now have very short life-cycles, e.g. personal computers. In addition many products have very high costs which are incurred before the good is launched, e.g. development of new cars.

Traditional costing techniques based around annual periods may give a misleading impression of the costs and profitability of a good.

The commitment of a high proportion of a product's life-cycle costs at the very early stages of the cycle has led to the need for accounting systems that compare the revenues from a product with all the costs incurred over the entire product life cycle.

**Life-cycle costing:**

- is the profiling of cost over a product's life, including the pre-production stage

- tracks and accumulates the actual costs and revenues attributable to each product from inception to abandonment

- enables a product's true profitability to be determined at the end of its economic life.

### Illustration 8 – Life-cycle costing in a manufacturing environment

- In an advanced manufacturing environment, where products have low labour content, the direct unit cost is relatively low.

- A very high proportion of the total costs over the product's life cycle will be in the form of initial development, design and production setup costs, and ongoing fixed costs that are committed to at this stage.

### Test your understanding 10

**Suggest two manufacturing industries where products tend to have low and decreasing direct labour costs but high initial development, design and production setup costs.**

## 3.2 The costs involved at different stages in the product life-cycle

Most products have a distinct product life-cycle:

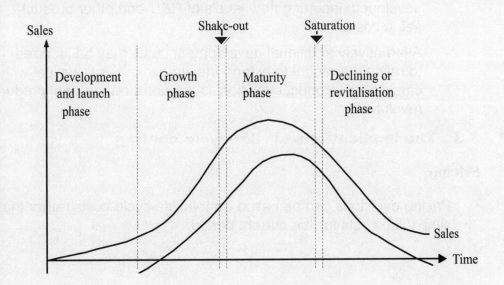

Specific costs may be associated with each stage.

1   Development and launch stage

–   A high level of setup costs will already have been incurred by this stage (preproduction costs), including research and development (R&D), product design and building of production facilities.

–   Success depends upon awareness and trial of the product by consumers, so this stage is likely to be accompanied by extensive marketing and promotion costs.

2   Growth stage

–   Marketing and promotion will continue through this stage.

–   In this stage sales volume increases dramatically, and unit costs fall as fixed costs are recovered over greater volumes.

3   Maturity stage

–   Initially profits will continue to increase, as initial setup and fixed costs are recovered.

–   Marketing and distribution economies are achieved.

–   However, price competition and product differentiation will start to erode profitability as firms compete for the limited new customers remaining.

4   Decline stage

–   Eventually, the product will move towards obsolescence as it is replaced by new and better alternatives.

–   The product will be abandoned when profits fall to an unacceptable level, or when further capital commitment is required.

–   Meanwhile, a replacement product will need to have been developed, incurring new levels of R&D and other product setup costs.

–   Alternatively additional development costs may be incurred to refine the model to extend the life-cycle (this is typical with cars where 'product evolution' is the norm rather than 'product revolution').

### 3.3   The implications of  life-cycle costing

**Pricing**

•   Pricing decisions can be based on total life-cycle costs rather than simply the costs for the current period.

## Test your understanding 11

The following details relate to a new product that has finished development and is about to be launched.

| | Development | Launch | Growth | Maturity | Decline |
|---|---|---|---|---|---|
| Time period | Finished | 1 year | 1 year | 1 year | 1 year |
| R&D costs ($ million) | 20 | | | | |
| Marketing costs ($ million) | | 5 | 4 | 3 | 0.9 |
| Production cost per unit ($) | | 1.00 | 0.90 | 0.80 | 0.90 |
| Production volume (millions) | | 1 | 5 | 10 | 4 |

The launch price is proving a contentious issue between managers. The marketing manager is keen to start with a low price of around $8 to gain new buyers and achieve target market share. The accountant is concerned that this does not cover costs during the launch phase and has produced the following schedule:

| Launch phase: | | $million |
|---|---|---|
| Amortised R&D costs | (20 ÷ 4) | 5.0 |
| Marketing costs | | 5.0 |
| Production costs | (1million × $1 per unit) | 1.0 |
| Total | | 11.0 |
| | | |
| Total production (units) | | 1 million |
| Cost per unit | | $11.00 |

**Prepare a revised cost per unit schedule looking at the whole lifecycle and comment.**

### Decision making

- In deciding to produce or purchase a product or service, a timetable of life-cycle costs helps show what costs need to be allocated to a product so that an organisation can recover its costs.

- If all costs cannot be recovered, it would not be wise to produce the product or service.

- Life-cycle costing allows an analysis of business function interrelationships, e.g. a decision towards lower R&D costs may lead to higher customer service costs in the future.

### Performance management - control

- Many companies find that 90% of the product's life-cycle costs are determined by decisions made in the development and launch stages. Focussing on costs after the product has entered production results in only a small proportion of life-cycle costs being manageable.

- Life-cycle costing thus reinforces the importance of tight control over locked-in costs, such as R&D in the development stage.

- Target costs should be set throughout the life-cycle and revised/ changed as needed.

### Performance management - reporting

- R&D, design, production setup, marketing and customer service costs are traditionally reported on an aggregated basis for all products and recorded as a period expense.

- Life-cycle costing traces these costs to individual products over their entire life cycles, to aid comparison with product revenues generated in later periods

## 4    Back-flush accounting

### 4.1   The basic concepts of back-flush accounting

- In traditional accounting systems inventory is a key item. Traditional manufacturing firms hold high levels of inventory for raw materials, work-in-progress (WIP) and finished goods.

- Much of the work of the management (or cost) accountant would be to place a value on this inventory, e.g. using process cost accounting.

- Back-flush accounting is an alternative approach to cost and management accounting that can be applied where:

  - the speed of throughput (or 'velocity' of throughput) is high, and

  - inventories of raw materials, WIP and unsold finished goods are very low.

- Instead of building up product costs sequentially from start to finish of production, back-flush accounting calculates product costs retrospectively, at the end of each accounting period.

> ### Expandable text
>
> The traditional approach is to track the cost of products through the sequential stages of production, building up costing records for the direct materials consumed, the direct labour cost and the overhead expense for each product or job. In this approach, the WIP control account represents the total costs of production for all the individual products, batches or jobs for which costing records are maintained.
>
> However, if the production cycle is short and there is only a small amount of WIP at any time, it is questionable whether there is much value in building up detailed cost records as items progress through production. This is key to back-flush accounting.
>
> Back-flush accounting is inappropriate for production systems where throughput is slow and the production process is long. It is also inappropriate where the business holds high levels of inventory, and inventory levels can increase or decrease substantially from one period to the next.

## 4.2 The accounting aspects of back-flush accounting

- Back-flush accounting offers an abbreviated and simplified approach to costing by getting rid of 'unnecessary' costing records.

- In the examination you will not be required to perform the double entry for back-flush accounting.

### A traditional system

- A traditional costing system will include the following 'T' accounts:

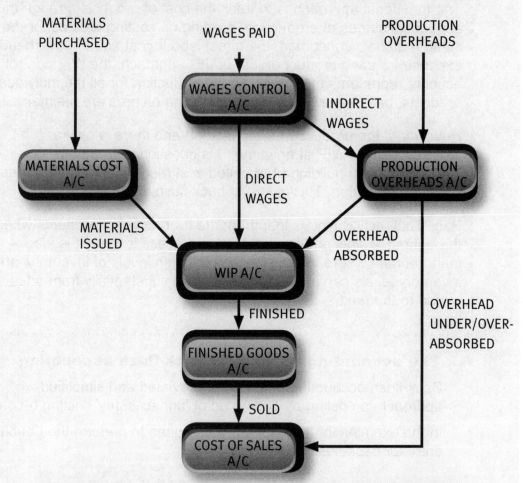

- The figures for closing inventory in materials, WIP and finished goods are the remaining balances carried forwards after other entries have been made.

- For example, in the WIP account the value of closing WIP is the balancing figure after the cost of finished goods has been transferred out to the finished goods account.

- The figures are built up from expenses being incurred through to cost of goods sold.

- Variances can be calculated at each stage (e.g. materials price, materials usage, etc.)

- Where process production is involved, these T-accounts will be repeated for each process with the output of one process being the input for the next.

### A back-flush accounting system

- The cost of raw materials is allocated to a 'raw materials and in progress' (RIP) account.

- Conversion costs (labour and production overheads) are allocated straight to the cost of goods sold account.

KAPLAN PUBLISHING

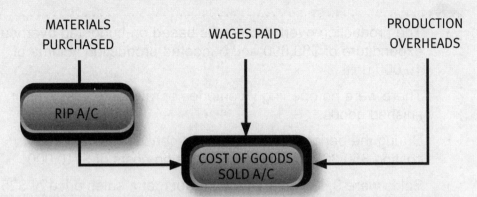

- At the end of the accounting period an inventory stock-take is carried out to determine closing balances for raw materials, WIP and finished goods. This is quick as there are few inventories. Inventory values are based on budget/standard costs.

- The closing inventory values for raw materials and WIP are then 'back-flushed' from the cost of goods sold account into the RIP account.

- Similarly the closing inventory value for finished goods is 'back-flushed' into the finished goods account.

- Thus with back-flush accounting there will be a significant reduction in accounting costs albeit at the cost of reduced detail. (e.g. a split of conversion costs between production labour and overhead is not available).

- However, as noted above, if the production cycle is short and there is only a small amount of WIP at any time, it is questionable whether there is much value in building up detailed cost records as items progress through production. This is key to back-flush accounting.

- In process production systems back-flush accounting often combines all processes into one.

**Expandable text**

**Illustration of double entry**

Even though you will not be asked to perform the double entry for back-flush accounting, it may be helpful to see the detail as follows:

A manufacturing company makes a single product which has the following budgeted cost:

|                     | $  |
|---------------------|----|
| Direct materials    | 5  |
| Direct labour       | 3  |
| Production overhead  | 8  |
|                     | 16 |

- The production overhead cost is based on budgeted overhead expenditure of $80,000 and budgeted production volume of 10,000 units.

- There were no opening inventories of raw materials, WIP or finished goods.

- During the period, the company purchased raw materials costing $50,300. It incurred conversion costs of $110,000.

- Sales were 9,800 units of the product, at a sales price of $25 per unit. Non-production overhead costs were $70,000.

- At the end of the period, a physical inventory count showed that there were $300 of raw materials, unfinished WIP amounted to 80 equivalent units of product and unsold finished goods amounted to 120 units.

- The company uses a system of back-flush accounting.

**Required:**

Prepare the accounts for the period.

**Solution**

**Step 1: Recording costs (and income)**

Before the closing inventory is valued, the accounts would be as follows.

### RIP account

|  | $ |  | $ |
|---|---|---|---|
| Trade payables | 50,300 | Cost of goods sold | 50,300 |

### Cost of goods sold account

|  | $ |  | $ |
|---|---|---|---|
| Conversion costs: |  |  |  |
| Bank or trade payables | 110,000 |  |  |
| RIP account | 50,300 |  |  |

### Other overheads account

|  | $ |  | $ |
|---|---|---|---|
| Trade payables | 70,000 |  |  |

### Sales account

|  | $ |  | $ |
|---|---|---|---|
|  |  | Trade receivables (9,800 × $25) | 245,000 |

## Step 2: Back-flushing

The next stage is to estimate a value for the closing inventory. Here, the raw materials inventory is valued at $300. The WIP of 80 equivalent units can be valued at the budgeted production cost of $16 per unit. Similarly the finished goods inventory should be valued at $16 per unit. These values are back-flushed to the RIP and finished goods accounts.

### RIP account

| | $ | | $ |
|---|---|---|---|
| Trade payables | 50,300 | Cost of goods sold | 50,300 |
| Cost of goods sold: | | | |
| raw materials | 300 | | |
| WIP | | | |
| (80 × $16) | 1,280 | | |

### Finished goods account

| | $ | | $ |
|---|---|---|---|
| Cost of goods sold | | | |
| (120 × $16) | 1,920 | | |

### Cost of goods sold account

| | $ | | $ |
|---|---|---|---|
| Conversion costs | 110,000 | RIP account: | |
| RIP account | 50,300 | raw materials | 300 |
| | | finished goods | 1,280 |
| | | Finished goods a/c | 1,920 |

## Step 3: Calculating the cost of sales and profit

The final stage in preparing the accounts is to prepare a costing income statement and carry forward the inventory values as opening balances for the next period.

### RIP account

| | $ | | $ |
|---|---|---|---|
| Trade payables | 50,300 | Cost of goods sold | 50,300 |
| Cost of goods sold: | | | |
| raw materials | 300 | | |
| WIP | 1,280 | Closing balance c/fwd | 1,580 |
| | 51,880 | | 51,880 |
| Opening balance b/fwd | 1,580 | | |

## Finished goods account

| | $ | | $ |
|---|---|---|---|
| Cost of goods sold | 1,920 | Closing balance c/fwd | 1,920 |
| | 1,920 | | 1,920 |
| Opening balance b/fwd | 1,920 | | |

## Cost of goods sold account

| | $ | | $ |
|---|---|---|---|
| Conversion costs | 110,000 | RIP account: | |
| RIP account | 50,300 | raw materials | 300 |
| | | finished goods | 1,280 |
| | | Finished goods a/c | 1,920 |
| | | Income statement | 156,800 |
| | 160,300 | | 160,300 |

## Other overheads account

| | $ | | $ |
|---|---|---|---|
| Trade payables | 70,000 | Income statement | 70,000 |

## Sales account

| | $ | | $ |
|---|---|---|---|
| Income statement | 245,000 | Trade receivables | 245,000 |

## Costing income statement

| | $ | | $ |
|---|---|---|---|
| Cost of goods sold | 156,800 | Sales | 245,000 |
| Other overheads | 70,000 | | |
| Profit | 18,200 | | |
| | 245,000 | | 245,000 |

In this example, actual costs have met budgeted expectations. There is no under/over-absorbed overhead, and given that budgeted or standard costs are used to value output and inventory, there are no variances to record. However, it is possible to record under/over-absorbed overhead (in the cost of goods sold account) and variances within a back-flush accounting system.

### 4.3 Back-flush accounting and traditional process accounting

**Advantages of switching to back-flush accounting:**

- It is a simpler costing system resulting in lower accounting costs.

- It avoids the need to record production costs sequentially as items move through step-by-step operations in the production process.

- When inventory levels are low or constant, it yields the same results as traditional costing methods would.

**Disadvantages of switching to back-flush accounting:**

- It provides less detailed management information than traditional costing systems.

- A more detailed audit trail is absent.

- There are additional costs for stocktaking.

- Extra training is necessary.

**Other comments**

- It is therefore appropriate in a mature just in time (JIT) environment where there is a short production cycle, and inventories are low.

- It is not appropriate for manufacturing environments where inventory levels are high, due to the problems of counting and valuing the inventory at the end of each period.

- It is probably inappropriate for production systems with a long production cycle. In such an environment, it is preferable to record the production costs as the work passes sequentially through each stage of the production system.

- Controlling production is more difficult under back-flush accounting as detail and variance information is lost. Other aspects, such as non-financial targets related to quality, need to be considered instead.

> **Test your understanding 12**
>
> **Comment on the suitability of back-flush accounting for a major construction firm (which makes bridges, roads, buildings, etc.).**

## 5 Throughput accounting

### 5.1 Throughput accounting

**Background**

- You should already be familiar with the use of key factor analysis to allocate scarce resources where there is one limiting constraint.

- In such cases alternatives may be ranked by examining the contribution per unit of scarce resource for each option.

- In throughput accounting traditional assumptions underlying contribution are challenged and the scarce resource relates to production bottlenecks.

## Main assumptions:

- The only totally variable cost is the purchase cost of raw materials and components that are bought from external suppliers.

- Direct labour costs are not wholly variable. Many employees are salaried and even if paid at a rate per unit, are usually guaranteed a minimum weekly wage.

- Fixed costs are 'less fixed' than they might have been in the past.

## Definitions

### Throughput

Throughput is the rate of converting raw materials and purchased components into products sold to customers.

Or

In money terms, throughput can therefore be defined as the extra money that is made for an organisation from selling its products:

Throughput = Revenue – Totally variable costs

Since totally variable costs are normally just raw materials and bought-in components, it is often convenient to define it as:

Throughput = Revenue – Raw material costs

### Inventory

Inventory is money tied up in assets so that the business can make the throughput.

### Operating expenses

This is all the money a business spends to produce the throughput (i.e. to turn the inventory into output).

### Illustration 9 – Throughput accounting

Hard Tiles recorded a profit of $120,000 in the accounting period just ended, using marginal costing. The contribution/sales ratio was 75%.

Material costs were 10% of sales value and there were no other variable production overhead costs. Fixed costs in the period were $300,000.

**Required:**

What was the value of throughput in the period?

**Solution**

|  | $ |
|---|---|
| Profit | 120,000 |
| Fixed costs | 300,000 |
| Contribution | 420,000 |
| Contribution/sales ratio | 75% |

|  | $ |
|---|---|
| Sales (420,000/75%) | 560,000 |
| Material costs (10% of sales) | 56,000 |
| Throughput | 504,000 |

## 5.2 The Throughput Accounting Ratio (TPAR)

When there is a bottleneck resource, performance can be measured in terms of throughput for each unit of bottleneck resource consumed.

There are three inter-related ratios:

| THROUGHPUT PER UNIT OF THE BOTTLENECK RESOURCE | OPERATING EXPENSE PER UNIT OF THE BOTTLENECK RESOURCE |
|---|---|

$$TPAR = \frac{\text{THROUGHPUT PER HOUR OF BOTTLENECK RESOURCES}}{\text{OPERATING EXPENCES PER HOUR OF BOTTLENECK RESOURCES}}$$

### Illustration 10 – Throughput accounting

A business manufactures a single product that it sells for $10 per unit. The materials cost for each unit of product sold is $3. Total operating expenses are $50,000 each month.

Labour hours are limited to 20,000 hours each month. Each unit of product takes 2 hours to assemble.

**Required:**

Calculate the throughput accounting ratio.

### Solution

Throughput per assembly hour $= \dfrac{\$(10 - 3)}{2 \text{ hours}} = \$3.50$

Operating expenses per assembly hour $= \dfrac{\$50,000}{20,000 \text{ hours}} = \$2.50$

Throughput accounting ratio $= \dfrac{\$3.50}{\$2.50} = 1.40$

### Test your understanding 13

X Limited manufactures a product that requires 1.5 hours of machining. Machine time is a bottleneck resource, due to the limited number of machines available. There are 10 machines available, and each machine can be used for up to 40 hours per week.

The product is sold for $85 per unit and the direct material cost per unit is $42.50. Total factory costs are $8,000 each week.

**Calculate**

a)   the return per factory hour

b)   the TPAR.

### Interpretation of TPAR

*   TPAR>1 would suggest that throughput exceeds operating costs so the product should make a profit.

*   TPAR<1 would suggest that throughput is insufficient to cover operating costs, resulting in a loss.

### Criticisms of TPAR:

*   It concentrates on the short-term, when a business has a fixed supply of resources and operating expenses are largely fixed.

*   It is more difficult to apply throughput accounting concepts to the longer-term, when all costs are variable, and vary with the volume of production and sales or another cost driver.

*   In the longer-term an ABC might be more appropriate for measuring and controlling performance.

## 5.3 Improving the TPAR

$$\text{TPAR} = \frac{\text{Throughput per hour of bottleneck resources}}{\text{Operating expences per hour of bottleneck resources}}$$

Options to improve the TPAR include the following:

- increase the sales price for each unit sold, to increase the throughput per unit

- reduce material costs per unit (e.g. by changing materials or switching suppliers)

- reduce total operating expenses, to reduce the cost per assembly hour

- improve the productivity of the assembly work force, and reduce the time required to make each unit of product. Throughput per assembly hour would increase, but the expenses per assembly hour would be unchanged; therefore the TPAR would increase.

### Illustration 11 – Throughput accounting

Suppose in the illustration above the following changes were made:

- the sales price were increased from $10 to $13.5

- the time taken to make each product fell from 2 hours to 1.75 hours

- the operating expenses fell from $50,000 to $45,000.

The TPAR would nearly double, increasing from 1.4 to 2.67.

$$\text{Throughput per assembly hour} = \frac{\$(13.5 - 3)}{1.75 \text{ hours}} = \$6.0$$

$$\text{Operating expenses per assembly hour} = \frac{\$45,000}{20,000 \text{ hours}} = \$2.25$$

$$\text{TPAR} = \frac{\$6.0}{\$2.25} = 2.67$$

### Expandable text

If there is no immediate demand for the products of a business from its customers, the business might produce assets to hold in inventory. At the same time, it might be looking for ways of improving labour efficiency.

However, producing items to hold in inventory does not make money – it costs money (raw material purchases) and so is bad for cash flow. A throughput accounting view would be that output should be limited to the volume of customer demand, and the focus of activity should be to find ways of raising customer demand to higher levels.

## 5.4 Multi-product decision making

Throughput accounting may be applied to a multi-product decision-making problem in the same way as conventional key factor analysis:

**Step 1:** calculate the throughput for each product.

**Step 2:** identify the bottleneck constraint.

**Step 3:** calculate the throughput per minute of the bottleneck resource for each product to rank the alternatives.

**Step 4:** allocate resources using this ranking.

### Illustration 12 – Throughput accounting

TPP Inc makes two products, A and B and has identified that a bottleneck occurs during assembly. Details of the products are as follows:

|  | Product A | Product B |
|---|---|---|
|  | $ | $ |
| Sales price | 25 | 16 |
| Materials cost | 5 | 3 |
| Direct labour cost | 10 | 8 |
|  | Minutes | Minutes |
| Assembly time per unit | 20 | 15 |

**Required:**

How should the two products be prioritised?

**Solution**

|  | Product A | Product B |
|---|---|---|
| Throughput ($) | 20 | 13 |
| Assembly time per unit | 20 | 15 |
| Throughput per minute | 1.00 | 0.87 |
| Ranking | 1st | 2nd |

## Test your understanding 14

Justin Thyme manufactures four products, A, B, C and D. Details of sales prices, costs and resource requirements for each of the products are as follows.

|  | Product A $ | Product B $ | Product C $ | Product D $ |
|---|---|---|---|---|
| Sales price | 1.40 | 0.80 | 1.20 | 2.80 |
| Materials cost | 0.60 | 0.30 | 0.60 | 1.00 |
| Direct labour cost | 0.40 | 0.20 | 0.40 | 1.00 |
|  | Minutes | Minutes | Minutes | Minutes |
| Machine time per unit | 5 | 2 | 3 | 6 |
| Labour time per unit | 2 | 1 | 2 | 5 |
|  | Units | Units | Units | Units |
| Weekly sales demand | 2,000 | 2,000 | 2,500 | 1,500 |

Machine time is a bottleneck resource and the maximum capacity is 400 machine hours each week. Operating costs, including direct labour costs, are $5,440 each week. Direct labour costs are $12 per hour, and direct labour workers are paid for a 38-hour week, with no overtime.

(a) **Determine the quantities of each product that should be manufactured and sold each week to maximise profit and calculate the weekly profit.**

(b) **Calculate the throughput accounting ratio at this profit-maximising level of output and sales.**

## Chapter summary

**ABC**
- Identify costs drivers
- Group costs into cost pools
- Estimate cost driver volume
- Calculate OH rate per cost driver
- Apportion costs on the basis of cost drivers.

**THROUGHPUT ACCOUNTING**
- Materials are the only variable cost
- Throughput = sales – materials
- TPAR = throughput per hour ffi operating expenses per hour.

**TARGET COSTING**
- Set selling price based on market competition
- Deduct required profit to identify target cost
- Try to close cost gap.

**ADVANCED COSTING METHODS**

**BACK-FLUSH ACCOUNTING**
- A simplified accounting system
- More appropriate for short production runs with low inventory.

**LIFECYCLE COSTING**
- Costs vary throughout the product lifecycle (PLC)
- Need to consider the whole of the PLC when assessing performance.

# Test your understanding answers

### Test your understanding 1

| | |
|---|---|
| Equipment preparation | Time taken or number of setups |
| Patient preparation | Time taken or number of patients |
| Patient aftercare | Time taken or number of patients |
| Film processing | Number of images |
| Film reporting | Number of images |

### Test your understanding 2

The company should establish:

- Directly attributable costs for each customer. These are the costs of printed materials and maps, hotel accommodation, meals and entrance costs.

- Costs that are directly attributable to each tour, which can then be charged to individual customers on the basis of the number of customers on each tour each year.

Suggested ways of charging costs according to cost drivers are:

| | |
|---|---|
| • Bookings and invoicing | Number of bookings received. |
| • Cost of tour guides | Charge directly to each tour. |
| • Vehicle hire | Charge directly to each tour. |
| • Customer services | Apportion on the basis of the number of bookings received, but with a weighting of x 2 for tours to the north and east. |
| • General overheads | Use a suitable recovery rate, perhaps a percentage of the sales revenue for each tour. |

## Test your understanding 3

| Activity | Total cost $ | Cost driver | | Product P $ | Product Q $ |
|---|---|---|---|---|---|
| Setting up | 20,000 | Cost per setup | 5,000 | 5,000 | 15,000 |
| Machining | 80,000 | Cost per machine hour | 40 | 4,000 | 76,000 |
| Order handling | 20,000 | Cost per order | 5,000 | 5,000 | 15,000 |
| Quality control | 20,000 | Cost per inspection | 4,000 | 4,000 | 16,000 |
| Engineering | 60,000 | Cost per engineering hour | 60 | 30,000 | 30,000 |
| | 200,000 | | | 48,000 | 152,000 |

| | Product P $ | Product Q $ |
|---|---|---|
| Direct materials | 1,500 | 19,000 |
| Direct labour | 2,000 | 38,000 |
| Overheads | 48,000 | 152,000 |
| Total cost | 51,500 | 209,000 |
| | | |
| Number of units | 100 | 950 |
| Cost per unit | $515 | $220 |

## Test your understanding 4

(a)  Traditional absorption costing

| | |
|---|---|
| Budgeted direct labour hours | 60,000 |
| (24,000 × 1.0) + (24,000 × 1.5) | |
| Budgeted overhead costs | $432,000 |
| Recovery rate per direct labour hour | $7.20 |

| | Plus $ | Doubleplus $ |
|---|---|---|
| Direct costs | 12.00 | 24.00 |
| Production overhead | 7.20 | 10.80 |
| Full production cost | 19.20 | 34.80 |

KAPLAN PUBLISHING

## (b) ABC

### Workings

|  | Plus | Doubleplus | Total |
|---|---|---|---|
| Batches | 12 | 240 | 252 |
| Setups | 12 | 720 | 732 |
| Special parts | 24,000 | 96,000 | 120,000 |
| Orders | 10 | 140 | 150 |
| Direct labour hours | 24,000 | 36,000 | 60,000 |

### Cost driver rates

| Setup costs | $73,200/732 | $100 per setup |
|---|---|---|
| Special parts handling | $60,000/120,000 | $0.50 per part |
| Order handling | $19,800/150 | $132 per order |
| Materials handling | $63,000/252 | $250 per batch |
| Other overheads | $216,000/60,000 | $3.60 per hour |

|  | Plus $ | Doubleplus $ | Total $ |
|---|---|---|---|
| Setup costs | 1,200 | 72,000 | 73,200 |
| Special parts handling costs | 12,000 | 48,000 | 60,000 |
| Order handling costs | 1,320 | 18,480 | 19,800 |
| Materials handling costs | 3,000 | 60,000 | 63,000 |
| Other overheads | 86,400 | 129,600 | 216,000 |
|  | 103,920 | 328,080 | 432,000 |

|  | Plus | Doubleplus |
|---|---|---|
| Number of units | 24,000 | 24,000 |
|  | $ | $ |
| Direct cost | 12.00 | 24.00 |
| Overhead cost per unit | 4.33 | 13.67 |
| Full cost | 16.33 | 37.67 |

**Note:** In the example above the full production costs were:

|  | Plus | Doubleplus |
|---|---|---|
| • Using traditional absorption costing | $19.20 | $34.80 |
| • Using ABC | $16.33 | $37.67 |
| • Assume the selling prices are | $25.00 | $40.00 |
| • Using absorption costing sales margins are | 23.2% | 13.0% |
| • ABC sales margins are | 34.7% | 5.8% |

Thus, using absorption costing it is apparent that Plus is approximately 6 times as profitable as Doubleplus and should therefore, subject to any other considerations, be given much greater emphasis than Doubleplus in terms of sales and production.

## Test your understanding 5

(a)

| Workings | M1 | M2 | Total |
|---|---|---|---|
| Number of batches | 4 | 80 | 84 |
| Number of setups | 4 | 240 | 244 |
| Special parts | 16,000 | 64,000 | 80,000 |
| Direct labour hours | 16,000 | 20,000 | 36,000 |

| Activity | Cost | | M1 | M2 |
|---|---|---|---|---|
| | $ | | $ | $ |
| Setups | 97,600 | Cost per setup $400 | 1,600 | 96,000 |
| Materials handling | 42,000 | Cost per batch $500 | 2,000 | 40,000 |
| Special parts handling | 50,000 | Cost per part $0.625 | 10,000 | 40,000 |
| Invoicing | 31,000 | Cost per order $100 | 6,000 | 25,000 |
| Other overheads | 108,000 | Cost per hour $3 | 48,000 | 60,000 |
| | 328,600 | | 67,600 | 261,000 |

| | M1 | | M2 | |
|---|---|---|---|---|
| | $ | $ | $ | $ |
| Sales | | 432,000 | | 584,000 |
| Direct materials | 88,000 | | 168,000 | |
| Direct labour | 128,000 | | 160,000 | |
| Overheads | 67,600 | | 261,000 | |
| Total costs | | 283,600 | | 589,000 |
| Profit/(loss) | | 148,400 | | (5,000) |
| Profit/loss per unit | | 18.55 | | (0.625) |

(b) The figures suggest that model M2 is not less profitable than M1. The sales manager should try to persuade the customer to buy model M1. Note that the apparent loss on M2 does not necessarily mean that production should be ceased. To assess this management should consider the incremental relevant cash flows involved - e.g. is the product making positive contribution, how many overheads are avoidable?

## Test your understanding 6

Cost plus pricing ignores:

- the price charged by competitors and
- the demand from the customer.

There may also be little incentive to control costs.

## Test your understanding 7

The information provided will give the following estimated product and company results:

|  | Product X | | Product Y | | |
|---|---|---|---|---|---|
| Company |  |  |  |  |  |
| Per unit | $ | $ | $ | $ | $ |
| Selling price |  | 75 |  | 90 |  |
| Less: variable costs |  |  |  |  |  |
| materials | 20 |  | 20 |  |  |
| conversion costs | 32 | (52) | 52 | (72) |  |
| Contribution |  | 23 |  | 18 |  |
| C/S sales ratio |  | 30.7% |  | 20% |  |
| Total for period |  |  |  |  |  |
| Sales |  | 900,000 |  | 648,000 | 1,548,000 |
| Contribution (sales × cont/unit) |  | 276,000 |  | 129,600 |  |
| Product-specific fixed costs |  | (170,000) |  | (90,000) |  |
|  |  | 106,000 |  | 39,600 | 145,600 |
| Company fixed costs |  |  |  |  | (50,000) |
| Net profit |  |  |  |  | 95,600 |
| Net profit margin on sales |  |  |  |  | 6.2% |

The company is falling considerably short of its 12% net profit margin target. If sales quantities and prices remain unchanged, costs must be reduced if the required return is to be reached.

## Test your understanding 8

c) is the correct answer.

## Test your understanding 9

Your answer may include:

- Substituting cheaper capital for relatively expensive labour.
- Using less packaging – e.g. a sheath rather than a box.
- Using plastics instead of metal for components.
- Using cheaper overseas labour.
- Sharing components between models. (This is widely used in the car industry and has helped to reduce costs dramatically.)
- Reduce stockholding costs through the introduction of JIT and lean production.

### Test your understanding 10

A large and increasing number of industries fall into this category. Examples would be the motor car and computer industries.

### Test your understanding 11

| Lifecycle costs | $million |
|---|---|
| Total RnD costs | 20.0 |
| Total Marketing costs    (5 + 4 + 3 + 0.9) | 12.9 |
| Total Production costs   $(1 \times 1 + 5 \times 0.9 + 10 \times 0.8 + 4 \times 0.9)$ | 17.1 |
| Total Lifecycle costs | 50.0 |
| Total production (units) (1 + 5 + 10 + 4) | 20 million |
| Cost per unit             (50÷20) | $2.50 |

**Looking at the whole lifecycle the marketing manager's proposal seems more reasonable.**

### Test your understanding 12

The long manufacturing cycle and high levels of WIP make back-flush accounting unsuitable.

### Test your understanding 13

Return per factory hour = ($85 − £42.50)/1.5 hours = $28.33

Cost per factory hour = $8,000/(10 × 40 hours) = $20

TPAR  = $28.33/$20 = 1.4165

## Test your understanding 14

**(a)**

|  | Product A $ | Product B $ | Product C $ | Product D $ |
|---|---|---|---|---|
| Sales price | 1.40 | 0.80 | 1.20 | 2.80 |
| Materials cost | 0.60 | 0.30 | 0.60 | 1.00 |
| Throughput | 0.80 | 0.50 | 0.60 | 1.80 |
| Machine time per unit | 5 minutes | 2 minutes | 3 minutes | 6 minutes |
| Throughput per minute | $0.16 | $0.25 | $0.20 | $0.30 |
| Priority | 4th | 2nd | 3rd | 1st |

400 machine hours available each week = 24,000 machine minutes.

The profit-maximising weekly output and sales volumes are as follows.

| Product | Units | Machine minutes $ | Throughput per unit $ | Total throughput |
|---|---|---|---|---|
| D | 1,500 | 9,000 | 1.80 | 2,700 |
| B | 2,000 | 4,000 | 0.50 | 1,000 |
| C | 2,500 | 7,500 | 0.60 | 1,500 |
|  | 20,500 |  |  |  |
| A (balance) | 700 | 3,500 | 0.80 | 560 |
|  |  | 24,000 |  | 5,760 |
| Operating expenses |  |  |  | 5,440 |
| Profit |  |  |  | 320 |

**(b)** Throughput per machine hour: $5,760/400 hours = $14.40.

Operating expenses per machine hour: $5,440/400 hours = $13.60.

TPAR: $14.40/$13.60 = 1.059.

# Planning with limiting factors

## Chapter learning objectives

Upon completion of this chapter you will be able to:

- select an appropriate technique, where there is one limiting factor/key factor, to achieve desired organisational goals

- select an appropriate technique, where there are several limiting factors/key factors, to achieve desired organisational goals

- formulate a linear programming problem involving two products

- determine the optimal solution to a linear programming problem using a graphical approach

- use simultaneous equations to determine where the two lines cross to solve a multiple scarce resource problem

- explain shadow prices (dual prices) and discuss their implications on decision making and performance management in multiple limited resource situations

- calculate shadow prices (dual prices) and discuss their specific implications on decision making and performance management

- explain the implications of the existence of slack, in multiple limited resource situations, for decision making and performance management

- calculate slack and explain the specific implications of the existence of the slack for decision making and performance management.

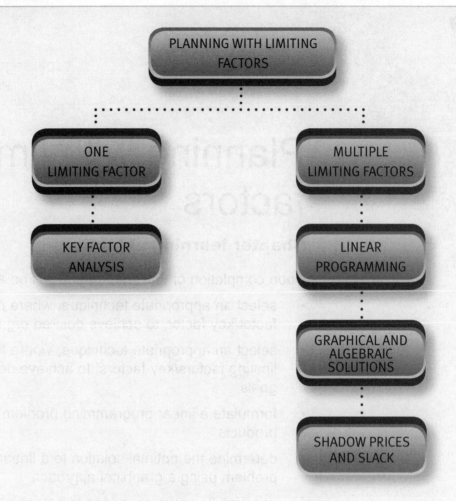

## 1   Planning with one limiting factor

Limiting factor analysis was covered in F2. In F5 the main difference is that the examination contains written questions so issues can be examined in more depth with scope for discussion. With linear programming the F5 syllabus also includes new aspects not seen before in F2.

### 1.1   Limiting factors

Firms face many constraints on their activity and plan accordingly:

*   limited demand

*   limited skilled labour and other production resources

*   limited finance ('capital rationing').

However, examination questions may focus on the problem of scarce resources that prevent the normal plan being achieved, e.g. a firm is facing a labour shortage this month due to sickness. How should its production plan be revised?

The usual objective in questions is to maximise profit. Given that fixed costs are unaffected by the production decision in the short run, the approach should be to maximise the contribution earned.

## 1.2  Key factor analysis – calculations

If there is one limiting factor, then the problem is best solved using key factor analysis where options are ranked using the contribution earned per unit of scace resource, e.g. if labour is the scarce resource, then rank the different options using contribution per labour hour.

---

### Illustration 1 – Key factor analysis

X Ltd makes three products, A, B and C, of which unit costs, machine hours and selling prices are as follows:

|  | Product A | Product B | Product C |
|---|---|---|---|
| Machine hours | 10 | 12 | 14 |
|  | $ | $ | $ |
| Direct materials @ 50c per kg | 7 (14 kg) | 6 (12 kg) | 5 (10 kg) |
| Direct wages @ $7.50 per hour | 9 (1.2 hours) | 6 (0.8 hours) | 3 (0.4 hours) |
| Variable overheads | 3 | 3 | 3 |
| Marginal cost | 19 | 15 | 11 |
| Selling price | 25 | 20 | 15 |
| Contribution | 6 | 5 | 4 |

Sales demand for the period is limited as follows.

| Product A | 4,000 |
|---|---|
| Product B | 6,000 |
| Product C | 6,000 |

Company policy is to produce a minimum of 1,000 units of Product A.

The supply of materials in the period is unlimited, but machine hours are limited to 200,000 and direct labour hours to 5,000.

**Required:**

Indicate the production levels that should be adopted for the three products in order to maximise profitability, and state the maximum contribution.

**Solution**

**Step 1:** First determine which is the limiting factor (this may be done for you in examination questions).

At potential sales level:

|  | Sales potential units | Total machine hours | Total labour hours |
|---|---|---|---|
| Product A | 4,000 | 40,000 | 4,800 |
| Product B | 6,000 | 72,000 | 4,800 |
| Product C | 6,000 | 84,000 | 2,400 |
|  |  | 196,000 | 12,000 |

Thus, labour hours are the limiting factor.

**Step 2:** Rank the options.

The next stage is to calculate contribution per labour hour.

Product A $\dfrac{\$6}{1.2} = \$5.00$

Product B $\dfrac{\$5}{0.8} = \$6.25$

Product C $\dfrac{\$4}{0.4} = \$10.00$

Thus, production should be concentrated first on C, up to the maximum available sales, then B, and finally A.

However, a minimum of 1,000 units of A must be produced.

**Step 3**: Allocate resources.

Taking these factors into account, the production schedule becomes:

|  | Units produced | Labour hours | Cumulative labour hours | Limiting factor |
|---|---|---|---|---|
| Product A | 1,000 | 1,200 | 1,200 | Policy to produce 1,000 units |
| Product C | 6,000 | 2,400 | 3,600 | Sales |
| Product B | 1,750 | 1,400 | 5,000 | Labour hours |

The maximum contribution is therefore as follows.

|  | $ |
|---|---|
| A (1,000 × $6) | 6,000 |
| B (1,750 × $5) | 8,750 |
| C (6,000 × $4) | 24,000 |
|  | 38,750 |

## Test your understanding 1

Z Inc makes two products which both use the same type of materials and grades of labour, but in different quantities as shown by the table below:

|  | Product A | Product B |
|---|---|---|
| Labour hours/unit | 3 | 4 |
| Material/unit | $20 | $15 |

During each week the maximum number of labour hours available is limited to 600, and the value of material available is limited to $6,000.

Each unit of product A made and sold earns Z Inc a contribution of $5 and each unit of product B earns $6 per unit. The demand for these products is limited to 100 of each per week.

**Advise Z Inc which product they should make.**

## 1.3 Key factor analysis – discussion aspects

**Assumptions**

- A single quantifiable objective – e.g. maximise contribution. In reality there may be multiple objectives such as maximising return while simultaneously minimising risk.

- Each product always uses the same quantity of the scarce resource per unit:

    - e.g. it always takes 2 hours to make a unit of X

    - in reality there may be economies of scale and/or learning effects that result in a unit of X taking fewer hours as volumes increase.

- The contribution per unit is constant. In reality this may not be the case:

    - the selling price may have to be lowered to sell more

    - discounts may be available as the quantity of materials needed increases

    - there may be economies of scale.

- Products are independent – it is possible to prioritise product A at the expense of B. In reality this may be difficult:

    - customers may expect to buy both products together

    - the products may be manufactured jointly together.

- The scenario is short term. This allows us to ignore fixed costs

    - a long timescale would introduce the possibilty of fixed costs changing.

A large supermarket is having some building work done for the next month. As a result shelf space is more limited than normal.

**Comment on the application of key factor analysis to this problem.**

## 2 Several limiting factors – linear programming

When there is only one scarce resource the method above (key factor analysis) can be used to solve the problem. However where there are two or more resources in short supply which limit the organisation's activities then linear programming is required to find the solution.

In examination questions linear programming is used to:

*   maximise contribution and/or
*   minimise costs.

**Expandable text**

A surprising number of problems can be solved with this relatively straightforward technique:

*   Mixing problems – a product is composed of several ingredients. The least costly mix of the ingredients that will produce a product of predetermined specification is required.

*   Job assignment problems – a number of jobs or products must be handled by various people and/or machines, and the least costly arrangement of assignments is required.

*   Capacity allocation problems – limited capacity is allocated to products so as to yield maximum profits. This is the most common application in examination questions.

*   Production scheduling – an uneven sales demand is met by a production schedule over a period of time, with given penalties for storage, overtime, and short-time working.

*   Transportation problems – various suppliers (or one company with several plants) throughout the country make the same products, which must be shipped to many outlets that are also widely distributed. This may involve different transportation costs and varying manufacturing costs. Linear programming can determine the best way to ship. It denotes which plant shall service any particular outlet. It can also evaluate whether it pays to open a new plant.

- Purchasing – multiple and complex bids can be evaluated, in order to ensure that the orders placed with suppliers comply with the lowest cost arrangement.

- Investment problems – the results of alternative capital investments can be evaluated when finance is in short supply.

- Location problems – linear programming can help to select an optimum plant or warehouse location where a wide choice is possible.

## 2.1 Formulating a linear programming problem involving two variables

The steps involved in linear programming are as follows:

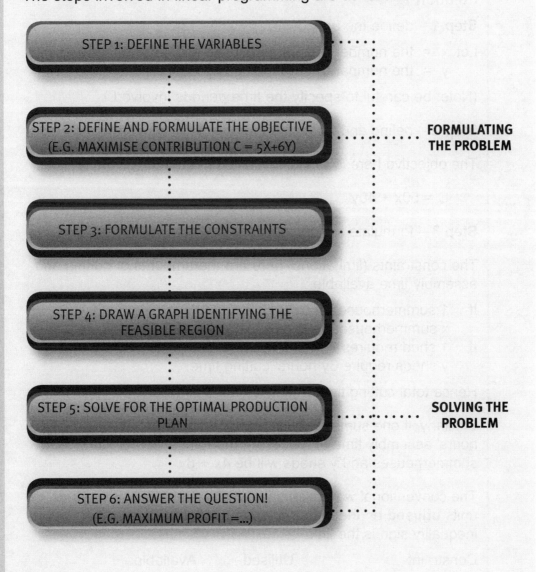

STEP 1: DEFINE THE VARIABLES

STEP 2: DEFINE AND FORMULATE THE OBJECTIVE (E.G. MAXIMISE CONTRIBUTION C = 5X+6Y)

**FORMULATING THE PROBLEM**

STEP 3: FORMULATE THE CONSTRAINTS

STEP 4: DRAW A GRAPH IDENTIFYING THE FEASIBLE REGION

STEP 5: SOLVE FOR THE OPTIMAL PRODUCTION PLAN

**SOLVING THE PROBLEM**

STEP 6: ANSWER THE QUESTION! (E.G. MAXIMUM PROFIT =...)

### Illustration 2 – Formulating the problem

Hebrus Inc manufactures summerhouses and garden sheds. Each product passes through a cutting process and an assembly process. One summerhouse, which makes a contribution of $50, takes six hours' cutting time and four hours' assembly time; while one shed makes a contribution of $40, and takes three hours' cutting time and eight hours' assembly time. There is a maximum of 36 cutting hours available each week and 48 assembly hours.

Cutters are paid $10 per hour and assembly workers $15 per hour.

**Required:**

Formulate the linear programming problem.

**Solution**

**Step 1** – define the unknowns.

Let $x$ = the number of summerhouses produced each week
    $y$ = the number of garden sheds produced each week.

(Note: be careful to specify the time periods involved.)

**Step 2** – define and formulate the objective function.

The objective here is to maximise contribution C, given by:

$$C = 50x + 40y$$

**Step 3** – formulate the constraints.

The constraints (limitations) here are the amounts of cutting and assembly time available.

If  1 summerhouse requires 6 hours' cutting time,
    $x$ summerhouses require $6x$ hours' cutting time.
If  1 shed requires 3 hours' cutting time,
    $y$ sheds require $3y$ hours' cutting time.

Hence total cutting time required = $6x + 3y$ hours.

Similarly, if one summerhouse and one shed require 4 and 8 hours' assembly time respectively, the total assembly time for $x$ summerhouses and $y$ sheds will be $4x + 8y$.

The conventional way of setting out the constraints is to place the units **utilised** on the left, and those **available** on the right; the inequality sign is the link.

| Constraint | | Utilised | | Available |
|---|---|---|---|---|
| Cutting time | (i) | $6x + 3y$ | ≤ | 36 |
| Assembly time | (ii) | $4x + 8y$ | ≤ | 48 |

In addition, two other logical constraints must be stated, i.e.

$x \geq 0$

$y \geq 0$

These simply state that negative amounts of garden sheds or summerhouses cannot be made.

### Test your understanding 3 – Alfred Co – part I

Alfred Co is preparing its production plan for the coming month. It manufactures two products, the flak trap and the sap trap. Details are as follows.

| | Product | | Price/wage rate |
| --- | --- | --- | --- |
| | Flak trap | Sap trap | |
| amount/unit: | | | |
| selling price ($) | 125 | 165 | |
| raw material (kg) | 6 | 4 | $5/kg |
| labour hours: | | | |
| skilled | 10 | 10 | $3/hour |
| semi-skilled | 5 | 25 | $3/hour |

The company's overhead absorption rate (OAR) is $1/labour hour (for both skilled and semi-skilled labour). The supply of skilled labour is limited to 2,000 hours/month and the supply of semi-skilled labour is limited to 2,500 hours/month. At the selling prices indicated, maximum demand for flak traps is expected to be 150 units/month and the maximum demand for sap traps is expected to be 80 units/month.

**Formulate the problem.**

## 2.2 Drawing the graph and identifying the feasible region

**Drawing the graph**

- Step 4 of the linear programming model is to represent the constraints as straight lines on a graph.

- In order to plot the constraints it is normally best to compute the intercepts of the equalities on the horizontal and vertical axes. Thus, x and y are each set equal to zero in turn and the value of y and x computed in these circumstances.

### Expandable text

Step 4 of the linear programming model is to represent the constraints as straight lines on a graph. We do this below. In the meantime, this section contains basic revision for students who are not familiar with the process of graphing a straight line.

To begin with, we must have a linear relationship between two measurements.

Examples
$$y = 3x + 1$$
$$y = 2x + 42 \text{ etc.}$$

**Note:**

1 To recognise a linear relationship the equation must have only 'x' not 'x' to the power of anything, e.g. $x^2$.

2 A straight line has two characteristics:

   (i) a slope or gradient – which measures the 'steepness' of the line

   (ii) a point at which it cuts the y axis – this is called the inter-cept:

$$y = (\text{slope} \times x) + \text{intercept}$$
$$\text{e.g.} \quad y = 2x + 3$$

∴ the gradient is 2 and the point at which the line cuts the y axis is 3.

To draw a straight line graph we only need to know two points that can then be joined.

Consider the following two equations:

(i) $y = 2x + 3$
(ii) $y = 2x - 2$

In order to draw the graphs of these equations it is necessary to decide on two values for x and then to calculate the corresponding values for y. Let us use x = 0 and 3. These calculations are best displayed in tabular form.

(i) (x=0, y=3) and (x=3, y=9)

(ii) (x=0, y=-2) and (x=3, y=4)

KAPLAN PUBLISHING

So to draw the first line we plot the points (0, 3) and (3, 9) and simply join them up. Similarly, for the second line we plot the points (0, -2) and (3, 4) and join them up.

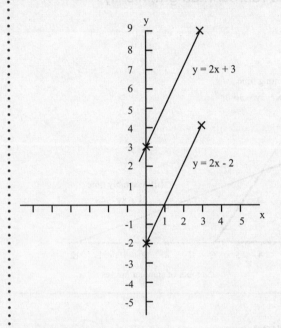

**Note:** The lines are parallel because the equations have the same gradient of 2.

## Illustration 3 – Drawing the graph and identifying the feasible region

The cutting time constraint is an inequality $6x + 3y \leq 36$ which represents a region on the graph. To identify this region we draw the line $6x + 3y = 36$ (equality) and then determine which side of the line is feasible. This process is repeated for each constraint.

For the equation        $6x + 3y = 36$ – cutting time constraint

when x = 0,            $y = \dfrac{36}{3} = 12$

when y = 0,            $x = \dfrac{36}{6} = 6$

To graph this constraint, we draw a straight line between the points (0, 12) and (6, 0).

For the equation        $4x + 8y = 48$ – assembly time constraint

when x = 0,            $y = \dfrac{48}{8} = 6$

when y = 0,            $x = \dfrac{48}{4} = 12$

To graph this constraint, we draw a straight line between the points (0, 6) and (12, 0).

The constraints can now be represented graphically:

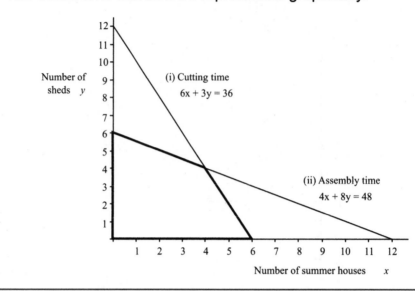

### Identifying the feasible region

• Having inserted the straight lines in the graph, we are then ready to work out what is called the feasible region.

• The feasible region shows those combinations of variables which are possible given the resource constraints.

• In the example above the original constraints were '≤' types, so the feasible region is shown by the area bounded by the thick black line on the graph. Production can be anywhere in this area.

• the lines drawn on the graph represent equations where the LHS equals the RHS. However, the original constraint was either '≤' or '≥'.

• A '≤' type constraint is represented by all points on the line AND all points in the area below the line (i.e. nearer to the origin - the point x=0,y=0)

• A '≥' type constraint is represented by all points on the line AND all points in the area above the line (i.e. away from the origin).

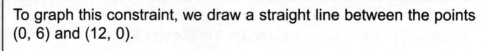

**Test your understanding 4 – Alfred Co – part II**

**Using the Alfred Co example again you are required to plot the constraints on a graph and indicate on the graph the feasible region.**

KAPLAN PUBLISHING

Note: The problem was to solve the following:

Maximise contribution, C, given by C = 50x + 40y, subject to the following constraints:

| | | | |
|---|---|---|---|
| Skilled labour | 10x + 10y | ≤ | 2,000 |
| Semi-skilled labour | 5x + 25y | ≤ | 2,500 |
| Max demand | x | ≤ | 150 |
| | y | ≤ | 80 |
| Non-negativity | x,y | ≥ | 0 |

Watch out in the examination for constraints that show minimum amounts required as well as maximum amounts of constraints available. Typically in questions these tend to be a government quota that a minimum amount of one of the output needs to be produced.

## 2.3 Finding the optimal solution using the graph

Having found the feasible region the problem now is to find the optimal solution within this feasible region.

There are two approaches to this final stage.

- By inspection it is clear that the maximum contribution will lie on one of the corners of the feasible region. The optimal solution can be reached simply by calculating the contributions at each corner.

- By drawing an iso-contribution line (an objective function for a particular value of C), which is a line where all points represent an equal contribution. This is the recommended approach, particularly for more complex problems.

### Illustration 4 – Finding the optimal solution

Using the Hebrus example, consider a contribution of $200. This would give the contribution line 50x + 40y = 200 and could be achieved by producing four summerhouses, or five sheds, or any combination on a straight line between the two.

Another iso-contribution line could be drawn at $240, i.e. $50x + 40y = 240$

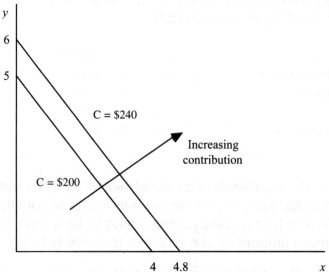

The iso-contribution lines move to and from the origin in parallel; the arrow indicates increasing contribution. The object is to get on the highest contribution line within (just touching) the binding constraints.

The optimum point is found by drawing an example of an iso-contribution line on the diagram (any convenient value of C will do), and then placing a ruler against it. Then, by moving the ruler away from the origin (in the case of a maximisation problem) or towards the origin (in the case of a minimisation problem) but keeping it parallel to the iso-contribution line, the last corner of the feasible solution space which is met represents the optimum solution.

KAPLAN PUBLISHING

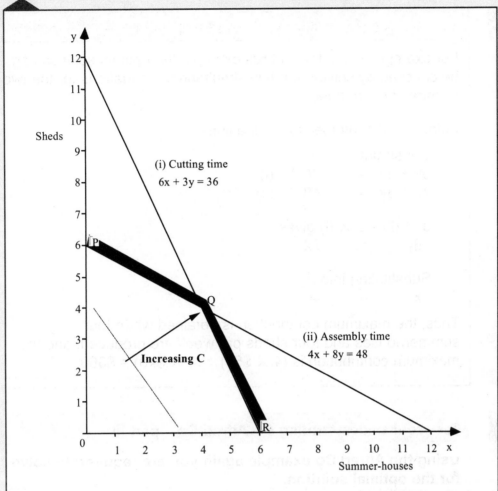

The highest available iso-contribution line occurs at point Q, where, reading from the graph, x = 4 and y = 4. This gives a maximum contribution of C = (50 × 4) + (40 × 4) = $360.

## 2.4 Solving the problem – using simultaneous equations

You may consider that the whole process would be easier by solving the constraints as sets of simultaneous equations and not bothering with a graph. This is possible and you may get the right answer, but such a technique should be used with caution and is not recommended until you have determined graphically which constraints are effective in determining the optimal solution. Furthermore if the question asks for a graphical solution, then a graph must be used.

The technique can, however, be used as a check, or to establish the exact quantities for the optimal solution when the graph does not give sufficient accuracy.

### Illustration 5 – Linear programming

For example, using the Hebrus example the optimal solution can be checked by solving the two simultaneous equations for the two constraint boundaries.

Point Q is the intersection of the lines:

Constraint
$6x + 3y = 36$   (i)
$4x + 8y = 48$   (ii)

$3 \times$ (ii) $- 2 \times$ (i) gives:
$18y = 72$

Substituting into (i)
$x = 4$

Thus, the maximum contribution is obtained when four summerhouses and four sheds per week are produced, and the maximum contribution is $(4 \times \$50) + (4 \times \$40) = \$360$.

### Test your understanding 5 – Alfred Co – part III

**Using the Alfred Co example again you are required to solve for the optimal solution.**

### Test your understanding 6 – Minimising costs

J Farms Ltd can buy two types of fertiliser which contain the following percentage of chemicals:

|        | Nitrates | Phosphates | Potash |
|--------|----------|------------|--------|
| Type X | 18       | 5          | 2      |
| Type Y | 3        | 2          | 5      |

For a certain crop the following minimum quantities (kg) are required:

Nitrates  100        Phosphates  50        Potash  40

Type X costs £10 per kg and type Y costs £5 per kg. J Farms Ltd currently buys 1,000 kg of each type and wishes to minimise its expenditure on fertilisers.

**(a) Write down the objective function and the constraints for J Farms Ltd.**

> **(b)** Draw a graph to illustrate all the constraints (equations/inequalities), shading the feasible region.
>
> **(c)** Recommend the quantity of each type of fertiliser which should be bought and the cost of these amounts.
>
> **(d)** Find the saving J Farms Ltd can make by switching from its current policy to your recommendation.

## 2.5 Linear programming assumptions

The assumptions made when using linear programming are the same as those given in section 1.3 above for key factor analysis.

**Assumptions**

- A single quantifiable objective.

- Each product always uses the same quantity of the scarce resource per unit. This ensures that the constraints are linear, giving straight lines on the graph.

- The contribution (and cost) per unit is constant for each product. This ensures that the objective function is a straight line and that its gradient doesn't change as it is moved out (in) on the graph.

- Products are independent.

- The scenario is short-term.

**Note:** the graphical approach is only feasible for problems with two variables. With more products an alternative, such as the Simpex algorithm, must be used. This is off-syllabus.

## 3 Shadow prices and slack

### 3.1 Introduction

**Slack**

- Slack is the amount by which a resource is under-utilised. It will occur when the optimum point does not fall on the given resource line.

- Slack is important because unused resources can be put to another use, e.g. hired out to another manufacturer.

---

**Illustration 6 – Slack**

In the Hebrus example, the optimum point Q lies on both the cutting and assembly time lines; therefore both resources are fully utilised. (These are referred to as the 'critical constraints' in this example.)

This can be checked from the constraint inequalities.

The optimal solution was $x = 4$, $y = 4$,

Cutting time:
available = 36, utilised = $6x + 3y = (6 \times 4) + (3 \times 4) = 36$

Assembly time:
available = 48, utilised = $4x + 8y = (4 \times 4) + (8 \times 4) = 48$

Hence all available time in both departments is utilised.

If, however, the optimum had been at P ($x = 0$, $y = 6$) then, because P does not lie on the cutting time line, there would be slack cutting time.

Cutting time utilised = $(6 \times 0) + (3 \times 6) = 18$.

Slack = $36 - 18 = 18$ hours.

---

**Shadow (or dual) prices**

- The shadow price of a resource is an increase in value (usually extra contribution) which would be created by having available one additional unit of a limiting resource at its original cost.

- It therefore represents the maximum premium that the firm should be willing to pay for one extra unit of each constraint. This aspect is discussed in more detail below.

- Non-critical constraints will have zero shadow prices as slack exists already.

### 3.2 Calculating shadow prices

The simplest way to calculate shadow prices for a critical constraint is as follows:

**Step 1:** add one unit to the constraint concerned, while leaving the other critical constraint unchanged.

**Step 2:** solve the revised simultaneous equations to derive a new optimal solution.

**Step 3:** calculate the revised optimal contribution. The increase is the shadow price for the constraint under consideration.

## Illustration 7 – Shadow prices

In Hebrus the optimal solution was determined to be x=4 and y=4 giving an optimal contribution of $360. This solution was at the intersection of the lines:

Cutting       6x + 3y   =   36
Assembly    4x + 8y   =   48

**Required:**

Calculate the shadow prices for cutting and assembly time.

### Solution

Suppose one extra hour was available for the cutting process each week. By how much would contribution (and profit) be increased?

We would then need to solve

Cutting       6x + 3y    =     37
Assembly    4x + 8y    =     48

These give y = 3.888... and x = 4.222...

This gives a revised contribution of C = (50×4.222...) + (40×3.888...) = $366.67.

The increase of $6.67 is the shadow price for cutting time per hour.

A similar calculation can be done for assembly time giving a shadow price of $2.50 per hour.

## Test your understanding 7

**Using the following data, calculate the shadow price for machining time.**

Maximise C = 80x + 75y    (contribution), subject to

(i)    20x + 25y   ≤    500    (machining time)

(ii)   40x + 25y   ≤    800    (finishing time)

The optimal solution at the intersection of the above constraints is: x = 15, y = 8.

### 3.3 Using shadow prices

- The relevant cost of a resource = the normal cost + the shadow price.

- Thus shadow prices can be used for decision making in the same way as any other relevant costs.

## Illustration 8 – Using shadow prices

Continuing the Hebrus example:

| Constraint | Normal cost | Shadow price | Relevant cost |
|---|---|---|---|
| Cutting time | $10/hour | $6.67/hour | $16.67/hour |
| Assembly time | $15/hour | $2.50/hour | $17.50/hour |

Thus the most Hebrus would pay for additional cutting time (e.g. through overtime or the use of temporary staff) would be $16.67 per hour. Similarly assembly time is worth $17.50 to the firm.

These figures can also be used to assess the impact of Hebrus losing hours for any reason, such as sickness.

## Test your understanding 8

Suppose a linear programming problem gives the following results.

| Constraint | Normal cost | Shadow price |
|---|---|---|
| Skilled labour | $20/hour | $12/hour |
| Unskilled labour | $10/hour | zero |
| Materials | $5/kg | $3/kg |

(a) Which two constraints give rise to the optimal solution?

(b) Overtime is paid at 'time-and-a-half'. Is it worth paying overtime to help relax constraints?

(c) A new product has been proposed with the following proposed costs and revenues

| | $ |
|---|---|
| Selling price | 80 |
| Skilled labour – 2 hours@$20/hour | (40) |
| Unskilled labour – 1 hour@$10/hour | (10) |
| Materials – 3kg@$5/kg | (15) |
| Profit per unit | 15 |

**Assuming that the constraints cannot be relaxed, should the new product be manufactured?**

## Chapter summary

```
          ┌─────────────────────────────────────┐
          │    PLANNING WITH LIMITING FACTORS     │
          └─────────────────────────────────────┘
```

**ONE LIMITING FACTOR**

**MULTIPLE LIMITING FACTORS**

**KEY FACTOR ANALYSIS**

Rank options using contribution per unit of limiting factor.

**LINEAR PROGRAMMING**

1. Define variables
2. Formulate objective
3. Formulate constraints
4. Draw graph and identify feasible region
5. Solve for optimal point
6. Answer question!

**ASSUMPTIONS**

- Single objective
- Constant selling price
- Constant variable cost per unit
- No economies of scale or learning effects
- Products are independent
- Short term.

**SHADOW PRICES AND SLACK**

- Critical constraints have no slack
- Shadow price = premium a firm is willing to pay for extra resources
- Only critical constraints have non-zero shadow prices
- Relevant cost = normal cost + shadow price.

## Test your understanding answers

### Test your understanding 1

**Step 1:** Determine the scarce resource.

Max labour hours needed = 100x3 + 100x4 = 700

Max materials needed = 100x20 + 100x15 = $3,500

Only labour is a limiting constraint.

**Step 2:** Calculate each product's contribution per unit of the scarce resource consumed by its manufacture.

Product A contribution per labour hour

=    $5/3 hours    =    $1.66 per hour

Product B contribution per labour hour

=    $6/4 hours    =    $1.50 per hour

Thus Z Ltd maximises its earnings by making and selling product A.

**Step 3:** Allocate scarce resource.

– Make 100 units of A using 300 hours.

– Use the remaining 300 hours to make 75 units of B.

### Test your understanding 2

Key factor analysis could be applied by ranking products using their contribution per square centimetre of shelf space used.

This is likely to result in the supermarket prioritising cigarettes and alcohol while stopping stocking cheap, bulky items such as bread.

This is unlikely to be acceptable to customers who expect the shop to provide a full range of products. If the supermarket stops selling bread, then customers may switch to a competitor to buy all the items they need.

### Test your understanding 3

**Step1: define variables**

Let  x = the number of units of flak traps produced per month.
     y = the number of units of sap traps produced per month.

## Step 2: objective function

The objective is to maximise contribution, C, given by C = 50x + 40y
(Working)

## Working:

Contribution per flak trap = 125 – (6 × 5) – (10 × 3) – (5 × 3) = 50
Contribution per sap trap = 165 – (4 × 5) – (10 × 3) – (25 × 3) = 40

## Step 3: constraints

| Skilled labour | 10x + 10y | ≤ | 2,000 |
|---|---|---|---|
| Semi-skilled labour | 5x + 25y | ≤ | 2,500 |
| Max demand | x | ≤ | 150 |
| | y | ≤ | 80 |
| Non-negativity | x,y | ≥ | 0 |

## Test your understanding 4

Skilled labour: x = 0, y = 2,000/10 = 200
y = 0, x = 2,000/10 = 200
We simply join up the points (0, 200) and (200, 0).

Semi-skilled labour: x = 0, y = 2,500/25 = 100
y = 0, x = 2,500/5 = 500
We join up the points (0, 100) and (500, 0).

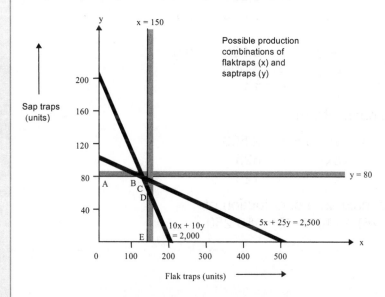

This gives a feasibility region of 0ABCDE.

Objective is to maximise contribution C = 50x + 40y.

The iso-contribution line C=5,000 has been drawn to establish the gradient and identify the optimal solution at point C:

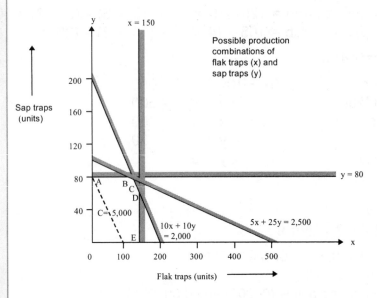

It is difficult to read the precise co-ordinates for point C but it is at the intersection of the two labour constraint lines. We thus need to solve:

| | | | | | |
|---|---|---|---|---|---|
| 5x | + | 25y | = | 2,500 | (i) |
| 10x | + | 10y | = | 2,000 | (ii) |

| | | | | | |
|---|---|---|---|---|---|
| 2×(i) | 10x | + | 50y | = | 5,000 | (iii) |
| (iii)-(ii) | | | 40y | = | 3,000 |
| | | | y | = | 75 |

Substituting back into (i)

| | | | | |
|---|---|---|---|---|
| 5x | + | 25×75 | = | 2,500 |
| | | 5x | = | 625 |
| | | x | = | 125 |

This gives a maximum contribution of
C = (50 × 125) + (40 × 75) = $9,250.

> **Test your understanding 6**
>
> (a)  The chemicals are given in percentage terms that are converted to decimals.
>
>   Let x = number of kg of X  purchased
>   Let y = number of kg of Y purchased
>
>   Total cost: z = 10x + 5y, the objective function which has to be minimised.
>
>   The constraints exist on the chemical composition of the fertilisers:
>
>   Nitrates:        0.18x + 0.03y  ≥  100
>   Phosphates:    0.05x + 0.02y  ≥   50
>   Potash:          0.02x + 0.05y  ≥   40
>   Non-negativity:   x ≥ 0, y ≥ 0
>
> (b)  In this example, all the points where the lines cut the axes are required, so that the easiest way to draw the constraints is to calculate these points.
>
> | Constraint | End points | |
> |---|---|---|
> | 0.18x + 0.03y = 100 | x = 0,  y = $\dfrac{100}{0.03}$ = 3,333.3 | y = 0, x = $\dfrac{100}{0.18}$ = 555.5 |
> | 0.05x + 0.02y = 50 | x = 0, y = $\dfrac{50}{0.02}$ = 2,500 | y = 0, x = $\dfrac{50}{0.05}$ = 1,000 |
> | 0.02x + 0.05y = 40 | x = 0, y = $\dfrac{40}{0.05}$ = 800 | y = 0, x = $\dfrac{40}{0.02}$ = 2,000 |

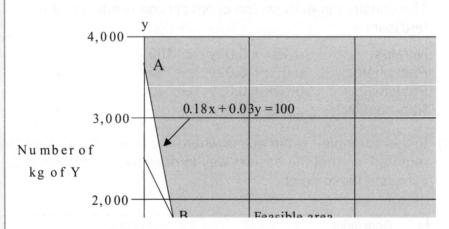

(c) Considering the vertices (i.e. corners) of the feasible area.

A:     $x = 0$     $y = 3,333.3$
      $z = 10x + 5y = 10(0) + 5(3,333.3) = \$16,666.50$

B:     Solving   $0.18x + 0.03y = 100$ and $0.05x + 0.02y = 50$
      gives     $x = 238.1$ and $y = 1,904.8$.
        $z = 10(238.1) + 5(1,904.8) = \$11,905$

C:     Solving   $0.05x + 0.02y = 50$ and $0.02x + 0.05y = 40$
      gives     $x = 809.5$ and $y = 476.2$
        $z = 10(809.5) + 5(476.2) = \$10,476$

D:     $x = 2,000$ $y = 0$
      $z = 10(2,000) + 5(0) = \$20,000$

Thus C gives the point of minimum cost with $x = 809.5$ and $y = 476.2$, i.e. 809.5 kg of X and 476.2 kg of Y, total cost $10,476.

or:

Alternatively, an iso-cost line for $z = 20,000$ (say) could be plotted and moved downwards. This would identify point C as the optimum point on the graph, and the values of x and y could be determined using simultaneous equations as above.

(d) The current policy costs: $1,000 (\$10) + 1,000 (\$5) = \$15,000$, so the saving made is of $\$(15,000 - 10,476) = \$4,524$.

## Test your understanding 7

Machining time – the constraints become:

    (i)        $20x + 25y \leq 501$
    (ii)      $40x + 25y \leq 800$

Subtracting (i) from (ii) gives $20x = 299$ and thus $x = 14.95$

Inserting into (i) gives

$$(20 \times 14.95) + 25y = 501$$
$$25y = 202$$
$$y = 8.08$$

Original contribution = $(15 \times \$80) + (8 \times \$75) = \$1,800$.

Amended contribution = $(14.95 \times \$80) + (8.08 \times \$75) = \$1,802$.

The shadow price per machine hour is thus $2.

## Test your understanding 8

(a) Critical constraints have non-zero dual prices, so the optimal solution will be at the intersection of skilled labour and materials.

(b) For skilled labour overtime will cost $30 per hour and the benefit will be $20+12=\$32$ per hour. The overtime is thus worth while and will generate a net $2 per hour benefit.

For unskilled labour there is already slack so overtime is not worth while.

(c) The profit statement can be revised using relevant costs as follows:

|  | $ |
|---|---|
| Selling price | 80 |
| Skilled labour – 2 hours@(20+12) | (64) |
| Unskilled labour – 1 hour@10 | (10) |
| Materials – 3kg@(5+3) | (24) |
| Loss per unit | (18) |

Incorporating the contribution lost elsewhere by reallocating scarce resources, the new product is not viable.

# Pricing

## Chapter learning objectives

Upon completion of this chapter you will be able to:

- explain the factors that influence the pricing of a product or service, e.g. costs, demand and competition

- define and explain the price elasticity of demand

- from supplied data, derive and manipulate a straight-line demand equation

- from supplied data, derive an equation for the total cost function excluding volume-based discounts

- from supplied data, derive an equation for the total cost function including volume-based discounts

- using data supplied or equations derived, advise on whether or not to increase production and sales levels considering incremental costs, incremental revenues and other factors

- explain, using a simple example, all forms of cost-plus pricing strategy

- calculate, for given data, a price using a cost-plus strategy

- explain, using a simple example, a market-skimming pricing strategy

- explain, using a simple example, a penetration-pricing strategy

- explain, using a simple example, a complementary-product pricing strategy

- explain, using a simple example, a product-line pricing strategy

- explain, using a simple example, a volume-discounting pricing strategy

- identify suitable pricing strategies for given situations from skimming, penetration, complementary product, product-line, volume discounting

- explain, using a simple example, a price-discrimination pricing strategy

- explain, using a simple example, a relevant-cost pricing strategy

- calculate, for given data, a price using a relevant cost strategy.

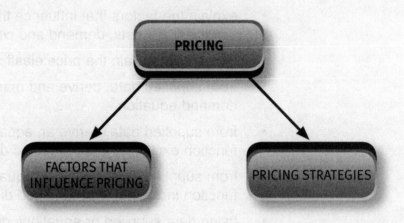

## 1 Introduction

Pricing is important because:

- It makes a pivotal contribution to profit maximisation – the overriding aim of most businesses.

- Businesses make profits by selling goods and services at a price higher than their cost.

- The amount that they are able to sell will often be determined by the price charged for the goods and services.

Pricing is one of the four components of the marketing mix, the others being:

- product

- place

- promotion.

Decisions in relation to all four components should be made within the context of the overall marketing strategy.

KAPLAN PUBLISHING

## 2    Important factors

Three important factors that influence the pricing of a product or service are:

- costs
- customers
- competition.

### 2.1   Cost-based pricing:  the accountant's approach

'Cost plus' pricing is a much favoured traditional approach to establishing the selling price by:

- calculating the unit cost
- adding a mark-up or margin to provide profit.

The unit cost may reflect:

- full cost
- manufacturing cost
- variable cost.

The mark-up is equally subjective and often reflects:

- the risk involved in the product
- competitors' mark-ups
- desired profit and/or ROCE (return on capital employed)
- type of cost used
- type of product, etc.

It is important to understand the difference between:

- Profit mark-up:  the profit is quoted as a percentage of the cost.
- Profit margin:   the profit is quoted as a percentage of the selling price.

### Illustration 1 – Important factors

If the full cost of an item is $540, calculate the selling price using a 25% mark up and a 25% profit margin:

**Solution**

- A 25% mark-up would produce a selling price of $675 ($540 x 1.25).

- A 25% profit margin would produce a selling price of $720 ($540/75 x 100).

## 2.2 Customer based pricing – the marketer's approach

Customer-based pricing reflects customers' perceptions of the benefits they will enjoy (e.g. convenience, status, etc.).

This approach:

*   has regard to costs – customer-based pricing must ensure that financial objectives are met.

but

*   Exploits the willingness of customers to pay a multiple of the cost price if they perceive the benefits to be substantial.

*   Has as its first step the production of a profile of the target customer.

*   Reflects a belief that the greater the understanding of the wants, needs and values of your customer the better placed you are to price the product.

### Illustration 2 – Customer-based pricing

On a remote beach in a hot country, the offer of food and drink to tourists on the beach will be perceived by them as being of significant benefit and they are likely to be prepared to pay a significant amount in excess of cost.

## 2.3 Competition-based pricing

Competition-based pricing means setting a price based upon the prices of competing products.

Competing products can be classified as:

*   The same type of product – easily distinguished from one's own products:

    –   price changes by competitors will not have a material impact.

*   The same type of product – not easily distinguished from one's own products:

    –   price changes by competitors will have a material impact.

*   Substitute products that may be bought instead of your type of product (e.g. buy ice cream instead of soft drinks on a hot day).

*   Impact of price changes will depend on relative price/performance of substitute.

## Illustration 3 – Important factors

Made-to-measure shoes and mass-manufactured shoes are examples of products that can be easily distinguished and where the price of one has little impact upon the price of the other.

If, however, one is a mass manufacturer of shoes it is very difficult to distinguish one's product from that of other mass manufacturers. The prices of competitors will have a material bearing on one's own prices.

## Test your understanding 1

**Of the three approaches to pricing discussed above:**

- **cost based**
- **customer based**
- **competition based,**

**which are most likely to maximise profits?**

## 3 Price elasticity of demand (PED)

When a business proposes to change the price of a product or service the key question is: 'to what degree will demand be affected?'.

### 3.1 Calculation

The price elasticity of demand can be calculated as follows:

$$\frac{\% \text{ Change in demand}}{\% \text{ Change in selling price}}$$

## Illustration 4 – Price elasticity of demand

- The price of a chocolate bar goes up from 40p to 60p.
- Sales of a retailer fall from 20 per day to 12 per day.

    %change in price =(20/40)= +50%
    %change in demand =(-8/20)= –40%
    PED = –40/+50 = –0.8

(a) If the % change in demand > the % change in price, then price elasticity > 1.

Demand is 'elastic', i.e. very responsive.

- Total revenue increases when price is reduced.
- Total revenue decreases when price is increased.

(b) If the % change in demand < the % change in price, then price elasticity < 1.

Demand is 'inelastic', i.e. not very responsive.

- Total revenue decreases when price is reduced.

- Total revenue increases when price is increased.

(c) If the % change in demand = the % change in price, then price elasticity = 1.

Demand is neither 'elastic' nor 'inelastic.'

Total revenue remains the same:

- When price is reduced   –   the price reduction is offset by increased demand.

- When price is increased  –   the price increase is offset by reduced demand.

### Test your understanding 2

- A retailer plans to increase the price of a text book from $20 to $22.

**Given that the PED=-1.25, what will be the impact of the price rise on sales (currently 300 per annum) and revenue?**

## 4 Straight-line demand equation

The equation of a straight line demand curve is represented by the following equation:

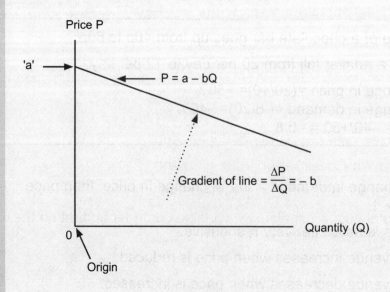

Price P

'a'

$P = a - bQ$

Gradient of line $= \dfrac{\Delta P}{\Delta Q} = -b$

Quantity (Q)

0

Origin

## Illustration 5 – Straight-line demand equation

**Required:**

Find the linear relationship between price (P) and the quantity demanded (Q) in relation to the following sales and demand data:

- Selling price of $200 = sales of 1,000 units per month.
- Selling price of $220 = sales of 950 units per month.

**Solution**

- b (gradient) $= \dfrac{220 - 200}{950 - 1000} = -0.4$
- remembering that price (P) = 200 when 1000 units are sold and substituting 2 0.4 for b
- 200 = a 2 (0.431,000)
- 200 = a 2 400
- a = 200 + 400 = 600
- So the equation is: P = 600 – 0.4Q.

## Test your understanding 3

**Find the linear relationship between price (P) and the quantity demanded (Q) in relation to the following sales and demand data:**

- **Selling price of $300 = sales of 500 units per month.**
- **Selling price of $330 = sales of 400 units per month.**

## 5 Equation for the total cost function

Cost equations are derived from historical cost data. Once a cost equation has been established, like the high/low method, it can be used to estimate future costs. In the exam, cost functions will be linear:

y = a + bx

- 'a' is the fixed cost per period (the intercept)
- 'b' is the variable cost per unit (the gradient)
- 'x' is the activity level (the independent variable)
- 'y' is the total cost = fixed cost + variable cost (dependent on the activity level).

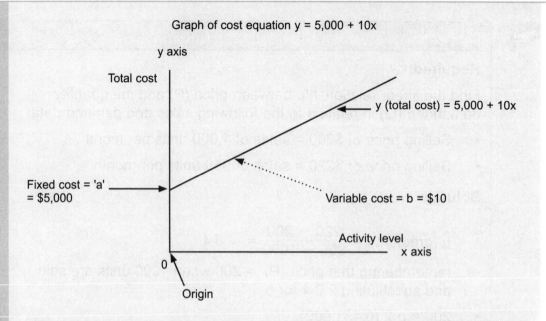

Graph of cost equation y = 5,000 + 10x

y axis

Total cost

y (total cost) = 5,000 + 10x

Fixed cost = 'a'
= $5,000

Variable cost = b = $10

Activity level
x axis

0

Origin

## Illustration 6 – Equation for the total cost function

If y = 8,000 + 40x

**Required:**

(a)  Fixed cost                    = $ ⬚

(b)  Variable cost per unit        = $ ⬚

(c)  Total cost for 200 units      = $ ⬚

**Solution**

(a)  Fixed cost                    = $ | 8,000 |

(b)  Variable cost per unit        = $ | 40 |

(c)  Total cost for 200 units      = $ | 16,000 |

**Working**
Fixed cost = $8,000
Variable cost = 200 × $40 = $8,000
Total cost + fixed cost + variable cost = $8,000 + $8,000 = $16,000

## Test your understanding 4

**Consider the linear function y = 1,488 + 20x and answer the following questions.**

**(a)  The line would cross the y axis at the point**

**(b)  The gradient of the line is**

**(c)  The independent variable is**

**(d)  The dependent variable is**

**Test your understanding 5**

**If the total cost of a product is given as:**

**Y = 4,800 + 8x**

**(a) The fixed cost is $**

**(b) The variable cost per unit is $**

**(c) The total cost of producing 100 units is $**

Suppose a cost has a cost equation of y = $5,000 + 10x, this can be shown graphically as follows:

## 6 Cost equations including volume-based discounts

Suppliers often offer discounts to encourage the purchase of increased volumes.

Where volume-based discounts are offered a total cost equation can be derived for each volume range.

**Illustration 7 – Equation including volume-based discounts**

- Fixed costs $100,000.

- Variable costs per unit $5 for volumes up to 1,000 units.

- Volumes above 1,000 units receive 5% discount on all units.

This gives:

- Y = 100,000 + 5x for x≤1000

- Y = 100,000 + 4.75x for x>1000.

The graphs of these two functions will therefore show a discontinuity at 1,000 units – see below.

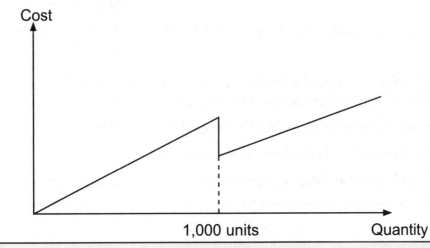

## Test your understanding 6

You are given the following cost data:

Fixed costs          $250,000.

Variable costs       $6 per unit up to 5000 units.
                     10% discount on all units purchased over
                     5000 units.

Derive equations for the total cost function.

# 7    Increasing sales and production levels

When an opportunity to increase sales and production levels arises in a business the key question to answer is:

What will be the effect upon net profit?  Will the:

*   increased contribution (sales less variable costs) generated by the increased sales exceed any additional fixed costs that will be incurred as a result of the increased sales level?

If the answer is 'yes' the opportunity should normally be pursued.

## Illustration 8 – Increasing sales and production levels

An opportunity arises to increase sales by 10,000 units:
*   Selling price of additional units      =   $10
*   Variable cost of  additional units     =   $6
*   Fixed costs will increase by           =   $50,000

The effect of the increased sales would be to reduce net profits by $10,000.

*   $100,000 increased sales

*   $60,000 increased variable costs      =   $40,000 additional contribution

*   less additional fixed costs of $50,000 =   $10,000 reduction in net profit.

Based on this analysis, the opportunity should be rejected. However, other factors need to be considered such as:

*   the impact on future sales beyond the current period

*   the impact of rejection on customer goodwill

*   whether the extra sales would help build the firm's brand.

## Illustration 9 – Increasing sales and production levels

An alternative is a tabular approach showing profits at different activity levels

**Tabular approach – increasing production and sales**

- XYZ Ltd is introducing a new product.

- Details of the costs are as follows:

  - Hire costs – hiring the machinery to manufacture the product will cost $200,000 pa. This machine will enable 60,000 units pa to be produced.

  - Additional machines can be hired at $80,000 pa. Each machine hired enables capacity to be increased by 20,000 units pa, but it is not possible to increase production beyond 90,000 units because of shortage of space.

  - The minimum rental period is for one year and the variable cost is estimated to be $6 per unit produced.

  - There are no other fixed costs that can be specifically traced to the product.

- Marketing management has estimated the maximum selling prices for a range of output from 50,000 units to 90,000 units. The estimates are as follows:

| Units sold | 50,000 | 60,000 | 70,000 | 80,000 | 90,000 | 90,000* |
|---|---|---|---|---|---|---|
| Selling price ($) | 22 | 20 | 19 | 18 | 17 | 15 |

\* At $15 demand will be in excess of 90,000 units but production capacity will limit the sales.

**Required:**

Present relevant financial information to management for the pricing and output decision.

**Solution**

| | $ | $ | $ | $ | $ | $ |
|---|---|---|---|---|---|---|
| Price per unit | 22 | 20 | 19 | 18 | 17 | 15 |
| Variable cost per unit | (6) | (6) | (6) | (6) | (6) | (6) |
| Contribution per unit | 16 | 14 | 13 | 12 | 11 | 9 |
| Number of units sold | 50,000 | 60,000 | 70,000 | 80,000 | 90,000 | 90,000 |
| Total contribution ($000) | 800 | 840 | 910 | 960 | 990 | 810 |
| Less fixed costs ($000) | (200) | (200) | (280) | (280) | (360) | (360) |
| Net profit ($000) | 600 | 640 | 630 | 680 | 630 | 450 |

Therefore produce 80,000 units of goods and sell at $18/unit.

## Test your understanding 7

A company produces and sells one product and its forecast for the next financial year is as follows:

|  | $000 | $000 |
|---|---|---|
| Sales 100,000 units @ $8 |  | 800 |
| Variable costs: |  |  |
| material | 300 |  |
| labour | 200 |  |
|  | 500 |  |
| Contribution ($3 per unit) |  | 300 |
| Fixed costs |  | 150 |
| Net profit |  | 150 |

As an attempt to increase net profit, two proposals have been put forward:

(a) To launch an advertising campaign costing $14,000. This will increase the sales to 150,000 units, although the price will have to be reduced to $7.

(b) To produce some components at present purchased from suppliers. This will reduce material costs by 20% but will increase fixed costs by $72,000.

**Decide whether these proposals should be pursued.**

## 8 Cost-plus pricing strategy

Cost-plus pricing strategies are widely used and simple to calculate if costs are known.

## Illustration 10 – Full cost-plus pricing strategy

The business needs to:

* Establish its full unit costs, e.g.:

  - raw materials — $40 per unit
  - variable production costs — $40 per unit
  - fixed costs based on planned volumes — $20 per unit
  - total cost — $100 per unit

- Add a profit margin:
  - 20% mark-up       =   selling price of $120 per unit
  - 20% sales margin     =   selling price of $125 per unit

Realisation of the target profit is dependent upon:

- accurate knowledge of costs
- the selling price arrived at being one which customers are prepared to pay
- selling the planned volume of goods.

The business must:

- establish its unit costs - e.g. prime, marginal, full
- add a mark-up or sales-margin.

| **Expandable text** |
| --- |

| Advantages of cost-plus pricing | Disadvantages of cost-plus pricing |
| --- | --- |
| <ul><li>Widely used and accepted.</li><li>Simple to calculate if costs are known.</li><li>Selling price decision may be delegated to junior management.</li><li>Justification for price increases.</li><li>May encourage price stability – if all competitors have similar cost structures and use similar mark-up.</li></ul> | <ul><li>Ignores the economic relationship between price and demand.</li><li>No attempt to establish optimum price.</li><li>Different absorption methods give rise to different costs and hence different selling prices.</li><li>Does not guarantee profit – if sales volumes are low fixed costs may not be recovered.</li><li>Must decide whether to use full cost, manufacturing cost or marginal cost.</li><li>This structured method fails to recognise the manager's need for flexibility in pricing.</li><li>Circular reasoning – for example, a price increase will reduce volume, thus increasing unit costs, resulting in pressure to increase the price further.</li></ul> |

A manufacturer has calculated that the total unit cost of a product is $250.

He proposes to sell the product at $300.

**Calculate:**

• the % mark-up involved in a price of $300.

• his profit margin on sales made at $300.

Cost-plus pricing is more suited to businesses that:

• sell in large volumes

• operate in markets dominated by price.

## 9 Market-skimming pricing strategy

Market skimming is an attempt to exploit those sections of the market which are relatively insensitive to price changes. Initially high prices may be charged to take advantage of the novelty appeal of a new product when demand is initially inelastic.

A skimming policy offers a safeguard against:

• unexpected future increases in costs

• a large fall in demand after the novelty appeal has declined.

Once the market becomes saturated the price can be reduced to attract that part of the market that has not been exploited.

Conditions suitable for a market-skimming strategy are:

• Where the product is new and different and has little direct competition:

– Customers are prepared to pay high prices so as to be 'one-up' on other people who do not own one.

• Where the strength of demand and the sensitivity of demand to price are unknown:

– It is much easier to lower prices than to increase them.

– From a psychological point of view it is far better to begin with a high price, which can then be lowered if the demand for the product appears to be more price sensitive than at first thought.

KAPLAN PUBLISHING

- Where high prices in the early stages of a product's life might generate high initial cash flows:
  - A firm with a liquidity problem may prefer market skimming for this reason.

- Where products have a short life cycle, and there is a need to:
  - recover their development costs
  - make a profit quickly.

With high prices being charged potential competitors will be tempted to enter the market. For skimming to be sustained one or more significant barriers to entry must be present to deter these potential competitors, e.g.:

- patent protection
- prohibitively high capital investment
- unusually strong brand loyalty.

## Illustration 11 – Market-skimming pricing strategy

Market skimming is often used in relation to electronic products when a new range (e.g. DVD players, plasma TV screens) are first released onto the market at a high price.

The target is the 'early adopters' of such products; their price sensitivity is relatively low because their interest in the product is substantial or they have a stronger appreciation of the qualities offered by the product.

## Test your understanding 9

**Which of the following features are often present when a market skimming strategy is used?**

1    Substantial development costs.

2    Product type is often attractive to early adopters.

3    Product features are tried and tested.

4    The likely level of demand and the price sensitivity is very difficult to gauge.

5    The initial price is subject to substantial reductions within a relatively brief period.

6    There are significant barriers to entry in this market.

## 10    Penetration pricing strategy

Penetration pricing is the charging of low prices when a product is initially launched in order to gain rapid acceptance of the product. Once market share is achieved, prices are increased.

The circumstances which favour a penetration policy are as follows:

- If the firm wishes to discourage new entrants from entering the market.

- If the firm wishes to shorten the initial period of the product's life cycle in order to enter the growth and maturity stages as quickly as possible.

- If there are significant economies of scale to be achieved from high-volume output, and so a quick penetration into the market is desirable in order to gain those unit cost reductions.

- If demand is highly elastic and so would respond well to low prices.

For penetration pricing to be effective:

- The total market in which the firm is operating must be substantial

- The anticipated market share must be significant.

Penetration pricing, if exploited to the full, becomes predatory pricing; its objective is to eliminate competition through use of unsustainably low prices. Predatory pricing is illegal.

### Illustration 12 – Penetration pricing strategy

The 2006 launch of Microsoft's anti-virus product, Windows Live OneCare, was described by commentators as an example of penetration pricing. Microsoft's competitors in this market (e.g. Symantec and McAfee) reportedly lost material market share within a few months of its launch.

### Test your understanding 10

**Which of the following are often features of penetration pricing?**

1    A substantial price reduction to gain market share following the use of a  successful market-skimming strategy

2    Demand is inelastic allowing acceptance of increased prices with little reduction in demand.

3    Production runs are usually of small size since unit cost is not an issue.

4    A high initial price followed by a substantial price reduction.

## 11    Complementary-product pricing

A complementary product is one that is normally used with another product.

An example is razors and razor blades – if sales of razors increase more razor blades will also be bought.

Other examples of complementary products are:

- game consoles and associated games

- printers and printer cartridges.

Complementary goods:

- Provide suppliers with additional power over the consumer.

- Potentially enable suppliers to lock consumers into an ongoing stream of purchases by ensuring that only proprietary consumables (e.g. printer cartridges) can be used in their products.

- Enable suppliers to increase the consumer's switching cost – in order to use cheaper cartridges the consumer would have to abandon his original printer and purchase one that allowed him to use non-proprietary cartridges.

### Illustration 13 – Complementary-product pricing

A complementary pricing strategy can take two forms:

- The major product (e.g. a printer or a camera) is priced at a relatively low figure – to encourage the purchase and lock the consumer into subsequent purchases of relatively high price consumables (e.g. printer cartridges or memory cards).

- The major product (e.g. membership of a fashionable sports or golf club) is priced at a relatively high figure – to create a barrier to entry and exit and the consumer is locked into subsequent purchases of relatively low-price facilities (e.g. court fees or green fees).

**Test your understanding 11**

**Which of the following accurately describe complementary pricing?**

1. The amount spent by consumers on the major product is, over time, often substantially exceeded by the amount spent on the complementary consumable product.

2. The supplier's margin on the major product is usually higher than the margin on the complementary product.

3. The supplier's objective is to lock the consumer into a stream of relatively low-value purchases of consumables.

## 12 Product-line pricing strategy

A product line is a range of products that are intended to meet similar needs of different target audiences. Thus all products within a product line are related but may vary in terms of style, colour, quality, etc.

Product-line pricing works by:

- capitalising on consumer interest in a number of products within a range.

- making the price entry point for the basic product relatively cheap.

- pricing other items in the range more highly – in order to 'complete the set' the consumer has to pay substantially more for the additional matching items.

**Illustration 14 – Product-line pricing strategy**

A dinner service is being promoted. The entry point (serving plates) will be relatively cheap. Other, less essential matching items in the same range (e.g. gravy boats) will have a higher price.

**Test your understanding 12**

**Which of the following is true of product-line pricing?**

1. The essential items within the range are relatively highly priced.

2. Product-line pricing relies on the wish of consumers to build up a matching set of items within a product range.

3. The less essential items within the range are relatively cheap since demand for these items is relatively low.

4. The product range has a short shelf life.

## 13 Volume-discounting pricing strategy

Volume discounting means offering customers a lower price per unit if they purchase a particular quantity (volume) of product. It takes two main forms:

- Quantity discounts – for customers that order large quantities.

- Cumulative quantity discounts – the discount increases as the cumulative total ordered increases. This may appeal to those who do not wish to place large individual orders but who purchase large quantities over time.

The volume discounter may enjoy the following benefits from this strategy:

- Increased customer loyalty – cumulative quantity discounts 'lock in' the customer since further purchases can be made at a lower cost per unit.

- Attracting new customers – an exceptional level of discount can be offered to new customers on a one-off basis, enabling the supplier to 'get his foot in the door'.

- Lower sales processing costs – an increased proportion of his sales take the form of bulk orders.

- Lower purchasing costs – his increased sales volumes enable him to enjoy discounts from his suppliers, creating a virtuous circle.

- Discounts help to sell items that are bought primarily on price.

- Competitive advantage – the discounts encouraging customers to concentrate their orders rather than try out new suppliers.

- Clearance of surplus stock – the discount level can be increased to clear unpopular items.

- Increased use of off-peak capacity – discounts are geared to particular off-peak periods.

### Illustration 14 – Volume discounting pricing strategy

A software vendor sells at a single unit price of $10 but offers a range of discounts for bulk purchases as follows:

- 2-5      10% discount

- 6-10     15% discount

- 11-25    20% discount

- 25+      25% discount.

**Which of the following is true of a volume-discounting pricing strategy?**

1   Volume discounting offers suppliers the opportunity to both increase their sales and to reduce their sales processing cost per unit.

2   Volume discounting is used to increase further the sales of items for which there is a strong demand and where the bulk of sales are made to regular customers.

3   Cumulative volume discounts are aimed at locking in the customer.

4   Volume discounting is concentrated in a small number of business sectors.

## 14   Pricing strategies for given situations

| Situation | Pricing Strategy |
|---|---|
| • Product is new and different (e.g. new electronic product).<br><br>• 'Early adopters' are prepared to pay high prices to achieve ownership.<br><br>• Significant barriers to entry exist (e.g. patent protection, high capital investment, or unusually strong brand loyalty) to deter competition – in order that skimming can be sustained.<br><br>• The product has a short life cycle so there is a need to recover development costs and make a profit quickly.<br><br>• The business has a liquidity problem and may be attracted by the high initial cash flows available in the early stages of a product's life.<br><br>• Strength of demand and the sensitivity of demand to price are unknown.  It is much easier to lower prices than to increase them. | Skimming |

| Situation (contd) | Pricing Strategy (contd) |
|---|---|
| • The business wishes to discourage newcomers from entering the market.<br><br>• The business wishes to shorten the initial period of the product's life cycle in order to enter the growth and maturity stages as quickly as possible.<br><br>• There are significant economies of scale to be achieved from high-volume output, and so a quick penetration into the market is desirable in order to gain those unit cost reductions.<br><br>• Demand is highly elastic and so would respond well to low prices. | Penetration |
| • Use of the product requires the purchase of an additional proprietary consumable item (e.g. memory cards for digital cameras, printer cartridges for printers). | Complementary-product |
| • A range of products is being marketed – the products within a product line are related but may vary in terms of style, colour, quality, etc. (e.g. dinner services, cutlery sets).<br><br>• Consumers will tend to buy a number of items within the range and be prepared to pay a relatively high price for the less essential items in order to build up a matching set. | Product-line |
| • The sales margin is substantial, allowing good profits to be made even after significant discounting (e.g. consumer software products).<br><br>• The product is traditionally bought on price – it is difficult to distinguish from competing products (e.g. car tyres).<br><br>• Products with a limited shelf life (e.g. fashion items). | Volume discounting |

---

**Test your understanding 14**

1   Which pricing strategies are aimed at the start of the product life cycle?

2   Which pricing strategies seek to attract sales by offering a product at a relatively low price?

3   Which pricing strategies lure the customer in with a relatively low-priced product in order to lock the customer in to subsequent additional purchases of similar items that are relatively highly priced?

4   Which pricing strategy is appropriate to items that are bought primarily on price.

---

## 15   Price-discrimination pricing strategy

A price-discrimination strategy is where a company sells the same products at different prices in different markets.

This is possible if:

*   the seller can determine the selling price

*   customers can be segregated into different markets

*   customers cannot buy at the lower price in one market and sell at the higher price in the other market.

Segmentation will usually be on the basis of one or more of the following:

*   time

*   age

*   gender

*   type of service

*   geographical location

*   quantity

*   type of customer.

---

**Illustration 16 – Price discrimination pricing strategy**

Examples of price discrimination include:

*   lower admission prices for children at certain sporting and entertainment events

*   discounts for Senior Citizens  in some pubs and restaurants

*   concessionary rail fares for students

*   lower admission prices for females at some nightclubs.

---

1    Identify four means of segmenting customers in relation to a price discrimination strategy.

2    Which services or products lend themselves to a price-discrimination strategy?

## 16    Using relevant costs to arrive at a price

The principles of relevant costing were met in paper F2. Here relevant costs are used to arrive at a minimum tender price for a one-off tender.

The use of relevant costs is only suitable for a one-off decision since:

*   fixed costs may become relevant in the long run

*   there are problems estimating incremental cash flows

*   there is a conflict between accounting measures such as profit and this approach.

### Illustration 17 – Using relevant costs to arrive at a price

Mr Smith has been asked to quote a price for a special contract. He has already prepared his tender but has asked you to review it for him.

He has pointed out to you that he wants to quote the minimum price as he believes this will lead to more lucrative work in the future.

Mr Smith's tender

|  |  | $ |
|---|---|---:|
| Material: | A 2,000 kgs @ $10 per kg | 20,000 |
|  | B 1,000 kgs @ $15 per kg | 15,000 |
|  | C 500 kgs @ $40 per kg | 20,000 |
|  | D 50 litres @ $12 per litre | 600 |
|  |  |  |
| Labour: | Skilled 1,000 hrs @ $25 per hr | 25,000 |
|  | Semi-skilled 2,000 hrs @ $15 per hr | 30,000 |
|  | Unskilled, 500 hrs @ $10 per hr | 5,000 |
|  |  |  |
| Fixed overheads 3,500 hrs @ $12 per hr |  | 42,000 |
|  |  |  |
| Costs of preparing the tender: |  |  |
|  | Mr Smith's time | 1,000 |
|  | other expenses | 500 |

| Minimum profit (5% of total costs) | 7,725 |
|---|---|
| Minimum tender price | 166,825 |

Other information

Material A

- 1,000 kgs of this material is in stock at a cost of $5 per kg.
- Mr Smith has no alternative use for his material and intends selling it for $2 per kg.
- However, if he sold any he would have to pay a fixed sum of $300 to cover delivery costs.
- The current purchase price is $10 per kg.

Material B

- There is plenty of this material in stock at a cost of $18 per kg.
- The current purchase price has fallen to $15 per kg.
- This material is constantly used by Mr Smith in his business.

Material C

- The total amount in stock of 500 kgs was bought for $10,000 some time ago for another one-off contract that never happened.
- Mr Smith is considering selling it for $6,000 in total or using it as a substitute for another material, constantly used in normal production.
- If used in this latter manner it would save $8,000 of the other material.
- Current purchase price is $40 per kg.

Material D

- There are 100 litres of this material in stock.
- It is dangerous and if not used in this contract will have to be disposed of at a cost to Mr Smith of $50 per litre.
- The current purchase price is $12 per litre.

Skilled labour

- Mr Smith only hires skilled labour when he needs it.
- $25 per hour is the current hourly rate.

Semi-skilled labour.

- Mr Smith has a workforce of 50 semi-skilled labourers who are currently not fully employed.

- They are on annual contracts and the number of spare hours currently available for this project are 1,500. Any hours in excess of this will have to be paid for at time-and-a-half.

- The normal hourly rate is $15 per hour.

Unskilled labour.

- These are currently fully employed by Mr Smith on jobs where they produce a contribution of $2 per unskilled labour hour.

- Their current rate is $10 per hour, although extra could be hired at $20 an hour if necessary.

Fixed overheads.

- This is considered by Mr Smith to be an accurate estimate of the hourly rate based on his existing production.

Costs of preparing the tender

- Mr Smith has spent 10 hours working on this project at $100 per hour, which he believes is his charge-out rate.

- Other expenses include the cost of travel and research spent by Mr Smith on the project.

Profit.

- This is Mr Smith's minimum profit margin which he believes is necessary to cover 'general day-to-day expenses of running a business'.

**Required:**

Calculate and explain for Mr Smith what you believe the minimum tender price should be.

**Solution**

|   |   |   | $ | $ |
|---|---|---|---|---|
| 1 | Material A | 1,000 kgs @ $2 – $300 | 1,700 | |
|   |   | 1,000 kgs @ $10 | 10,000 | |
|   |   |   |   | 11,700 |
| 2 | Material B | 1,000 kgs @ $15 | | 15,000 |
| 3 | Material C | 500 kgs – opportunity cost | | 8,000 |
| 4 | Material D | 50 litres @ $50 | | (2,500) |
| 5 | Skilled labour | 1,000 hrs @ $25 | | 25,000 |
| 6 | Semi-skilled labour | 500 hrs @ $22.50 | | 11,250 |
| 7 | Unskilled labour | 500 @ $12 (opportunity cost) | | 6,000 |
| | Minimum tender price | | | 74,450 |

## Notes

1 Presumably the 1,000 kgs in stock would otherwise be sold at a net gain of $1,700. This gain is therefore foregone as a result of using this material in the contract. (Note, however, that the gain forgone is less than the cost of buying the extra 1,000 kgs.)

2 As this material is constantly needed, the relevant cost is the cost of replacing it at the current purchase price.

3 How would this material be used if it were not required for the contract?

Option 1 – Sell it for $6,000.

Option 2 – Use it as a substitute and save $8,000.

Option 2 is preferable. This is therefore the opportunity cost of using it in the contract. (Also note that this opportunity cost is much less than the cost of buying it and is therefore the correct decision.)

4 The cost of disposing of 50 litres will be saved (@ $50/litre, i.e. $2,500). Saving this cost is a relevant benefit.

5 The incremental cost of paying for the labour needed.

6 The assumption is that the 1,500 spare hours have already been paid for as the workforce are on annual contracts. The additional cash flow is therefore the extra 500 hours that are needed at time-and-a-half.

7 For each hour diverted from their normal jobs contribution of $2 will be foregone. This together with the cost of paying the workers to do the project amounts to a relevant cost of $12 per kg. They would not be hired at $20 per hour as this is more expensive.

Alternatively

This typical problem can be looked at from the point of view of incremental cash flows.

|  | Cash flow normally $ | Cash flow with project $ |
|---|---|---|
| Revenue per hour | 12 | – |
| Labour per hour | (10) | (10) |
| Contribution | 2 | (10) |

Therefore difference in cash flow is from positive $2 to negative $10, i.e. a negative cost of $12 per hour.

8   Fixed overheads can be ignored as they are not incremental.

9   Costs of preparing the tender are all sunk costs and hence must be ignored.

10  Profit element should be ignored.

**Test your understanding 16**

1   Relevant cost principles require that only future incremental .... ..... should be included in the calculations. These arise from the alternative course of action under consideration.

2   Future incremental .... ..... are the differences between the actual .... .... if the course of action is taken and the actual .... .... if it is not.

3   Future incremental .... ..... relate to those costs and revenues which can ....... the decision under consideration or be ......... by it.

4   Which of the following are specifically excluded from relevant cost calculations:

   (a)  sunk costs

   (b)  non - cash flows (e.g. depreciation)

   (c)  historic costs – (e.g. of an asset)

   (d)  book values (e.g. inventory values)

   (e)  unavoidable costs

   (f)  opportunity costs and revenues

   (g)  apportioned fixed costs

   (h)  finance costs (e.g. interest – discounting deals with this).

## Chapter summary

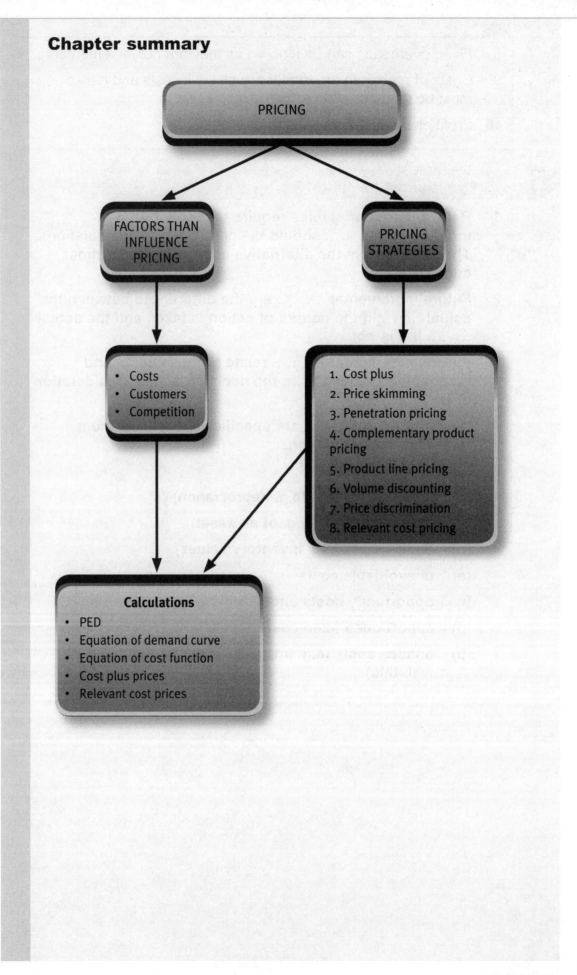

# Test your understanding answers

## Test your understanding 1

Customer-based and competition-based pricing are most likely to maximise profits since they take into account the behaviour of customers and competitors, as well as the need to recover costs or obtain a particular margin on sales. Cost-based pricing, in contrast, simply reflects the objective of cost recovery or achieving a margin on sales and ignores the potential to exploit the level of customers' interest in the product or the strength of the product in the marketplace relative to competitors.

## Test your understanding 2

The %change in price = +10%
The %change in demand = -1.25 x 10 = -12.5%
The demand thus drops to 300 x 87.5% = 262.5 units pa
Total revenue currently = 300x20 = $6,000
New revenue = 262.5 x 22 = $5,775
A price rise with elastic demand has resulted in a fall in revenue.

## Test your understanding 3

- $P = a - bQ$

- b (gradient) = $(330 - 300) \div (400 - 500) = -0.3$

- remembering that price (P) = 300 when 500 units are sold and substituting $-0.3$ for b

- $300 = a - (0.3 \times 500)$

- $300 = a - 150$

- $a = 300 + 150 = 450$

- So the linear relationship (or demand function equation) is: $P = 450 - 0.3Q$.

## Test your understanding 4

(a) The line would cross the y axis at the point     1,488

(b) The gradient of the line is     20

(c) The independent variable is     x

(d) The dependent variable is     y

## Test your understanding 5

(a) The fixed cost is $     4,800

(b) The variable cost per unit is $     8

(c) The total cost of producing 100 units is $     5,600

**Working**

Fixed cost = $4,800

Variable cost = 100 × $8 = $800

Total cost = fixed cost + variable cost = $4,800 + $800 = $5,600

## Test your understanding 6

$y = 250,000 + 6x$ for $x \leq 5000$.

$y = 250,000 + 5.4x$ for $x > 5000$.

## Test your understanding 7

Proposal (a) will increase the sales revenue but the increase in costs will be greater:

|  | $000 |
|---|---|
| Sales 150,000 @ $7 | 1,050 |
| Variable costs | 750 |
|  | 300 |
| Fixed costs plus advertising | 164 |
| Net profit | 136 |

Proposal (a) is therefore of no value and sales must be increased by a further 7,000 units to maintain net profit:

| Advertising cost | $14,000 |
|---|---|
| Contribution per unit | $2 |
| ∴ Additional volume required | 7,000 units |

Proposal (b)

- reduces variable costs by $60,000

- but increases fixed costs by $72,000 and is therefore not to be recommended unless the total volume increases as a result of the policy (e.g. if the supply of the components were previously a limiting factor).

The increase in sales needed to maintain profit at $150,000 (assuming the price remains at $8) would be as follows:

| | |
|---|---|
| Reduced profits at 100,000 units | $12,000 |
| Revised contribution per unit | $3.60 |
| ∴ Additional volume required | 3,333 units. |

### Test your understanding 8

- The mark up is 20%        50/250.
- His profit margin is 16.7%        50/300.

### Test your understanding 9

All the features listed – save for No.3. – are typical elements of a market-skimming strategy. Product features are likely to be new and different rather than tried and tested.

### Test your understanding 10

None of the four options listed are features of penetration pricing which is characterised by:

- a substantial price increase once material market share is achieved

- highly-elastic demand

- large production runs

- a low initial price to gain market share.

### Test your understanding 11

Numbers 1 and 3 accurately describe complementary pricing. The supplier's margin on the complementary product is usually substantially higher than the margin on the main product which can be a 'loss leader'.

### Test your understanding 12

Only statement No. 2 is true.

The essential items are relatively inexpensive in order to lure the consumer into the purchase of an initial set of items. The less essential items are relatively expensive but the customer is 'forced' to buy them in order to have a matching set.

The product range often has a long shelf life to enable customers to build up their set over a long period.

### Test your understanding 13

Statements 1 and 3 are true. Volume discounting is often applied to items:

- for which demand is uncertain and possibly time limited (e.g. raffle tickets)

- that are of low unit value (e.g. biros)

- where price is key to making a sale (e.g. PC components)

- that are bought infrequently and by a changing population of customers (e.g. printer cartridges)

- that are spread over a wide range of business sectors.

### Test your understanding 14

1 Skimming and the penetration-pricing strategies.

2 Penetration and volume discounting rely substantially on relatively low-price offers; this is also true to a lesser extent of complementary and product line pricing strategies.

3 Complementary and product-line pricing strategies.

4 Volume discounting.

### Test your understanding 15

1 Age (e.g. Senior Citizens), time (e.g. admission to clubs at off peak times), type of customer (e.g. students), geographical location (e.g. beer in central london versus lower provincial prices).

2 Examples include:

(a) Entertainment, where the vendor is seeking to attract.

KAPLAN PUBLISHING

families – children attracting lower prices. (e.g. Alton Towers)

(b) meals and drinks which can be offered at different prices in different parts of the country reflecting the relative affluence of the area

(c) clubs and bars where one gender (girls) is offered concessionary prices to enter in order to attract other customers (boys)

(d) services such as meals at concessionary prices (e.g. for Senior Citizens) where the seller controls the price and the service is personal to the purchaser and cannot be sold at a higher price in another market.

## Test your understanding 16

1 Relevant cost principles require that only future incremental cash flows should be included in the calculations. These arise from the alternative course of action under consideration.

2 Future incremental cash flows are the difference between the actual cash flow if the course of action is taken and the actual cash flow if it is not.

3 Future incremental cash flows relate to those costs and revenues which can affect the decision under consideration or be affected by it.

4 All the items listed should be excluded save for f) opportunity costs and revenues, all of which should be included.

# Make or buy and other short-term decisions

## Chapter learning objectives

Upon completion of this chapter you will be able to:

- explain the practical issues surrounding make versus buy and outsourcing decisions

- for given data, calculate and compare 'make' costs with 'buy-in' costs

- for given data, compare in-house costs and outsource costs of completing tasks and consider other issues surrounding this decision

- for given data, apply relevant costing principles in situations involving make or buy, shut down, one-off contracts and joint product further processing decisions.

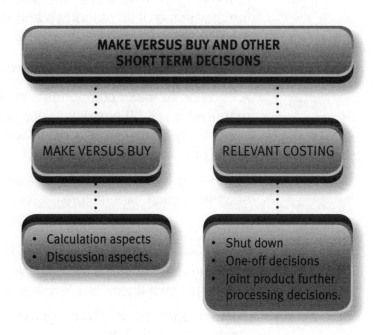

# 1 Introduction

Many businesses are considering which products/services to produce in-house and which to outsource with the current trend being towards outsourcing.

This chapter discusses the 'make versus buy' decision in terms of both the financial and other longer term implications.

Any short term decision should be approached using relevant costing principles. These are applied to a range of scenarios later in the chapter.

# 2 Make versus buy

## 2.1 Calculations

When assessing the differences in costs between making a product in-house or outsourcing, a key consideration is whether spare capacity does or would exist. If there is spare production capacity available the following issues arise:

- Production resources may be idle if the component is purchased from outside.

- The fixed costs of those resources are irrelevant to the decision in the short-term as they will be incurred whether the component is made or purchased.

- Purchase would be recommended, therefore, only if the buying price were less than the variable costs of internal manufacture.

- In the long-term, however, the business may dispense with or transfer some of its resources and may purchase from outside if it thereby saves more than the extra cost of purchasing.

If there is not spare capacity available the following issues arise:

- A decision to make components in-house might displace the manufacture of other existing products. This could give rise to opportunity costs of lost contribution or additional costs of buying in those products (if cheaper).

- In the longer-term, management may look to other alternatives, such as capital expenditure.

**Illustration 1 – Make versus buy**

A company manufactures an assembly used in the production of one of its product lines.

- The department in which the assembly is produced incurs fixed costs of $24,000 pa.

- The variable costs of production are $2.55 per unit.

- The assembly could be bought outside at a cost of $2.65 per unit.

The current annual requirement is for 80,000 assemblies per year.

**Required:**

Should the company continue to manufacture the assembly, or should it be purchased from the outside suppliers?

**Solution**

- A decision to purchase outside would cost the company $(2.65 − 2.55) = 10c per unit, which for 80,000 assemblies would amount to $8,000 pa.

- Thus, the fixed costs of $24,000 will require analysis to determine if more than $8,000 would actually be saved if production of the assembly were discontinued.

## Test your understanding 1

A factory's entire machine capacity is used to produce essential components. The production costs of using the machines are as follows.

|          | $      |
|----------|--------|
| Variable | 30,000 |
| Fixed    | 50,000 |
| Total    | 80,000 |

If all component production was outsourced, then the machines could be used to produce other items that would generate additional contribution of $50,000.

**What is the maximum price that the company should be willing to pay to the outside supplier for the components?**

A   $130,000
B   $80,000
C   $50,000
D   $30,000

## Test your understanding 2

A company plans to build an extension to its factory. The estimated costs of carrying out the work in-house are as follows:

|  | € |
|---|---|
| Materials | 58,500 |
| Labour | 32,800 |
| Additional overheads | 17,200 |
| Allocated fixed overheads | 8,200 |
|  | 116,700 |

If the extension is built internally, interference to normal production will result in lost contribution to profits of €28,500.

An outside contractor has bid €110,000 for the job.

**What is the net gain or loss if the company does its own construction work?**

A €35,200 loss
B €27,000 loss
C €6,700 loss
D €1,500 gain

## Test your understanding 3

Robust Ltd makes four components A, B, C and D and the associated annual costs are as follows:

|  | A | B | C | D |
|---|---|---|---|---|
| Production volume (units) | 1,500 | 3,000 | 5,000 | 7,000 |
| Unit variable costs | $ | $ | $ | $ |
| Direct materials | 4 | 4 | 5 | 5 |
| Direct labour | 8 | 8 | 6 | 6 |
| Variable production overheads | 2 | 1 | 4 | 5 |
| Total | 14 | 13 | 15 | 16 |
| Fixed costs directly attributable are: | 3,000 | 6,000 | 10,000 | 7,000 |
| The unit prices of an external supplier are: | 12 | 16 | 20 | 24 |

**Determine whether any of the products should be bought in from the external supplier.**

## 2.2 Other issues

Management need to consider a number of factors before deciding to outsource.

- Continuity and control of supply. Can the outside company be relied upon to meet the requirements in terms of:
    - quantity
    - quality
    - delivery dates
    - price stability
    - security.

**Note** – there are a variety of methods available to improve the chances of standards being met or surpassed. These usually involve gearing the level of reward to the level of standard achieved.

- Specialist skills:
    - Does the external supplier possess specialist skills in this area of work that are not available in-house and which add to the quality of the product or service?

- Alternative use of resources:
    - Can the resources used to make this article be transferred to another activity which will save cost or increase revenue?
    - For example, will valuable skilled staff be who could be usefully deployed elsewhere in the business, be freed up
    - Does the article require substantial in-house expertise which will be lost if it is outsourced?

- Social/legal
    - Will the decision affect contractual or ethical obligations to employees or business connections?
    - Potential difficulties in agreeing and enforcing contract terms.
    - The length of the contract (the risk of being 'locked in').

- Confidentiality
    - Is there a risk of loss of confidentiality, particularly if the external supplier performs similar work for rival companies.

- Operational gearing
    - Would outsourcing enable overheads to be reduced?
    - If so, what would be the impact on operational gearing and what would be the level of improvement in the margin of safety?

- Scheduling:
  - Will the outsourcing necessitate any re-scheduling of deliveries to customers?
  - If so, what will be the impact on customers and can the re-scheduling be negotiated without compensation being payable to customers?

- Customer reaction:
  - Do customers attach importance to the components being manufactured in-house?
  - If they do, it may be necessary to confirm with them that they would be happy for the components to be outsourced and to provide any assurances that they may require.

- Rebadging:
  - Would any of the outsourced items have to be rebadged?
  - What would be the cost of any re-badging?

**Test your understanding 4**

KRS Ltd is considering whether to administer its own purchase ledger or to use an external accounting service. It has obtained the following cost estimates for each option:

Internal service department:

| | | Volume |
|---|---|---|
| Purchase computer software | | |
| Hardware/software maintenance | $750 pa | |
| Accounting stationery | $500 pa | |
| Part-time accounts clerk | $6,000 pa | |
| External services: | | |
| Processing of invoices/credit notes | $0.50 per document | 5,000 pa |
| Processing of cheque payments | $0.50 per cheque | 4,000 pa |
| Reconciling supplier accounts | $2.00 per supplier per month | 150 suppliers |

**Determine the cost effectiveness of outsourcing the accounting activities and identify the broad qualitative factors involved.**

### Test your understanding 5

Company X, a manufacturer, has received an offer from Company Y to supply it with a component at a price of $4 per unit. Company X currently incurs variable costs (material and labour) totalling $5 per unit.

**Detail some of the non-financial issues Company X should consider when evaluating this offer.**

## 3 Applying relevant costing principles

The relevant costs are the future, incremental, cash flows arising from any decision. These cash flows are the difference between:

- the actual cash flow if the course of action is taken, and
- the actual cash flow if it is not.

These principles have already been applied to pricing decisions and make versus buy. In this section we look at further short-term decisions.

### 3.1 Shut-down situations

Part of a business may appear to be unprofitable. The segment may, e.g. be:

- a product
- a channel of distribution.
- any other profit centre.

In evaluating closure the cost accountant should identify:

- loss of contribution from the segment
- savings in specific fixed costs from closure
- penalties resulting from the closure, e.g. redundancy, compensation to customers
- alternative use for resources released
- non-quantifiable effects
- knock-on impact, e.g. supermarkets often stock some goods which they sell at a loss. This is to get customers through the door, who they then hope will purchase other products which have higher profit margins for them.

**Make or buy and other short-term decisions**

**Illustration 4 – Applying relevant costing principles**

Harolds fashion store comprises three departments – Men's Wear, Ladies' Wear and Unisex. The store budget is as follows:

|  | Men's $ | Ladies' $ | Unisex $ | Total $ |
|---|---|---|---|---|
| Sales | 40,000 | 60,000 | 20,000 | 120,000 |
| | | | | |
| Direct cost of sales | 20,000 | 36,000 | 15,000 | 71,000 |
| Department costs | 5,000 | 10,000 | 3,000 | 18,000 |
| Apportioned store costs | 5,000 | 5,000 | 5,000 | 15,000 |
| Profit/(loss) | 10,000 | 9,000 | (3,000) | 16,000 |

It is suggested that Unisex be closed to increase the size of Men's and Ladies' Wear.

**Required:**

Determine what information is relevant or required.

**Solution**

Possible answers are as follows:

(a) Unisex earns $2,000 net contribution (apportioned costs will still be incurred and thus reapportioned to other departments).

(b) Possible increase in Men's/Ladies' sales volume.

(c) Will Unisex staff be dismissed or transferred to Men's/Ladies'?

(d) Reorganisation costs, e.g. repartitioning, stock disposal.

(e) Loss of custom because Unisex attracts certain types of customer who will not buy in Men's/Ladies'.

## Test your understanding 6

The management of Fiona Co is considering the closure of one of its operations and the financial accountant has submitted the following report.

| Department | 1 | 2 | 3 | Total |
|---|---|---|---|---|
| Sales (units) | 5,000 | 6,000 | 2,000 | 13,000 |
| Sales ($) | 150,000 | 240,000 | 24,000 | 414,000 |
| Cost of sales | | | | |
| Direct material | 75,000 | 150,000 | 10,000 | 235,000 |
| Direct labour | 25,000 | 30,000 | 8,000 | 63,000 |
| Production overhead | 5,769 | 6,923 | 2,308 | 15,000 |
| Gross profit | 44,231 | 53,077 | 3,692 | 101,000 |
| Expenses | (15,384) | (18,461) | (6,155) | (40,000) |
| Net profit ($) | 28,847 | 34,616 | (2,463) | 61,000 |

In addition to the information supplied above, you are told that:

- production overheads of $15,000 have been apportioned to the three departments on the basis of unit sales volume

- expenses are head office overhead, again apportioned to departments on sales volume.

As management accountant, you further ascertain that, on a cost driver basis:

- 50% of the production overheads can be directly traced to departments and so could be allocated on the basis 2:2:1.

- Similarly 60% of the expenses can be allocated 3:3:2.

- In addition:

  - 80% of the so-called direct labour is fixed and cannot be readily allocated

  - the remaining 20% can be better allocated on the basis of sales volume.

**Prepare a report for management including a restatement of the financial position in terms of contribution made by each department and making a clear recommendation.**

## 3.2 One-off contracts

When a business is presented with the opportunity of a one-off contract it should apply relevant costing principles, i.e. it should identify the incremental cash flows associated with the project.

**Illustration 5 – – Applying relevant costing principles**

On 1 January a company prepared the following budget for a one-off contract.

|  | $ |
|---|---|
| Research and development | 50,000 |
| Material | 15,000 |
| Machinery | 5,000 |
| Labour | 35,000 |
| Allocated fixed overhead | 25,000 |
|  | 130,000 |
| Budgeted selling price | 200,000 |
| Profit | 70,000 |

In March, having spent $30,000 of the research costs and having contracted for the machinery, the company realises that the completed contract would be sold for only $100,000.

**Required:**

Determine whether the project should be continued.

**Solution**

The relevant cost of the project is as follows.

|  | $ |
|---|---|
| R&D (the part not yet spent) | (20,000) |
| Material | (15,000) |
| Machinery (a committed cost) | – |
| Labour | (35,000) |
| Allocated overhead (a common cost) | – |
| Net relevant cost | (70,000) |
| Revenue | 100,000 |
| Net benefit | 30,000 |

The project should be continued since the potential proceeds ($100,000) exceed the relevant cost ($70,000).

### Test your understanding 7

A research contract, which to date has cost the company $150,000, is under review.

If the contract is allowed to proceed:

- it will be completed in approximately one year

- the results would then be sold to a government agency for $300,000.

Shown below are the additional expenses which the managing director estimates will be necessary to complete the work.

Materials

- This material for the contract has just been purchased at a cost of $60,000.

- It is toxic; if not used in this contract it must be disposed of at a cost of $5,000.

Labour

- Skilled labour is hard to recruit.

- The workers concerned were transferred to the contract from a production department, and at a recent meeting the production manager claimed that if the men were returned to him they could generate sales of $150,000 in the next year.

    - The prime cost of these sales would be $100,000, including $40,000 for the labour cost itself.

    - The overhead absorbed into this production would amount to $20,000.

Research staff

- It has been decided that when work on this contract ceases, the research department will be closed.

- Research wages for the year are $60,000, and redundancy and severance pay has been estimated at $15,000 now, or $35,000 in one year's time.

Equipment

- The contract utilises a special microscope which cost $18,000 three years ago.

- It has a residual value of $3,000 in another two years, and a current disposal value of $8,000.

- If used in the contract it is estimated that the disposal value in a year's time will be $6,000.

Share of general building services

- The contract is charged with $35,000 pa to cover general building expenses.

- Immediately the contract is discontinued the space occupied could be sub-let for an annual rental of $7,000.

**Advise the managing director as to whether the contract should be allowed to proceed, explaining the reasons for the treatment of each item.**

(**Note:** Ignore the time value of money.)

## Test your understanding 8

Mike Inc has been asked to quote a price for a one-off contract. Management has drawn up the following schedule:

|  |  | $ |
|---|---|---:|
| Contract price (cost plus 20%) |  | 60,780 |
| Costs: |  |  |
| materials: | V (300 kg at $10/kg) | 3,000 |
|  | I (1,000 litres at $7/litre) | 7,000 |
|  | C (550 kg at $3/kg) | 1,650 |
| labour: | Department 1 (1,500 hours at $8/hour) | 12,000 |
|  | Department 2 (2,000 hours at $10/hour) | 20,000 |
| overheads: | Absorbed on a budgeted labour hour basis |  |
|  | 3,500 hours at $2/labour hour) | 7,000 |
| Total costs |  | 50,650 |

The following is also relevant:

Material V

- The cost of $10 is the original purchase cost incurred some years ago.

- This material is no longer in use by the company and if not used in the contract then it would be sold for scrap at $3/kg.

Material I

- This is in continuous use by the business.

- $7 is the historic cost of the material although current supplies are being purchased at $6.50.

Material C

- Mike Limited has 300 kg of this material in stock and new supplies would cost $4/kg.

- If current stocks are not used for the contract then they would be used as a substitute for material Y in another production process costing $7/kg.

- 2 kg of C replaces 1 kg of Y.

Department 1

- This department has spare labour capacity sufficient for the contract and labour would be retained.

Department 2

- This department is currently working at full capacity.

- Mike Inc could get the men to work overtime to complete the contract paid at time-and-a-half, or they could divert labour hours from the production of other units that currently average $3 contribution per labour hour.

Overheads

- These are arbitrarily absorbed at a pre-determined rate.

- There will be no incremental costs incurred.

**Calculate the minimum contract price that Mike Inc could accept to break even using relevant costing techniques.**

## 3.3 Joint product further processing decisions

Joint product costing was met in paper F2. Key aspects of such systems are as follows:

- Joint products arise where the manufacture of one product makes inevitable the manufacture of other products.

- The specific point at which individual products become identifiable is known as the split-off point.

- Costs incurred before the split-off point (joint or pre-separation costs) must be shared between joint products produced (e.g. for inventory valuation purposes).

- After separation products may be sold immediately or may be processed further. Any post-separation costs (further processing costs) are allocated directly to the product on which they are incurred.

When deciding whether to process a product further or to sell after split-off only future incremental cash flows should be considered:

- Any difference in revenue.

- Any extra costs – both further processing costs and any differences in selling costs.

- Note: pre-separation costs are sunk at this stage and thus not relevant to the decision.

## Illustration 6 – Applying relevant costing principles

A joint product can be further processed at a cost of €5 per kg and sold for €20 per kg. Alternatively it can be sold at the split-off point for €17 per kg.

Should it be further processed?

**Solution**

|  | € |
|---|---|
| Extra costs | (5) |
| Extra revenue (20 – 17) | 3 |
| Incremental loss | (2) |

Therefore do not process further.

## Test your understanding 9

A firm makes three joint products, X, Y and Z, at a joint cost of $400,000. Joint costs are apportioned on the basis of weight. Products X and Z are currently processed further.

| Product | Weight at split-off (tonnes) | Further processing costs (variable) $000 | Sales $000 |
|---|---|---|---|
| X | 600 | 800 | 980 |
| Y | 200 | – | 120 |
| Z | 200 | 400 | 600 |

An opportunity has arisen to sell all three products at the split-off point for the following prices.

| X | $200,000 |
|---|---|
| Y | $120,000 |
| Z | $160,000 |

**Which of products X and Z should the firm process further?**

# Chapter summary

**MAKE VERSUS BUY AND OTHER SHORT TERM DECISIONS**

**MAKE VERSUS BUY**

**RELEVANT COSTING**

## Calculation aspects

- Compare incremental costs of manufacture versus buy
- Does spare capacity exist?

## Discussion aspects

- Quality
- Skills/competences
- Alternative use of resources
- Social/legal aspects
- Confidentiality
- Operating gearing
- Scheduling
- Customer reaction
- Re-badging.

## Shut down

- Are fixed overheads avoided?
- Will staff be sacked or relocated?
- Include redundancy and other closure costs.

## One-off decisions

- Only include incremental cash flows in calculations
- Discuss wider implications – e.g. effect on long term sales.

Joint product processing decisions

- Joint costs are not relevant.

## Test your understanding answers

### Test your understanding 1

**B**

|  | $ |
|---|---|
| Variable costs saved | 30,000 |
| Contribution earned | 50,000 |
|  | 80,000 |

**Note.** Assumes no change in fixed costs.

### Test your understanding 2

**B**

Relevant costs if built in-house

|  | €000 |
|---|---|
| Materials | 58.5 |
| Labour | 32.8 |
| Additional overheads | 17.2 |
| Lost contribution | 28.5 |
|  | 137.0 |
| Contract price of outside supplier | 110.0 |
| Difference = Loss if done in-house | 27.0 |

### Test your understanding 3

|  | $ | $ | $ | $ |
|---|---|---|---|---|
| Making in house – unit variable cost | 14 | 13 | 15 | 16 |
| Buying in – unit variable cost | 12 | 16 | 20 | 24 |
| Additional variable costs of buying in | –2 | 3 | 5 | 8 |

|  | $ | $ | $ | $ |
|---|---|---|---|---|
| Annual requirements | 1,500 | 3,000 | 5,000 | 7,000 |
| Annual variable cost savings if bought in | 3,000 | (9,000) | (25,000) | (56,000) |
| Annual fixed cost savings if bought in | 3,000 | 6,000 | 10,000 | 7,000 |
| Total annual savings if bought in | 6,000 | (3,000) | (15,000) | (49,000) |

Robust Ltd should buy in product A since it would achieve savings of $6,000 pa Buying in any of the other products would increase its costs.

## Test your understanding 4

It would not be cost effective to outsource the accounting activities. The present costs of $7,570 would rise to $8,100 pa

Annual internal processing costs

| | |
|---|---|
| • Hardware and software | $320 |
| • Hardware/software annual maintenance | $750 |
| • Accounting stationery | $500 |
| • Part time accounts clerk | $6,000 |
| Total | $7,570 |

Annual outsourcing costs

| | | |
|---|---|---|
| • Processing of invoices/credit notes | $2,500 | 5,0003$0.50 |
| • Processing of cheque payments | $2,000 | 4,0003$0.50 |
| • Reconciling supplier accounts | $3,600 | 15032.00312 |
| Total | $8,100 | |

Broad qualitative factors:

• the reliability of supply

• the quality of supply

• security of information.

## Test your understanding 5

How critical is this component to Company X?

• This is the critical question – it is not worth risking the business to achieve a modest reduction in costs.

• If the component is not available to Company X at the right time, at the right quality and in the right quantities can Company X survive? E.g. by drawing on a stockpile of the component until such time as it can resume production itself or it can find another supplier.

Company X will need to satisfy itself as to the ability of Company Y to:

• manufacture the component to the required quality

• deliver the component in the required quantities at the required times

• maintain the finally-agreed price for the agreed contract period.

What is the size and reputation of Company Y?

- Has Company Y previously carried out work for Company X?

    - If yes, was the work fully satisfactory in terms of quality, quantity, delivery dates and price?

    - If no, can company X speak to other customers of Company Y for whom they have done similar work for a significant period?

- Can Company X inspect the production facilities of Company Y and meet the staff who would be working on the component?

Company X will need to consider the implications for their employees in the light of the significance of the component in question:

    - What proportion of the workforce is involved in its production?

    - What level of skill is involved in its production?

    - How easy/difficult is it to recruit staff with these skills?

- Will it be possible to redeploy the existing staff without risking the loss of key skilled workers?

### Test your understanding 6

First of all we must restate the figures so that they present the situation in its true light. This will enable each department to be readily evaluated on its locally controllable performance.

Appendix

| Department | 1 | 2 | 3 | Total |
|---|---|---|---|---|
| Sales volume (units) | 5,000 | 6,000 | 2,000 | 13,000 |
| Sales value ($) | 150,000 | 240,000 | 24,000 | 414,000 |
| Cost of sales | | | | |
| Direct material | 75,000 | 150,000 | 10,000 | 235,000 |
| Direct labour | 4,846 | 5,815 | 1,939 | 12,600 |
| Overhead | 3,000 | 3,000 | 1,500 | 7,500 |
| Expenses | 9,000 | 9,000 | 6,000 | 24,000 |
| Contribution ($) | 58,154 | 72,185 | 4,561 | 134,900 |
| Other costs | | | | |
| Labour | | | | (50,400) |
| Overhead | | | | (7,500) |
| Expenses | | | | (16,000) |
| Net profit | | | | 61,000 |

**To:** Management
**From:** Management Accountant
**Date:** 18/04/X6
**Subject:** Report to management on the advisability of closing Department 3

Introduction

In response to the request to appraise the advisability of closing Department 3:

- We have first considered the way the original financial information was presented.

- This was found to be misleading, since the figures included apportioned fixed costs over which the operations managers had no control. Indeed, the method of apportionment was such as to actually penalise an effective manager especially when her sales volumes were considerably higher than those of her colleagues irrespective of the contribution those sales might make to the overall business.

- Consequently we have restated the figures, eliminating from the contribution calculations all figures which cannot be objectively allocated to the departments and over which the local managers have no control. This identifies the overall contribution made by each department to the corporate entity. It makes no difference to the final bottom line.

Findings

From the restated figures it can be seen that:

- Department 3 is making a contribution of $4,561 to the overall profit of the business

- the apparent loss arises purely from inappropriate apportionment of overheads and expenses

- if the department were closed:

  - there would be a loss of $4,561 contribution to the business and

  - on the assumption there would be no further saving on fixed costs, the profit would be reduced to $56,439.

Other considerations

The figures make no allowance for:

- the closure of Department 3 and the redundancy costs and losses on any equipment disposal

> • the possible loss of business due to products from Department 3 being unavailable to customers who buy from the other departments at the same time.
>
> Conclusions and recommendations
>
> Department 3 should be kept open:
>
> • it makes a small but useful contribution to the business
>
> • it may be necessary to review whether it is making a meaningful use of the assets committed to it.
>
> Consideration must be given to:
>
> • the effectiveness of the reporting methodology and cost apportionment procedures, since they are likely to mislead management in their present form.
>
> • to that end, control reporting should be done on a marginal costing basis, with operations management assessed for effectiveness on sales and the costs for which they are responsible and can control.
>
> Other costs should be looked at very carefully to see what value the company is deriving from them:
>
> • At present, over 20% of the costs structure cannot be assigned directly to products and could be construed as being costs which do not add value.
>
> • These costs need careful attention.

**Test your understanding 7**

| Costs and revenues of proceeding with the contract. | $ |
|---|---|
| (1) Costs to date of $150,000 sunk – ignore. | – |
| (2) Materials – purchase price of $60,000 is also sunk. There is an opportunity benefit of the disposal costs saved. | 5,000 |
| (3) Labour cost – the direct cost of $40,000 will be incurred regardless of whether the project is undertaken or not – and so is not relevant. Opportunity cost of lost contribution = $150,000 – ($100,000 – $40,000) The absorption of overheads is irrelevant – it is merely an apportionment of existing costs. | (90,000) |
| (4) Research staff costs | |
| Wages for the year | (60,000) |
| Increase in redundancy pay ($35,000 – $15,000) | (20,000) |

(5)  Equipment
Deprival value if used in the project = disposal value          (8,000)
Disposal proceeds in one year                                    6,000
(All book values and depreciation figures are irrelevant)
(6)  General building services
Apportioned costs – irrelevant
Opportunity costs of rental foregone                            (7,000)
                                                               (174,000)
Sales value of contract                                         300,000
Increased contribution from contract                            126,000

**Advice.**  Proceed with the contract.

## Test your understanding 8

### Mike Inc

Relevant cost statement

|               | Note | $      |
|---------------|------|--------|
| Material V    | 1    | 900    |
| Material I    | 2    | 6,500  |
| Material C    | 3    | 2,050  |
| Department 1  | 4    | –      |
| Department 2  | 5    | 26,000 |
| Overheads     | 6    | –      |
| Minimum contract price |  | 35,450 |

### Notes

1  The historical cost of $10 is not relevant, as it is a sunk cost.
   The relevant cost is the opportunity cost relating to lost scrap
   proceeds:

   = 300 × $3 = $900.

2  Again, the historical cost is irrelevant, as it is a sunk cost. Since
   the material is in continuous use in the business, the relevant
   cost is the current replacement cost of the material:

   = 1,000 × $6.50 = $6,500.

3  Since there is only 300 kg in stock, 250 kg would need to
   be purchased at the current replacement cost = 250 × $4
   = $1,000. If the current stock of 300 kg is not used for the
   contract, it would be used to replace material Y in an alternative
   production process.

   Therefore the relevant cost for the stock of 300 kg is = 300 ×
   $7/2 = $1,050, bearing in mind the 2-for-1 substitution.

Total relevant cost for material C = $1,000 + $1,050 = $2,050.

4   Since there is spare capacity in this department, there is no relevant cost.

5   For this department, the two alternatives need to be considered:

Cost of working overtime = 2,000 × $10 × 1.5 = $30,000

Cost of diverting labour = 2,000 × ($10 + $3) = $26,000

It would be cheaper to divert the labour from the other production processes, so the relevant cost for department 2 is $26,000.

6   There will be an increase in overhead expenditure for the relevant costs.

7   The minimum price is the price that just covers the relevant costs of the contract.

### Test your understanding 9

The pre-separation (i.e. "joint") costs are not incremental and so can be ignored. The only incremental cash flows are as follows:

| Product | X $000 | Y $000 | Z $000 |
|---|---|---|---|
| Additional revenue | 780 | – | 440 |
| Separable costs | 800 | – | 400 |
| Benefit | (20) | | 40 |

Thus only Z should be processed further.

# Risk and uncertainty

## Chapter learning objectives

Upon completion of this chapter you will be able to:

- describe generally available research techniques to reduce uncertainty, e.g. focus groups, market research

- suggest for a given situation, suitable research techniques for reducing uncertainty

- explain, using a simple example, the use of simulation

- explain, calculate and demonstrate the use of expected values and sensitivity analysis in simple decision-making situations

- for given data, apply the techniques of maximax, maximin and minimax regret to decision making problems including the production of profit tables.

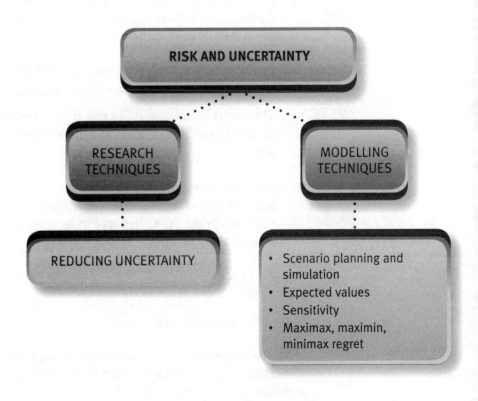

# 1 Introduction

## 1.1 Risk and uncertainty

Risk in business is the chance that future events or results may not be as expected. This can take two forms:

- Downside exposure ('pure risk') – outcomes are less favourable than expected. For example, costs may be higher than anticipated.

- Upside exposure ('speculative risk') – outcomes are more favourable than expected. For example, sales growth is higher than budgeted.

Risk is important as we normally assume rational investors (e.g. the firm's shareholders) to be **'risk averse'**. This means that they are only willing to accept higher risk if there is the expectation of a higher return to compensate. How much higher will depend on the individual investor but the key issue is that risk is often discussed in the context of a risk/return trade-off.

While many people use the terms interchangeably, some writers make a distinction between 'risk' and 'uncertainty':

- The term 'risk' is used for scenarios where it is possible to identify different possible outcomes and assign probabilities to them.

  For example, based on past experience, a sales team may estimate that they have a 60% chance of winning a particular sales pitch and a 40% chance of losing the tender.

  Such scenarios can be analysed using a range of different techniques, such as expected values.

- The term 'uncertainty' is used for scenarios where it is not possible to identify different possible outcomes and assign probabilities to them.

  For example, when trying to predict the likely behaviour of a new entrant into a market, some possible actions may be identifiable, such as price cuts, but trying to assign probabilities may be very speculative at best.

  The lack of probabilities limits the range of techniques available to assess the situation.

## 1.2 Risk management

Risk management is the process of understanding and managing the risks that the organisation is inevitably subject to in attempting to achieve its corporate objectives.

**IDENTIFY POSSIBLE SOURCES OF RISK**

**Measure and assess risks**
- Carry out research
- Identify possible outcomes
- Investigate implications of different outcomes
- Attempt to assign probabilities
- Numerical analysis

**FORMULATE RISK STRATEGY**

## 2 Research techniques

Market research is an important means of assessing and reducing uncertainty about the likely responses of customers to new products, new advertising campaigns, price changes, etc.

### Illustration 1 – Research techniques

A typical problem could be that of a falling market share for one or more of the organisation's products or services. To be able to clarify the problem and put it in perspective, a number of questions could be posed, for example:

Regarding the marketplace:

- Is the market stable, expanding or declining?

- Is the threat from domestic competitors, or from overseas?

- What is the situation for competitors?

- What advantages, if any, do the competitors products have?

Regarding customers:

- What is the organisation's reputation with its existing customers?

- How often do customers purchase?

- How likely are they to purchase from you?

- What is the expected market price?
- How do they select a vendor?
- Are there enough customers to build a viable business?
- What are the main factors considered by customers in a purchase decision?

Market research can be pursued via the analysis of:

- secondary data (desk research)
- primary data (field research).

### 2.1 Desk research

Features of desk research are:

- The information is collected from secondary sources.
- It obtains existing data by studying published and other available sources of information.
- It can often eliminate the need for extensive field work.
- It may not be exactly what the researcher wants and not be totally up to date, but it is cheaper and quicker than field research.
- You do not know if the findings are accurate, or how relevant they will be to your product or service.

**Expandable text**

There are three main types of information that can be collected by desk research:

- Economic intelligence can be defined as information relating to the economic environment within which a company operates. It is concerned with such factors as gross national product (GNP), investment, expenditure, population, employment, productivity and trade. It provides an organisation with a picture of past and future trends in the environment and with an indication of the company's position in the economy as a whole. A great deal of information is freely available in this area from sources such as government ministries, the nationalised industries, universities and organisations such as the OECD.

- Market intelligence is information about a company's present or possible future markets. Such information will be both commercial and technical, for example, the level of sales of competitors' products recorded by the Business Monitor or Census of Production; the product range offered by existing or potential competitors; the number of outlets forming the distribution network for a company's products; the structure of that network by size, location and relation to the end user; and the best overseas markets for a company.

- Internal company data is perhaps the most neglected source of marketing information. Companies tend to record their sales information for accountancy purposes or for the management of the sales force. Conversely, many companies, especially blue-chips and public services, can often be seen to produce reams of data for no apparent reason, or because 'we always have done'. Rarely is the information collected in a form in which it can readily be used by marketing management.

## 2.2 Field research

Field (or primary) research is research by direct contact with a targeted group of potential customers. It falls into two chief types:

- motivational research
- measurement research.

**Motivational research** – the objective is to unearth factors that influence why consumers do or do not buy particular products.

### Expandable text

Some of the more common techniques in motivational research are:

- Depth interviewing – undertaken at length by a trained person who is able to appreciate conscious and unconscious associations and motivations and their significance.

- Group interviewing – where between six and ten people are asked to consider the relevant subject (object) under trained supervision.

- Word association testing – on being given a word by the interviewer, the first word that comes into the mind of the person being tested is noted.

- Triad testing – where people are asked which out of a given three items they prefer. If the three are brands of a given type of product (or three similar types), replies may show a great deal about which features of a product most influence the buying decision.

**Measurement research** – the objective here is to build on the motivation research by trying to quantify the issues involved.

Sample surveys are used to find out how many people buy the product(s), what quantity each type of buyer purchases, and where and when the product is bought. This sort of information is often collected in retail environments at the point of sale.

### Expandable text

It is also possible (less accurately) to assess roughly the importance of some reasons for buying or not buying a product. The main types of measurement are:

**Random sampling** – where each person in the target population has an equal chance of being selected. Such samples are more likely to be representative, making predictions more reliable. However, the technique may be unfeasible in practice.

**Quota sampling** – where samples are designed to be representative with respect to pre-selected criteria.

- For example, if the target population is 55% women and 45% men, then a sample of 200 people could be structured so 110 women and 90 men are asked, rather than simply asking 200 people and leaving it up to chance whether or not the gender mix is typical.

- The main disadvantage of quota sampling is that samples may still be biased for non-selected criteria.

**Panelling** – where the sample is kept for subsequent investigations, so trends are easier to spot.

**Surveying by post** – the mail shot method. Unfortunately the sample becomes self-selecting and so may be biased.

**Observation** – e.g. through the use of cameras within supermarkets to examine how long customers spend on reading the nutritional information on food packaging.

## 2.3 Focus groups

Focus groups are a form of market research that has attracted a lot of attention as a result of their extensive use by political parties in the UK and overseas.

Online focus groups offer the opportunity for smaller businesses to gauge customer reactions in a relatively low-cost way. Their popularity is growing, particularly in the US.

Focus groups are:

- small groups (typically eight to ten individuals) selected from a broader population

- interviewed through facilitator-led round table discussions in an informal setting

- questioned in order to gather their opinions and reactions to a particular subject or marketing-orientated issues, known as test concepts

- a common market research tool.

Features of focus groups include:

- Results are qualitative and are not statistically significant.

- They can provide marketing managers, product managers, and market researchers with much helpful information.

- Their use as a research tool however is limited in that it is difficult to measure the results objectively.

- Their cost and logistical complexity is frequently cited as a barrier, especially for smaller companies.

- They can aid businesses in decision making and in the development of marketing strategies and promotional campaigns, by providing qualitative information from well-defined target audiences.

Some difficulties of focus groups have been highlighted above. Other problems include the following:

- given their small size, group membership not be representative.

- groups may feel pressured to give the "right" answer to questions.

- dominant individuals can skew discussion

- focus groups require a skilled moderator

- individuals may feel under pressure to agree with other members rather than expressing their own opinions.

## Using focus groups

Focus groups have often been used:

- to gather qualitative data from target groups of consumers in relation to consumer products

- in the new product development process, e.g. to test consumer reaction to new product concepts and prototypes

- to ascertain both perceptions of and reactions to a brand image

- to test marketing programmes, as they can provide an indication of how consumers will react to specific advertising messages and other types of marketing communications

- to learn more about consumer habits, product usage, and service expectations.

### Illustration 2 – Research techniques

Focus groups have been used by:

- television companies to obtain voters' reactions to possible candidates for political party leadership contests

- banks to assess consumer reactions to new electronic banking products

- pharmaceutical companies to test reactions to new drug concepts.

### Test your understanding 1

A company is thinking of adding a new baby milk substitute to its existing range of baby foods.

**Suggest secondary sources of information for its market research (also referred to as desk research).**

## 3 Reducing uncertainty in particular situations

Situations where it is particularly important for an organisation to reduce uncertainty include:

- further development of existing products

- entry into a new market

- launch of a new product or service

- diversification.

e.g

**Illustration 3 – Reducing uncertainty in particular situations**

Company X, a manufacturer of TVs, is considering diversifying into the manufacture of cameras.

It wishes to gain an understanding of the market and, in particular,

- the product range offered by existing and potential competitors
- the number of outlets forming the distribution network for competitor products
- the structure of these networks by size, location and their relation to the end user
- the best overseas markets for its planned products.

The company wishes to minimise its research costs and to gather the data as rapidly as possible.

Suggested research technique: **Desk research.**

Desk research, involving the collection of information from secondary sources:

- would meet the criteria of speed and low cost
- would be cheaper and quicker than field research
- might not, however,
  - be entirely accurate
  - be totally up to date.

Subject to these caveats desk research should enable the management to form an initial impression of the prospects for its proposed new product range and to decide whether it wishes to take its research to the next stage.

**Illustration 4 – Reducing uncertainty in particular situations**

Company B, a drinks manufacturer, is considering the development of a new drink for teenagers and wishes to obtain their reactions to the new product.

Suggested research technique: **Online focus group**.

This is an effective means of gathering consumer reactions and would offer the advantages of:

- relatively low cost
- allowing all those employees with an internet connection to view the focus group on their PC screen.

However:

- results are qualitative and are not statistically significant
- it is difficult to measure the results objectively.

If, however, the results are strongly positive the company can then consider taking the research to the next step.

## Illustration 5 – Reducing uncertainty in particular situations

Company A, a drinks manufacturer, is considering the launch of its products in a new overseas market. It wishes to gain an initial understanding of this country's economic environment: e.g. it is interested in levels of investment, expenditure, productivity and trade.

Suggested research technique: **Desk research**.

A great deal of information is freely available in this area from sources such as government ministries, the nationalised industries, universities and organisations such as the OECD.

## Test your understanding 2

A major food retailer is considering diversifying into the provision of financial services which will involve offering its customers loans and insurance policies.

The retailer wishes to establish the likely response of its customers and, in particular, the likely level of take up of these new services.

**What form of market research would be appropriate?**

## 4 Scenario planning and simulation

### 4.1 Scenario planning

When the business environment has a high degree of uncertainty due to complexity and/or rapid change, it may be impossible to predict a single picture of how the firm will be affected in the future.

Scenarios are detailed and plausible views of how the business environment might develop in the future based on groupings of key environmental influences and drivers of change about which there is a high degree of uncertainty.

Scenario planning involves the following steps.

1    Identify high-impact, high-uncertainty factors in the environment

Relevant factors and driving forces could be identified through a strategic analysis framework such as the PEST analysis considered in paper F1. Once identified, factors need to be ranked according to importance and uncertainty.

For example, in the oil industry there may be a need to form a view of the business environment up to 25 years ahead and issues such as crude oil availability, price and economic conditions are critical.

2    For each factor, identify different possible futures.

For example, oil companies would consider the possible outcomes of elections in different countries and the attitudes of the possible governments to climate change, pollution and energy policy.

Precision is not possible but developing a view of the future against which to evaluate and evolve strategies is important.

3    Cluster together different factors to identify various consistent future scenarios.

For example, two key factors may have been identified as:

(a)  the threat of new entrants into the industry and

(b)  new legislation that may reduce the industry potential for profit.

Clearly if new legislation is passed that reduces industry profit potential, then the likelihood of new entrants will fall.

4    'Writing the scenario' - for the most important scenarios (usually limited to three), build a detailed analysis to identify and assess future implications.

The result of this detailed scenario construction should include:

–    financial implications - anticipated net profits, cash flow, and net working capital for each of three versions of the future

–    strategic implications – possible opportunities and risks

–    assigning probabilities to key variables

–    financial analysis, such as Monte Carlo simulation, discussed in section 4.2 below.

5    For each scenario identify and assess possible courses of action for the firm.

6    Monitor reality to see which scenario is unfolding.

7    Revise scenarios and strategic options as appropriate.

## 4.2 Simulation

Simulation is a modelling technique that is often used in capital investment appraisal, especially as part of scenario planning.

Simulation involves the construction of a mathematical model and has the following features:

- It produces a range of possible outcomes and their probability distribution.

- It is a relatively easily understood technique.

Monte Carlo simulation, which uses statistical simulation methods, is a simulation method that is capable of addressing the most complex applications. It involves:

- the constant random generation of values for uncertain variables to simulate a model

- the consideration of all possible combinations of variables (unlike sensitivity analysis which considered the effect of changing just one variable at a time).

Monte Carlo simulation can include all random events that might affect the success or failure of a proposed project, as identified in the scenario planning. For example:

- a competitor appearing

- changes in consumer taste

- changes in inflation or exchange rates, etc.

There are major drawbacks of simulation.

- It is not a technique for making a decision, only for obtaining more information about the possible outcomes.

- Models can become extremely complex, particularly where dependent probabilities are involved.

- Thus the time and costs involved in their construction can be more than is gained from the improved decisions.

- Probability distributions may be difficult to formulate.

### Illustration 6 – Simulation

The simulation process breaks down into three stages, and is greatly helped by the use of a computer.

**Stage 1:** Specify major areas of uncertainty and their implications for variables.

Variables will differ between investment projects but typical examples are as follows:

(i) Market details
- market size
- selling price
- market growth rate
- market share.

(ii) Investment costs
- investment required
- residual value of investment.

(iii) Operating costs
- variable costs
- fixed costs
- taxation
- useful life of plant.

**Stage 2:** Specify the relationships between variables to calculate an NPV.

- Sales revenue = market size 3 market share 3 selling price.

- Net cash flow = sales revenue – (variable costs + fixed costs + taxation), etc.

**Stage 3:** Simulate the environment.

- Attach a probability distribution to each variable

- For example, we may have the following estimates of variable cost:

| Variable cost per unit ($) | 4.00 | 4.50 | 5.00 |
|---|---|---|---|
| Probability | 0.3 | 0.5 | 0.2 |

- Random numbers are then assigned to represent the above probability distribution.

| Variable cost per unit ($) | 4.00 | 4.50 | 5.00 |
|---|---|---|---|
| Probability | 0.3 | 0.5 | 0.2 |
| Random number range | 00-29 | 30-79 | 80-99 |

- If two digit random numbers are then generated, the probability of occurrence of each range will reflect the underlying probability distribution.

- Probability distributions and random number ranges are assigned to each variable. Care must be taken at this stage to allow for dependence between variables.

- For example, selling price and market share could clearly be related and it could be necessary to specify a probability distribution of market shares for each selling price.

- Finally to simulate the project we need to do the following:

  - draw a random number for each variable (most computers can generate random numbers)

  - select the value of each variable corresponding with the selected random number and compute an NPV

  - repeat the process many times until we have a probability distribution of returns.

### Results of simulation

- The results of a simulation exercise will be a probability distribution of NPVs.

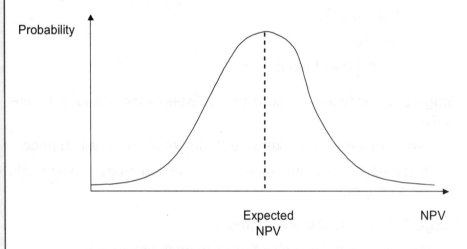

Instead of choosing between expected values, decision makers can now take the dispersion of outcomes and the expected return into account.

### Test your understanding 3

**Assess the use of simulation for a chain of betting shops.**

KAPLAN PUBLISHING

# 5 Expected values (EVs) in decision making

## 5.1 Expected values

When considering a scenario it may be possible to make several predictions about alternative future outcomes and to assign probabilities to each outcome.

An expected value is computed by multiplying the value of each possible outcome by the probability of that outcome, and summing the results.

An expected value can therefore be defined as a weighted average value, calculated from probability estimates.

### Illustration 7 – EVs in decision making

Cash flows from a new restaurant venture may depend on whether a competitor decides to open up in the same area. We make the following estimates:

| Competitor opens up | Probability | Project NPV $ | EV |
|---|---|---|---|
| Yes | 0.3 | (10,000) | (3,000) |
| No | 0.7 | 20,000 | 14,000 |
| | | | 11,000 |

The expected NPV of this venture is $(0.3 \times -10,000) + (0.7 \times 20,000) = \$11,000$.

The simple decision rules using EVs are:

- to accept projects with a positive expected NPV as above.

- when choosing between projects accept those projects with the highest expected NPVs.

A matrix can be a useful way to represent and analyse a scenario where there is a range of possible outcomes and a variety of possible responses.

Advantages of EVs

- Recognises that there are several possible outcomes and is, therefore, more sophisticated than single value forecasts.

- Enables the probability of the different outcomes to be quantified.

- Leads directly to a simple optimising decision rule.

- Calculations are relatively simple.

Limitations of EVs

- By asking for a series of forecasts the whole forecasting procedure is complicated. Inaccurate forecasting is already a major weakness in project evaluation. The probabilities used are also usually very subjective.

- The EV is merely a weighted average of the probability distribution, indicating the average pay-off if the project is repeated many times. This has little meaning for a one-off project.

- The EV gives no indication of the dispersion of possible outcomes about the EV. The more widely spread out the possible results are, the more risky the investment is usually seen to be. The EV ignores this aspect of the probability distribution. In the above example, the EV is positive but there is still a 30% chance of making a loss.

- In ignoring risk, the EVT also ignores the investor's attitude to risk. Some investors are more likely to take risks than others.

Conclusions on EVs

The simple EV decision rule is appropriate if three conditions are met or nearly met:

- There is a reasonable basis for making the forecasts and estimating the probability of different outcomes.

- The decision is relatively small in relation to the business. Risk is then small in magnitude.

- The decision is for a category of decisions that are often made. A technique which maximises average pay-off is then valid.

### Illustration 8 – EVs in decision making

- Hofgarten Newsagents stocks a weekly magazine which advertises local second-hand goods. Marie, the owner, can:
    - buy the magazines for 15c each
    - sell them at the retail price of 25c

- At the end of each week unsold magazines are obsolete and have no value.

- Marie estimates a probability distribution for weekly demand which looks like this:

| Weekly demand in units | Probability |
|:---:|:---:|
| 10 | 0.20 |
| 15 | 0.55 |
| 20 | 0.25 |
| | 1.00 |

**Required:**

(i) What is the expected value of demand?

(ii) If Marie is to order a fixed quantity of magazines per week how many should that be? Assume no seasonal variations in demand.

**Solution**

(i) EV of demand = $(10 \times 0.20) + (15 \times 0.55) + (20 \times 0.25)$ = 15.25 units per week.

(ii) The first step is to set up a decision matrix of possible strategies (numbers bought) and possible demand, as follows:

| Outcome (number demanded) | Strategy (number bought) | | |
|---|---|---|---|
| | 10 | 15 | 20 |
| 10 | | | |
| 15 | | | |
| 20 | | | |

The 'pay-off' from each combination of action and outcome is then computed:

No sale: cost of 15c per magazine.
Sale: profit of 25c – 15c = 10c per magazine

Pay-offs are shown for each combination of strategy and outcome.

**Workings**

(i) If 10 magazines are bought, then 10 are sold no matter how many are demanded and the payoff is always $10 \times 10c$ = 100c.

(ii) If 15 magazines are bought and 10 are demanded, then 10 are sold at a profit of $10 \times 10c$ = 100c, and 5 are scrapped at a loss of $5 \times 15c$ = 75c, making a net profit of 25c

(iii) The other contributions are similarly calculated.

| Probability | Outcome (number demanded) | Decision (number bought) | | |
|---|---|---|---|---|
| | | 10 | 15 | 20 |
| 0.20 | 10 | 100 | 25 | (50) |
| 0.55 | 15 | 100 | 150 | 75 |
| 0.25 | 20 | 100 | 150 | 200 |
| 1.00 | EV | 100c | 125c | 81.25c |

The expected values of each strategy are listed on the bottom line, in cents. From this it can be seen that the strategy which gives the highest expected pay-off is to stock 15 magazines each week.

### Test your understanding 4

A bar owner is considering whether to offer lunchtime meals. He has estimated that daily demand will either be for 10 meals (probability 0.7) or 20 meals (probability 0.3). Each meal costs $5 to prepare and would be priced at $15 to customers. Meals must be prepared in advance.

(a) **Calculate the expected demand per day.**

(b) **Prepare a pay-off matrix showing the outcomes if the owner decides to make in advance 10, 20 and the EV number of meals demanded. Use this to determine the optimal strategy.**

## 6 Sensitivity and EVs

Sensitivity analysis is a technique which is similar to the 'what if?' facility provided by a computer spreadsheet.

By using this technique it is possible to establish which estimates (variables) are more critical than others in affecting a decision.

The process is as follows:

- Best estimates for variables are made and a decision arrived at. For example, a NPV calculation may indicate accepting a project.

- Each of the variables is analysed in turn to see how much the original estimate can change before the original decision is reversed. For example, it may be that the estimated selling price can fall by 5% before the NPV becomes negative and the project would be rejected.

- Estimates for each variable can then be reconsidered to assess the likelihood of the decision being wrong. For example, what is the chance of the selling price falling by more than 5%?

### 6.1 Strengths of sensitivity analysis

- There is no complicated theory to understand.

- Information will be presented to management in a form which facilitates subjective judgement to decide the likelihood of the various possible outcomes considered.

- It identifies areas which are crucial to the success of the project. If the project is chosen, those areas can be carefully monitored.

- It indicates just how critical are some of the forecasts which are considered to be uncertain.

## 6.2 Weaknesses of sensitivity analysis

- It assumes that changes to variables can be made independently, e.g. material prices will change independently of other variables. This is unlikely. If material prices went up the firm would probably increase the selling price at the same time with little overall effect on the NPV. Simulation allows us to change more than one variable at a time.

- It only identifies how far a variable needs to change; it does not look at the probability of such a change. For example sales volume may appear to be the most crucial variable, but if the firm were facing volatile raw material markets a 65% change in raw material prices would be far more likely than a 29% change in sales volume.

- It is not an optimising technique. It provides information on the basis of which decisions can be made. It does not point to the correct decision directly.

### Illustration 9 – EVs

A manager has identified the following two possible outcomes for a process

| Outcome | Probability | Financial implications ($000s) |
| --- | --- | --- |
| Poor | 0.4 | Loss of 20 |
| Good | 0.6 | Profit of 40 |

The expected value has been calculated as EV = (0.4 x -20) + (0.6 × 40) = +16. This would suggest that the opportunity should be accepted.

**(a) Sensitivity to the estimated loss if a poor outcome materialises**

However, suppose the likely loss if results are poor has been underestimated. What level of loss would change the decision? In effect we want a break-even estimate.

Let the loss be "-L".
EV = (0.4 x -L)+ (0.6 × 40) = 24 – 0.4L
Setting the EV to be zero gives 24 - 0.4L = 0,
so L = 24/0.4 = 60

Thus the potential loss would have to be $60,000 (i.e. 200% larger) before invalidating the decision to accept.

**(b) Sensitivity to the estimated probability**

However, suppose the probability of a loss has been underestimated. What is the break-even probability?

Let the probability of a loss be "p". Thus the probability of a good outcome would change to (1-p)
EV = p x -20+ (1-p) × 40 = 40 – 60p
Setting the EV to be zero gives 40 - 60p=0
so p = 40/60 = 2/3 or 0.67

Thus the probability of a poor outcome would have to be 0.67 before the decision to accept was wrong.

### Test your understanding 5

A manager is considering a make v buy decision based on the following estimates:

|  | If made in-house € | If buy in and re-badge € |
|---|---|---|
| Variable production costs | 10 | 2 |
| External purchase costs | - | 6 |
| Ultimate selling price | 15 | 14 |

**Assess the sensitivity of the decision to the external purchase price.**

## 7  Maximax, maximin and minimax regret

When probabilities are not available, there are still tools available for incorporating risk into decision making.

### 7.1 Maximax

The maximax rule applies to an optimist who seeks to maximise the maximum possible gain of possible outcomes.

### Illustration 10 – Applying maximax

A company is choosing which of three new products to make (A, B or C) and has calculated likely pay-offs under three possible scenarios (I, II or III), giving the following pay-off table.

| Profit/(loss) Scenario | Product chosen A | B | C |
|---|---|---|---|
| I | 20 | 80 | 10 |
| II | 40 | 70 | **100** |
| III | 50 | (10) | 40 |

Using maximax, an optimist would consider the best possible outcome for each product and pick the product with the greatest potential.

Here C would be chosen with a maximum possible gain of 100.

## 7.2 Maximin

The maximin rule involves selecting the alternative that maximises the minimum pay-off achievable.

This approach would be appopriate for a pessimist who: seeks to achieve the best results if the worst happens

### Illustration 11 – Applying maximin

Apply the maximin rule to the example in the A/B/C case above:

*   identify the minimum pay-off achievable for A, B and C

    A: worst case scenario = gain of 20

    B: worst case scenario = loss of 10

    C: worst case scenario = gain of 10

*   detemine which product would ensure the maximum pay-off if the worst result were to happen in each case.

The pessimist would thus chose product A.

## 7.3 The minimax regret rule

The minimax regret strategy is the one that minimises the maximum regret. Essentially this is the technique for a 'sore loser' who does not wish to make the wrong decision.

'Regret' in this context is defined as the opportunity loss through having made the wrong decision.

### Illustration 12 – Applying minimax regret rule

In the pay-off matrix above, if the market state had been scenario I:

*   The correct decision
    would have been:                    B (net income $80).

*   If A had been chosen instead:   the company would have been
                                     out of pocket by $60
                                     (i.e. 80 – 20)

*   If C had been chosen:           It would have been out of pocket
                                     by $70 (i.e. 80 – 10)

- The opportunity loss associated with each product is:
A = $60, B =$0, C = $70.

The opportunity losses for a given market state are obtained by subtracting each value in the row from the highest value in that row.

The completed opportunity loss ('regret') table is thus as follows.

| State | Decision | | |
|---|---|---|---|
| | A | B | C |
| I | 60 | 0 | 70 |
| II | 60 | 30 | 0 |
| III | 0 | 60 | 10 |
| Maximum regret | 60 | 60 | 70 |

The maximum regret value for:

A  = $60
B  = $60
C  = $70

The minimum value of these is $60, hence the minimax regret strategy would be either A or B.

B would probably be adopted because its second-highest regret outcome ($30) is lower than the second-highest for A ($60).

**Expandable text**

**Decision-making criteria**

In the A/B/C example given above, it is by no means clear which decision is going to produce the most satisfactory result, since each product gives the most desirable outcome at one level of demand.

Three possible criteria for choosing between A, B and C in this situation were:

- maximisation of EVs

- maximin rule

- minimax regret rule.

It is important to appreciate that no one criterion can be 'right or wrong'. They are alternatives and the one that is adopted in any given situation depends on circumstances and the attitude to risk of the decision maker.

KAPLAN PUBLISHING

## Test your understanding 6

Using the payoff matrix from the Hofgarten Newsagents example from illustration 8:

| Profit/(loss) | Decision = Number bought | | |
|---|---|---|---|
| | 10 | 15 | 20 |
| Number demanded | | | |
| 10 | 100 | 25 | (50) |
| 15 | 100 | 150 | 75 |
| 20 | 100 | 150 | 200 |

**Recommend how many magazines should be bought based on the following criteria:**

**(a) Maximax**

**(b) Maximin**

**(c) Minimax regret**

## Chapter summary

**Risk and uncertainty**
- Variability in returns
- Risk aversion
- Upside v downside
- Risk v uncertainty

**Research techniques**
- Desk research
- Field research
- Focus groups

**MODELLING TECHNIQUES**

- Scenario planning and simulation
- Expected values - long term average
- Sensitivity of decision to key estimates
- Maximax – optimist
- Maximin – pessimist
- Minimax – sore loser.

# Test your understanding answers

## Test your understanding 1

Possible sources of secondary information include:

(a) Past market research. It is quite probable that the company will have under-taken relevant research in connection with similar products.

(b) Existing sales. These indicate current consumer preferences which together with past sales may show trends.

- Government health departments may have significant information regarding baby foods together with current advice to parents.

- Industry groups, such as the Milk Marketing Board in the UK, may have undertaken relevant research or have useful information regarding trends.

- Supermarket/baby food retailers may have analyses regarding consumer choices and apparent preferences.

- Other sources of information include trade organisations, universities and colleges, welfare organisations and specialist consumer groups.

## Test your understanding 2

Measurement research – a form of primary market research – would be appropriate since direct contact with customers will be required. The objective here is to quantify the issues involved.

Sample surveys would be used to find out:

- how many people would be likely to buy the products

- the likely volume of purchases by each customer

- the situations in which a purchase is likely to be made.

## Test your understanding 3

Simulation would be particularly useful on an operational level for analysing the possible implications of a single event, such as a major horse race or football match:

- Possible outcomes are easy to identify (e.g. win, lose, draw, 2-1, 3-0, etc)

- Quoted odds can help estimate probabilities

- The outcomes of the simulation could be used to assess impact on cash flow, whether bets should be laid off with other betting agents to reduces risk, etc

Simulation could also be used for wider strategic analysis such as for assessing the possibility and implications of stricter anti-gambling legislation.

### Test your understanding 4

(a) EV = (0.3 x 10) + (0.7 x 20) = 17 meals per day.

(b) Pay off matrix

| Demand | Probability | Decision – number of meals prepared | | |
|---|---|---|---|---|
| | | 10 | 17 | 20 |
| 10 | 0.3 | 100 | 65 | 50 |
| 20 | 0.7 | 100 | 170 | 200 |
| **Expected value** | | **100** | **138.50** | **155** |

The optimal plan is thus to prepare 20 meals per day.

**Note:** choosing to prepare the expected demand of 17 meals per day is not optimal. You will always find that the optimal decision correlates to a possible demand level in these 'sandwich shop' type questions.

### Test your understanding 5

Comparing contribution figures, the product should be outsourced:

| | If made in-house | If buy in and re-badge |
|---|---|---|
| | € | € |
| Contribution | 5 | 6 |

For indifference, the contribution from outsourcing needs to fall to €5 per unit. Thus the external purchase price only needs to increase by €1 per unit (or 17%).

**Note**: Often a common-sense approach will work without the need to solve equations.

chapter **5**

## Test your understanding 6

(a), (b)

| Profit/(loss) | Decision = Number bought | | |
|---|---|---|---|
| | 10 | 15 | 20 |
| Number demanded | | | |
| 10 | 100 | 25 | (50) |
| 15 | 100 | 150 | 75 |
| 20 | 100 | 150 | 200 |
| | | | |
| Max. profit | 100 | 150 | 200 |
| Worst case | 100 | 25 | (50) |

(a) Using maximax, an optimist would choose to buy 20 magazines giving a maximum possible profit of 200.

(b) Using maxmin a pessimist would choose to buy 10 magazines giving a minimum profit of 100.

(c) Minimax regret

| Regret | Decision = Number bought | | |
|---|---|---|---|
| | 10 | 15 | 20 |
| Number demanded | | | |
| 10 | 0 | 75 | 150 |
| 15 | 50 | 0 | 75 |
| 20 | 100 | 50 | 0 |
| | | | |
| Max. regret | 100 | 75 | 150 |

Using minimax regret a sore loser would choose to buy 15 magazines limiting the opportunity loss to 75.

# Budgeting 1

## Chapter learning objectives

Upon completion of this chapter you will be able to:

- explain why organisations use budgeting
- explain how budgetary systems fit within the performance hierarchy
- explain how budgets can contribute to performance management
- describe the factors which influence behaviour at work
- discuss the issues surrounding setting the difficulty level for a budget
- explain the benefits and difficulties of the participation of employees in the negotiation of targets
- explain how corporate and divisional objectives may differ and can be reconciled
- identify and resolve conflicting objectives, explaining the implications of the conflict and method of resolution.

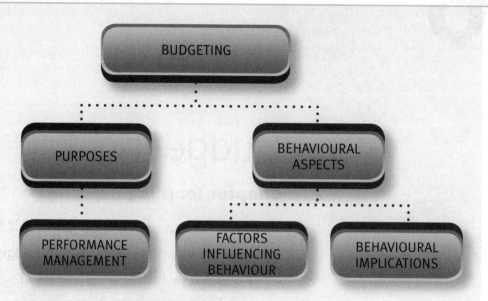

## 1 Purpose of budgets

### 1.1 Why do organisations use budgets?

A budget is a quantitative plan prepared for a specific time period. It is normally expressed in financial terms and prepared for one year.

| Illustration 1 – Purpose of budgets |
| --- |

A frequently-asked question in formulating the corporate plan is 'Where do we see ourselves in ten years' time?' To answer this successfully the firm must consider:

- what it wants to achieve (its objectives)

- how it intends to get there (its strategy)

- what resources will be required (its operating plans)

- how well it is doing in comparison to the plan (control).

The budget is a short-term operating plan, linked to the corporate plan, and will be used for detailed control.

Aims of budgeting:

- Planning

  A budgeting process forces a business to look to the future. If a business does not look to the future it will fail in the short, medium or long-term. It will fail because the organisation will become 'out of kilter' with its environment.

- Control

  Actual results are compared against the budget and action is taken as appropriate. In many respects this is the most important aspect of budgeting.

- Communication

  The budget may form the basis of the reporting hierarchy. It is a formal communication channel that allows junior and senior managers to converse.

- Co-ordination

  The budget allows the business to co-ordinate all diverse actions towards a common corporate goal.

- Evaluation

  The budget may be used to evaluate the financial results of a part of the business such as a cost centre. It may further be used to evaluate the actions of a manager within the business. The costs and revenues appraised must be within the control of that which we are evaluating.

- Motivation

  The budget may be used as a target for managers to aim for. Reward should be given for operating within or under budgeted levels of expenditure.

- Authorisation and delegation.

**Test your understanding 1**

**Explain the difference between a budget and a forecast.**

## 1.2 The performance hierarchy

As you may recall from paper F1, firms have a planning hierarchy:

- Strategic planning is long term, looks at the whole organisation and defines resource requirements.

- Tactical planning is medium term, looks at the department / divisional level and specifies how to use resources.

- Operational planning is very short term, very detailed and is mainly concerned with control. Most budgeting activities fall within operational planning and control.

Strategic plans will have to be translated into medium term tactical plans, which in turn need to be converted into detailed budgets. Similarly a firm's mission will be translated into strategic goals, which are then expressed as tactical targets, which again end up as short term operational targets. For example:

- Strategic plan – to develop new products in response to changing customer needs.

- Tactical plan – to make use of existing production spare capacity and to train staff to acquire the additional skills required.

- Operational plan – budgets for the new products to include advertising spend, sales forecasts, inventory policies, etc.

The aim is that if a manager achieves short-term budgetary targets than there is more chance of meeting tactical goals and ultimately success for strategic plans.

## 1.3 Budgets and performance management

 Responsibility accounting divides the organisation into budget centres, each of which has a manager who is responsible for its performance.

The budget is the target against which the performance of the budget centre or the manager is measured. The advantages of this approach are that:

- There is a clear published target known throughout the organisation that is linked to the overall organisation aims (goal congruence).

- Managers may be involved in setting the targets, which may make them more realistic.

- Budget targets can be linked to individual rewards, which may provide motivation to improve performance.

The disadvantages of the approach are that:

- Managers may work towards specific short-term budget targets to the detriment of long-term organisational goals.

- Managers may distort results to try to exceed targets and gain rewards.

 Management by exception is the practice of focusing on activities which require attention and ignoring those which appear to be conforming to expectations.

When measuring performance it may be appropriate to concentrate on activities which are deviating from plan.

- Managers should use a flexed budgeting approach to adjust fixed budget targets to reflect actual volumes of output achieved.

- Managers should only be assessed against costs and revenues' that are within their control (the 'controllability principle'). Failure to do this can be demotivating if, say, a manager fails to achieve a target due to factors outside their control.

### Illustration 2 – Purpose of budgets

A simplified performance report for an operating division is shown below.

|  | $000 |
|---|---|
| Sales | 750 |
| Variable costs | 420 |
| Contribution | 330 |
| Controllable fixed costs | 110 |
| Key measure for assessing managerial performance | 220 |
| Uncontrollable fixed costs (e.g. share of general overhead) | 150 |
| Profit | 70 |

### Test your understanding 2

**A wage award for production staff is agreed which exceeds the allowance incorporated in the budget. Discuss whether this is a controllable cost.**

## 2 Behavioural aspects of budgeting

### 2.1 Budgets and behaviour

Individuals react to the demands of budgeting and budgetary control in different ways and their behaviour can damage the budgeting process.

Behavioural problems include dysfunctional behaviour and budget slack.

Dysfunctional behaviour is when individual managers seek to achieve their own objectives at the expense of the objectives of the organisation. A key performance management issue is to ensure that the system of targets and measures used does not encourage such behaviour but rather encourages goal congruence.

Budget slack (or bias) is a deliberate over-estimation of expenditure and/or under-estimation of revenues in the budgeting process. This can happen because managers want easy targets (e.g. for an "easy life" or to ensure targets are exceeded and bonuses won) or simply to "play the system". Either way, this results in a budget that is poor for control purposes and meaningless variances.

## 2.2 Management styles (Hopwood)

Hopwood described three management styles that can be applied to budgets and performance management:

- Budget constrained.

- Profit conscious.

- Non-accounting.

### Expandable text

Research was carried out by **Hopwood (1973)** into the manufacturing division of a US steelworks, involving a sample of more than 200 managers with cost centre responsibility. **Hopwood** identified three distinct styles of using budgetary information to evaluate management performance.

- Budget-constrained style – Here, the main emphasis in performance evaluation is the manager's success in meeting budget targets in the short-term, with no consideration for other aspects of performance that are not targeted in the budget. A manager is criticised for poor results compared to the budget, for example if his actual spending exceeds the budget limit.

- Profit-conscious style – The performance of a manager is measured in terms of his ability to increase the overall effectiveness of his area of responsibility, in relation to meeting the longer-term objectives of the organisation. At a cost centre level of responsibility, performance might be judged in terms of reducing costs over the longer-term, rather than meeting short-term cost targets. Short-term budgetary information needs to be used with care and in a flexible way to achieve this purpose.

- Non-accounting style – With this style, performance evaluation is not based on budgetary information, and accounting information plays a relatively unimportant role. Other, non-accounting performance indicators , such as quality, are as important as the budget targets.

**Hopwood's** research suggested that each style of performance evaluation had the following behavioural effects.

- With the budget-constrained style, much attention was given to costs and there was a high degree of job-related pressure and tension. This often led to the manipulation of data in accounting reports.

- With the profit-conscious style, there was still a high involvement with costs but less job-related pressure. Consequently, there was less manipulation of accounting data.

Relationships between managers and their colleagues and superiors were also better than with a budget-constrained style.

- With the non-accounting style, the results were very similar to the profit-conscious style, except for a much lower concern with cost information.

- Hopwood found some evidence that better managerial performance was achieved where a profit-conscious or non-accounting style was in use. Poor performance was often associated with a budget-constrained style.

Subsequent studies by **Otley (1978)** involving profit centre managers in the UK coal mining industry contradicted **Hopwood's** earlier findings. One particular area of difference was that the UK study showed a closer link between the budget-constrained style and good performance. The manager evaluated on a rather tight budget-constrained basis tended to meet the budget more closely than if it was evaluated in a less rigid way.

**Test your understanding 3**

**A manager is awarded a bonus for achieving monthly budgetary targets. State three possible behavioural implications of this policy. What should be done to try to improve the process ?**

## 2.3 Setting the difficulty level of a budget

Targets will assist motivation and appraisal if they are at the right level. They should not be too difficult, as this will demotivate staff, but also not too easy, as managers are unlikely to strive for optimal performance.

An **expectations** budget is a budget set at current achievable levels. This is unlikely to motivate managers to improve but may give more accurate forecasts for resource planning.

An **aspirations** budget is a budget set at a level which exceeds the achievable level. This will motivate managers to improve if it is seen as attainable but may always result in an adverse variance. This must be managed carefully.

Note the potential for conflict between using a budget for planning/control purposes and using one to motivate staff.

Targets should be:

- communicated in advance

- dependent on factors controllable by the individual

- based on quantifiable factors

- linked to appropriate rewards and penalties

- chosen carefully to ensure goal congruence.

**Illustration 3 – Behavioural aspects of budgeting**

The concept of budget difficulty can be demonstrated diagrammatically as follows:

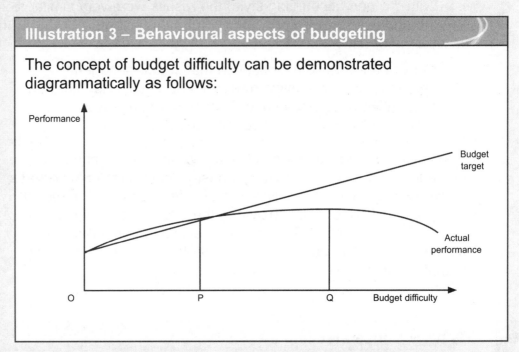

**Test your understanding 4**

**By referring to the diagram above, explain whether an organisation should set an expectations budget or an aspirations budget.**

## 2.3  Participation in setting targets

Managers may be involved in setting targets or these may be imposed by senior management without consultation.

Advantages of participation include:

- increased motivation (ownership of target)

- better understanding of an individual manager's aspiration level so that the target can be set at a suitable level for an individual.

Disadvantages of participation:

- time consuming

- may result in a wide range of targets which are seen as unfair

- managers may understate targets to make them easier to achieve (i.e. incorporate budgetary slack)

- negotiation may become a political process, which draws attention from running the business.

A sales manager has achieved $550,000 of sales in the current year. Business is expected to grow by 10% and price inflation is expected to be 3%.

**Suggest a suitable budget target for the forthcoming year.**

## 3 Conflicting objectives

Throughout this chapter there have been examples of conflicting objectives that occur in budgeting. The implications of the conflicts and the method of resolution will often be specific to the organisation and will depend on:

- the specific purpose for which the budget is to be used

- the management style and culture of the organisation

- the knowledge and experience of the managers preparing budgets.

**Illustration 4 – Conflicting objects**

| Type of conflict | Examples | Resolution |
|---|---|---|
| Company versus division. | • The company wishes to increase shareholder wealth. This should involve the use of NPV but divisions are assessed on accounting targets such as profit.<br><br>• Similarly shareholder wealth is determined by the long term but divisions are set short term targets (see below). | • Some companies try to insist that projects are assessed using NPV but then still impose accounting targets.<br><br>• Cash based targets.<br><br>• Give managers share options so they focus on shareholder wealth. |

| Type of conflict | Examples | Resolution |
|---|---|---|
| | • Managers reject projects that dilute divisional performance, even though they beat company target. (this is discussed in more detail in chapter 12) | |
| Division versus division. | • Divisions may compete for limited financial resources when setting budgets. | • Prioritisation (e.g. using zero based budgeting – covered in chapter 7).<br>• Negotiation and compromise.<br>• 'Satisfycing' – ensuring each manager gets a satisfactory result, though not as much as they wanted. |
| Short-termism. | • Managers cut RnD to hit short term targets but erode long term competences.<br>• Managers reject projects that are "slow starters" even though they have positive NPV. | • Use more non-financial indicators that focus on key long term issues such as quality, productivity, etc. (These are discussed in more detail in later chapters).<br>• Link bonuses to longer time periods. |
| Individualism. | • The risk of budgetary slack when managers participate in target setting. | • Greater scrutiny of budgets.<br>• Better training of managers. |

### Test your understanding 6

**A manager is planning to retire at the end of the current period. Suggest some performance management issues this raises and how they can be resolved.**

## Chapter summary

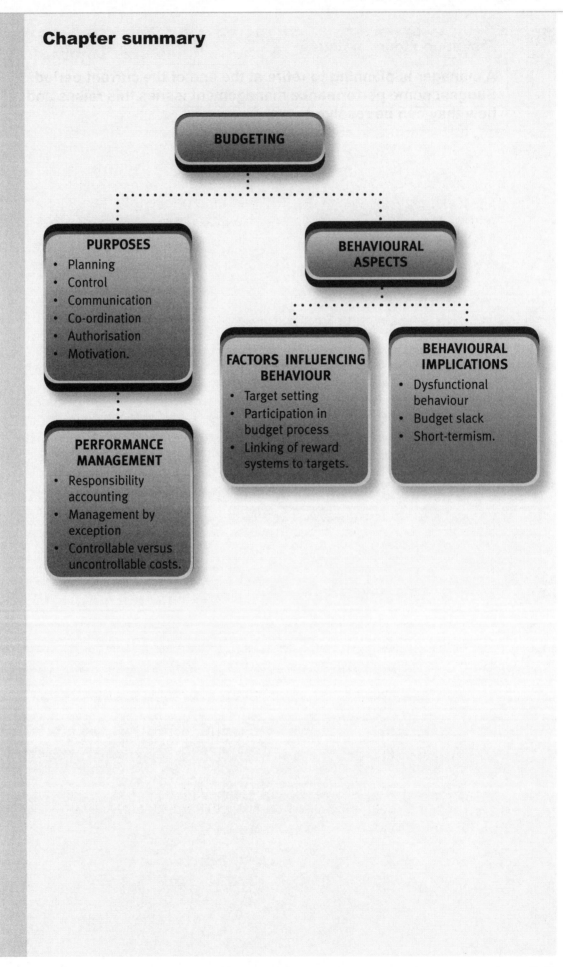

# Test your understanding answers

### Test your understanding 1

An organisation may produce a range of forecasts under different scenarios to explore possible courses of action. Forecasts can normally be updated as and when new/better information comes to light. The budget is the agreed plan towards which all of the organisation is working and which is used to measure actual performance. A budget is usually fixed for a period (perhaps a quarter) – this helps maintain a stable benchmark, and makes it easier to bridge back to the point in time when the budget was produced.

### Test your understanding 2

The key point here is that the answer depends on who awarded the pay increase.

If this was the production manager's decision, they the cost would be controllable. Depending on the culture of the firm, the manager would then be under pressure to explain why they departed form the budget in this instance.

If awarded by, say, the board of directors, then the cost increase was not controllable by the manager and should not feature in their appraisal.

### Test your understanding 3

The manager may try to:

*   delay discretionary short-term expenditure, e.g. maintenance, at the expense of long-term performance to improve results.

*   manipulate results to make sure the relevant targets are achieved.

*   incorporate budgetary slack into the targets to make them easier to achieve.

The process can be improved by measuring performance against a variety of targets, including non-financial targets, and linking performance to long-term objectives.

### Test your understanding 4

A budget has many purposes including:

- planning
- control
- performance evaluation
- motivation.

An expectations budget (e.g. at point P on the graph) is useful for planning, control and performance evaluation but is unlikely to encourage managers to improve. An aspirations budget (e.g. at point Q on the graph) sets targets which exceed current performance and provide a target for improvement. While this may result in the highest performance from managers, they are likely to fall short of targets set. In the long run aspirations targets will be viewed as unfair. Managers may decide to set two budget targets to overcome this problem.

### Test your understanding 5

Sales are expected to be $500,000 × 10% × 3% = $623,150. The manager may accept this as a fair target for performance appraisal, planning and control purposes. To encourage the manager to improve further an aspirations target incorporating a further improvement, say to $650,000, could be used and linked to the reward system.

### Test your understanding 6

The key issue is short-termism - the manager may act to increase profit for this period (thus increasing his final bonus) without any consideration of longer term implications. These could include:

- cutting RnD
- cutting marketing expenditure
- cutting back on training
- rejecting projects that do not have high returns in year 1
- sacking non-core staff.

It will be difficult to link the bonus to a longer time scale as the manager will have retired. Instead a non-accounting style focussing on quality, productivity, brand awareness, market share, etc should be adopted, if not already in place.

# Budgeting 2

## Chapter learning objectives

Upon completion of this chapter you will be able to:

- explain and evaluate 'top down' and 'bottom up' budgetary systems

- explain and evaluate a 'rolling' budgetary system

- explain and evaluate an 'activity-based' budgetary system

- explain and evaluate an 'incremental' budgetary system

- explain and evaluate 'feed-forward' budgetary control

- explain and evaluate a 'zero-based' budgetary system

- explain and evaluate a 'master' budget

- explain and evaluate functional budgets

- explain and evaluate a 'flexible' budget

- select and justify an appropriate budgetary system for a given organisation

- describe the information used in various budgetary systems and the sources of the information needed

- explain the difficulties of changing a budgetary system and type of budget used

- explain how budget systems can deal with uncertainty in the environment

- explain the major benefits and dangers in using spreadsheets in budgeting.

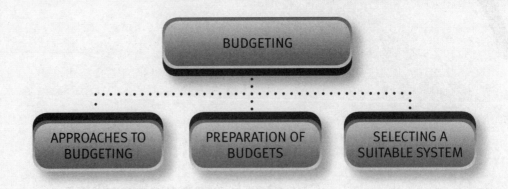

## 1 Approaches to budgeting

### 1.1 Top down and bottom up budgeting

The issues of allowing staff to participate in target setting were discussed in the previous chapter. Here the discussion is widened to look at the extent to which managers should participate in the budgeting process.

**Top down budget**

A budget that is set without allowing the ultimate budget holder to have the opportunity to participate in the budgeting process. Also called 'authoritative' or 'non-participative'.

**Bottom up budget**

A system of budgeting in which budget holders have the opportunity to participate in setting their own budgets. Also called participative budgeting. Even here budgets prepared by junior managers would be reviewed and challenged by senior management.

Advantages of participative budgets:

- increased motivation (ownership of budget)
- should contain better information, especially in a fast-moving or diverse business
- increases managers' understanding and commitment
- better communication
- senior managers can concentrate on strategy.

Disadvantages of participative budgets:

- senior managers may resent loss of control
- bad decisions from inexperienced managers
- budgets may not be in line with corporate objectives as managers lack a strategic perspective and will focus just on divisional concerns.
- budget preparation is slower and disputes can arise

- figures may be subject to bias if junior managers either try to impress or set easily achievable targets (budgetary slack)

- certain environments may preclude participation, e.g. sales manager may be faced with long-term contracts already agreed.

### Illustration 1 – Approaches to budgeting

- Budgeting is a political process. Imposed budgets may give senior managers an opportunity to impose their ideas and targets. Participative budgets may lead to bargaining strategies such as introducing slack, spending up to a target, forming alliances to protect budget allowances and offering to cut 'vital' services such as health and safety.

### Test your understanding 1

Bottom up budgeting is generally seen as preferable because it leads to improved managerial motivation and performance. However, there are situations for which top down budgeting is preferable.

**Describe three situations where top down budgeting would be more applicable.**

## 1.2 Rolling budgets

A budget kept continuously up to date by adding another accounting period (e.g. month or quarter) when the earliest accounting period has expired.

Aim: To keep tight control and always have an accurate budget for the next 12 months.

Suitable if accurate forecasts cannot be made, or for any area of business that needs tight control.

Advantages of rolling budgets:

- the budgeting process should be more accurate

- there should be much better information upon which to appraise the performance of management

- the budget will be much more 'relevant' by the end of the traditional budgeting period

- it forces management to take the budgeting process more seriously.

Disadvantages of rolling budgets:

- they are more costly and time consuming

- an increase in budgeting work may lead to less control of the actual results

- there is a danger that the budget may become the last budget 'plus or minus a bit'.

### Illustration 2 – Approaches to budgeting

A typical rolling budget might be prepared as follows:

1    A budget is prepared for the coming year (say January – December) broken down into suitable, say quarterly, control periods.

2    At the end of the first control period (31 March) a comparison is made of that period's results against the budget. The conclusions drawn from this analysis are used to update the budgets for the remaining control periods and to add a budget for a further three months, so that the company once again has budgets available for the coming year (this time April – March).

3    The planning process is repeated at the end of each three-month control period.

### Test your understanding 2

A company uses rolling budgeting and has a sales budget as follows;

|  | Quarter 1 $ | Quarter 2 $ | Quarter 3 $ | Quarter 4 $ | Total $ |
|---|---|---|---|---|---|
| Sales | 125,750 | 132,038 | 138,640 | 145,572 | 542,000 |

Actual sales for Quarter 1 were $123,450. The adverse variance is fully explained by competition being more intense than expected and growth being lower than anticipated. The budget committee has proposed that the revised assumption for sales growth should be 3% per quarter.

**Update the budget as appropriate.**

### 1.3   Incremental budgets

An incremental budget starts with the previous period's budget or actual results and adds (or subtracts) an incremental amount to cover inflation and other known changes.

It is suitable for stable businesses, where costs are not expected to change significantly. There should be good cost control and limited discretionary costs.

Advantages:

- quickest and easiest method

- assuming that the historic figures are acceptable, only the increment needs to be justified

- avoids 'reinventing the wheel'.

Disadvantages:

- builds in previous problems and inefficiencies, e.g. an overspend may result in a larger budget allowance next year.

- uneconomic activities may be continued, e.g. the firm may continue to make a component in-house when it might be cheaper to outsource.

- managers may spend unnecessarily to use up their budgeted expenditure allowance this year, thus ensuring they get the same (or a larger) budget next year.

## Illustration 3 – Incremental budgeting

AW Inc produces two products, A and C. In the last year (20X4) it produced 640 units of A and 350 units of C incurring costs of $672,000. Analysis of the costs has shown that 75% of the total costs are variable. 60% of these variable costs vary in line with the number of A produced and the remainder with the number of C.

The budget for the year 20X5 is now being prepared using an incremental budgeting approach. The following additional information is available for 20X5:

- All costs will be 4% higher than the average paid in 20X4.

- Efficiency levels will remain unchanged.

- Expected output of A is 750 units and of C is 340 units.

What is the budgeted total variable cost of product C (to the nearest $100) for the full year 20X5?

**Solution**

**20X4 costs:**

| | |
|---|---|
| Total variable costs | = 75% x $672,000 = $504,000 |
| Proportion relating to product C | = 40% x $504,000 = $201,600 |
| Cost per unit of product C | = $201,6000/350 = $576 |

**20X5 budget costs:**

| | | |
|---|---|---|
| Inflated cost per unit of C | = 1.04 x $576 | = $599.04 |
| Total variable cost for product C | = 340 x $599.04 | = $203,673.6 |

i.e. $203,700 to the nearest $100.

**Test your understanding 3**

**Using the information relating to AW Inc, calculate the budgeted cost per unit of product A.**

## 1.4 Activity-based budgeting

Traditionally, there has been a tendency to take an incremental approach to budgeting for overhead costs, and prepare next year's budget by simply adding a percentage to the current year's budget, to allow for inflation. ABB is an alternative method which may produce more accurate budgets and enable greater control of overhead expenditure.

ABB is defined as: 'a method of budgeting based on an activity framework and utilising cost driver data in the budget-setting and variance feedback processes'.

The advantages of ABB are similar to those provided by activity-based costing (ABC).

- It draws attention to the costs of 'overhead activities'. This can be important where overhead costs are a large proportion of total operating costs.

- It provides information for the control of activity costs, by assuming that they are variable, at least in the longer term.

- It provides a useful basis for monitoring and controlling overhead costs, by drawing management attention to the actual costs of activities and comparing actual costs with what the activities were expected to cost.

- It also provides useful control information by emphasising that activity costs might be controllable if the activity volume can be controlled.

- ABB can provide useful information for a total quality management (TQM) programme, by relating the cost of an activity to the level of service provided (for example, stores' requisitions processed) – do the user departments feel they are getting a cost-effective service?

Disadvantages of ABB

- A considerable amount of time and effort might be needed to establish an ABB system, for example to identify the key activities and their cost drivers.

- ABB might not be appropriate for the organisation and its activities and cost structures.

- A budget should be prepared on the basis of responsibility centres, with identifiable budget holders made responsible for the performance of their budget centre. A problem with ABB could be to identify clear individual responsibilities for activities.

- It could be argued that in the short-term many overhead costs are not controllable and do not vary directly with changes in the volume of activity for the cost driver. The only cost variances to report would be fixed overhead expenditure variances for each activity.

## Illustration 4 – ABB

The operating divisions of Z plc have in the past always used a traditional approach to analysing costs into their fixed and variable components. A single measure of activity was used which, for simplicity, was the number of units produced. The new management does not accept that such a simplistic approach is appropriate for budgeting in the modern environment and has requested that the managers adopt an activity-based approach in future.

Explain how ABB would be implemented by the operating divisions of Z plc.

**Solution**

**Step 1**    Identify cost pools and cost drivers.

**Step 2**    Calculate a budgeted cost driver rate based on budgeted cost and budgeted activity.

**Step 3**    Produce a budget for each department or product by multiplying the budgeted cost driver rate by the expected usage.

An activity-based budget can be constructed by preparing an activity matrix. This identifies the activities in each column, and the resources required to carry out the activities in each row.

The following 'activity matrix' shows the resources used (rows) and major functions/activities (columns) of a stores department. In this example, all the identified activities occur within a single department.

- The total current annual costs of each resource consumed by the department are shown in the final column; they have then been spread back over the various activities to establish the cost pools. The allocation of resource costs between activities will, to some extent, be subjective.

- Each of the first four activities has an identifiable cost driver, and the total resource cost driver rates can be determined (cost per unit of activity).

- The last two activities that occur within the department are non-volume related, and are sometimes referred to as 'sustaining costs'. They are necessary functions and should not be ignored in the budgeting process; however, they should not be attributed to particular cost drivers, as this would not reflect their true cost behaviour and would result in inappropriate budgets being set.

Activity cost matrix for stores department

| Activity: | Receiving deliveries | Issuing from store | Stock ordering | Stock counting | Keeping records | Supervision | Total |
|---|---|---|---|---|---|---|---|
| Cost driver: | Deliveries | Store requisitions | Number of orders | Number of counts | – | – | |
| Number: | 400 | 800 | 400 | 12 | | | |
| | $000 | $000 | $000 | $000 | $000 | $000 | $000 |
| Management salary | – | – | – | 1 | 4 | 25 | 30 |
| Basic wages | 20 | 25 | 6 | 4 | 11 | – | 66 |
| Overtime payments | 5 | – | – | 5 | 5 | – | 15 |
| Stationery, etc | 1 | 2 | 2 | 1 | 3 | – | 9 |
| Other | 6 | 5 | 2 | 1 | 1 | 5 | 20 |
| **Total** | **32** | **32** | **10** | **12** | **24** | **30** | **140** |
| Cost per activity unit | $80 | $40 | $25 | $1,000 | | | |

Sustaining costs will effectively be treated as fixed costs. However, for control purposes, activity-based costs can be assumed to be variable, and actual costs can be compared with the expected costs for the given level of activity.

## Test your understanding 4

A company has prepared an activity-based budget for its stores department. The budgeted costs are:

|  | Cost driver | Budgeted cost |
|---|---|---|
| Receiving goods | Number of deliveries | $80 per delivery |
| Issuing goods from store | Number of stores' requisitions | $40 per requisition |
| Ordering | Number of orders | $25 per order |
| Counting stock | Number of stock counts | $1,000 per count |
| Keeping records | – | $24,000 each year |
| Supervision | – | $30,000 each year |

Actual results for April were:

| Activity | Quantity | Actual cost $ |
|---|---|---|
| Receiving goods | 45 orders delivered | 3,450 |
| Issuing goods | 100 requisitions | 4,400 |
| Ordering | 36 orders | 960 |
| Counting | 2 stock counts | 1,750 |
| Record keeping |  | 1,900 |
| Supervision |  | 2,700 |
|  |  | 15,160 |

**Prepare a variance report for the month.**

## Test your understanding 5

**Which statement is correct regarding the benefits to be gained from using ABB?**

Answer options:

A   If there is much inefficiency within the operations of a business then ABB will identify and remove these areas of inefficiency.

B   In a highly direct labour intensive manufacturing process, an ABB approach will assist management in budgeting for the majority of the production costs.

C   In an organisation currently operating efficiently, where the next period will be relatively unchanged from the current one, then ABB will make the budgeting process simpler and quicker.

D   If an organisation produces many different types of output using different combinations of activities then ABB can provide more meaningful information for budgetary control.

## 1.5 Feed-forward control

Feed-forward control is defined as the 'forecasting of differences between actual and planned outcomes and the implementation of actions before the event, to avoid such differences'.

Whereas feedback is based on a comparison of historical actual results with the budget for the period to date, feed-forward looks ahead and compares:

• the target or objectives for the period, and

• the actual results forecast.

### Illustration 5 – Feed-forward control

A sales manager receives monthly control reports about sales values. The budgeted sales for the year to 31 December are $600,000 in total. At the end of April the manager might receive the following feedback control report.

| | Sales report for April | | | | | |
| | Month | | | Cumulative | | |
| | Budget | Actual | Variance | Budget | Actual | Variance |
| Product | $000 | $000 | $000 | $000 | $000 | $000 |
| P1 | 35 | 38 | 3 (F) | 90 | 94 | 4 (F) |
| P2 | 20 | 14 | 6 (A) | 50 | 39 | 11 (A) |
| P3 | 25 | 23 | 2 (A) | 50 | 45 | 5 (A) |
| Total | 80 | 75 | 5 (A) | 190 | 178 | 12 (A) |

Alternatively, the sales manager might be presented with a feed-forward control report, as follows:

| | Sales report, April | | |
| | Budget | Latest forecast for the year | Expected variance |
| Product | $000 | $000 | $000 |
| P1 | 240 | 250 | 10 (F) |
| P2 | 150 | 120 | 30 (A) |
| P3 | 210 | 194 | 16 (A) |
| Total | 600 | 564 | 36 (A) |

As with much theory, in practice companies often put a combination of the options above into use. This may involve comparing monthly actual, cumulative actual, and full-year forecast to budget.

Variance analysis of this nature is only as good as the commentary that accomodates it and the actions that it is used to drive.

Advantages

- It informs managers of what is likely to happen unless control action is taken.

- It encourages managers to be proactive and deal with problems before they occur.

- Reforecasting on a monthly or continuous basis can save time when it comes to completing a quarterly or annual budget.

Disadvantages

- It may be time consuming as control reports must be produced regularly.

- It may require a sophisticated forecasting system, which might be expensive.

### Test your understanding 6

**Explain why feed-forward control may be particularly appropriate for the capital expenditure budget.**

## 1.6  Zero-based budgeting (ZBB)

A 'method of budgeting that requires each cost element to be specifically justified, as though the activities to which the budget relates were being undertaken for the first time. Without approval, the budget allowance is zero'.

It is especially useful for:

- service departments such as stores, maintenance, marketing, finance, etc.

- discretionary costs such as research and development

- public sector organisations such as local authorities.

It is important that managers involved in ZBB examine their current practices very carefully. Questions they should ask themselves include:

- Is the activity essential? What would happen if it ceased?

- Is the provision of the activity at the correct level?

- Are there other alternatives for achieving the same effect?

There are four distinct stages in the implementation of ZBB:

1   Managers should specify, for their responsibility centres, those activities that can be individually evaluated.

2   Each of the individual activities is then described in a decision package. The decision package should state the costs and revenues expected from the given activity. It should be drawn up in such a way that the package can be evaluated and ranked against other packages.

3   Each decision package is evaluated and ranked usually using cost/ benefit analysis.

4   The resources are then allocated to the various packages.

Advantages

- Inefficient or obsolete operations can be identified and discontinued.

- It creates an inquisitorial attitude, rather than one which assumes that current practices represent value for money.

- Wasteful expenditure is avoided.

- Managers are forced to consider alternative methods of achieving their objectives.

- ZBB leads to increased staff involvement at all levels. This should lead to better communication and motivation.

- Attention is focused on outputs in relation to value for money.

- Knowledge and understanding of the cost behaviour patterns of the organisation will be enhanced.

- Resources should be allocated efficiently and economically.

Disadvantages

- The time involved and the cost of preparing the budget is much greater than for less elaborate budgeting methods. In some organisations because of the heavy paperwork involved ZBB has become known as 'Xerox-based budgeting'.

- It may emphasise short-term benefits to the detriment of long-term benefits.

- There is a need for management skills that may not be present in the organisation.

- Managers, staff and unions may feel threatened;.

- The rankings of packages may be subjective where the benefits are of a qualitative nature.

- It is difficult to compare and rank completely different types of activity.

- The budgeting process may become too rigid and the company may not be able to react to unforeseen opportunities or threats.

- Incremental costs and benefits of alternative courses of action are difficult to quantify accurately.

**Expandable text**

A decision package was defined by **Peter Pyhrr** (who first formulated the ZBB approach at Texas Instruments) as:

'A document that identifies and describes a specific activity in such a manner that senior management can:

(a) evaluate and rank it against other activities competing for limited resources, and

(b) decide whether to approve or disapprove it.'

A decision package is a document that:

- analyses the cost of the activity (costs may be built up from a zero base, but costing information can be obtained from historical records or last year's budget)

- states the purpose of the activity

- identifies alternative methods of achieving the same purpose

- assesses the consequence of not doing the activity at all, or performing the activity at a different level

- establishes measures of performance for the activity.

**Pyhrr** identifies two types of package.

(i) Mutually exclusive packages: these contain different methods of obtaining the same objective.

(ii) Incremental packages: these divide the activity into a number of different levels of activity. The base package describes the minimum effort and cost needed to carry out the activity. The other packages describe the incremental costs and benefits when added to the base.

## Illustration 6 – ZBB

A company is conducting a ZBB exercise, and a decision package is being prepared for its materials handling operations.

- The manager responsible has identified a base package for the minimum resources needed to perform the materials handling function. This is to have a team of five workers and a supervisor, operating without any labour-saving machinery. The estimated annual cost of wages and salaries, with overtime, would be $375,000.

- In addition to the base package, the manager has identified an incremental package. The company could lease two fork lift trucks at a cost of $20,000 each year. This would provide a better system because materials could be stacked higher and moved more quickly. Health and safety risks for the workers would be reduced, and there would be savings of $5,000 each year in overtime payments.

- Another incremental package has been prepared, in which the company introduces new computer software to plan materials handling schedules. The cost of buying and implementing the system would be $60,000, but the benefits are expected to be improvements in efficiency that reduce production downtime and result in savings of $10,000 each year in overtime payments.

The base package would be considered essential, and so given a high priority. The two incremental packages should be evaluated and ranked. Here, the fork lift trucks option might be ranked more highly than the computer software.

In the budget that is eventually decided by senior management, the fork lift truck package might be approved, but the computer software package rejected on the grounds that there are other demands for resources with a higher priority.

## Test your understanding 7

For a number of years, the research division of Z Inc has produced its annual budget (for new and continuing projects) using incremental budgeting techniques. The company is now under new management and the annual budget for 20X4 is to be prepared using ZBB techniques.

**Explain how Z Inc could operate a ZBB system for its research projects.**

# 2 Budget preparation

## 2.1 The master budget

The master budget is the budget into which all subsidiary budgets are consolidated. The master budget normally comprises:

- budgeted income statement
- budgeted balance sheet
- budgeted cash flow statement (cash budget).

Assuming that the level of demand is the principal budget factor, the various functional, departmental and master budgets will be drawn up in the following order.

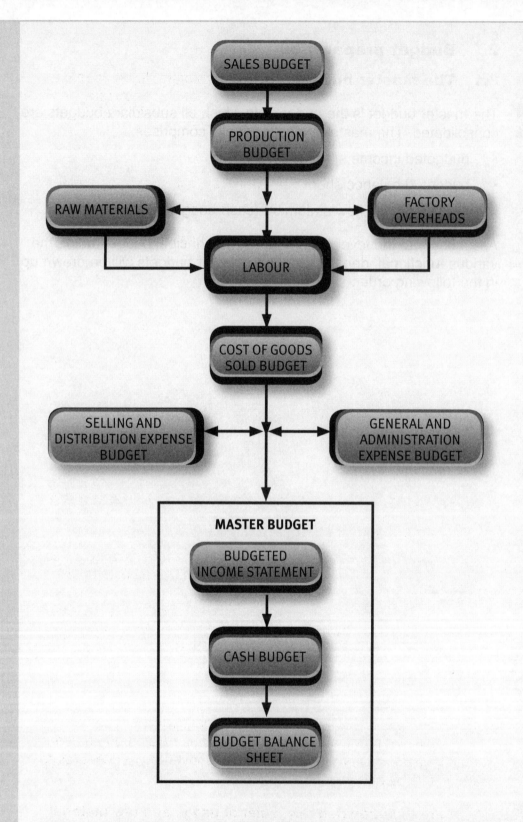

Budget preparation was covered in F2 and it is highly unlikely the F5 examiner will ask you to perform such calculations again.

## 2.2 Functional budgets

Functional budgets are prepared and consolidated to produce the master budget. The normal assumption is that demand is the principal budget factor. A recap of functional budgets is useful for variance analysis.

### Production budget

| | | |
|---|---|---|
| Budgeted production | = | Forecast sales + Closing inventory – Opening inventory |

or

| | | |
|---|---|---|
| Budgeted production | = | Forecast sales + Increase in inventory |

### Test your understanding 8

The sales forecast of a product for January is 2,000 units and finished goods inventory at the start of January is expected to be 200 units. Budgeted closing inventory is 500 units of finished goods at the end of January.

**What is the production budget?**

### Material usage budget

| | | |
|---|---|---|
| Materials usage | = | Usage per unit x units produced |

### Materials purchase budget

| | | |
|---|---|---|
| Materials purchases budget | = | Forecast materials usage + Closing inventory – Opening inventory |

or

| | | |
|---|---|---|
| Materials purchases budget | = | Forecast materials usage + Increase in inventory |

### Test your understanding 9

In the previous illustration, the raw material usage is 6 kg per unit of finished product. Raw material inventory is 1,000 kg at the beginning of January and we expect new inventory procedures to reduce this by half during the month.

**What are the budgeted raw material usage and raw material purchases for January?**

### Losses

If we expect to lose part of our input, we must reflect that in the cost of the output from that process. The only thing we must remember is that the loss percentage will be based on the input units and not the outputs.

### Test your understanding 10

We have budgeted to sell 5,000 units of output. The production units pass through a quality control point at which 5% are expected to be rejected.

**What is budgeted production?**

### Test your understanding 11

A company plans to sell 400 units in the forthcoming year. Inventories of 100 units of finished goods and 300 kg of raw materials are held at the current year end. They are both expected to fall by 25% during next year due to more efficient stockholding procedures. A loss of 10% is expected on all raw materials received from suppliers. One unit of output requires 5 kg of raw material.

**What are the budgeted production units, raw material usage and raw material purchases?**

## 2.3 Flexible budgeting

### Fixed budget

A budget prepared at a single level of activity.

### Flexible budget

A budget prepared with the cost behaviour of all cost elements known and classified as either fixed or variable. The budget may be prepared at a number of activity levels and can be 'flexed' or changed to the actual level of activity for budgetary control purposes.

### Illustration 12 – Budget preparation

A firm has prepared the following cost card per unit based on producing and selling 10,000 units in a month:

|  | $ |
|---|---|
| Selling price | 10 |
| Variable production costs | 3 |
| Fixed production costs | 1 |
| Profit per unit | 6 |

Actual sales and production for month 1 were for 12,000 units and gave the following profit:

|                        | $   |
|------------------------|-----|
| Sales                  | 125 |
| Variable production costs | (40) |
| Fixed Production costs  | (9) |
| Profit                 | 76  |

Prepare a table showing the original budget, the flexed budget, the actual results and total variances.

**Solution**

|                | Original budget | Flexed budget | Actual | Variance |
|----------------|-----------------|---------------|--------|----------|
| Sales          | 100             | 120           | 125    | 5 favourable |
| Variable costs | (30)            | (36)          | (40)   | 4 adverse |
| Fixed costs    | (10)            | (10)*         | (9)    | 1 favourable |
| Profit         | 60              | 74            | 76     | 2 favourable |

*Be careful not to change the total fixed costs when flexing the budget unless there is a stepped element to include. The budgeted profit per unit of $6 no longer applies once the budget is flexed.

## Test your understanding 12

**Using the budgeted figures from the above example, prepare a revised performance table for month 2 when actual sales and production volumes were 20,000 units. Assume that the fixed costs have a step where by they are expected to increase by $5,000 once production exceeds 15,000 units.**

Actual results for month 2 were as follows:

|                         | $000 |
|-------------------------|------|
| Sales                   | 196  |
| Variable production costs | (62) |
| Fixed production costs  | (16) |
| Profit                  | 118  |

## Test your understanding 13

You have been provided with the following operating statement, which represents an attempt to compare the actual performance for the quarter that has just ended with the budget.

|                          | Budget | Actual | Variance |
|--------------------------|--------|--------|----------|
| Number of units sold (000) | 640    | 720    | 80       |

|  | $000 | $000 | $000 |
|---|---|---|---|
| Cost of sales (all variable) | | | |
| Materials | 168 | 144 | 24 |
| Labour | 240 | 288 | (48) |
| Overheads | 32 | 36 | (4) |
|  | 440 | 468 | (28) |
| | | | |
| Fixed labour cost | 100 | 94 | 6 |
| Selling and distribution costs | | | |
| Fixed | 72 | 83 | (11) |
| Variable | 144 | 153 | (9) |
| | | | |
| Administration costs | | | |
| Fixed | 184 | 176 | 8 |
| Variable | 48 | 54 | (6) |
|  | 548 | 560 | (12) |
| Total costs | 988 | 1,028 | (40) |
| Sales | 1,024 | 1,071 | 47 |
| Net profit | 36 | 43 | 7 |

(a) **Using a flexible budgeting approach, redraft the operating statement so as to provide a more realistic indication of the variances, and comment briefly on the possible reasons (other than inflation) why they have occurred.**

(b) **Explain why the original operating statement was of little use to management.**

(c) (i) **Discuss the problems associated with the forecasting of figures which are to be used in flexible budgeting.**

   (ii) **Further analysis has indicated that the 'variable' overheads for cost of sales are, in fact, only semi-variable. Whilst the budgeted overheads for 640,000 units is indicated to be $32,000, it is felt that the budget for 760,000 units would be $37,000. Included in this later cost is $1,000 incurred when the activity reached 750,000 units due to extra hiring capacity.**

   **Produce a revised flexed budget for the overheads contained in cost of sales for an activity level of 720,000 units.**

# 3 Selecting a suitable budgetary system

## 3.1 Selecting a suitable budgetary system

There are many approaches to budgeting and an organisation will wish to select a system which is most appropriate.

Factors, which will determine suitability include:

- type of organisation
- type of industry
- type of product and product range
- culture of the organisation.

### Illustration 13 – Selecting a suitable budgetary system

A hospital operates in a relatively stable financial environment, has a very high proportion of fixed costs and a diverse range of activities. Factors to consider when selecting a suitable budgetary system may be:

- An incremental approach may be suitable for all routine activities. New ventures may use a zero-based approach.

- The fixed costs may need close control and therefore some form of ABB may be appropriate.

- The culture of the organisation may dictate whether a participative or imposed budgeting style is more effective. If there are managers who are trained in budgeting and costs are mainly controllable then it may be preferable to adopt a participative approach to empower and motivate staff. If costs are mainly uncontrollable it may be preferable to use a centrally controlled, imposed budget.

### Test your understanding 14

**Select and justify a suitable budgeting system for a company operating in the mobile phone market.**

## 3.2 Information for budgeting

Budgeting requires a great deal of information that can be drawn from many sources.

The main sources of information for budgeting purposes are:

- previous year's actual results
- other internal sources which may include manager's knowledge concerning the state of repair of fixed assets, training needs of staff, long-term requirements of individual customers, etc.

- estimates of costs of new products using work study techniques, technical estimates from research and development, etc.

- statistical techniques such as linear regression may help to forecast sales. EOQ may be used to forecast optimal inventory levels

- external sources of information may include suppliers' price lists, estimates of inflation and exchange rate movements, strategic analysis of the economic environment. Senior managers may incorporate assumptions concerning competitor actions based on the analysis of the market.

### Expandable text

The PESTL model met in paper F1 is useful for identifying change factors:

#### Political change

A change in government policy, for example fiscal policy, may affect the demand for an organisation's products, and/or the costs incurred in providing them. Any such changes will affect both short-term and long-term planning. This is one reason why planning is a continuous process.

#### Social change

Changes in social responsibilities and people's attitude towards them affect every organisation. In recent years there has been much more concern about social responsibilities, some of which are now recognised by law. All of these factors may impinge on the plans of the organisation.

#### Economic change

When there is a change in the economic climate from boom through to recession, the demands upon people's income become more focused. Money tends to be spent on necessary goods with little left for 'luxury goods' and savings. The lack of savings deters investment, with the result that plans have to be modified if they are to be realistic targets.

#### Technological change

When plans are made, they are based upon the use of certain methods and equipment. As technology advances, the older methods are proven to be inefficient, with the result that decisions are taken to update the operation. As a consequence, the aspects of the budgets and plans which related to the old method are no longer relevant. Revised plans must now be drawn up on the basis of the new technology.

**Legal change**

When plans are made they are based on the current legal framework and known changes to this are also factored in over time. However, changes to the legal framework can cause information that is used when pulling budgets together to become redundant. An example of this might be the government introducing legislation that bans fast food from being advertised during the intervals between children's TV programmes.

> **Test your understanding 15**
>
> **Describe the sources of information required for a company's cash budget.**

### 3.3 Changing a budgetary system

A budget system is an important system for planning, control and decision making in an organisation and changing the system must be carefully planned and implemented.

Changing a budgetary system is a very time consuming process and the following issues should be considered:

- Are suitably trained staff available to implement the change successfully?

- Will changing the system take up management time which should be focusing on production or sales?

- All staff involved in the budgetary process will need to be trained in the new system and understand the procedure to be followed in changing to the new approach. A lack of understanding builds resistance to change.

- All costs of the systems change should be evaluated against the perceived benefits. These may include new system costs, training, downtime of existing staff, consultancy fees, development of new statistical models and sources of information suitable for the new budgetary system. Benefits may be difficult to quantify and therefore a rigorous investment appraisal of the project may be difficult to prepare. Note: the above issues can result in an organization continuing to use a budgeting system it knows to be sub-optimal.

A large holiday complex currently uses incremental budgeting but is concerned about its very high proportion of overhead costs and is considering changing to an activity based budgeting system. Demand follows a fairly predictable seasonal pattern.

**Discuss the issues that should be considered before changing to a new budgetary system.**

### 3.4 Budgeting and uncertainty

Since budgets are predictions and plans for the future, non-controllable events will make the outcome of particular actions uncertain.

There are a number of factors which contribute to the uncertainty surrounding the budget-setting and budgetary-control process.

- Some of the factors may be internal to the organisation but not controllable in the short-term. These would include productivity and efficiency factors which may be controlled in the longer-term by re-training and investment.

- External factors may include:

    (i)     sales may be lower owing to recession

    (ii)    customers may be lost owing to lack of goods because of lower productivity

    (iii)   inflation

    (iv)    government fiscal policy

    (v)     natural disasters

    (vi)    changes in supplier costs and terms of supply.

**Dealing with uncertainty**

There are several techniques available to help deal with uncertainty. These have been discussed before and include:

- rolling budgets

- sensitivity analysis ('what-if?' analysis)

- scenario planning and simulation.

Different assumptions or variables can be changed, and a large number of 'what if?' budgets produced. The impact of the different assumptions on profits and cash flow can be tested. For example, 'what if?' questions that might be asked are:

- What would happen if sales of a particular product or service are only 75% of the budgeted volume?

- What would happen if the direct labour workforce is given a 5% pay rise in return for productivity improvements of 3%?

- What would happen if the launch of a new product is delayed by three months?

- What would happen if bad debts rose to 3% and credit customers took 30 days longer to pay invoices?

- What would happen if interest rates went up by 2%, or if the /US$ exchange rate changed to 1.40?

- What would happen if inventory levels were increased by 5%?

With a spreadsheet model or other budget model, each 'what if?' question can be evaluated easily and quickly, simply by altering the value of the relevant variable in the model. Alternatively a range of different budgets based on different possible outcomes can be prepared.

## 3.5 Spreadsheets in budgeting

A spreadsheet is a computer package which stores data in a matrix format where the intersection of each row and column is referred to as a cell.

### Advantages of spreadsheets

- A typical spreadsheet can handle approximately 8,000 rows and over 200 columns, enough to accommodate a very complex model.

- Formulae and look up tables can be used so that if any figure is amended, all the figures will be immediately recalculated. This is very useful for carrying out sensitivity analysis.

- The results can be printed out or distributed to other users electronically quickly and easily.

- Most programs can also represent the results graphically e.g. balances can be shown in a bar chart:

**Closing cash balances**

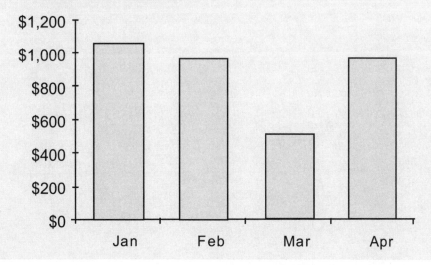

**Disdvantages of spreadsheets:**

- Spreadsheets for a particular budgeting application will take time to build up and develop. There is no benefit in taking many hours to develop a spreadsheet which is then only used occasionally to complete a task which could easily be done efficiently using a manual method.

- Data can be accidentally changed (or deleted) without the user being aware of this occurring.

- Errors in design, particularly in the use of formulae, can produce invalid output. Due to the complexity of the model, these design errors may be difficult to locate.

- The manipulation of the data using such a mathematical approach may lead to the loss of the original concepts, these being replaced with a seemingly accurate set of output reports. In the context of budgets and forecasts it must be remembered that such output is based on data which are estimates and which may therefore be incorrect.

- Security issues, whether due to unauthorized access (e.g. hacking) or a loss of back-up files.

### Illustration 16 – Selecting a suitable budgetary system

When producing a master budget manually the major problem is ensuring that any initial entry in the budget or any adjustment to a budget item is dealt with in every budget that is relevant – in effect, budgets need to comply with normal double entry principles to be consistent.

Suppose, for instance, that sales in the last month were expected to rise by $10,000, what adjustments would be necessary?

THE SALES BUDGET WOULD NEED TO BE INCREASED.

IF CUSTOMERS TAKE MORE THAN ONE MONTH TO PAY, YEAR-END RECEIVABLES WOULD NEED TO BE INCREASED.

COST OF SALES WOULD INCREASE.

PURCHASES WOULD NEED TO BE INCREASED.

EITHER PAYABLES OR CASH PAYMENTS WOULD BE INCREASED.

INVENTORY AT A MONTH END MAY HAVE TO BE INCREASED, BUT NOT THE FINAL YEAR-END INVENTORY.

PROFIT WOULD INCREASE.

Using spreadsheets all of the above adjustments could be processed automatically if the relevant formulae were set up properly. Receivables, cost of sales, purchases, payables, cash, inventory and profit could change instantly on adjusting sales of month 12.

**Test your understanding 17**

Cash budgeting is commonly carried out using spreadsheets.

**Explain the advantages of using spreadsheets for cash budgeting and any possible dangers.**

# Chapter summary

BUDGETING

## APPROACHES TO BUDGETING
- Top down/bottom up budgeting
- Rolling budgets
- Activity-based budgets
- Incremental budgets
- Feed-forward budgets
- Zero-based budgets.

## PREPARATION OF BUDGETS
- Master budgets
- Functional budgets
- Flexible budgets.

## SELECTING A SUITABLE SYSTEM
- Dealing with change
- Incorporating uncertainty
- Use of spreadsheets.

# Test your understanding answers

## Test your understanding 1

1   Operational managers may not have the knowledge and experience to set a budget. For example, in a small business only the owner may be involved in all aspects of the business and may therefore set the budget.

2   In times of crisis there may be insufficient time to set a participative budget and targets may have to be imposed to ensure survival.

3   Participation has to be genuine for it to result in improved motivation. Pseudo-participation, where senior managers seek the opinions of the ultimate budget holders but do not act on these views, may lead to demotivation.

## Test your understanding 2

The revised budget should incorporate 3% growth starting from the actual sales figure of Quarter 1 and should include a figure for Quarter 1 of the following year.

|  | Quarter 2 $ | Quarter 3 $ | Quarter 4 $ | Quarter 1 $ | Total $ |
|---|---|---|---|---|---|
| Sales | 127,154 | 130,969 | 134,898 | 138,945 | 531,966 |

## Test your understanding 3

### 20X4 Costs

| | | |
|---|---|---|
| Total variable cost | = 75% × $672,000 = | $504,000 |
| Proportion relating to product A | = 60% × $504,000 = | $302,400 |
| Cost per unit of product A | = $302,400/640     = | $472.50 |

### 20X5 Costs

| | | |
|---|---|---|
| Inflated cost per unit of A | = $472.50 × 1.04  = | $491.40 |

### Test your understanding 4

| Activity | | Expected cost $ | Actual cost $ | Variance $ | |
|---|---|---|---|---|---|
| Receiving goods | 45 orders delivered | 3,600 | 3,450 | 150 | (F) |
| Issuing goods | 100 requisitions | 4,000 | 4,400 | 400 | (A) |
| Ordering | 36 orders | 900 | 960 | 60 | (A) |
| Counting | 2 stock counts | 2,000 | 1,750 | 250 | (F) |
| Record keeping | | 2,000 | 1,900 | 100 | (F) |
| Supervision | | 2,500 | 2,700 | 200 | (A) |
| | | 15,000 | 15,160 | 160 | (A) |

### Test your understanding 5

D is the correct answer.

Situation A would be best suited by implementing Zero Base Budgeting. Situation B does not require ABB since it has relatively low overheads. Situation C would be suitable for incremental budgeting. ABB will certainly not be quicker.

### Test your understanding 6

Capital expenditure is often long-term in nature. It is more useful to compare actual costs to forecast completion costs so that action can be taken when a project is in progress rather than waiting for completion.

### Test your understanding 7

The managers/researchers responsible for each project should decide which projects they wish to undertake in the forthcoming period. These projects will be a mixture of continued projects and new projects.

For the projects which have already been started and which the managers want to continue in the next period, we should ignore any cash flows already incurred (they are sunk costs), and we should only look at future costs and benefits. Similarly, for the new projects we should only look at the future costs and benefits.

Different ways of achieving the same research goals should also be investigated and the projects should only go ahead if the benefit exceeds the cost.

Once all the potential projects have been evaluated if there are insufficient funds to undertake all the worthwhile projects, then the funds should be allocated to the best projects on the basis of a cost-benefit analysis.

ZBB is usually of a highly subjective nature. (The costs are often reasonably certain, but usually a lot of uncertainty is attached to the estimated benefits.) This can be shown by the example of a research division where the researchers may have their own pet projects, which they are unable to view in an objective light.

### Test your understanding 8

Production = 2,000 + 500 − 200 = 2,300 units.

### Test your understanding 9

| | | |
|---|---|---|
| Raw material usage | = | 2,300 × 6 = 13,800 kg |
| Raw material purchases | = | 13,800 + 500 − 1,000 = 13,300 kg |

### Test your understanding 10

| | | |
|---|---|---|
| Output | = | 95% of input |
| Sales | = | 5,000 = 0.95 × production |
| Production | = | $\dfrac{5,000}{0.95}$ = 5,263.16 or rounded up = 5,264. |

### Test your understanding 11

| | | | | |
|---|---|---|---|---|
| Budgeted production | = | 400 + 75 − 100 | = | 375 |
| Raw material usage | = | 375 × 5 | = | 1875 kg |
| Raw material purchases (excluding losses) | = | 1,875 + 225 − 300 | = | 1,800 kg |
| Actual purchases | = | $\dfrac{1,800}{0.9}$ | = | 2,000 kg |

### Test your understanding 12

| $000 | Original budget | Flexed budget | Actual | Variances |
|---|---|---|---|---|
| Sales | 100 | 200 | 196 | 4 adverse |
| Variable costs | (30) | (60) | (62) | 2 adverse |
| Fixed costs | (10) | (15) | (16) | 1 adverse |
| Profit | 60 | 125 | 118 | 7 adverse |

## Test your understanding 13

(a)

|  | Flexible budget | Actual | Variance |
|---|---|---|---|
| Number of units sold (000) | 720 | 720 | 80 |
|  | $000 | $000 | $000 |
| Sales | 1,152 | 1,071 | (81) |
| Variable cost of sales |  |  |  |
| Materials | 189 | 144 | 45 |
| Labour | 270 | 288 | (18) |
| Overheads | 36 | 36 | 0 |
| Fixed labour cost | 100 | 94 | 6 |
|  | 595 | 562 | 33 |
| Gross profit | 557 | 509 | (48) |
| Selling and distribution costs |  |  |  |
| Fixed | 72 | 83 | (11) |
| Variable | 162 | 153 | 9 |
| Administration costs |  |  |  |
| Fixed | 184 | 176 | 8 |
| Variable | 54 | 54 |  |
|  | 472 | 466 | 6 |
| Net profit | 85 | 43 | (42) |

Possible reasons

Sales (adverse) – the volume variance is favourable so the adverse variance must be due to price being less than planned.

Materials (favourable) – could be due to bulk purchase, resulting in a lower unit price.

Variable labour (adverse) – could be due to inefficient working by direct labour.

Fixed labour (favourable) – could be due to employees leaving and not being replaced.

Fixed selling overheads (adverse) – could be due to additional fixed advertising costs.

Variable selling overheads (favourable) – could be due to lower running costs of distribution vehicles.

Fixed administration overheads (favourable) – better computer systems reduces the number of accountants needed!

**Note:** There are many other possible reasons for the variances.

(b) The original statement was of no use as there were volume variances comparing 640,000 units with 720,000 units. To be fair, the budget needs to be flexed to the actual level of 720,000 in order to compare 'like with like'.

(c) (i) Problems of forecasting with flexible budgets include the following:

General problems: These must be overcome in any budgeting system, e.g. predicting volume and other internal estimates along with macroeconomic factors such as inflation and the interest rate.

Separation of fixed and variable costs: Whereas separating out a gas bill between standing charge and usage is relatively straightforward, labour is more convoluted especially if pay structure is complicated and involves an element of both (e.g. piece rate plus fixed bonuses).

Nature of fixed costs: In the long-term, all costs are variable. An apparently fixed cost will turn out to be a stepped cost, e.g. the need to hire a new machine once output reaches a certain level.

Historical information: Standards must be kept up to date as much as possible but the past is not necessarily an indicator of the future, e.g. increased mechanisation may alter the standard times taken.

(ii)

|  | 640 | 760 | **Change** |
|---|---|---|---|
| Activity level (000): | 640 | 760 | 120 |
| Overheads ($000) | 32 | 37 | |
| Stepped cost | | (1) | |
| | 32 | 36 | 4 |

Variable cost per unit $= \dfrac{4}{120} = 0.0333$

Fixed cost $= 32 - 0.03333 \times 640 = 10.667$

Therefore flexed budget for 720 would be ($000):

| | |
|---|---|
| Fixed cost | 10.667 |
| Variable cost (720 x 0.0333) | 24.000 |
| | 34.667 |

### Test your understanding 14

The mobile phone market is intensely competitive so a company will need sophisticated systems to gather information about the market and competitors. The market is also fast changing so a rolling budget approach may be suitable to keep budget targets up to date. It will be very important to incorporate the latest information into budgets and a participative approach will be important as production managers and sales managers may have local knowledge which would improve the budgeting process.

### Test your understanding 15

Internal information will be required from the:

*   sales department relating to volume and estimated collection periods

*   the production manager will estimate material, labour and overhead usage

*   the purchasing manager will estimate material prices and payment terms

*   human resources will forecast pay rates, bonus payments and overtime requirements

*   the finance office may forecast payments of interest, dividends and general office costs.

External information may be required relating to forecast interest rates, tax rates, payment terms for tax, exchange rates, inflation, etc.

## Test your understanding 16

An analysis of overheads should be carried out to determine the proportion that have identifiable cost drivers which differ from the normal volume related cost drivers which may be used when carrying out incremental budgeting. If a substantial volume of overhead is non-volume related then implementing ABB may lead to more accurate planning and control.

Issues, which should then be considered include:

- the development or purchase of a suitable computer system to support an ABB process;

- training of staff to operate and interpret the information produced;

- development of an implementation plan and whether this should run in tandem with the existing process for a trial period.

## Test your understanding 17

Advantages

- Standard format can be used which is easily understood throughout the organisation.

- 'What-if?' analysis can be carried out easily to test different assumptions.

- Cash budget can be linked to other functional budgets and the income statement and balance sheet so that changes can be linked between budgets.

- Look up tables can be used so that, for example, if price levels change these can be input in one place in the spreadsheet and the effects can be carried throughout the budget.

- Different managers may be able to input information into the spreadsheet if it is held on a shared drive.

Dangers:

- If there is an error in the cash budgeting model this may be overlooked and the organisation will be using inaccurate information.

- Information may be accidentally changed or deleted.

- Data used will still be forecast and subject to a high degree of uncertainty. There is a danger that it will be used incorrectly.

# Quantitative analysis

## Chapter learning objectives

Upon completion of this chapter you will be able to:

- explain and evaluate the use of high/low analysis to separate the fixed and variable elements of total cost

- explain and evaluate the use of regression analysis to separate the fixed and variable elements of total cost

- explain the use of time series analysis as a forecasting technique

- predict a future value from time series analysis data using both the additive and proportional data

- explain the use of a simple average growth model as a forecasting technique

- explain the use of judgement and experience in forecasting

- explain the learning curve effect

- estimate the learning effect and apply this to a budgetary problem

- calculate production times when the learning curve has reached a steady state

- explain the limitations of the learning curve model.

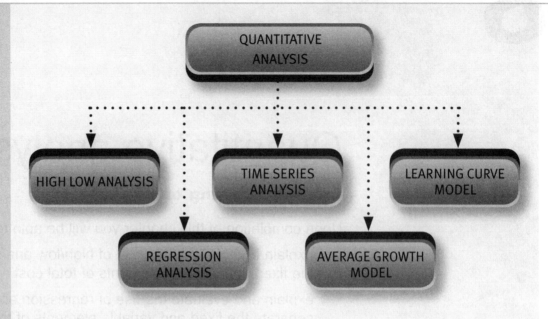

## 1 High/low analysis

A method of analysing a semi-variable cost into its fixed and variable elements based on an analysis of historical information about costs at different activity levels.

The approach is as follows:

**Step 1**

Select the highest and lowest **activity** levels, and their costs.

(**Note:** do not take the highest and lowest costs).

**Step 2**

Find the variable cost/unit.

$$\text{Variable cost/unit} = \frac{\text{Cost at high level of activity} - \text{Cost at low level activity}}{\text{High level activity} - \text{Low level activity}}$$

**Step 3**

Find the fixed cost, using either the high or low activity level.

Fixed cost         = Total cost at activity level − Total variable cost

The high-low method has the enormous advantage of simplicity. It is easy to understand and easy to use.

The limitations of the high-low method are:

- It assumes that activity is the only factor affecting costs.

- It assumes that historical costs reliably predict future costs.

- It uses only two values, the highest and the lowest, so the results may be distorted due to random variations in these values.

## Illustration 1 – Hi/low analysis

Cost data for the six months to 31 December 20X8 is as follows:

| Month | Units | Inspection costs $ |
|---|---|---|
| July | 340 | 2,240 |
| August | 300 | 2,160 |
| September | 380 | 2,320 |
| October | 420 | 2,400 |
| November | 400 | 2,360 |
| December | 360 | 2,280 |

The variable element of a cost item is estimated by calculating the unit cost between high and low volumes during a period.

| Six months to 31/12/X8 | Units produced | Inspection costs $ |
|---|---|---|
| Highest month | 420 | 2,400 |
| Lowest month | 300 | 2,160 |
| Range | 120 | 240 |

Variable cost per unit = $240/120 = $2 per unit

Fixed inspection costs are, therefore:

$2,400 – (420 units x $2) = $1,560 per month
or $2,160 – (300 units x $2) = $1,560 per month.
i.e. the relationship is of the form y = $1,560 + $2x.

## Test your understanding 1

| Output (Units) | Total cost ($) |
|---|---|
| 200 | 7,000 |
| 300 | 8,000 |
| 400 | 9,000 |

(a)  **Find the variable cost per unit.**

(b)  **Find the total fixed cost.**

(c)  **Estimate the total cost if output is 350 units.**

(d)  **Estimate the total cost if output is 600 units.**

## 2    Regression analysis

Regression involves using historical data to find the line of best fit between two variables (one dependent on the other), and use this to predict future values.

The dependent variable is y and must always be on the vertical axis

The independent variable is x and always goes on the horizontal axis.

**Scatter diagram**

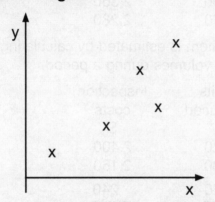

The scatter of the points is caused by the other factors affecting y.

Our objective is to find the best line (the 'line of best fit') through the centre of this diagram.

**Equation of a straight line**

The equation of a straight line is:

y = a + bx

where:

a    is the intercept:              the y value when x equals zero, and

b    is the gradient or slope:   the change in y when x increases by one unit.

If b is negative, the line will be downwards sloping – as x increases, y decreases. This is called a negative relationship.

To find the line of best fit we need to calculate a and b using the historical data for x and y. The formulae for these are:

$$b = \frac{n\sum xy - \sum x \sum y}{n\sum x^2 - (\sum x)^2}$$

$$a = \frac{\sum y}{n} - b\frac{\sum x}{n}$$

where n = sample size

Both of these formulae are given in the examination.

### Illustration 2 – Regression analysis

A company has recorded expenditure on advertising and resulting sales for six months as follows:

| Month | Advertising expenditure | Sales |
| --- | --- | --- |
| | x | y |
| | $000 | $000 |
| March | 20 | 170 |
| April | 40 | 240 |
| May | 50 | 260 |
| June | 60 | 300 |
| July | 30 | 220 |
| August | 40 | 250 |

**Required:**

(a)  Plot the data on a scatter diagram and comment.

(b)  Calculate the line of best fit through the data, and interpret your values of a and b.

(c)  Forecast sales when advertising expenditure is:

   (i)   $50,000

   (ii)  $100,000

   and comment on your answers.

**Solution**

(a)

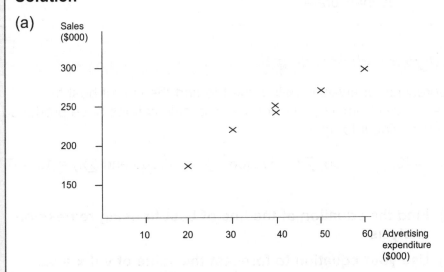

There appears to be a positive linear relationship between advertising expenditure and sales.

(b)

| x | y | xy | $x^2$ | $y^2$ |
|---|---|---|---|---|
| 20 | 170 | 3,400 | 400 | 28,900 |
| 40 | 240 | 9,600 | 1,600 | 57,600 |
| 50 | 260 | 13,000 | 2,500 | 67,600 |
| 60 | 300 | 18,000 | 3,600 | 90,000 |
| 30 | 220 | 6,600 | 900 | 48,400 |
| 40 | 250 | 10,000 | 1,600 | 62,500 |
| 240 | 1,440 | 60,600 | 10,600 | 355,000 |

$$b = \frac{6 \times 60,600 - 240 \times 1,440}{6 \times 10,600 - 240^2} = \frac{18,000}{6,000} = 3$$

$$a = \frac{1,440}{6} - 3\frac{240}{6} = 120$$

Line is:  y = 120 + 3x

This means that when advertising expenditure is zero, sales will be $120,000, and for every $1 spent on advertising, sales will increase by $3.

(c) (i)  Advertising is $50,000 x = 50;  y = 120 + (3 x 50) = 270

Forecast sales are $270,000

This is an interpolation within the sample range of values and is likely to be fairly accurate.

(ii)  Advertising is $100,000 x = 100;  y = 120 + (3 x 100) = 420

Forecast sales are $420,000

This is an extrapolation outside the sample range and may be inaccurate.

### Test your understanding 2

Regression analysis is being used to find the line of best fit (y = a + bx) from 11 pairs of data. The calculations have produced the following information:

$\sum x$ = 440, $\sum y$ = 330, $\sum x^2$ = 17,986, $\sum y^2$ = 10,366 and $\sum xy$ = 13,467

**(a) Find the equation of the line of best fit using regression analysis.**

**(b) Use your equation to forecast the value of y if x = 42.**

**Note:** You may recall form paper F2 that the strength of the linear relationship between the two variables (and hence the usefulness of the regression line equation) can be assessed by calculating the correlation coefficient ("r") and the coefficient of determination ("$r^2$"), where

$$r = \frac{n \sum xy - \sum x \sum y}{\sqrt{\left(n \sum x^2 - \left(\sum x\right)^2\right)\left(n \sum y^2 - \left(\sum y\right)^2\right)}}$$

Using the data from illustration 2 above:

$$r = \frac{6 \times 60,600 - 240 \times 1,440}{\sqrt{\left(6 \times 10,600 - 240^2\right)\left(6 \times 355,000 - 1,440^2\right)}} = 0.97849\ldots$$

$r^2 = 0.957$

Thus 95.7% of the observed variation is sales can be explained as being due to changes in the advertising spend. This would give strong assurances that the forecasts made using the regression equation are valid.

## 3    Time series analysis

A time series is a series of figures relating to the changing value of a variable over time. The data often conforms to a certain pattern over time. This pattern can be extrapolated into the future and hence forecasts are possible. Time periods may be any measure of time including days, weeks, months and quarters.

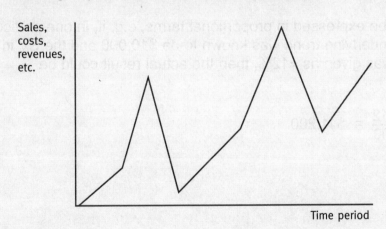

The four components of a time series are:

*   The trend – this describes the long-term general movement of the data.

*   Seasonal variations – a regular variation around the trend over a fixed time period, usually one year.

- Cyclical variations – economic cycle of booms and slumps.
- Residual variations – irregular, random fluctuations in the data usually caused by factors specific to the time series. They are unpredictable.

In examination problems there is generally insufficient data to evaluate the cyclical variations, hence, they are ignored. The residual influences are also, effectively, ignored. They should actually be eliminated by using some averaging techniques.

**The numerical analysis**

This is performed by carrying out two distinct steps:

- establishing the long-term underlying trend
- establishing the regular seasonal variations.

You will not be asked to derive the time series relationship. Instead you could be given this information and asked to forecast future sales.

**The additive model**

This is based upon the idea that each actual result is made up of two influences.

Actual = Trend + Seasonal Variation (SV)

The SV will be expressed in absolute terms.

**The multiplicative model**

Actual = Trend x SV factor

The SV will be expressed in proportional terms, e.g. if, in one particular period the underlying trend was known to be $10,000 and the SV in this period was given as +12%, then the actual result could be forecast as:

$$\$10,000 \times \frac{112}{100} = \$11,200.$$

**Test your understanding 3**

A company has found that the trend in the quarterly sales of its furniture is well described by the regression equation

$$y = 150 + 10X$$

where  y equals quarterly sales ($000)
  x  = 1 represents the first quarter of 20X0
  x  = 2 represents the second quarter of 20X0
  x = 5 represents the first quarter of 20X1, etc.

It has also been found that, based on a multiplicative model, i.e.

  Sales  =  Trend $\times$ Seasonal $\times$ Random

The mean seasonal quarterly index for its furniture sales is as follows:

| Quarter | 1 | 2 | 3 | 4 |
|---|---|---|---|---|
| Seasonal index | 80 | 110 | 140 | 70 |

**(a) Explain the meaning of this regression equation, and set of seasonal index numbers.**

**(b) Using the regression equation, estimate the trend values in the company's furniture sales for each quarter of 20X5**

**(c) Using the seasonal index, prepare sales forecasts for the company's quarterly furniture sales in 20X5**

**(d) State what factors might cause your sales forecasts to be in error.**

**Test your understanding 4**

The number of customers to a health centre has been increasing and it is estimated that the underlying trend is for an increase of 50 customers each month. However, the numbers fluctuate depending on the month of the year.

The underlying trend value for customers in December Year 1 is 4,300.

SVs for some of the months are:

| | SV factor |
|---|---|
| May | 116 |
| June | 107 |
| July | 94 |
| August | 82 |
| September | 106 |

**Prepare a forecast for the number of customers in each of the months May to September, Year 2.**

## 5 Average growth models

Strategic plans may incorporate an objective of a target average growth of profit or sales over a number of years. There may also be requirements for a target average growth rate of productivity over a number of years.

### Illustration 6 – Average growth models

Sales are forecast to increase, on average, by 2% per quarter. Sales are currently $250,000 pa. Calculate the budgeted sales figures for each quarter of the forthcoming year.

Show how you could have found the average growth rate given the final figure.

**Solution**

| | | Sales ($) |
|---|---|---|
| Quarter 1 | ($250,000/4 x 1.02) | 63,750 |
| Quarter 2 | ($63,750 x 1.02) | 65,025 |
| Quarter 3 | ($65,025 x 1.02) | 66,326 |
| Quarter 4 | ($66,325.5 x 1.02) | 67,652 |
| | | $262,753 |

The problem may be to find the average growth rate given the original and final sales figure.

Let  g = the unknown growth rate
     O = the original figure
     F = the final figure
     n = number of periods of growth.

$F = O (1+g)^n$

In this problem $67,652 = $62,500 $(1+g)^3$

So g = ($67,652/62,500)$^{1/3}$ – 1 = 2.0%

### Test your understanding 5

A company is producing a budget relating to a new product to be introduced. Sales volume is expected to be 1,000 units in the first quarter of the year and is forecast to grow by 10% per quarter. The sale price is to be set at $125 initially but will be reduced by 5% each quarter. Variable costs per unit are forecast to be $65 initially but productivity improvements of 2% per quarter are expected. Assume that no inventories are held.

**Calculate the budgeted contribution for each quarter and the average growth per quarter of contribution over the year.**

## 6 The use of judgement and experience in forecasting

Judgement and experience are important in forecasting. The quantitative models available are mainly based on past information and extrapolate these results into the future. Managers will have access to many sources of information to help them judge whether past results are likely to be good predictors of future results.

### Illustration 7 – The use of judgement and experience in forecasting

A regression analysis has been carried out linking sales to advertising expenditure. Managers may use their judgement to modify the forecasts if they know that, for example:

- a competitor has recently launched a new product in the market

- a new advertising medium is to be used

- general forecasts of growth in the economy are less favourable

- consumers view the product as being almost out of date.

Managers may:

- forecast more than one scenario, using the regression formula or other quantitative;analysis as an initial estimate and then modifying this to give a most likely, a pessimistic and an optimistic scenario

- use probabilities, estimated using their own judgement and experience, to determine the expected value of a forecast.

### Test your understanding 6

A manager has forecast the following sales revenues and probabilities based on a given level of advertising.

|  | Probability | Sales revenue ($) |
|---|---|---|
| Pessimistic | 0.1 | 100,000 |
| Most likely | 0.6 | 125,000 |
| Optimistic | 0.3 | 140,000 |

**Explain how this information may be used when preparing the budget.**

## 7 Learning curves

### 7.1 The learning curve effect

As workers become more familiar with the production of a new product, average time (and average cost) per unit will decline.

**Wrights Law:** as cumulative output doubles, the cumulative average time per unit falls to a fixed percentage (referred to as the learning rate) of the previous average time.

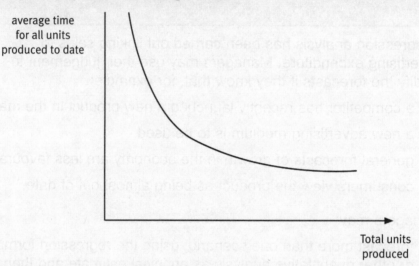

As can be seen on the graph, eventually the curve becomes almost horizontal when many units have been produced, as the learning effect is lost and production time per unit becomes a constant.

The learning curve effect can be calculated by:

- reducing cumulative average time by the learning rate each time output doubles in a table:

- using the formula:

$$y = ax^b$$

where  $y$ = cumulative average time (or average cost) per unit or per batch

$a$ = time (or cost) for first unit or per batch

$b = \dfrac{\log r}{\log 2}$ ($r$ = rate of learning, expressed as a decimal)

$x$ = cumulative output in units or in batches

Conditions for the learning effect to apply:

- the activity is labour intensive

- a repetitive process for each unit

- low turnover of labour

- early stages of production

- no prolonged breaks in production.

Applications of the learning effect:

- pricing decisions – prices will be set too high if based on the costs of making the first few units

- work scheduling – less labour per unit will be required as more units are made

- limiting factor decisions

- standard setting

- budgeting.

Cessation of the learning effect (steady state):

- machine efficiency restricts further improvements

- machines have reached the limits of safe running speeds

- 'go slow' agreements.

## Illustration 8 – Learning curve

Assume that it has taken 400 direct labour hours to manufacture the first unit of a new product. As in the past for this business it is anticipated that a 75% learning curve will occur. A schedule can be drawn up with the following headings and calculations:

| (1)<br>Cumulative number<br>of units | (2)<br>Cumulative average<br>time per unit | (1) × (2)<br>Cumulative total<br>hours |
|---|---|---|
| 1 | 400 | 400 |
| 2 | 300 (75% of 400) | 600 |
| 4 | 225 (75% of 300) | 900 |

Once 2 units have been produced, and the learning process continues, the production of 2 more units will take only (900 – 600), i.e. 300 hours. This represents 150 hours per unit.

### Test your understanding 7

**Determine the cumulative total hours for eight units and hence determine the total time to make the last four units.**

## Illustration 9 – Learning curve

Use the formula to calculate the cumulative average time to produce four units in the previous illustration.

First calculate the exponent b: $\dfrac{\text{logarithm of rate of learning}}{\text{logarithm of 2}}$

Therefore, for a 75% learning curve the coefficient of learning is given by:

$$b = \frac{\log 0.75}{\log 2}$$

$$= \frac{-(0.1249)}{0.3010}$$

$$= -0.415$$

**Note:** The log of a number less than one is always negative, therefore b will always be negative.

Then use the formula,

$$Y = 400 \times 4^{-0.415} = 225 \text{ hours, as before.}$$

## Test your understanding 8

**Assume that it takes 400 direct labour hours to produce the first unit of a new product and an 85% learning curve applies. Calculate the total time to produce the third unit.**

### 7.2 Application of the learning effect to budgeting

A standard cost of a product is the planned unit cost of the product during a specific period of time. If the product enjoys a learning effect, but the effect is ignored, then the standard cost will be too high, since the fact that the products will take progressively less labour will have been ignored.

- Budgeted costs must therefore take into account any expected learning curve when they are being formulated.

KAPLAN PUBLISHING

## Illustration 10 – Learning curve

Rachel plc expects to produce four machines next month. Each machine will require $200 of components to be incorporated into a frame costing $100. The first machine is expected to require 100 hours of labour, although a 90% learning effect will apply throughout the month. Labour is paid $8 per hour, while variable overheads are charged at $12 per hour. Calculate the budgeted average cost per machine produced next month.

**Solution**

Hours for first machine = 100

∴ Average hours for first four machines = 100 x 0.92 = 81 hours
∴ Total hours for first four machines = 4 x 81 = 324 hours

Total cost next month will be:

|  |  | $ |
|---|---|---|
| Materials | 4 x ($200 + $100) | 1,200 |
| Labour | 324 x $8 | 2,592 |
| Overheads | 324 x $12 | 3,888 |
|  |  | 7,680 |

The budgeted average per machine is $\dfrac{\$7,680}{4}$ = $1,920.

## Test your understanding 9

A company wishes to determine the minimum price it should charge a customer for a special order. The customer has requested a quotation for 10 machines, but might subsequently place an order for a further 10. Material costs are $30 per machine. It is estimated that the first batch of 10 machines will take 100 hours to manufacture and an 80% learning curve is expected to apply. Labour plus variable overhead costs amount to $3 per hour. Setup costs are $1,000 regardless of the number of machines made.

(a) **What is the minimum price the company should quote for the initial order if there is no guarantee of further orders?**

(b) **What is the minimum price for the follow-on order?**

(c) **What would be the minimum price if both orders were placed together?**

(d) **Having completed the initial orders for a total of 20 machines (price at the minimum levels recommended in (a)**

> and (b)), the company thinks that there would be a ready market for this type of machine if it brought the unit selling price down to $45. At this price, what would be the profit on the first 140 'mass-production' models (i.e. after the first 20 machines) assuming that marketing costs totalled $250?

## 7.3 The learning curve and the steady state

The learning effect will only apply for a certain range of production. Once the steady state is reached the direct labour hours will not reduce any further and this will become the basis on which the budget is produced.

### Illustration 11 – Learning curve

The first batch of a new product took 20 hours to produce. The learning rate is 90%.

If the learning effect ceases after 72 batches (i.e. all subsequent batches take the same time as the 72nd), how long will it take to make a grand total of 100 batches?

**Solution**

$y = ax^b$

$a = 20$ hours

$b = \dfrac{\log 0.9}{\log 2} = -0.152$

$x = 72$ batches

$y = 20 \times 72^{-0.152} = 10.44$ hrs/batch

$x = 71$ batches

$y = 20 \times 71^{-0.152} = 10.46$ hrs/batch

| | | | |
|---|---|---|---|
| Batches | 1-71 will take 71 × 10.46 = | | 742.66 hrs |
| Batches | 1-72 will take 72 × 10.44 = | | 751.68 hrs |
| | | | |
| Batch | 72 will take | | 9.02 hrs |
| | | | |
| Batches | 1-72 will take | | 751.68 hrs |
| Batches | 73-100 will take 28 × 9.02 = | | 252.56 hrs |
| | | | |
| Batches | 1-100 will take | | 1,004.24 hrs |

## Test your understanding 10

Devon Ltd manufactures specialised electronic instruments for the medical profession. The company's major problem is finding sufficient suitably trained staff. Thanks to an extensive training programme Devon has managed to maintain a steady workforce of 40 assembly staff but sees no chance of increasing that number.

A contract is being considered by the board to supply a new type of dartmeter for the next four years. The meter will sell for $2,000, will require components costing $300 and will take two days to assemble and test. The company is only prepared to put 25% of its staff on production of the dartmeter. Even this will mean that they will have to be taken from other work which will result in a loss of contribution of $120 per man day (calculated after charging the $80 per day labour cost).

Devon Ltd feels that it will be able to sell all the output that this team can produce in the 250 working days a year.

The figures of $300 for components and two days for production are initial basic estimates. If output exceeds 2,600 units in any one year, the components supplier will reduce the cost by 10%. Two days is the time that it is anticipated that the first component will take a member of staff to produce. Learning effects will cause this to fall in the conventional manner.

The learning rate for Devon staff is 90%, but learning stops once a member of staff has produced 50 units.

**Calculate the relevant cash flow in year 1 and subsequent years.**

## 7.4 Limitations of the learning curve model

The learning curve, whilst being an important factor to be taken into account if it exists, is based on specific assumptions which may or may not apply in a modern manufacturing environment. The model applies if the process is:

- labour intensive
- no breaks in production
- new product
- complex
- repetitive.

It may also be difficult to identify the learning effect in practice.

In any given scenario you should think carefully about whether the learning effect may be present and be prepared to discuss the limitations of your analysis.

## Illustration 12 – Learning curve

Discuss whether the learning curve is likely to apply in a modern manufacturing environment.

### Solution

The following points may be relevant.

- Modern manufacturing environments may be very capital intensive and the learning effect cannot apply if machines limit the speed of labour.

- Products have short lives in a modern manufacturing environment and therefore new products will be introduced on a regular basis. This makes it likely that there will be learning effects.

- The more complex the product the more likely that the learning curve will be significant and the longer it will take for the learning curve to reach a plateau (beyond which no more learning can take place).

- The learning effect requires that production is repetitive with no major breaks in which the learning effect may be lost. JIT production has moved towards multiskilled and multitasked workers. It is possible that some of the benefits of the learning effect in a single tasking environment may be lost.

- The production of small batches of possibly different products in response to customer demand may also lead to the loss of some of the learning effect.

## Test your understanding 11

**There are many limitations to the learning curve model but the implications of ignoring it when it is present can be very serious. Describe how the learning curve effect may impact on the operation of a business.**

**Chapter summary**

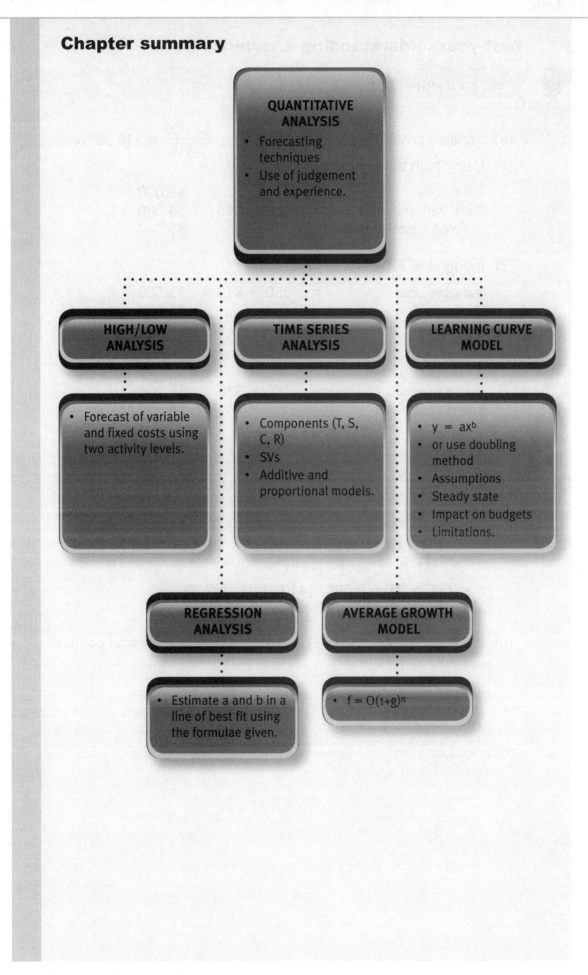

## Test your understanding answers

### Test your understanding 1

(a)  Variable cost/unit $= \dfrac{\$9{,}000 - \$7{,}000}{400 - 200} = \dfrac{\$2{,}000}{200} = \$10$ per unit

(b)  Using high activity level:

| | | |
|---|---|---|
| Total cost | = | $9,000 |
| Total variable cost | = 400 × $10 | $4,000 |
| ∴ Fixed cost | = | $5,000 |

(c)  If output is 350 units:

| | | |
|---|---|---|
| Variable cost | = 350 × $10 = | $3,500 |
| Fixed cost | = | $5,000 |
| Total cost | = | $8,500 |

(d)  If output is 600 units:

| | | |
|---|---|---|
| Variable cost | = 600 × $10 | $6,000 |
| Fixed cost | = | $5,000 |
| Total cost | = | $11,000 |

### Test your understanding 2

(a)  Use the formulae to find the values of a and b.

$$b = \frac{11 \times 13{,}467 - (440 \times 330)}{(11 \times 17{,}986) - (440)^2} = 0.6917$$

$a = (330 \div 11) - 0.6917\,(440 \div 11) = 2.33$

The equation of the line is $y = 2.33 + 0.6917x$

(b)  If $x = 42$, $y = 2.33 + 0.6917 \times 42 = 31.38$ (to 2 decimal points)

## Test your understanding 3

(a)  y = 150 + 10x

The 150 represents the trend when x = 0, i.e. the final quarter of 20W9.

The 10 represents the increase in trend each quarter, that is we expect the trend to rise by 10 each quarter.

The seasonal indices can be interpreted as follows:

Quarter 1 = 80 – Means that we expect sales to be 80% of the trend value, i.e. 20% below the trend in quarter 1.

Quarter 2 = 110 – Means that we expect sales to be 10% above the trend in quarter 2.

Quarter 3 = 140 – Means that we expect sales to be 40% above the trend in quarter 3.

Quarter 4 = 70 – Means that we expect sales to be 30% below the trend in quarter 4.

(b)  In 20X5, the 4 'x' values and hence the trend will be:

| Quarter | x | Trend |
|---------|----|---------------------------|
| 1 | 21 | 150 + 10 × 21 = 360 |
| 2 | 22 | 150 + 10 × 22 = 370 |
| 3 | 23 | 150 + 10 × 23 = 380 |
| 4 | 24 | 150 + 10 × 24 = 390 |

(c)

| Quarter | Trend | Seasonal | Sales forecast |
|---------|-------|----------|---------------------|
| 1 | 360 | 80 | 360 × 0.8 = 288 |
| 2 | 370 | 110 | 370 × 1.1 = 407 |
| 3 | 380 | 140 | 380 × 1.4 = 532 |
| 4 | 390 | 70 | 390 × 0.7 = 273 |

(d)  The two main factors that may cause errors are:

(1)  Extrapolation error – we may be forecasting too far beyond the original regression.

(2)  We are ignoring any residual variation, that is:

T × S × R

Ignoring R may cause our forecast of y to be wrong.

## Test your understanding 4

|  | Trend | Seasonal factor | Forecast |
|---|---|---|---|
| May | 4,550 | × 1.16 | 5,278 |
| June | 4,600 | × 1.07 | 4,922 |
| July | 4,650 | × 0.94 | 4,371 |
| August | 4,700 | × 0.82 | 3,854 |
| September | 4,750 | × 1.06 | 5,035 |

## Test your understanding 5

|  | Q1 $ | Q2 $ | Q3 $ | Q4 $ |
|---|---|---|---|---|
| Sales units | 1,000 | 1,100 | 1,210 | 1,331 |
| Sales price | 125 | 118.75 | 112.81 | 107.17 |
| Variable cost per unit | 65 | 63.7 | 62.426 | 61.177 |
| Sales revenue | 125,000 | 130,625 | 136,500 | 142,643 |
| Variable costs | 65,000 | 70,070 | 75,535 | 81,427 |
| Contribution | 60,000 | 60,555 | 60,965 | 61,216 |

Average growth = ($61,216/60,000)$^{1/3}$ − 1 = 0.67%

## Test your understanding 6

The manager may:

- Calculate an expected value of sales revenue $(100,000 x 0.1 + 125,000 x 0.6 + 140,000 x 0.3 = 127,000) and use this as the sales budget.

- Include the most likely estimate in the budget as the best indication of likely results.

- Include the optimistic estimate in the budget to give sales staff a challenging target but accept that this may lead to adverse variances.

- Prepare a flexible budget with all 3 scenarios analysed.

## Test your understanding 7

| Cumulative number of units | Cumulative average time per unit | Cumulative total hours |
|---|---|---|
| 8 | 168.75 (75% of 225) | 1,350 |

Therefore, time for last 4 items = 1,350 − 900 = 450 hours.

**Test your understanding 8**

$$b = \frac{\log(0.85)}{\log 2}$$

$$b = \frac{-0.0706}{0.3010} = -0.234$$

The cumulative average time to produce the first two units is
$y = 400 \times 2^{-0.234} = 340.1$.

The cumulative average time to produce the first three units is
$y = 400 \times 3^{-0.234} = 309.3$.

The total time to produce the first two units    = 340.1 x 2 = 680.2.

The total time to produce the first three units = 309.3 x 3 = 927.9.

The time to produce the third unit = 927.9 – 680.2 = 247.7 direct labour hours.

**Test your understanding 9**

(a) **Initial order**

If there is no guarantee of a follow-up order, the setup costs must be recovered on the initial order. Costs are, therefore, as follows.

|  | $ |
|---|---|
| Material (10 × $30) | 300 |
| Labour and variable overhead (100 × $3) | 300 |
| Setting-up cost | 1,000 |
| Total | $1,600 |
| Minimum price each ($1,600 ÷ 10) | $160 |

(b) **Follow-on order**

The set-up costs have been recovered on the initial order. Output is doubled; therefore, average time for each group of 10 machines is reduced to

100 x 0.8 = 80 hours

i.e. cumulative time for 20 machines = 160 hours

∴Time for second group of 10 = time for first 20 – time for first 10
= 160 – 100
= 60 hours

Costs are therefore:

| | $ |
|---|---|
| Material (10 × $30) | 300 |
| Labour and variable overhead (60 × $3) | 180 |
| Total | $480 |
| Minimum price each | $48 |

### (c) Both orders together

Total costs are:

| | $ |
|---|---|
| Material | 600 |
| Labour (160 hours) | 480 |
| Set-up cost | 1,000 |
| Total | $2,080 |
| Minimum price each | $104 |

This is, of course, the mean of the two previous prices: cumulative costs are the same but they are recorded evenly over 20 units instead of most of the cost being 'loaded' onto the first 10 units.

### (d) Mass production

The time spent on the first 140 mass production models is calculated as follows:

If a 'unit' is a batch of 10 machines, $y = ax^b$ where

$$a = 100$$

$$b = \frac{\log (0.8)}{\log 2}$$

$$= -0.3219$$

Average time/unit for first 2 units (i.e. first 20 machines)

$= 100 \times 2^{-0.3219} = 80$ hours

Total time for first 2 units = 80 × 2 = 160 hours (as before).

Average time per unit for first 16 units (i.e. first 160 machines)

$= 100 \times 16^{-0.3219} = 40.96$ hours.

Total time for first 16 units = 40.96 × 16 = 655.36 hours.

Hence total time for units 3 to 16, i.e. the 140 mass-produced units) = (655.36 – 160) hours = 495.36 hours.

Cost of first 140 mass-production models:

|  | $ |
|---|---|
| Material (140 × $30) | 4,200 |
| Labour and variable overhead (495.36 x $3) | 1,486 |
| Marketing | 250 |
| Total cost | 5,936 |
| Revenue | 6,300 |
| Profit | 364 |

### Test your understanding 10

| Number | Log value |
|---|---|
| 0.9 | – 0.0458 |
| 2.0 | 0.3010 |

b = – 0.0458/0.3010 = – 0.152.
y = ax$^b$ where a = 2 and b = – 0.152.

Since the learning effect stops after 50 units, we need to calculate the average unit time for the first 50 units. We also need the average unit time for the first 51 units, because this gives us an average time for the 51st unit. From this we can calculate the time per unit for the 51st unit and all subsequent units.

When x = 50, the average time per unit is 1.1035 days.
When x = 51, the average time per unit is 1.1002 days.

|  |  | Total time required Days |
|---|---|---|
| 1st 50 units | (50 x 1.1035) | 55.175 |
| 1st 51 units | (51 x 1.1002) | 56.110 |
|  |  | 0.935 |

Rounding these estimates, we can assume that the first 50 units for each employee require a total of 55 days, and thereafter, each unit takes 1 day.

Each employee in the first year will therefore be able to make 50 + (250 days – 55 days) = 245 units.

There are 10 employees available, so total annual production in year 1 will be 2,450 units.

In subsequent years, total annual production will be 2,500 units.

|  | Year 1 $ | Years 2-4 $ |
|---|---|---|
| Materials at $300 | 735,000 | 750,000 |
| Labour (2,500 hours at $200) | 500,000 | 500,000 |
| Extra fixed costs | 850,000 | 850,000 |
|  | 2,085,000 | 2,100,000 |
| Sales at $2,000 | 4,900,000 |  |
|  | 5,000,000 |  |
| Cash profit | 2,815,000 | 2,900,000 |

### Test your understanding 11

The learning curve effect can impact on:

- The labour budget, including the number of staff required, overtime requirements, bonus schemes.

- The level of raw material inventory required. If production is faster than expected this could lead to stockouts.

- The level of finished goods inventory required. If production is faster than expected then this may lead to excess stockholding.

- The standard cost per unit. This may need to reflect the steady state and adverse variances should be expected until the steady state is reached.

- The cash budget. There will be lower costs per unit but working capital may be required earlier than expected.

- The initial viability of the product may be questioned if a learning curve effect is overlooked.

- Pricing strategy may be affected. A company can afford a low price to keep competitors out of the market if high volumes can be achieved quickly.

# Standard costing and basic variances

## Chapter learning objectives

Upon completion of this chapter you will be able to:

- explain the purpose and principles of standard costing
- describe the methods used to derive standard costs
- prepare standards that allow for idle time and waste
- explain how standard costs may be used to flex a budget
- explain and apply the principle of controllability
- calculate the sales price and volume variances and explain their possible causes
- calculate the materials total, price and usage variances and explain their possible causes
- calculate labour total, rate and efficiency variances and explain their possible causes
- calculate variable overhead total, expenditure and efficiency variances and explain their possible causes
- calculate fixed overhead total, expenditure, volume, capacity and efficiency variances and explain their possible causes
- produce an operating statement to reconcile budgeted and actual profit under standard absorption costing
- produce an operating statement to reconcile budgeted and actual profit or contribution under standard marginal costing
- explain how the learning curve will affect labour variances
- explain the major causes of idle time and waste, suggest methods for their control and calculate their effect on variances
- calculate simple activity-based costing (ABC) variances
- explain whether or not to investigate the cause of a variance.

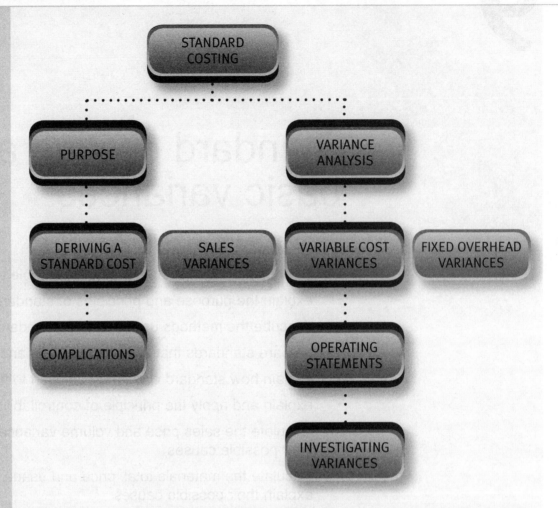

Standard costing and the basics of variance analysis were encountered in F2. In F5 you will have to cope with the following:

- new variances

- more complex calculations

- discussion of the results and implications of your calculations.

# 1 Standard costing

## 1.1 What is standard costing?

A **standard cost** for a product or service is a **predetermined** (planned) unit cost set under **specified working conditions**.

The key aspects of this definition are as follows:

- unit cost

- predetermined

- under specificied working conditions.

The main purposes of standard costing are:

- to provide control by exception reporting

- to form a basis for performance measurement

- to value inventories
- to simplify accounting.

---

### Test your understanding 1

**Which of the following organisations may use standard costing?**

    **(i)  a bank**

    **(ii) a kitchen designer**

    **(iii) a food manufacturer**

**A**   (i), (ii) and (iii)

**B**   (i) and (ii) only

**C**   (ii) and (iii) only

**D**   (i) and (iii) only

---

## 1.2 Preparing standard costs

A **standard cost** is based on technical specifications for the materials, labour time and other resources required and the prices and rates for the materials and labour.

---

### Test your understanding 2

K Ltd makes two products. Information regarding one of those products is given below:

Budgeted output for the year:   900 units
Standard details for one unit:
Direct materials:               40 square metres at $5.30 per square metre
Direct wages:                 Bonding department: 24 hours at $5.00 per hour
                          Finishing department: 15 hours at $4.80 per hour

Budgeted costs and hours pa:

|  | $ | Hours |
|---|---|---|
| Variable overhead: | | |
|    Bonding department | 45,000 | 30,000 |
|    Finishing department | 25,000 | 25,000 |
| Fixed overhead apportioned to this product: | | |
|    Production | $36,000 | |
|    Selling, distribution and administration | $27,000 | |

Note: Variable overheads are recovered (absorbed) using hours, fixed overheads are recovered on a unit basis.

**(a)  Prepare a standard cost card for one unit and enter on the standard cost card the following subtotals:**

(i)   Prime cost

(ii)  Variable production cost

(iii) Total production cost

(iv) Total cost.

**(b)  Calculate the selling price per unit allowing for a profit of 25% of the selling price.  Calculate the resulting contribution per unit and the profit per unit before non-production overheads.**

There is a whole range of bases upon which standards may be set within a standard costing system. This choice will be affected by the use to which the standards will be put and includes:

*   attainable standards which are based upon efficient (but not perfect) operating conditions

*   basic standards which are long-term standards which remain unchanged over a period of years

*   current standards which are standards based on current working conditions

*   ideal standards which are based upon perfect operating conditions.

**Expandable text**

**Attainable standards**

These are the most frequently-encountered types of standard. They are based upon efficient (but not perfect) operating conditions. The standard will include allowances for normal material losses, realistic allowances for fatigue, machine breakdowns, etc.  Attainable standards must be based on a high performance level so that its achievement is possible, but has to be worked for.

**Basic standards**

These are long-term standards which remain unchanged over a period of years.  Their sole use is to show trends over time for such items as material prices, labour rates and efficiency and the effect of changing methods. They cannot be used to highlight current efficiency. Basic standards are the least used and the least useful types of standard.

### Current standards

These are standards based on current working conditions. They are useful when current conditions are abnormal and any other standard would provide meaningless information. The disadvantage is that they do not attempt to improve upon current conditions.

### Ideal standards

These are based upon perfect operating conditions, i.e. no wastage or scrap, no breakdowns, no stoppages or idle time; in short, no inefficiencies. In their search for perfect quality, Japanese companies use ideal standards for pinpointing areas where close examination may result in large cost savings. Ideal standards may have an adverse motivational impact.

## Test your understanding 3

**Explain why standards are usually set on an attainable basis.**

## 1.3   Idle time and waste

Attainable standards are set at levels which include an allowance for idle time and waste.

## Illustration 1 – Standard costing

Lunches Ltd makes sandwiches for sale to offices and over the counter. Contents of their 'spicy meat special' are as follows:

    2 slices of bread
    88 grams of spicy meat mix
    44 grams of grated cheese
    20 grams of pickle

It is company policy to guarantee the cooked weight of meat mix to be a minimum of 88 grams. There is a 20% loss of mix weight during cooking. Losses due to accidental damage, dropped sandwiches, etc. are estimated to be 5% of completed sandwiches.

Anticipated prices of raw materials for the coming period are:

| | |
|---|---|
| Bread | 54p per loaf of 18 useable slices |
| Spicy meat mix (uncooked) | $3.20 per kg |
| Cheese | $3 per kg |
| Pickle | $1.60 per kg |

Prepare the standard ingredients cost of one 'spicy meat special' sandwich.

**Solution**

|  |  | $ |
|---|---|---|
| 2 slices bread | 2/18 x $0.54 | 0.060 |
| Spicy meat mix | 88g cooked weight = | |
| | 88/0.8 uncooked weight @ $3.20/kg | 0.352 |
| Grated cheese | 44g @ $3/kg | 0.132 |
| Pickle | 20g @ $1.60/kg | 0.032 |
| Cost per sandwich started (95%) | | 0.576 |
| Allowance due to anticipated losses (5%) | | 0.030 |
| Standard ingredients cost (100%) | | 0.606 |

**Test your understanding 4**

The fastest time in which a batch of 20 'spicy meat special' sandwiches has been made was 32 minutes, with no hold-ups. However, work studies have shown that, on average, about 8% of the sandwich makers' time is non-productive and that, in addition to this setup time (getting ingredients together etc.), is 2 minutes.

**If the sandwich-makers are paid $4.50 per hour, what is the attainable standard labour cost of one sandwich?**

## 1.4 Standard costs and the flexing of budgets

Standard costs may be used to help prepare budgets. The budget is based on a given level of output. If actual output is different from budgeted output a flexed budget can be prepared which provides a more meaningful estimate of expected costs than the original fixed budget.

Fixed costs do not change when output levels change.

**Test your understanding 5**

The World History Museum has an Education Department which specialises in running courses in various subjects. The courses are run on premises which the museum rents for the purpose and they are presented by freelance expert speakers. The courses are of a standard type and format and can therefore be treated alike for budgetary control purposes.

The museum currently uses fixed budgets to control expenditure. The following data shows the actual costs of the Education Department for the month of April compared with the budgeted figures.

**Education Department – April**

| | Actual | Budget | Variance |
|---|---|---|---|
| Number of courses run | 5 | 6 | (1) |
| | $ | $ | $ |
| Expenditure | | | |
| Speakers' fees | 2,500 | 3,180 | 680 |
| Hire of premises | 1,500 | 1,500 | – |
| Depreciation of equipment | 200 | 180 | (20) |
| Stationery | 530 | 600 | 70 |
| Catering | 1,500 | 1,750 | 250 |
| Insurance | 700 | 820 | 120 |
| Administration | 1,650 | 1,620 | (30) |
| | 8,580 | 9,650 | 1,070 |

The following information is available;

1 Depreciation of equipment is a fixed cost.
2 Administration is a fixed cost.
3 The budget figures for the catering costs and insurance costs include a fixed element as follows.
   Catering          $250
   Insurance         $100
   The remaining elements of the catering and insurance costs follow linear variable patterns.
4 All other costs follow linear variable patterns.

(a) **Use the above information to produce a budgetary control statement for April, based on a flexed budget for the actual number of courses run.**

(b) **Calculate the revised variances based on your flexed budget.**

## 1.5 Controllable and non-controllable costs

A cost is controllable if a manager is responsible for it being incurred or is able to authorise the expenditure.

Managers may become demotivated if they are made responsible for non-controllable costs.

Factors which should be taken into consideration.

• Over a long enough time span most costs are controllable at some management level.

• Some costs are unavoidable.

• Some costs may have joint responsibility.

### Illustration 2 – Standard costing

The materials purchasing manager is given a target which includes:

- total material expenditure for the organisation
- the cost of introducing safety measures in accordance with revised government legislation
- a notional rental cost for the material storage area.

Discuss whether these costs are controllable by the manager and if they should be included in a target for performance appraisal purposes.

### Solution

The total material expenditure for the organisation will be dependent partly on the prices negotiated by the purchasing manager and partly by the requirements and performance of the production department. If it is included as a target for performance appraisal the manager may be tempted to purchase cheaper material which may have an adverse effect elsewhere in the organisation.

The requirement to introduce safety measures may be imposed but the manager should be able to ensure that implementation meets budget targets.

A notional rental cost is outside the control of the manager and should not be included in a target for performance appraisal purposes.

### Test your understanding 6

**Explain whether a production manager should be accountable for direct labour materials cost variances.**

## 2 Revision of basic variance analysis

### 2.1 Sales variances

$$
\left.\begin{array}{ll}
\text{Actual quantity sold} & \times \text{ Actual price} \\
\text{Actual quantity sold} & \times \text{ Budget price}
\end{array}\right\} \text{Sales price variance}
$$

$$
\left.\begin{array}{ll}
\text{Actual quantity sold} & \times \text{ Standard margin} \\
\text{Budget quantity sold} & \times \text{ Standard margin}
\end{array}\right\} \text{Sales volume variance}
$$

Note: 'margin' = contribution (marginal costing) or profit (absorption costing) per unit.

The calculation of the sales volume variance will be different for a marginal costing system and an absorption costing system.

## Expandable text

An alternative layout when calculating sales price and sales volume variances is as follows:

| **Sales price variance** | $ |
|---|---|
| Actual selling price | X |
| Budgeted selling price | X |
| Difference in price | X |

Price variance = difference in price x actual quantity sold.

| **Sales volume variance, absorption costing** | units |
|---|---|
| Budgeted sales | X |
| Actual sales | X |
| Sales volume variance in units | X (F) or (A) |
| | |
| Standard profit per unit | X |
| Sales volume variance in $ | X (F) or (A) |

| **Sales volume variance, marginal costing** | units |
|---|---|
| Budgeted sales | $X |
| Actual sales | $X |
| Sales volume variance in units | X (F) or (A) |
| | |
| Standard contribution per unit | $X |
| Sales volume variance in £ | $X (F) or (A) |

**Causes of sales variances**

Sales price variances have many causes which may include:

- higher or lower discounts than expected offered to customers

- a greater or lesser proportion of higher priced products sold than expected

- more or less price competition from competitors.

Sales volume variances may be caused by:

- changes in customers' buying habits

- successful or unsuccessful marketing campaigns

- higher demand as a result of price cuts, or vice versa.

## Test your understanding 7

W Ltd budgeted sales of 6,500 units but actually sold only 6,000 units. Its standard cost card is as follows:

|  | $ |
|---|---|
| Direct material | 25 |
| Direct wages | 8 |
| Variable overhead | 4 |
| Fixed overhead | 18 |
| Total standard cost | 55 |
| Standard gross profit | 5 |
| Standard selling price | 60 |

The actual selling price for the period was $61.

**Calculate the sales price and sales volume variance for the period (using absorption costing). Suggest two possible causes of each variance.**

## 2.2 Materials variances

Actual quantity bought × Actual price
Actual quantity bought × Standard price
} Price variance

Actual quantity used × Standard price
Actual quantity used × Standard price
(for actual production)
} Usage variance

## Expandable text

An alternative layout for the calculation of material variances is as follows:

|  | $ |
|---|---|
| Actual price paid per bag | X |
| Budget priceper kg | X |
| Difference in price | X |

Materials price variance = difference in price x actual quantity purchased.

If actual purchase cost exceeds standard cost, the variance is adverse. If actual purchase cost is less than standard cost, the variance is favourable.

| | | Quantity |
|---|---|---|
| Actual output produced | should use | X |
| | did use | X |
| Materials usage variance (in quantities) | | X (F) or (A) |
| x Standard price per unit of material | | $X |
| Materials usage variance (in $) | | $X (F) or (A) |

If actual usage exceeds standard usage, the variance is adverse.
If actual usage is less than standard usage, the variance is favourable.

Possible reasons for price variance:

- wrong budgeting
- higher/lower quality of material used
- careful/careless purchasing
- losing/gaining bulk discounts by buying smaller/larger quantities
- change of supplier.

Possible reasons for usage variance:

- wrong budgeting
- higher/lower quality of materials used
- higher/lower grade of worker
- stricter quality control
- theft
- change in product specification.

### Test your understanding 8

James Marshall Co makes a single product with the following budgeted material costs per unit:

2 kg of material A at $10/kg

Actual details:
Output 1,000 units
Material purchased and used 2,200 kg
Material cost $20,900

**Calculate material price and usage variances and suggest two possible causes for each variance.**

## 2.3 Labour variances

Actual hours     x     Actual rate     } Rate variance

Actual hours     x     Standard rate

Standard hours   x     Standard rate    } Efficiency variance
(for actual production)

---

**Expandable text**

An alternative approach to calculating labour variances is as follows:

|                                    | $      |
|------------------------------------|--------|
| Actual labour rate paid per hour   | X      |
| Budgeted labour rate per hour      | X      |
| Difference                         | X      |

Labour rate variance = difference in rate x actual hours paid.

If the actual labour cost exceeds standard cost, the variance is adverse (A). If the actual labour cost is less than standard cost, the variance is favourable (F).

|                          |            | Hours        |
|--------------------------|------------|--------------|
| Actual output produced   | should take| X            |
|                          | did take   | X            |
| **Labour efficiency variance (in hours)** |  | X (F) or (A) |
| Standard rate per labour hour |       | $X           |
| Labour efficiency variance (in $) |   | $X (F) or (A)|

If actual hours exceed standard hours, the variance is adverse. If actual hours are less than standard hours produced, the variance is favourable.

---

Possible reasons for rate variance:

- wrong budgeting
- higher rate being paid due to wage award
- higher/lower grade of worker
- payment of unplanned overtime or bonus.

Possible reasons for efficiency variance:

- wrong budgeting
- higher/lower grade of worker
- higher/lower grade of material to work with
- more or less efficient working through motivation.

## Test your understanding 9

Extract from the standard cost card for K Ltd

 |$
---|---
Direct labour:|
   Finishing (15 hours @ $4.80 per hour)|72

Actual direct wages for the period were;
Finishing    15,500 hours costing $69,750 in total
Actual units produced 1,000

**Calculate the labour rate and labour efficiency variances in the finishing department and give two possible causes of each variance.**

## 2.4 Variable overhead variances

Actual hours   x Actual rate per hour   } Expenditure (rate) variance

Actual hours   x Standard rate per hour
Standard hours x Standard rate per hour   } Efficiency variance
(for actual production)

## Expandable text

An alternative approach to calculating variable overhead variances is as follows;.

 |$
---|---
Actual variance overhead rate per hour|X
Budget variance overhead rate per hour|X
Difference in hourly rate|$\overline{X}$

Expenditure (rate) variance = difference in rate x actual hours worked.

If the actual variable overhead cost exceeds standard cost, the variance is adverse (A). If the actual variable overhead cost is less than standard cost, the variance is favourable (F).

 |Hours|
---|---|---
Actual output produced|should take|X
 |did take|X
Efficiency variance (in hours)||$\overline{X}$ (F) or (A)
x Standard rate per hour for variable overhead||$X
**Variable overhead efficiency variance (in $)**||$X (F) or (A)

If actual hours exceed standard hours, the variance is adverse. If actual hours are less than standard hours produced, the variance is favourable.

Possible reasons for expenditure variance:

*   wrong budgeting

*   overheads consist of a number of items, such as: indirect materials, indirect labour, maintenance costs, power, etc. Consequently, any meaningful interpretation of the expenditure variance must focus on individual cost items.

Possible reasons for efficiency variance (as for labour efficiency):

*   wrong budgeting
*   higher/lower grade of worker
*   higher/lower grade of material to work with
*   more or less efficient working through motivation.

---

**Test your understanding 10**

Extract from the standard cost card for K Ltd

| | $ |
|---|---|
| Variable overhead: | |
| Finishing (15 hours @ $1 per hour) | 15 |

Actual variable overheads for the period were:

| Finishing | (15,500 hours) | Total cost | $14,900 |
|---|---|---|---|

Actual units produced 1,000

**Calculate the variable overhead expenditure and variable overhead efficiency variances in the finishing department and give to possible causes of each variance.**

---

## 2.5 Fixed overhead variances

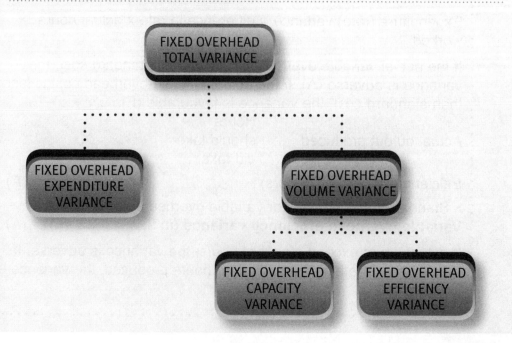

## Marginal costing system

With a marginal costing profit and loss, no overheads are absorbed, the amount spent is simply written off to the income statement.

So with marginal costing the only fixed overhead variance is the difference between what was budgeted to be spent and what was actually spent.

Actual expenditure
Budgeted expenditue $\Big\}$ Fixed overhead expenditure variance

## Absorption costing system

Under absorption costing we use an overhead absorption rate to absorb overheads. Variances will occur if this absorption rate is incorrect (just as we will get over/under-absorption).

The fixed overhead total variance is equal to the level of over/under absorbed overhead.

- Over-absorption = a favourable variance
- Under-absorption = an adverse variance

Actual expenditure
Actual units x FOAR $\Big\}$ total variance

## Expenditure and volume variances

The total fixed overhead variance can be split between expenditure and volume variances.

- The fixed overhead volume variance is used to calculate whether the company absorbed as much overhead as it expected.

- The fixed overhead expenditure variance is used to calculate whether the company incurred as much overhead as it expected.

The expenditure variance is the same as earlier.

## Fixed overhead expenditure variance

Actual expenditure
Budgeted expenditue $\Big\}$ Expenditure variance

## Fixed overhead volume variance

Budgeted expenditure
Actual units x FOAR per unit $\Big\}$ Volume variance

## Illustration 3 – Variance analysis

K Ltd makes two products. The budgeted data relating to one of these products is as follows;

Budgeted output for the year 900 units
Fixed overhead apportioned to this product:

| | |
|---|---|
| Production | $36,000 |
| Selling, distribution and administration | $27,000 |

**Note:** fixed overheads are recovered on a unit basis.
Actual data is as follows:
Actual output 1,000 units
Fixed overheads apportioned to this product:

| | |
|---|---|
| Production | $38,000 |
| Non-production | $24,000 |

### Required:

Calculate the following:
(i)   Total variance for production overheads.
(ii)  Expenditure variance for production overheads.
(iii) Volume variance for production overheads

### Solution

**Total production overhead variance**

The overhead absorption rate is $36,000/900 = $40 per unit

| | | |
|---|---|---|
| Overheads absorbed | 1,000 x $40 | $40,000 |
| Overheads incurred | | $38,000 |
| Over-absorption | | $2,000 |

The total production fixed overhead variance is $2,000 Favourable

**Non-production overheads expenditure variance**

| | |
|---|---|
| Budgeted expenditure | $27,000 |
| Actual expenditure | $24,000 |
| | $3,000 F |

**Production overheads expenditure variance**

| | |
|---|---|
| Budgeted expenditure | $36,000 |
| Actual expenditure | $38,000 |
| | $2,000 A |

**Production overheads volume variance**

| | | |
|---|---|---|
| Actual units x FOAR | 1,000 x $40 | $40,000 |
| Budgeted units x FOAR | 900 x $40 | $36,000 |
| | | $4,000 F |

| Total production overheads variance | | |
|---|---|---|
| Expenditure | $2,000 | A |
| Volume | $4,000 | F |
| Total | $2,000 | F |

### Test your understanding 11

A business has budgeted to produce and sell 10,000 units of its single product. The standard cost per unit is as follows:

| Direct materials | $15 |
|---|---|
| Direct labour | $12 |
| Variable overhead | $10 |
| Fixed production overhead | $8 |

During the period the actual results were:

| Production and sales | 11,500 units |
|---|---|
| Fixed production overheads | $84,000 |

**(a) The fixed production overhead expenditure variance is:**

- A $4,000 favourable
- B $4,000 adverse
- C $8,000 favourable
- D $8,000 adverse

**(b) The fixed production overhead volume variance is:**

- A $8,000 favourable
- B $8,000 adverse
- C $12,000 favourable
- D $12,000 adverse

### Capacity and efficiency variances

The fixed overhead volume variance can be further split between capacity and efficiency variances

### Fixed overhead capacity variance

Budgeted expenditure
Actual hours x FOAR per hour } Capacity variance

### Fixed overhead efficiency variance

Actual hours x FOAR per hour
Standard hours x FOAR per hour } Efficiency variance

The sum of the above two is equal to the volume variance.

### Expandable text

You might find the following summary useful for remembering how to calculate fixed production overhead cost variances

| Fixed overhead expenditure variance | $ |
|---|---|
| Budgeted fixed overheads | X |
| Actual fixed overhead | X |
| Fixed overhead expenditure variance | X (F) or (A) |

If the actual costs exceed budgeted costs, the variance is adverse.

If the actual costs are less than budget, the variance is favourable.

| Fixed overhead volume variance | Units or standard hours of output |
|---|---|
| Budgeted production volume | X |
| Actual production volume | X |
| Fixed overhead volume variance (in units or standard hours) | X (F) or (A) |
| Standard fixed overhead rate per unit/standard hour of output | $X |
| Fixed overhead volume variance (in $) | $X (F) or (A) |

The fixed overhead volume variance can be analysed into an efficiency variance and a capacity variance.

Fixed overhead efficiency variance:

Efficiency variance in hours = same as for direct labour and variable production overhead (see above)

Efficiency variance in $ =

Efficiency variance in hours x Standard fixed overhead rate per hour.

| Fixed overhead capacity variance | Hours |
|---|---|
| Budgeted hours of work | X |
| Actual hours of work | X |
| Fixed overhead capacity variance (in hours) | X (F) or (A) |
| Standard fixed overhead rate per hour | $X |
| Fixed overhead capacity variance (in $) | $X (F) or (A) |

## Illustration 4 – Variance analysis

The following information is available for J Ltd for Period 4:

Budget
Fixed production overheads                 $22,960
Units                                        6,560
The standard time to produce each unit is 2 hours
Actual
Fixed production overheads                 $24,200
Units                                        6,460
Labour hours                           12,600 hrs

### Required:

Calculate the following:

(a) (i)   FOAR per unit
    (ii)  Fixed overhead expenditure variance
    (iii) Fixed overhead volume variance
(b) (i)   FOAR per hour
    (ii)  Fixed overhead expenditure variance
(iii) Fixed overhead capacity variance
(iv) Fixed overhead efficiency variance

### Solution

(a) (i)   OAR  = $22,960/6,560 = $3.50 per unit

| | | |
|---|---|---|
| | Actual expenditure | $24,200 |
| (ii) | **Expenditure variance** | $1,240 (A) |
| | Budgeted expenditure | $22,960 |
| (iii) | **Volume variance** | $350 (A) |
| | Actual units x OAR = 6,460 x $3.50 | $22,610 |

(b) (i)   OAR  = $22,960/13,120 = $1.75 per hour

| | | |
|---|---|---|
| | Actual expenditure | $24,200 |
| (ii) | **Expenditure variance** | $1,240 (A) |
| | Budgeted expenditure | $22,960 |
| (iii) | **Capacity variance** | $910 (A) |
| | Actual hours x OAR = 12,600 x $1.75 | $22,050 |
| (iv) | **Efficiency variance** | $560 (F) |
| | Standard hours x OAR = 6,460 x 2 x $1.75 | $22,610 |

## Causes of variances

Fixed overhead expenditure variance:

- changes in price relating to fixed overhead items

- seasonal effect.

Fixed overhead volume variance:

- changes in production volume due to change in demand or alterations to stockholding policy

- changes in productivity of labour or machinery

- production lost through strikes, etc.

Fixed overhead capacity variance:

- hours worked different from original budget
- change in production volume
- change in productivity
- strikes, overtime

Fixed overhead efficiency variance:

- same as for labour and/or variable overhead efficiency.

### Test your understanding 12

Budgeted annual fixed production overheads at Budd Limited are $637,500. The company makes a single product, for which the standard direct labour production time is 1.25 hours. The budgeted production for 20X4 was 60,000 units.

During 20X4, 63,000 units of the product were made in 79,600 hours, and fixed production overheads were $632,000.

(a) **For 20X4, calculate the fixed overhead expenditure, efficiency and capacity variances, if the company uses a standard absorption costing system with overheads absorbed at a standard rate per direct labour hour.**

(b) **Explain one possible cause of each variance.**

## 2.6 Operating statement under absorption costing

The purpose of calculating variances is to identify the different effects of each item of cost/income on profit compared to the expected profit. These variances are summarised in a reconciliation statement or operating statement.

### Illustration 5 – Variance analysis

Using the variances for K Ltd calculated previously the operating statement would be shown as follows;

|  | $ |  |
|---|---|---|
| Budgeted profit (original profit based on 900 units) | 157,500 |  |
| Sales volume profit variance | 20,500 | F |
| Standard profit on actual sales (= flexed budget profit) | 178,000 |  |
| Selling price variance | 50,000 | A |
|  | 128,000 |  |

| Cost variances: | F | A |
|---|---|---|
| | $ | $ |
| Material price | | 3,900 |
| Material usage | 5,300 | |
| Labour rate – bonding | | 11,950 |
| Labour efficiency – bonding | 500 | |
| Labour rate – finishing | 4,650 | |
| Labour efficiency – finishing | | 2,400 |
| Variable overhead rate – bonding | | 2,390 |
| Variable overhead efficiency – bonding | 150 | |
| Variable overhead rate – finishing | 600 | |
| Variable overhead efficiency – finishing | | 500 |
| Fixed production overhead expenditure variance | | 2,000 |
| Fixed production overhead volume variance | 4,000 | |
| Fixed non-production overhead expenditure variance | 3,000 | |
| Total | 18,200 | 23,140 |

| | | |
|---|---|---|
| | 4,940 | A |
| Actual profit | 123,060 | |

## Test your understanding 13

Riki Ltd, produces and sells one product only. The standard cost and price for one unit being as follows:

| | $ |
|---|---|
| Direct material A – 10 kilograms at $12 per kg | 120 |
| Direct material B – 6 kilograms at $5 per kg | 30 |
| Direct wages – 5 hours at $8 per hour | 40 |
| Fixed production overhead | 60 |
| Total standard cost | 250 |
| Standard gross profit | 50 |
| Standard selling price | 300 |

The fixed production overhead included in the standard cost is based on an expected monthly output of 750 units. Riki Ltd use an absorption costing system.

During April 2000 the actual results were as follows:

|  | $ |
|---|---|
| Sales 700 units @ $320 | 224,000 |
| Direct materials: | |
| A: 7,500 Kg | 91,500 |
| B: 3,500 Kg | 20,300 |
| Direct wages 3,400 hours | 27,880 |
| Fixed production overhead | |
| | 37,000 |
| | 176,680 |
| Gross profit | 47,320 |

**You are required to reconcile budgeted profit with actual profit for the period, calculating the following variances:**

**Selling price, sales volume, material price, material usage, labour rate, labour efficiency, fixed overhead expenditure and fixed overhead volume.**

## 2.7 Operating statement under marginal costing

The operating statement under marginal costing is the same as that under absorption costing except;

- a sales volume contribution variance is included instead of a sales volume profit variance

- the only fixed overhead variances are the expenditure variances

- the reconciliation is from budgeted to actual contribution then fixed overheads are deducted to arrive at a profit.

### Illustration 6 – Variance analysis

Using the variances for K Ltd calculated previously the operating statement would be shown as follows;

|  | $ |
|---|---|
| Budgeted contribution | |
| (original contribution based on 900 units) | 220,500 |
| Sales volume contribution variance | 24,500 F |
| | |
| Standard contribution on actual sales | |
| (= flexed budget contribution) | 245,000 |
| Selling price variance | 50,000 A |
| | 195,000 |

Cost variances:

| | F $ | A $ | $ |
|---|---|---|---|
| Material price | | 3,900 | |
| Material usage | 5,300 | | |
| Labour rate – bonding | | 11,950 | |
| Labour efficiency – bonding | 500 | | |
| Labour rate – finishing | 4,650 | | |
| Labour efficiency – finishing | | 2,400 | |
| Variable overhead rate – bonding | | 2,390 | |
| Variable overhead efficiency – bonding | 150 | | |
| Variable overhead rate – finishing | 600 | | |
| Variable overhead efficiency –finishing | | 500 | |
| | | | |
| Total | 11,200 | 21,140 | 9,940 A |
| | | | |
| Actual contribution | | | 185,060 |
| | | | |
| Budgeted fixed overheads | | | |
| Production | | | (36,000) |
| Non-production | | | (27,000) |
| Fixed overhead expenditure variance – production | 2,000 | | |
| Fixed overhead expenditure variance – non-production | 3,000 | | 1,000 F |
| | | | |
| Actual profit | | | 123,060 |

## Test your understanding 14

Chapel Ltd manufactures a chemical protective called Rustnot. The following standard costs apply for the production of 100 cylinders:

| | | $ |
|---|---|---|
| Materials | 500 kgs @ 80c per kg | 400 |
| Labour | 20 hours @ $1.50 per hour | 30 |
| Fixed overheads | 20 hours @ $1.00 per hour | 20 |
| | | 450 |

The monthly production/sales budget is 10,000 cylinders.
Selling price = $6 per cylinder.

For the month of November the following production and sales information is available:

| | | |
|---|---|---|
| Produced/sold | 10,600 | cylinders |
| Sales value | $63,000 | |
| Materials purchased and used 53,200 kgs | $42,500 | |

| | |
|---|---|
| Labour 2,040 hours | $3,100 |
| Fixed overheads | $2,200 |

**You are required to prepare an operating statement in a marginal costing format for November detailing all the variances.**

## 3 Further aspects of variances

### 3.1 The learning curve effect and labour variances

When production is complex and labour intensive it may be the case that unit labour times reduce as the workforce become more familiar with the task. The learning curve effect is a mathematical model which quantifies this reduction in time taken.

The learning curve model states that each time the number of units produced doubles, the cumulative average time per unit is reduced by a constant percentage.

The learning curve model will affect labour variances since;

• The initial standard time taken to produce the item will become rapidly out of date.

• Variances calculated using out-of-date standards will quickly become meaningless for planning and control.

### Illustration 7 – Further aspects of variances

A company has introduced a new product which is complex and labour intensive and it is expected that an 80% learning curve applies. The standard cost card for the product, based on estimates for the time required to produce the first unit, includes standard labour time of 100 hours at a cost of $8 per hour.

The first 4 units took 270 hours to produce at a cost of $2,187.

Calculate the labour rate and efficiency variances based on

(a) the initial labour standard
(b) a labour standard for 4 units which takes into account an 80% learning curve effect.

**Solution**

(a) Labour rate variance = 270 x $8 – $2,187 = $27 A

Labour efficiency variance (4 x 100 – 270) x $8 = $1,040 F

(b) Taking into account the learning curve effect:

- the average standard time per unit for 4 units would be 100 x 0.8 x 0.8 = 64 hours.

- the total expected time for 4 units is therefore 64 x 4 = 256 hours

Labour rate variance is unchanged.

Labour efficiency variance is now (256 – 270) x $8 = $112 A taking into account the learning curve effect has changed the labour efficiency variance from $1,040 F to $112 A. This is because the actual learning rate was slower than expected, possibly linked to the adverse rate variance. In this type of scenario the firm could consider having different labour standards for different volumes of production.

### Test your understanding 15

A company has introduced a new product and it is anticipated that a 90% learning curve applies. The standard cost card for the product, based on estimates for the time required to produce the first unit, includes standard labour time of 200 hours at a cost of $8 per hour.

The first 8 units took 1,150 hours to produce at a cost of $9,430.

**Calculate the labour rate and efficiency variances based on a labour standard which takes into account the learning curve effect.**

### 3.2 Idle time and waste

Idle time and waste are unavoidable in many businesses and must be incorporated into attainable standards and considered when calculating variances.

### Illustration 8 – Idle time

PQ Ltd operates a 40-hour week and pays its employees $4.05 per hour. As part of its normal activity it is usual for there to be non-productive time equal to 10% of hours paid. Employee wages are paid at the same rate of $4.05 per hour for both productive and non-productive time. Calculate the adjusted hourly rate to compensate for the idle time expected.

**Solution**

| | |
|---|---|
| Cost of 40 hours attendance = 40 x $4.05 | $162 |
| Productive time 90% of 40 hours | 36 hours |
| Adjusted hourly rate = $162/36 hours | $4.50 |

An alternative solution method is:

$$\frac{\$4.05}{(1 - \% \text{ idle time})} = \frac{\$4.05}{0.90} \qquad \$4.50$$

Idle time may relate to labour hours or machine hours and could be caused by:

- poor production planning
- stockouts
- lack of demand.

Waste may also be a normal part of a process and could be caused by:

- evaporation
- scrap
- sediment
- testing.

Idle time could affect labour or overhead efficiency variances and could be a cause of the sales volume variance. Waste could affect material usage variances.

For labour, this gives us the following variances:

| | |
|---|---|
| Actual hours paid x Actual rate | } **Rate variance** |
| Actual hours paid x Standard rate | **(as before)** |
| Actual idle time x Standard grossed up rate | } **Excess idle time** |
| Standard idle time x Standard grossed up rate | **variance** |
| Actual hours worked x Standard grossed up rate | } **Productive** |
| Standard hours x Standard grossed up rate | **efficiency** |
| **(For actual production)** | **variance.** |

**e.g**

## Illustration 9 – Idle time variances

ZS plc has a target time (standard time) of 0.5 hours per unit, and expects there to be non-productive time equal to 5% of hours paid. The following details relate to the month of December:

| | |
|---|---|
| Units produced | 5,400 |
| Hours paid | 3,000 |
| Non-productive hours | 165 |
| Wage cost | $15,000 |
| Wage rate variance | $Nil |

Calculate the overall labour efficiency variance and analyse it between productive efficiency and excess idle time variances.

**Solution**

Actual wage rate = 15,000/3,000 = $5 per hour.

Rate variance is zero, so the standard wage rate must also be $5 per hour.

| | |
|---|---|
| Standard productive hours for 5,400 units | 2,700 |
| Standard paid hours for 5,400 units = 2,700/0.95 | 2,842 |
| Actual paid hours | 3,000 |
| Total efficiency variance [(2,842 x 3,000 hours) = | |
| 158 hours] x $5 | $790 (A) |
| Actual productive hours (3,000 – 165) | 2,835 |

Productive efficiency variance [(2,700 – 2,835 hours) =

135 hours x $\dfrac{\$5}{0.95}$ ........................................ $711 (A)

Excess idle time variance

| | |
|---|---|
| Expected idle time 3,000 hours x 5% | 150 |
| Actual idle time | 165 |
| | 15 |

15 hours x $\dfrac{\$5}{0.95}$ ........................................ $79 (A)

Note:

- Variances and calculations of hours have been made to the nearest $1 and complete hour respectively.

- The total efficiency variance is valued using the standard hourly rate; but the sub-analysis into productive efficiency and idle time uses the adjusted hourly rate to value the differences in hours.

## Test your understanding 16

The following data relates to T plc for the month of January:

Standard productive time per unit 2 hours

| | |
|---|---|
| Standard wage rate per paid hour | $4.00 |
| Actual production | 1,200 units |
| Standard idle time as a percentage of hours paid | 4% |
| Actual hours paid | 2,600 |
| Actual idle time hours | 110 |

**Calculate the labour efficiency variance and analyse it between productive efficiency and idle time.**

### 3.3 Standard costing and activity-based costing (ABC)

ABC is a method of allocating overhead costs to product using cost drivers. Standard costs can be derived and variances calculated to aid control of the cost.

**Illustration 10 – Further aspects of variances**

A hospital uses ABC to allocate some of its costs, which would otherwise be treated as overheads, to various different surgical procedures. The following budgeted information was prepared for a period;

| Activity | Cost pool | Cost driver information |
|---|---|---|
| Theatre preparation | $120,000 | Number of setups |
| Disposable equipment | $90,000 | Number of operations |
| Recovery nursing | $360,000 | Nursing hours |

| | |
|---|---|
| Number of setups | 30 |
| Number of operations | 300 |
| Number of nursing hours | 900 |

One particular surgical procedure was expected to use:

| | |
|---|---|
| Number of setups | 5 |
| Number of operations | 32 |
| Number of nursing hours | 400 |

Actual information for the period relating to the surgical procedure was;

| | | | |
|---|---|---|---|
| Number of setups | 6 at a cost of | $22,500 |
| Number of operations | 36 at a cost of | $11,800 |
| Number of nursing hours | 425 at a cost of | $176,375 |

| Actual costs | |
|---|---|
| Theatre preparation | $22,500 |
| Disposable equipment | $11,160 |
| Recovery nursing | $165,000 |

Calculate suitable total, expenditure and efficiency variances for disposable equipment and theatre preparation costs.

**Solution**

The unit of output for the hospital is the operation. First find the standard cost for an operation.

**Disposable equipment**

The standard cost per operation is $90,000/300 = $300
A total variance can be calculated;

| | $ |
|---|---|
| 36 operations should cost | 10,800 |
| did cost | 11,160 |
| Total variance | 360   Adverse |

No information has been given relating to the price and usage of disposable equipment therefore no sub-analysis is possible.

**Theatre preparation**

The standard cost per setup for theatre preparation is
    $120,000/30 = $4,000
The standard cost per operation  is

| | | |
|---|---|---|
| 5 setups at $4,000 per setup | | $20,000 |
| or   $20,000/32 | | $625 per operation |

| | | |
|---|---|---|
| Actual cost is 6 setups at $3,750 per setup | | $22,500 |

The total variance is

| | | |
|---|---|---|
| 36 operations should cost | x $625 | $22,500 |
| did cost | | $22,500 |
| | | Nil |

For this cost usage of setups and the rate per setup has been given so the total variance can be sub-analysed into expenditure and efficiency elements.

The expenditure variance is:
Actual number of set ups x (actual cost per set up – standard cost per set up)
    6 x ( $4,000 – $3,750) = $1,500 Favourable

To calculate the efficiency variance first calculate the standard usage.

32 operations expect to need 5 setups.
So 1 operation would expect to need 5/32 = 0.15625 of a setup.
36 operations would be expected to require 0.15625 x 36 = 5.625 setups.
The efficiency variance is:
(actual number of set ups - how many it should have taken) x standard cost per set up
    (6 – 5.625) x $4,000 = $1,500 Adverse

The expenditure variance +  the efficiency variance = the total variance.

It can be seen that variance analysis is very similar to the calculation of variable overhead variances.

**Test your understanding 17**

**Using the example of a hospital, calculate appropriate total, expenditure and efficiency variances for recovery nursing.**

## 3.4 Investigating the cause of a variance

Variances arise naturally in standard costing because a standard cost is a long-term average cost. In any period actual costs may be higher or lower than standard but in the long run these should cancel out if the process is under control.

Variances may also arise because of:

- poor budgeting
- poor recording of cost
- operational reasons (the key emphasis in exam questions)
- random factors.

It is important to identify the reason for a variance so that appropriate action can be taken, but time and effort will be wasted if all variances are investigated as many will arise as a normal part of the process.

### When should a variance be investigated?

Factors to consider include the following:

- the size of the variance
- whether favourable/adverse – firms often treat adverse variances as more important than favorable
- correction costs versus benefits
- ability to correct
- past pattern
- budget reliability
- reliability of measurement/recording systems.

Criteria or techniques for variance investigation:

- Fixed size of variance: investigate all variances over $5,000.

- Fixed percentage rule: investigate all variances over 10% of budget.

- Statistical decision rule: this involves studying past patterns of the data to determine how likely a variance is to arise. A decision rule can then be set to investigate, e.g. all variances of which there is a likelihood of less than 5% that it could have arisen randomly.

**Expandable text**

Consider an operational process for which the mean time is 50 minutes with a standard deviation of 10 minutes. It is known from statistical theory that the pattern of actual times is likely to form a normal distribution about the mean.

Furthermore, it is known that specific proportions of the times will be within specified standard deviations of the mean.

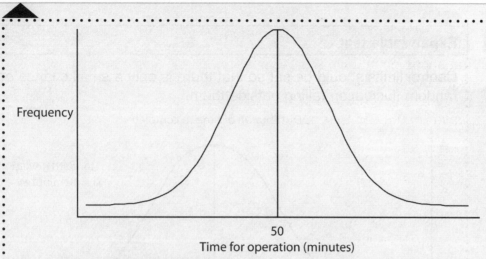

The values are approximately:

- 1 standard deviation      68%   (68.26%)
- 2 standard deviations    95%   (95.44%)
- 3 standard deviations    99.7% (99.73%)

This information can be used to create a statistical control chart. The mean time forms the standard. The control limits are set a given number of standard deviations from the mean. Control limits are quantities/values outside which managerial operation is triggered.

## Illustration 11 – Variance analysis

A process has a standard time of 50 minutes. Control limits may be set as a fixed amount, a fixed percentage or using a statistical model. Assume they are set at 30 and 70 minutes, and actual times recorded as follows:

Time to complete operation:

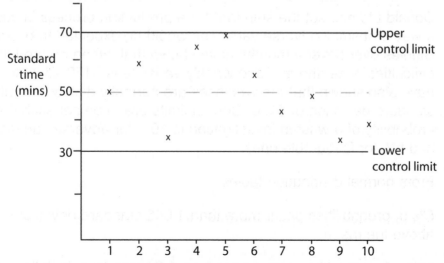

If the actual time taken falls within the bands, the variance is not significant.

## Expandable text

Control limits should be set so that there is only a small chance of a random fluctuation falling outside them.

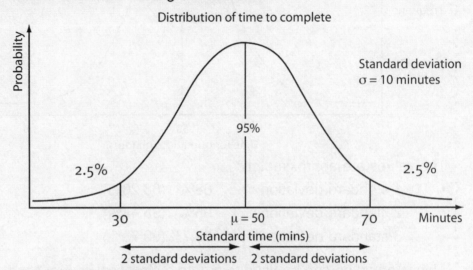

Distribution of time to complete

- In this example the control limits are set two standard deviations from the mean. Thus, 95% of the recorded process times should lie within the control limits.

- The actual time is recorded on the chart after the completion of each process. It will soon be apparent if the mean time is shifting from 50 minutes, as the recorded times move outside the control limits.

- If more than 5% of the observed results do lie outside the control limits, then the system may be referred to as being statistically out of control. At this stage management must decide what further action to take.

## Test your understanding 18

Donald Ltd has set the standard for a production process in such a way that small adverse variances would be expected to occur. Studies over several months have shown that, when no production difficulties arise, the average weekly variance is $150 adverse. They have also shown that the variances are normally distributed with a standard deviation of $100. Control limits are to be set such that the probability of a wasted investigation is 10% for adverse variances and 5% for favourable ones.

From normal distribution tables:

5% of probabilities occur more than 1.645 standard deviations above the mean.

10% of probabilities occur more than 1.28 standard deviations below the mean.

(a) **Suggest a reason why the standard has been set in this way.**

(b) **Calculate the control limits.**

## Chapter summary

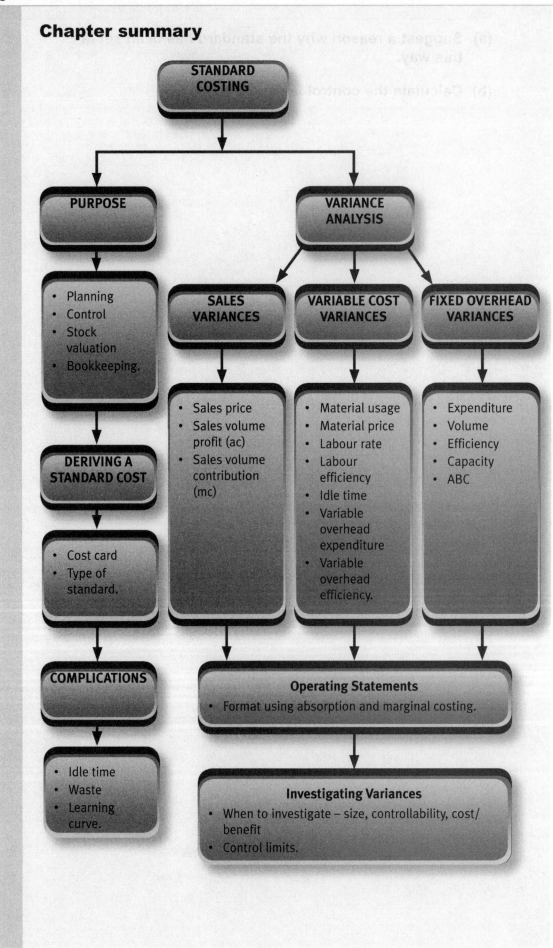

# Test your understanding answers

## Test your understanding 1

**D**

A bank and a food manufacturer would have similar repetitive output for which standard costs could be calculated whereas a kitchen designer is likely to work on different jobs specified by the customer.

## Test your understanding 2

|  | $ |
|---|---|
| Direct materials (40 x $5.30) | 212 |
| Direct labour: |  |
| Bonding (24 hours x $5.00) | 120 |
| Finishing (15 hours at $4.80) | 72 |
| **Prime cost** | 404 |
| Variable overhead: |  |
| Bonding (24 hours at $1.50 per hour) | 36 |
| Finishing (15 hours at $1 per hour) | 15 |
| **Variable production cost** | 455 |
| Production overheads | 40 |
| **Total production cost** | 495 |
| Non-production overheads | 30 |
| **Total cost** | **525** |

(b)

$$\text{Profit} \left( \frac{25}{75} \times 525 \right) \qquad 175$$

| **Price** | 700 |
|---|---|

Contribution per unit = $700 – $455 = $245

Profit per unit before non-production overheads
= $700 – $495 = $205

## Test your understanding 3

Ideal standards may be useful for highlighting the maximum improvement possible but generally attainable standards are used because:

- attainable standards are the most useful for planning, control and motivation
- basic standards are out of date
- current standards do not incorporate targets for improvement
- ideal standards may be seen to be unachievable.

## Test your understanding 4

|  |  | Per batch of 20 |  |
|---|---|---:|---|
| Ideal time | (92%) | 32.0 | minutes |
| Non-productive time | (8%) | 2.8 | minutes |
|  | (100%) | 34.8 | minutes |
| Setup time |  | 2.0 | minutes |
| Total time |  | 36.8 | minutes |
| Total cost @ $4.50/hr |  | | $2.76 |
| Standard labour cost per sandwich (/20) |  | | $0.138 |

## Test your understanding 5

### Analysis of budgeted costs

|  | Fixed cost | Variable cost | Variable per course |
|---|---:|---:|---:|
|  | $ | $ | $ |
| Speakers' fees | – | 3,180 | 530 |
| Hire of premises | – | 1,500 | 250 |
| Depreciation of equipment | 180 | – | – |
| Stationery | – | 600 | 100 |
| Catering | 250 | 1,500 | 250 |
| Insurance | 100 | 720 | 120 |
| Administration | 1,620 | – | – |

### Flexible budget control statement for April

| Expenditure | Fixed cost allowance | Variable cost allowance | Total cost allowance | Actual cost | Variance |
|---|---:|---:|---:|---:|---:|
|  | $ | $ | $ | $ | $ |
| Speakers' fees | – | 2,650 | 2,650 | 2,500 | 150 |
| Hire of premises | – | 1,250 | 1,250 | 1,500 | (250) |
| Depreciation of equipment | 180 | – | 180 | 200 | (20) |
| Stationery | – | 500 | 500 | 530 | (30) |
| Catering | 250 | 1,250 | 1,500 | 1,500 | – |
| Insurance | 100 | 600 | 700 | 700 | – |
| Administration | 1,620 | – | 1,620 | 1,650 | (30) |
|  | 2,150 | 6,250 | 8,400 | 8,580 | (180) |

## Test your understanding 6

The production manager will be responsible for managing direct labour and direct material usage but may not be able to influence material prices or labour rates. Performance should be measured against the element of direct cost which the manager can control.

## Test your understanding 7

| | | | | |
|---|---|---|---|---|
| Price variance = ($60 – $61) x 6000 | = | $6,000 | (F) |
| Volume Variance = (6,500 – 6,000) x $5 | = | $2,500 | (A) |
| | | $3,500 | (F) |

The sales price variance may be favourable due to lower discounts being offered than expected or due to unexpected increases in the cost of the product leading to a decision to increase prices. The sales volume variance may be adverse due to the increase in sales prices or due to increased competition in the market.

## Test your understanding 8

| Material variances | $ | $ |
|---|---|---|
| Actual quantity x Actual price = | 20,900 | |
| Price variance | | 1,100 (F) |
| Actual quantity x Standard price | | |
| = 2,200 x $10 = | 22,000 | |
| Usage variance | | 2,000 (A) |
| Standard quantity x Standard price | | |
| = 1,000 x 2 x $10 = | 20,000 | |
| Total variance | | 900 (A) |

The favourable price variance could have been caused by buying lower quality material or by buying in larger quantities and gaining bulk discounts. The adverse usage variance could have been caused by using cheaper material or by less experienced staff using more material.

### Test your understanding 9

**Labour variances in finishing department**

| | | |
|---|---|---|
| Actual quantity x Actual price | $69,750 | |
| Rate variance | | $4,650  F |
| Actual quantity x Standard price | | |
| 15,500 x $4.80 | $74,400 | |
| Efficiency variance | | $2,400  A |
| Standard quantity x Standard price | | |
| (For actual production) | | |
| 1,000 x 15 x $4.80 | $72,000 | |

The favourable rate variance may have been caused by less experienced staff being utilised or work being completed with less overtime than expected. The adverse efficiency variance may have been caused by less experienced staff taking longer to make products or lower quality material making it more difficult to carry out the work.

### Test your understanding 10

**Variable overhead variances in finishing department**

| | | |
|---|---|---|
| Actual quantity x Actual price | $14,900 | |
| Expenditure variance | | $600  F |
| Actual quantity x Standard price | | |
| 15,500 x $1.00 | $15,500 | |
| Efficiency variance | | $500  A |
| Standard quantity x Standard price | | |
| (For actual production) | | |
| 1,000 x 15 x $1 | $15,000 | |

## Test your understanding 11

**(a) B**

Expenditure variance ($8 x 10,000) – $84,000 = $4,000 A

**(b) C**

Volume variance (11,500 – 10,000) x $8 = $12,000       F

**Capacity and efficiency variances**

The volume variance that was calculated above assumed that fixed overheads were absorbed using units, however, this may not be the case.

Overheads might be absorbed using labour or machine hours. This means that:

* the number of units might be different to budgeted

* the number of hours used might be different from what would be expected.

## Test your understanding 12

**(a)**

| | $ |
|---|---|
| Budgeted fixed production overhead | 637,500 |
| Actual fixed production overhead | 632,000 |
| Fixed production overhead expenditure variance | 5,500 (F) |

The expenditure variance is favourable because fixed overhead expenditure was less than expected.

| | |
|---|---|
| Budgeted direct labour hours (60,000 x 1.25) | 75,000 hours |
| Budgeted fixed overheads | $637,500 |
| Fixed overhead absorption rate per hour | $8.50 |
| | Hours |
| 63,000 units should take (x 1.25 hours) | 78,750 |
| Did take | 79,600 |
| Efficiency variance in hours | 850 (A) |
| Standard fixed overhead rate per hour | $8.50 |
| Fixed production overhead efficiency variance in $ | $7,225 (A) |

The efficiency variance is adverse because the time required to make the units was longer than expected.

|  | Hours |
|---|---|
| Budgeted hours of work | 75,000 |
| Actual hours of work | 79,600 |
| Capacity variance in hours | 4,600 (F) |

| | |
|---|---|
| Standard fixed overhead rate per hour $8.50 | |
| Fixed production overhead capacity variance in $ | $39,100 (F) |

The capacity variance is favourable because more hours were worked than budgeted (which should result in more units being manufactured but note the adverse efficiency variance in this case).

Note:

The fixed overhead variances together explain the under- or over-absorbed fixed overhead in the period. The standard fixed overhead cost per unit is

|  | $ |
|---|---|
| 1.25 hours x $8.50 per hour = $10.625 per unit. | |
| Absorbed fixed overheads (63,000 units x $10.625) | 669,375 |
| Actual fixed overheads | 632,000 |
|  | 37,375 (F) |

| Variances | |
|---|---|
| Fixed overhead expenditure | 5,500 (F) |
| Fixed overhead efficiency | 7,225 (A) |
| Fixed overhead capacity | 39,100 (F) |
| | |
| Total variances | 37,375 (F) |

**(b)** The fixed overhead expenditure variance may be favourable due to the reduction in price of rent. The efficiency variance may be adverse due to less experienced staff being used. The capacity variance may be favourable due to overtime being worked.

### Test your understanding 13

| Material A variances: | $ | $ |
|---|---|---|
| Actual quantity x Actual price | 91,500 | |
| Price variance | | 1,500 (A) |
| Actual quantity x Standard price – $7,500 x $12 | 90,000 | |
| Usage variance | | 6,000 (A) |
| Standard quantity x Standard price = 700 x 10 x $12 | 84,000 | |

| Material B variances: | $ | $ |
|---|---|---|
| Actual quantity x Actual price $20,300 | | |
| Price variance | | 2,800 (A) |
| Actual quantity x Standard price – 3,500 x $5 | 17,500 | |
| Usage variance | | 3,500 (F) |
| Standard quantity x Standard price = 700 x 6 x $5 | 21,000 | |

| Labour variances: | $ | $ |
|---|---|---|
| Actual hours x Actual rate | 27,880 | |
| Rate variance | | 680 (A) |
| Actual hours x Standard rate = $3,800 x $8 | 27,200 | |
| Efficiency variance | | 800 (F) |
| Standard hours x Standard rate = 700 x 5 x $8 | 28,000 | |

| Fixed overhead variances: | $ | $ |
|---|---|---|
| Actual overheads | 37,000 | |
| Expenditure variance | | 8,000 (F) |
| Budgeted overheads = 750 x $60 | 45,000 | |
| Volume variance | | 3,000 (A) |
| Flexed budget overheads = 700 x $60 | 42,000 | |
| Sales price variance ($300 – 320) x 700 = | $14,000 F | |
| Sales volume variance ($750 – 700) x 50 = | $2,500 A | |

**Operating statement**

| | $ |
|---|---|
| Budgeted profit | 37,500 |
| Sales volume variance | 2,500 A |
| Standard profit on actual sales | 35,000 |
| Selling price variance | 14,000 F |
| | 49,000 |

| Cost variances: | F | A | |
|---|---|---|---|
| | $ | $ | |
| Material price (combined) | | 4,300 | |
| Material usage (combined) | | 2,500 | |
| Labour rate | | 680 | |
| Labour efficiency | 800 | | |
| Fixed overhead expenditure | 8,000 | | |
| Fixed overhead volume | | 3,000 | |
| Total | 8,800 | 10,480 | (1,680) |
| Actual profit | | | 47,320 |

### Test your understanding 14

Standard contribution = $6 – $4.30 = $1.70 per cylinder
Sales volume variance = (10,600 – 10,000) x $1.70 = $1,020 F
Sales price variance = $6 x 10,600 – $63,000 = $600 A
Material price = 53,200 x 0.8 – $42,500 = $60 F
Wages rate = 2,040 x $1.50 – $3,100 = $40 A
Material usage = (10,600 x 5 – 53,200) x 0.8 = $160 A
Labour efficiency = (10,600 x 0.2 – 2,040) x $1.50 = $120F

| | | | $ |
|---|---|---|---|
| Budgeted contribution (10,000 x $1.70) | | | 17,000 |
| Add: Sales volume variance | | | 1,020 |
| Standard contribution on actual sales (W10) | | | 18,020 |

| Less: Variances: | A | F | |
|---|---|---|---|
| | $ | $ | $ |
| Sales price | 600 | | |
| Materials price | | 60 | |
| Wages rate | 40 | | |
| Materials usage | 160 | | |
| Labour efficiency | | 120 | |
| | 800 | 180 | |
| | | 620 | |
| Actual contribution | | | 17,400 |
| Budgeted fixed overhead | | | 2,000 |
| Fixed overhead expenditure variance | | | 200 A |
| Actual profit | | | 15,200 |

## Test your understanding 15

Labour rate variance = 1,150 x $8 – $9,430 = $230 A

Revised standard hours for 8 units taking into account the learning curve:

= 200 x 0.9 x 0.9 x 0.9 = 145.8 x 8 = 1,166.4 hours

Labour efficiency variance = 1,166.4 – 1,150 = 16.4 x $8 = $131.20 F

## Test your understanding 16

**Labour efficiency variance**

Standard paid hours = $\dfrac{1,200 \times 2}{0.96}$      2,500

Actual hours paid      2,600

Variance: 100 hours x $4.00/hour      $400 (A)

Productive efficiency:

(2,400 hours – 2,490 hours) x $\dfrac{\$4.00}{0.96}$      $375 (A)

Idle time

[(2,600 x 4%) – 110] x $\dfrac{\$4.00}{0.96}$      $25 (A)

## Test your understanding 17

The standard cost per nursing hour for recovery nursing is $360,000/900 = $400

The standard cost per operation is $400 x 400 = $160,000/32 = $5,000 per operation.

The total variance is

|  |  | $ |
|---|---|---|
| 36 operations should cost x $5,000 |  | 180,000 |
| did cost |  | 176,375 |
|  |  | 3,625   F |

Actual cost per nursing hour is $176,375/425 = $415
The expenditure variance is
425 x (415 – 400) = $6,375 A

32 operations expect to need 400 nursing hours.
So 1 operation would expect to need 400/32 = 12.5 nursing hours.
36 operations would have expected to require 12.5 x 36 = 450 nursing hours.
Efficiency variance = (450 – 425) x $400 = $10,000 F
$10,000 F + $6,375 A = $3,625 F

---

**Test your understanding 18**

**(a) Harshly set standards**

Whilst it is accepted that standards should not be set too harshly or too loosely, it is thought that a standard slightly tougher than is actually expected to be achieved will motivate staff to work harder. This standard will have been set to get the best out of staff.

**(b) Control limits**

When tackling questions to do with normal distributions it is useful to draw a diagram to represent the problem, as shown below.

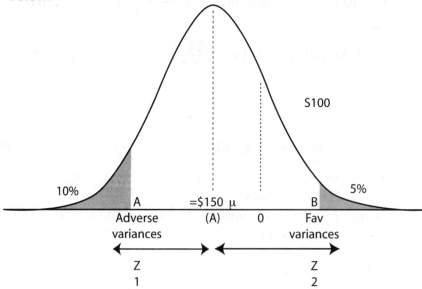

The tails of the distribution show the relevant 10% and 5% areas mentioned in the question.

Control limits:

A   = $150 (A) + (1.28 x $100)   =   $278 (A)

B   = $150 (A) – (1.645 x $100) =   $15 (F)

# Advanced variances

## Chapter learning objectives

Upon completion of this chapter you will be able to:

- define, for a manufacturing company, material mix and yield variances

- calculate, from information supplied, material mix and yield variances

- for given or calculated material mix and yield variances, interpret and explain possible causes, including possible interrelationships between them

- explain, using simple non-numerical examples, the wider issues involved in changing mix, e.g. cost, quality and performance measurement issues

- identify and explain the interrelationship between price, mix and yield, using a simple numerical example

- suggest and justify alternative methods of controlling production processes in manufacturing environments

- using revised standards supplied, calculate a revised budget

- from supplied data, calculate planning and operational variances for sales (including market size and market share)

- from supplied data, calculate planning and operational variances for materials

- from supplied data, calculate planning and operational variances for labour

- identify and explain those factors that, in general, should and should not be allowed to revise an original budget

- explain and resolve the typical manipulation issues in revising budgets

- describe the dysfunctional nature of some variances in the modern environment of Just-in-time (JIT) and total quality management (TQM)

- describe the major behavioural problems resulting from using standard costs in rapidly changing environments

- discuss the major effects that variances have on staff motivation and action.

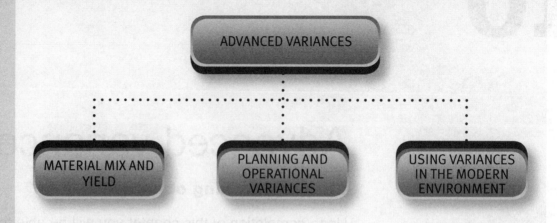

# 1   Material mix and yield

## 1.1   Material mix and yield variances

In certain industries it is possible that the materials (and other components) input to the product are interchangeable. In this situation it makes sense to identify variances related to the substitution of one material for another. Mix and yield variances are a sub-analysis of the usage variance. Where material inputs are not interchangeable then conventional materials usage variances should be calculated for each input.

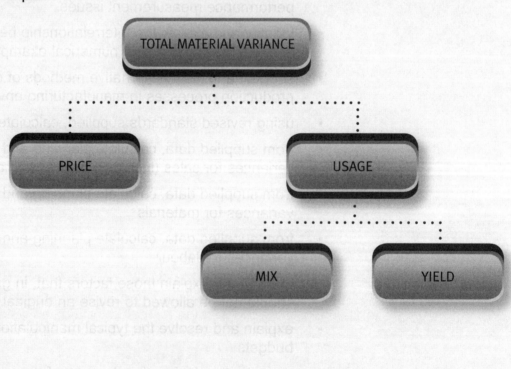

**Illustration 1 – Material mix and yield**

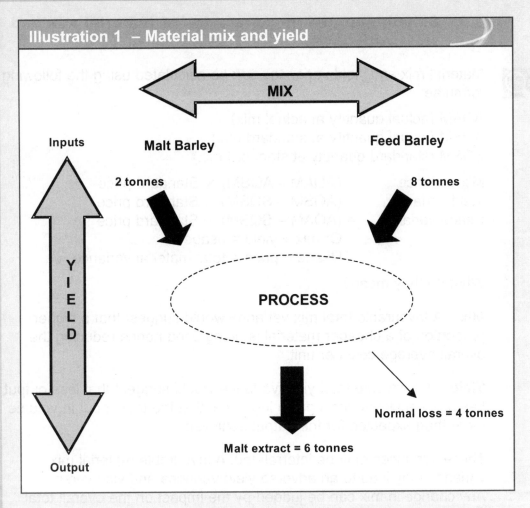

**Material mix** – The relationship of one material input to another. The standard mix shows the proportion of a material that we expect to use in a given mix. The mix variance identifies the amount by which the actual proportion differs from the standard mix. In the above example it is possible that the amount of feed barley (say) is more or less than 80% of the total. The mix variance would evaluate the cost effect of that difference.

**Material yield** – the relationship of inputs in total to the outputs. In most questions of this type there is a yield loss. This means that the input is expected to be greater than the output and there is an expected or 'normal' loss in the process. A yield variance identifies if the inputs (in total) are greater or less than expected for a given output.

**Test your understanding 1**

**Explain the circumstances under which a materials mix variance is relevant to managerial control.**

## 1.2 Calculation and interpretation of material mix and yield variances.

Material mix and yield variances can be calculated using the following formulae:

AQAM (actual quantity at actual mix)
AQSM (actual quantity at standard mix)
SQSM (standard quantity at standard mix)

| | |
|---|---|
| Mix variance | = (AQAM – AQSM) × Standard price |
| Yield variance | = (AQSM – SQSM) × Standard price |
| Usage variance | = (AQAM – SQSM) × Standard price |
| | Or mix + yield = usage |
| | Usage + price = total material variance |

What do they mean?

**Mix** – A favourable total mix variance would suggest that a higher proportion of a cheaper material is being used hence reducing the overall average cost per unit.

**Yield** – An adverse total yield variance would suggest that less output has been achieved for a given input, i.e. that the total input in volume is more than expected for the output achieved.

These variances may be interrelated. A favourable material mix variance may lead to an adverse yield variance and vice versa. Any change in mix can be judged by the impact on the overall total materials variance.

### Expandable text

The analysis required can be summarised as follows:

| Actual total quantity in actual proportions at actual prices | Actual total quantity in actual proportions at standard prices | Actual total quantity in standard proportions at standard prices | Standard total quantity in standard proportions at standard prices |
|---|---|---|---|

PRICE          MIX          YIELD

Illustration 2 – Material mix and yield

The following shows the standard input and cost for 6 tonnes of output

|  | Tonnes |  | $ |
|---|---|---|---|
| Malt barley | 2.0 | @ $230 | 460 |
| Feed barley | 8.0 | @ $110 | 880 |
| Total | 10.0 |  | 1,340 |
| Yield loss 40% | (4.0) |  | 0 |
| Expected output | 6.0 |  | 1,340 |

The actual input, output and costs are shown below:

| Production | 270 tonnes |
|---|---|
| Input – Malt barley | 70 tonnes costing $16,100 |
| – Feed barley | 430 tonnes costing $48,355 |

**Required:**

Prepare all material variances and discuss their causes.

**Price variance**

| Material: | Malt barley | Feed barley | Total |
|---|---|---|---|
| AQAP |  |  |  |
| AQSP |  |  |  |
| Variance |  |  |  |

**Usage variances**

Workings (Tonnes)

| Material: | Malt barley | Feed barley | Total |
|---|---|---|---|
| 1 AQAM (Actual quantity at actual mix) |  |  |  |
| 2 AQSM (Actual quantity at standard mix) |  |  |  |
| 3 SQSM (Standard quantity at standard mix for actual output) |  |  |  |
| 4 Standard price ($) |  |  |  |

Variances (all at standard price)

| Material: | Malt barley | Feed barley | Total |
|---|---|---|---|
| Mix | | | |
| Yield | | | |
| Usage | | | |

### Solution

### Price variance

| Material: | Malt barley | Feed barley | Total |
|---|---|---|---|
| AQAP | 16,100 | 48,355 | |
| AQSP | 16,100 | 47,300 | |
| Variance | 0 | 1,055 A | 1,055 A |

### Usage variances

### Workings

| Material: | Malt barley | Feed barley | Total |
|---|---|---|---|
| 1 AQAM | 70 | 430 | 500 |
| 2 AQSM | 100 | 400 | 500 |
| 3 SQSM | 90 | 360 | 270/0.6 = 450 |
| 4 Standard price ($) | $230 | $110 | |

Variances

| Material: | Malt barley | Feed barley | Total |
|---|---|---|---|
| Mix | 30 × 230 = 6,900 F | 30 × 110 = 3,300 A | 3,600 F |
| Yield | 10 × 230 = 2,300 A | 40 × 110 = 4,400 A | 6,700 A |
| Usage | 20 × 230 = 4,600 F | 70 × 110 = 7,700 A | 3,100 A |

The total material variance can be calculated:

| | | |
|---|---|---|
| Standard material cost for 270 tonnes of output ($1,340/6 × 270) | $60,300 | |
| Actual material cost | $64,455 | |
| Total material variance | $4,155 | A |

This is made up of:

| | | |
|---|---|---|
| Price variance | $1,055 | A |
| Mix variance | $3,600 | F |
| Yield variance | $6,700 | A |

The sum of the mix and yield variances is the usage variance.

Causes:

- The price variance is adverse because the feed barley price is higher than expected.

- The mix variance is favourable because a greater proportion of feed barley has been used than would normally be used in the standard mix. Feed barley is a cheaper material than malt barley.

- The yield variance is adverse because less output has been achieved than was expected from the materials input.

- It is possible that changing the mix to include a greater proportion of cheaper feed barley has led to the reduction in yield.

- Overall this has led to a total adverse usage variance of $3,100 and this will adversely affect profit.

## Test your understanding 2

Pan-Ocean Chemicals has one product, which requires inputs from three types of material to produce batches of product Synthon. Standard cost details for a single batch are shown below.

| Material type | Materials | | Labour | |
|---|---|---|---|---|
| | Standard kg | Standard price per kg $ | Standard hours | Standard rate per hour $ |
| S1 | 8 | 0.30 | 1 | 5.00 |
| S2 | 5 | 0.50 | | |
| S3 | 3 | 0.40 | | |

A standard loss of 10% of input is expected. Actual production was 15,408 kg for the previous week. Details of the materials used were:

**Actual material used (kg)**

| | |
|---|---|
| S1 | 8,284 |
| S2 | 7,535 |
| S3 | 3,334 |

Total labour cost for the week was $6,916 for 1,235 hours worked.

**Calculate total material mix, yield and usage variances.**

Using the variances calculated for Pan-Ocean Chemicals write a report to management, which explains and interprets your results.

The report should pay particular attention to:

- explaining what is meant by mix and yield variances in respect of materials: and

- possible reasons for all the results you have derived.

## 1.3 Alternative calculations for mix and yield variances

Mix and yield variance calculations can be made quicker by the use of weighted average costs of inputs and outputs.

**Using the barley example above:**

Ten tonnes of input should cost $1,340 if in standard mix at standard prices. This should result in six tonnes of output, so the:

- standard cost of input in standard mix = 1,340/10 = $134 per tonne

- standard cost of output = 1,340/6 = $223.33 per tonne.

**Mix variance**

AQAMSP = (70 tonnes Malt x $230) + (430 tonnes feed × $110) = $63,400.

AQSMSP = 500 tonnes × $134 standard cost of input = $67,000.

The difference gives the mix variance of $3,600 (F) as before.

**Note:** this approach has the advantage that we have not had to split the total input of 500 tonnes into standard mix for each input.

**Yield variance**

AQSMSP = $67,000 as above.

SQSMSP can be calculated as 270 tonnes output x $223.33 = $60,300, using the standard cost of output.

The difference is the yield variance of $6,700 (A) as before.

**Note:**

Some students wonder if yield variances can be calculated by looking at yields (i.e. output) rather than inputs. This can be done as follows.

The 500 tonnes of input should have produced a yield of 500 x 0.6 = 300 tonnes.

The actual yield was 270 tonnes, thus there was a shortfall in yield of 30 tonnes.

Using the standard cost of output, this gives:

- yield variance = 30 x 223.33 = $6,700 (A) as before.

---

**Test your understanding 4**

Hordru Inc operates a standard costing system.

The standard direct material mix to produce 1,000 kgs of output is as follows:

| Material grade | Input quantity (kg) | Standard price per kilo input $ |
|---|---|---|
| A | 600 | 1.10 |
| B | 240 | 2.40 |
| C | 360 | 1.50 |

During April the actual output of the product was 21,000 kilos.

The actual materials issued to production were:

| Material grade | Quantity (kg) |
|---|---|
| A | 14,000 |
| B | 5,500 |
| C | 5,500 |

**Calculate material mix and yield variances.**

---

## 1.4   Changing mix – the wider issues

It has already been shown that changing the mix of material input can affect the material yield of the process. It can impact on:

- cost
- quality
- performance measurement.

## Illustration 3 – Material mix and yield

A company produces pre-cast concrete sections for the construction industry. The mix of materials used to produce the concrete can be varied and different mixes are suitable for different products. Discuss the issues that management should consider when setting standard material costs.

**Solution**

For each product management should consider the optimum mix of input materials that will maximise profits to the business. This may involve consideration of:

- the relationship between cost, quality and price. Reducing the cost of input materials by using a greater proportion of a cheaper material may reduce the quality of the product and lead to a reduction in the price that can be charged;

- costs of reduced quality. Using a greater proportion of a cheaper input material may lead to higher quality failure costs;

- impact on other variances. Increasing the proportion of a cheaper input material may result in increased labour costs or overhead costs if this leads to more time having to be spent producing a product. Increased rejects may lead to higher overhead costs.

It may be the case that, whilst changing a material mix could lead to an overall favourable material variance this could have an adverse impact on the profitability of the business if prices have to be reduced because of reduced quality or quality failure costs exceed material cost savings. Thus it is important to set the standard mix at the level which optimises profit taking all factors into consideration.

## Test your understanding 5

**Discuss how the performance measurement system should be designed when the mix of input materials can be varied in a process.**

## 1.5 The control of production processes in manufacturing environments

As well as variances, organisations can also use other performance measures and targets for controlling production processes, e.g.:

- detailed timesheets
- % idle time
- productivity
- % yield

- % waste
- quality measures e.g. reject rate
- average cost of inputs
- average cost of output
- average prices achieved for finished products
- average margins
- % on-time deliveries
- customer satisfaction ratings.

# 2 Planning and operational variances

## 2.1 Revised standards and budgeting

Traditionally when comparing standards to actual results the comparison has suffered from the time delay between setting the standard and the occurrence of the actual results. The standard is set as part of the budgeting process which occurs before the period to which it relates. This means that the difference between standard and actual may arise partly due to an unrealistic budget and not solely due to operational factors. The budget may need to be revised to enable actual performance to be compared with a standard that reflects these changed conditions.

**Planning variances**

Aims to update the original standards to reflect the change in conditions and environment. They compare original standards with revised standards. Calculations are the same as for conventional variances ('actual versus budget') except 'actual' becomes 'revised standards' and 'budget' becomes 'original budget'.

Often deemed to be uncontrollable. Management may not be held responsible.

**Operational variances**

Compare revised standards to actual results. Calculations are the same as for conventional variances except a revised budget is used.

Deemed controllable. Management held responsible for operational variances.

In effect a planning/operating variance approach means that calculations need to be done twice for each type of variance.

Original budget ('ex-ante') } planning variances

Revised budget ('ex-post') }
} operating variances
Actual }

## 2.2 Planning and operational variances for sales

Many different planning and operational variances may be calculated for sales price and sales volume. Two you need to be aware of are market share and market size variances.

Planning ⟶ market volume variance.

Operational ⟶ market share variance.

### Illustration 4 – Planning and operational variances

Hudson Inc has a sales budget of 400,000 units for the coming year based on 20% of the total market. On each unit, Hudson makes a profit of $3. Actual sales for the year were 450,000, but industry reports showed that the total market volume had been 2.2 million.

(a) Find the traditional sales (margin) volume variance.

(b) Split this into planning and operational variances (market volume and market share).

### Solution

(a) Traditional sales volume variance

= (Actual units sold – Budgeted sales) x Standard profit per unit

= (450,000 – 400,000) x $3 = $150,000 F.

(b) Planning and operational variances

The revised (ex-post) budget would show that Hudson Ltd should expect to sell 20% of 2.2 million units = 440,000 units.

Original budget: 400,000 x $3 = $1,200,000  Planning ('Market volume') variance

Revised budget: 440,000 x $3 = $1,320,000  Operational ('Market share') variance

Actual results: 450,000 x $3 = $1,350,000

|  | $ |  |
|---|---:|---|
| Planning (or market volume) variance | | |
| = $1,320,000 – $1,200,000 | 120,000 | F |
| Operational (or market share) variance | | |
| = $1,350,000 – $1,320,000 | 30,000 | F |
| Total sales volume variance    = | 150,000 | F |

Most of the favourable sales volume variance can be attributed to the increase in the overall market volume. However some can be put down to effort by the sales force which has increased its share of the market a little from 20% to $\left(\dfrac{450,000}{2,200,000}\right)$ = 20.5%.

## Test your understanding 6

A company sets its sales budget based on an average price of $14 per unit and sales volume of 250,000 units. Competition was more intense than expected and the company only achieved sales of 220,000 and had to sell at a discounted price of $12.50 per unit. The company was unable to reduce costs so profit per unit fell from $4 per unit to $2.50 per unit. It was estimated that the total market volume grew by 10% from 1,000,000 units to 1,100,000 units.

(a) **Calculate the sales price and volume variances.**

(b) **Analyse the volume variances into market share and market size.**

(c) **Discuss whether the price variance is a planning or operational variance.**

## 2.3 Planning and operating cost variances

When applying planning and operating principles to cost variances, care must be taken over flexing the budgets. The accepted approach for use in the exam is to flex both the original and revised budgets to actual production levels:

Original (flexed) budget

                      Planning variances

Revised (flexed) budget

                      Operating variances

Actual results

## Illustration 5 – Planning and operational variances

Rhodes Co manufactures Stops which it is estimated require 2 kg of material XYZ at $10/kg In week 21 only 250 Stops were produced although budgeted production was 300. 450 kg of XYZ were purchased and used in the week at a total cost of $5,100. Later it was found that the standard had failed to allow for a 10% price increase throughout the material supplier's industry. Rhodes Ltd carries no stocks.

**Planning and operational analysis**

The first step in the analysis is to calculate:

1    Original flexed budget (ex-ante).

2    Revised flexed budget (ex-post).

3    Actual results.

**(W1)**    Original flexed budget (ex-ante)

250 units at 2kg per unit for $10/kg  =  $5,000   ↑ Planning variance

**(W2)**    Revised flexed budget (ex-post)

250 units at 2kg per unit for $11/kg  =  $5,500   ↓

**(W3)**    Actual results

450kg for                                              $5,100   ↓ Operational variance

## Test your understanding 7

A transport business makes a particular journey regularly, and has established that the standard fuel cost for each journey is 20 litres of fuel at $2 per litre. New legislation has forced a change in the vehicle used for the journey and an unexpected rise in fuel costs. It is decided retrospectively that the standard cost per journey should have been 18 litres at $2.50 per litre.

**Calculate the original and revised flexed budgets if the journey is made 120 times in the period.**

## 2.4  Planning and operational variances for materials

Planning and operational variances can be calculated for materials in the same way as above.

## Illustration 8 – Planning and operational variances

The standard cost per unit of raw material was estimated to be $5 per unit. The general market price at the time of purchase was $5.20 per unit and the actual price paid was $5.18 per unit. 10,000 units of the raw materials were purchased during the period. Calculate the planning and operational materials price variances.

**Solution**

**Planning variance:**

|  |  | $ |
|---|---|---|
| AQ RSP | 10,000 × $5.20 | 52,000 |
| AQ SP | 10,000 × $5 | 50,000 |
| Price variance | | 2,000  A |

**Operational variance:**

|  |  |  |
|---|---|---|
| AQ AP | 10,000 × 5.18 | 51,800 |
| AQ RSP | 10,000 × 5.20 | 52,000 |
| Price variance | | 200  F |

## Test your understanding 8

Holmes Ltd uses one raw material for one of their products. The standard cost per unit at the beginning of the year was $28, made up as follows:

Standard material cost per unit = 7 kg per unit at $4 per kg = $28.

In the middle of the year the supplier had changed the specification of the material slightly due to problems experienced in the country of origin, so that the standard had to be revised as follows:

Standard material cost per unit = 8 kg per unit at $3.80 per kg = $30.40.

The actual output for November was 1,400 units. 11,000 kg of material was purchased and used at a cost of $41,500.

**Calculate**

(a) **material price and usage variances using the traditional method**

(b) **all planning and operational material variances.**

## 2.5 Planning and operational variances for labour

Planning and operational variances for labour can be calculated in the same way as for materials.

## Illustration 7 – Planning and operational variances

The standard hours per unit of production for a product is 5 hours. Actual production for the period was 250 units and actual hours worked were 1,450 hours. The standard rate per hour was $10. Because of a shortage of skilled labour it has been necessary to use unskilled labour and it is estimated that this will increase the time taken by 20%. Calculate the planning and operational efficiency variances.

### Solution

**Planning variance:**

|  |  | $ |  |
|---|---|---|---|
| RSH SR | 6 × 250 × $10 | 15,000 |  |
| SH SR | 5 × 250 × $10 | 12,500 |  |
| Efficiency variance |  | 2,500 | A |

**Operational variance:**

|  |  |  |  |
|---|---|---|---|
| AH RSR | 1,450 × $10 | 14,500 |  |
| RSH RSR | 6 × 250 × $10 | 15,000 |  |
| Efficiency variance |  | 500 | F |

## Test your understanding 9

POV Ltd uses a standard costing system to control and report upon the production of its single product.

An abstract from the original standard cost card of the product is as follows:

|  | $ | $ |
|---|---|---|
| Selling price per unit |  | 200 |
| Less: 4 kgs materials @ $20 per kg | 80 |  |
| 6 hours labour @ $7 per hour | 42 |  |
|  |  | 122 |
| Contribution per unit |  | 78 |

For period 3, 2,500 units were budgeted to be produced and sold but the actual production and sales were 2,850 units.

The following information was also available:

(1) At the commencement of period 3 the normal material became unobtainable and it was necessary to use an alternative. Unfortunately, 0.5 kg per unit extra was required and it was thought that the material would be more difficult to work with. The price of the alternative was expected to be $16.50 per kg In the event, actual usage was 12,450 kg at $18 per kg

(2) Weather conditions unexpectedly improved for the period with the result that a 50c per hour bad weather bonus, which had been allowed for in the original standard, did not have to be paid. Because of the difficulties expected with the alternative material, management agreed to pay the workers $8 per hour for period 3 only. During the period 18,800 hours were paid for.

After using conventional variances for some time, POV Ltd is contemplating extending its system to include planning and operational variances.

(a) **Prepare a statement reconciling budgeted contribution for the period with actual contribution, using conventional material and labour variances.**

(b) **Prepare a similar reconciliation statement using planning and operational variances.**

(c) **Explain the meaning of the variances shown in statement (b).**

## 2.6 When should a budget be revised ?

There must be a good reason for deciding that the original standard cost is unrealistic. Deciding in retrospect that expected costs should be different from the standard should not be an arbitrary decision, aimed perhaps at shifting the blame for poor results from poor operational management to poor cost estimation.

A good reason for a change in the standard might be:

- a change in one of the main materials used to make a product or provide a service

- an unexpected increase in the price of materials due to a rapid increase in world market prices (e.g. the price of oil or other commodities)

- a change in working methods and procedures that alters the expected direct labour time for a product or service

- an unexpected change in the rate of pay to the workforce.

The aim of variance reporting should be to:

- identify responsibilities for performance, and

- attempt to put a realistic value to the costs or benefits arising from that performance.

If different managers are responsible for planning and operations, the responsibility for the variances can be attributed to the appropriate manager, and the principles of responsibility accounting can be properly applied.

However, frequent 'errors' in the ex-ante standard should not happen, except in unusual circumstances, and the need to report planning and operational variances should therefore be occasional rather than a regular event.

## Illustration 8 – Planning and operational variances

A company is operating in a fast changing environment and is considering whether analysing existing variances into a planning and operational element would help to improve performance. Discuss the advantages and disadvantages of the approach.

**Solution**

Advantages may include:

- Variances are more relevant, especially in a turbulent environment.

- The operational variances give a 'fair' reflection of the actual results achieved in the actual conditions that existed.

- Managers are, theoretically, more likely to accept and be motivated by the variances reported which provide a better measure of their performance.

- It emphasises the importance of planning and the relationship between planning and control and is a better guide for cost control.

- The analysis helps in the standard-setting learning process, which will hopefully result in more useful standards in the future.

Disadvantages:

- The establishment of ex-post budgets is very difficult. Managers whose performance is reported to be poor using such a budget are unlikely to accept them as performance measures because of the subjectivity in setting such budgets.

- There is a considerable amount of administrative work involved first to analyse the traditional variances and then to decide on which are controllable and which are uncontrollable.

- The analysis tends to exaggerate the interrelationship of variances, providing managers with a 'pre-packed' list of excuses for below standard performance. Poor performance is often excused as being the fault of a badly set budget.

- Frequent demands for budget revisions may result in bias.

### Test your understanding 10

It might be argued that only operational variances have significance for performance measurement. Planning variances cannot be controlled and so have little or no value for performance reporting.

**State briefly, with your reason or reasons, whether you agree with this point of view.**

## 3 Using variance analysis

### 3.1 Modern manufacturing environments

There are two aspects of modern manufacturing that you need to be familiar with – Total Quality Management (TQM) and Just in Time (JIT).

**Total Quality Management**

TQM is the continuous improvement in quality, productivity and effectiveness through a management approach focusing on both process and the product.

Fundamental features include:

- prevention of errors before they occur;

- importance of total quality in the design of systems and products;

- real participation of all employees;

- commitment of senior management to the cause;

- recognition of the vital role of customers and suppliers;

- recognition of the need for continual change (Kaizen).

### JIT

JIT is a pull-based system of planning and control pulling work through the system in response to customer demand. This means that goods are only produced when they are needed, eliminating large stocks of materials and finished goods.

Key characteristics for successfully operating such a system are:

High quality: possibly through deploying TQM systems.

Speed:    rapid throughput to meet customers' needs.

Reliability:   computer-aided manufacturing technology will assist.

Flexibility:   small batch sizes and automated techniques are used.

Low costs:   through all of the above.

### 3.2 Variance analysis in the modern manufacturing environment

Standard product costs are associated with traditional manufacturing systems producing large quantities of standard items. Key features of companies operating in a JIT and TQM environment are:

- high level of automation

- high levels of overheads and low levels of direct labour costs

- customised products produced in small batches

- low stocks

- emphasis on high quality.

Variance analysis may not be appropriate because:

- Standard product costs apply to manufacturing environments in which quantities of an identical product are output from the production process. They are not suitable for manufacturing environments where products are non-standard or are customised to customer specifications.

- It is doubtful whether standard costing is of much value for performance setting and control in automated manufacturing environments. There is an underlying assumption in standard costing that control can be exercised by concentrating on the efficiency of the workforce. Direct labour efficiency standards are seen as a key to management control. However, in practice, where manufacturing systems are highly automated, the rates of production output and materials consumption, are controlled by the machinery rather than the workforce.

- Variances are the difference between actual performance and standard, measured in cost terms. The significance of variances for management control purposes depends on the type of standard cost used. For example, adverse variances with an ideal standard have a different meaning from adverse variances calculated with a current standard.

- Standard costing and adherence to a preset standard is inconsistent with the concept of continuous improvement, which is applied within TQM and JIT environments.

- When standard costing was first devised, the main elements of product costs were direct materials and direct labour. In modern manufacturing, production overhead costs are often a high proportion of total production costs. Standard costing is therefore not an appropriate system of performance measurement or effective management control.

- Variance analysis is often carried out on an aggregate basis (total material usage variance, total labour efficiency variance and so on) but in a complex and constantly changing business environment more detailed information is required for effective management control.

- Variance analysis control reports tend to be made available to managers at the end of a reporting period. In the modern business environment managers need more 'real time' information about events as they occur.

- Shorter product life cycles in the modern business environment mean that standard costs will need to be reviewed and updated frequently. This will increase the cost of operating a standard cost system but, if the standards are not updated regularly, they will be of limited use for planning and control purposes. The extra work involved in maintaining up-to-date standards might limit the usefulness and relevance of a standard costing system.

> **Test your understanding 11**
>
> **Comment on whether standard costing applies in both manufacturing and service businesses and how it may be affected by modern initiatives of continuous performance improvement and cost reduction.**

### 3.3 Standard costs and behavioural issues

Standard costs are set with a view to measuring actual performance against the standard, and reporting variances to the managers responsible. The aims of setting standards include:

- setting a target for performance

- motivating the managers responsible to achieve those targets

- holding these managers accountable for actual performance

- perhaps rewarding managers for good performance and criticising them for poor performance.

Managers and employees might respond in different ways to standard setting.

### Standards as a target for achievement

Individuals might respond to standards in different ways, according to the difficulty of achieving the standard level of performance.

- When a standard level of performance is high, e.g. an ideal standard, employees and their managers will recognise that they cannot achieve it. Since the target is not achievable, they might not even try to get near it.

- When the standard of performance is not challenging (e.g. a current standard), employees and their managers might be content simply to achieve the standard without trying to improve their performance.

- An attainable standard might be set which challenges employees and their managers to improve their performance. If this attainable standard is realistic, it might provide a target that they try to achieve.

## Standard costs and motivation

An argument in favour of setting attainable standards is that they can be used to motivate employees and their managers to improve performance. However, this argument is based on the assumption that individuals are motivated by challenging targets. This is not necessarily the case.

- If the standard is too difficult, it could have the opposite effect and de-motivate individuals.

- Even if the standard is attainable, individuals will not necessarily be motivated to achieve it. It might be necessary to provide motivation in the form of a bonus or other type of reward for achieving the standard.

- Individuals might prefer standards to be set at a low level of performance, in order to avoid the need to work harder.

## Participation in standard setting

It has been suggested that if managers and employees can participate in the standard-setting process, their motivation will improve.

- Employees might become involved in trying to improve performance levels.

- Having set the standards, employees will be motivated to try to achieve the targets they have set for themselves.

Participation in standard setting could therefore be a way of achieving improvements in performance.

However, the effectiveness of participation in setting standards depends on a variety of factors, such as the type of staff involved, the attitudes of their managers, the organisation structure and culture, and the nature of the work.

| Arguments in favour of participation | Arguments against participation |
|---|---|
| It could motivate employees to set higher standards for achievement. | Senior management might be reluctant to share responsibilities for budgeting. |
| Staff are more likely to accept standards that they have been involved in setting. | The standard-setting process could be time-consuming. |

| Morale and actual performance levels might be improved. | Staff might want to set standards that they are likely to achieve, rather than more challenging targets. They might try to build some 'slack' into the budget. |
| Staff will understand more clearly what is expected of them. | The standard-setting process could result in conflicts rather than co-operation and collaboration. |
| | Staff might feel that their suggestions have been ignored. |

## Pay as a motivator

If standards are used as a way of encouraging employees to improve their performance, motivation could be provided in the form of higher pay (or other rewards) if targets are reached or exceeded.

However, if employees are offered a bonus for achieving standard costs, this could increase their incentive to set low standards of performance, and include 'slack' in the standard cost. Lower standards will increase the probability that the standards will be achieved and a bonus will be earned.

### Illustration 9 – Using variance analysis

Variance reporting should prompt positive responses, but in practice could result in negative and defensive actions by the manager responsible.

- If there is a culture of 'blame' when adverse variances occur, managers might try to disguise their poor results (e.g. by deferring essential spending or rushing work though in order to improve efficiency regardless of quality).

- The response to adverse variances needs to be more positive. The aim of reporting adverse variances is to indicate problems that might have occurred, and encourage managers to take action to deal with their cause.

### Test your understanding 12

**Which one of the following is not an advantage of participation in standard setting?**

A   The time taken to reach decisions will be quicker via assorted committee meetings.

B   The quality of decisions should improve with collective decision making.

C   There will be improved communication between staff.

D   Staff are more likely to accept standards that they have helped set.

### Test your understanding 13

**What are the major behavioural problems resulting from using standard costs in rapidly-changing environments?**

# Chapter summary

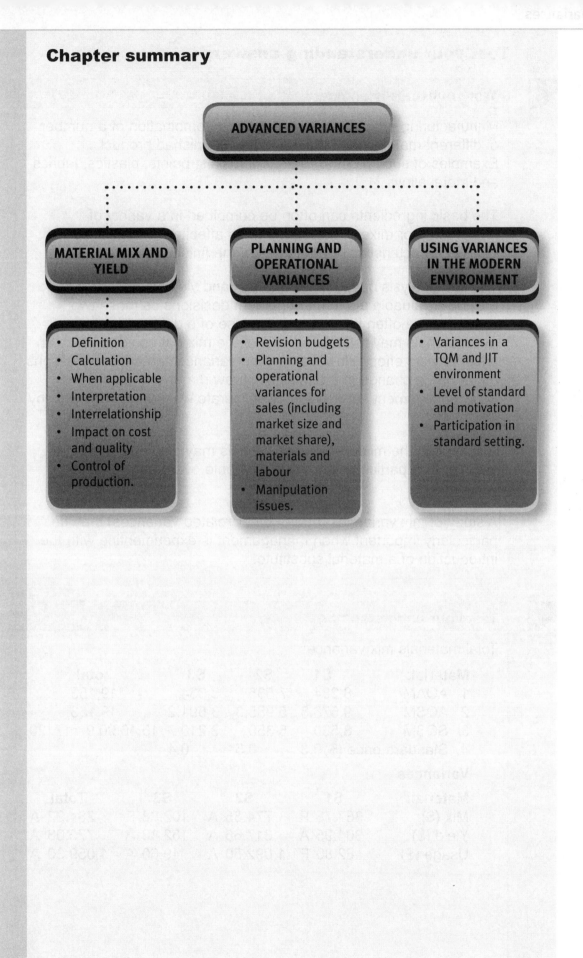

**ADVANCED VARIANCES**

**MATERIAL MIX AND YIELD**

- Definition
- Calculation
- When applicable
- Interpretation
- Interrelationship
- Impact on cost and quality
- Control of production.

**PLANNING AND OPERATIONAL VARIANCES**

- Revision budgets
- Planning and operational variances for sales (including market size and market share), materials and labour
- Manipulation issues.

**USING VARIANCES IN THE MODERN ENVIRONMENT**

- Variances in a TQM and JIT environment
- Level of standard and motivation
- Participation in standard setting.

## Test your understanding answers

### Test your understanding 1

Manufacturing processes often entail the combination of a number of different materials to obtain one unit of finished product. Examples of such processes are chemicals, paints, plastics, fabrics and metal alloys.

The basic ingredients can often be combined in a variety of proportions (or mixes), without perhaps affecting the specified quality characteristics or properties of the finished product.

The sub-analysis of variances into mix and yield components can provide a valuable aid to management decisions as these two variances are often interrelated. The use of a different mixture of raw materials may reduce the cost of the mix but could produce an adverse yield effect. However, a yield variance can arise for reasons other than a change in the mixture of raw materials, e.g. due to poor management supervision or deliberate wastage of materials by operatives.

A change in the mixture of raw materials may also affect other variances, in particular labour and variable overhead efficiency variances.

A study of mix variances (and of other related variances) may be particularly important when management is experimenting with the introduction of a material substitute.

### Test your understanding 2

Total materials mix variance:

| Material: | S1 | S2 | S3 | Total |
|---|---|---|---|---|
| 1  AQAM | 8,284 | 7,535 | 3,334 | 19,153 |
| 2  AQSM | 9,576.5 | 5,985.3 | 3,591.2 | 19,153 |
| 3  SQSM | 8,560 | 5,350 | 3,210 | 15,408/0.9 =17120 |
| 4  Standard price ($) | 0.3 | 0.5 | 0.4 | |

**Variances**

| Material: | S1 | S2 | S3 | Total |
|---|---|---|---|---|
| Mix ($) | 387.75 F | 774.85 A | 102.88 F | 284.22 A |
| Yield ($) | 304.95 A | 317.65 A | 152.48 A | 775.08 A |
| Usage ($) | 82.80 F | 1,092.50 A | 49.60 A | 1,059.30 A |

## Test your understanding 3

### Analysis of variance for Pan-Ocean Chemicals

**Circulation:** Pan-Ocean Chemicals: Senior Management
**Author:**
**Date:** xx/xx/xx

### General

The appendix to this report (results in part (a)) details mix, yield and usage variances for materials and rate and efficiency variances for labour over the last seven days. The purpose of this report is to explain what is meant by the analysis undertaken and to interpret the results derived.

### Materials variances

Materials variances can be categorised in four ways: usage, mix, yield and price. We are concerned only with mix and yield for the purposes of this report.

The three types of material used to produce Synthon (S1, S2 and S3) are not always used in the same proportions. Whilst it is the intention of the production team to use a constant or standard mix, this is not always achieved. In practice, the proportions of input chemicals used can vary for many reasons, mostly associated with the physical properties of the chemicals (which need not concern us here). To the extent that the standard mix is not used in the production of Synthon, then mix variances arise which simply record the cost implications of the change in mix.

Materials yield variances record the differences arising in what inputs should have been used for the output achieved against what inputs have actually been used. Essentially, yield variances are a description of how efficiently inputs have been used.

The adverse yield variance should give rise to some concern since such results indicate an inefficient use of inputs against what was expected. The adverse variance may have arisen, e.g. because of a batch of poor quality input chemicals or because of inefficient working practices, which have led to a significant degree of spoilage.

It must also be borne in mind that mix and yield variances do not incorporate any indication of the quality of output. The adverse yield variance could have been due to stricter quality control, for example. Other performance measures would be needed to monitor quality.

---

### Final comments

Variances of any type should be a signal for some sort of investigative action by management. This can involve either looking to see how the variances have arisen or re-assessing the suitability of the standards that have been set. It might have to be accepted that the standard by which materials is being measured might not be an accurate one.

---

## Test your understanding 4

**Mix variance**

|  | Material A kg | Material B kg | Material C kg | Total kg |
|---|---|---|---|---|
| 1  Actual input | 14,000 | 5,500 | 5,500 | 25,000 |
| 2  Actual input in std proportions 50%:20%:30% | 12,500 | 5,000 | 7,500 | 25,000 |
| 3  Difference in quantity | 1,500 A | 500 A | 2,000 F |  |
| 4  x standard price | x 1.10 | x 2.40 | x 1.50 |  |
| 5  Mix variance | $1,650 | $1,200 A | $3,000 | $150 F |

**Yield variance**

Std cost per kg of output =

$$\frac{(600 \times 1.10) + (240 \times 2.40) + (360 \times 1.50)}{1.2} = \$1.776/kg$$

|  |  | kg |
|---|---|---|
| 1  Std yield | $25,000 \times \dfrac{1,000}{1,200}$ | 20,833.33 |
| 2  Actual yield |  | 21,000 |
| 3 |  | 166.67  F |
| 4  x Standard price/cost per kg of output |  | x 1.176 |
| Yield variance |  | 296    F |

---

## Test your understanding 5

In a performance measurement system managers are often rewarded for improving the performance of cost and/or revenues under their control. The production manager may be responsible for the material mix decision and, if the reward system is based on achieving cost savings, then the cheapest mix may be used. This may have a detrimental effect on company profit if quality is reduced and this leads to a lower price or quality failure costs.

It may therefore be preferable to reward managers on the basis of total company profit so that the full impact of the mix decision is taken into account.

## Test your understanding 6

(a) Sales price variance
= 220,000 × ($14 − $12.50) = $330,000 A
Sales volume variance
= (250,000 − 220,000) × $4 = $120,000 A

(b) Budgeted market share = 250,000/1,000,000 = 25%

The company would have expected to achieve sales of 25% × 1,100,000 = 275,000 in the actual market conditions.

The market size variance
= (275,000 − 250,000) × $4 = $100,000 F
The market share variance
= (275,000 − 220,000) × $4 = $220,000 A
The increased market size is favourable as the company should sell more if market share can be maintained. The market share variance was adverse as market share fell from 25% to 220,000/1,100,000 = 20%.

(c) It could be argued that the increased competition in the market was not foreseen when the budget was set and the variance is thus a planning variance. However, this line of reasoning would suggest that any unforeseen issues give rise just to planning variances. Perhaps sales managers should have identified potential threats sooner? Also, once extra competition was experienced, managers had to decide how to respond. This could have involved additional advertising rather than price cuts, e.g. it could be argued that price cuts were made to try (unsuccessfully) to protect market share, in which case managers should be held (at least partly) responsible for such a decision.

## Test your understanding 7

Original flexed budget:

| 120 × 20 × $2 | $4,800 |

Revised flexed budget:

| 120 × 18 × $2.50 | $5,400 |

## Test your understanding 8

(a) **Traditional variances**

| | | | |
|---|---|---|---|
| AQAP | | $41,500 | |
| | | | Price variance $2,500 F |
| AQSP | 11,000 x $4 | $44,000 | |
| | | | Usage variance $4,800 A |
| SQSP | 1400 x 7 x $4 | $39,200 | |

(b) **Planning variances**

| | | | |
|---|---|---|---|
| RSQ x RSP | 1,400 x 8 x $3.80 | $42,560 | |
| | | | Price variance $2,240 F |
| RSQ x SP | 1,400 x 8 x $4 | $44,800 | |
| | | | Usage variance $5,600 A |
| SQ x SP | 1,400 x 7 x $4 | $39,200 | |

**Operational variances**

| | | | |
|---|---|---|---|
| AQ x AP | | $41,500 | |
| | | | Price variance $300 F |
| AQ x RSP | 11,000 x $3.80 | $41,800 | |
| | | | Usage variance $760 F |
| RSQ x RSP | 1,400 x 8 x $3.80 | $42,560 | |

## Test your understanding 9

(a) Reconciliation of budgeted and actual contribution using conventional variances

| | | | Variances $ | Favourable $ | Adverse |
|---|---|---|---|---|---|
| Budgeted contribution: | 2,500 × $78 | | | | 195,000 |
| Sales volume | | | 27,300 | | |
| Direct material | – | Price | | 24,900 | |
| | – | Usage | | | 21,000 |
| Direct labour | – | Rate | | | 18,800 |
| | – | Efficiency | | | 11,900 |
| | | | 52,200 | 51,700 | |
| | | | | | 500 |
| Actual contribution | | | | | 195,500 |

**Assumption:** No sales price variance.

**Workings**

**Conventional variances**

(i) **Materials**

Price = (Actual material purchased × standard price) − (Actual cost of material purchased)

= (12,450 × $20) − (12,450 × $18)

= $249,000 − $224,100

= $24,900 F

Usage = (Standard quantity for actual production × standard price) − (Actual material used at standard price)

= (2,850 × 4 × $20) − (12,450 × $20)

= $228,000 − $249,000

= $21,000 A

(ii) **Labour**

Rate = (Actual hours worked × standard direct labour rate) − (Actual hours worked × actual hourly rate)

= (18,800 × $7) − (18,800 × $8)

= $131,600 − $150,400

= $18,800 A

Efficiency = (Standard hours of actual production × standard rate) − (Actual hours worked × standard rate)

= (2,850 × 6 × $7) − (18,800 × $7)

= $119,700 − $131,600

= $11,900 A

(iii) **Sales volume contribution**

= (Budgeted sales units × standard contribution per unit) − (Actual sales units × standard contribution per unit)

= (2,500 × $78) − (2,850 × $78)

= $195,000 − $222,300

= $27,300 F

(b) Reconciliation statement using planning and operational variances

| | | $ |
|---|---|---|
| Budgeted contribution for actual sales: | 2,850 x $78 | 222,300.00 |

| Planning variances | | Favourable | Adverse |
|---|---|---|---|
| | | $ | $ |
| Material | – Price | 44,887.50 | |
| | – Usage | | 28,500 |
| Labour | – Rate: weather | 8,550.00 | |
| | – Rate: material | | 25,650 |
| | | 53,437.50 | 54,150 |
| | | | (712.50) |
| Revised budgeted contribution ($77.75 × 2,850) | | | 221,587.50 |

| Operational variances | | Favourable | Adverse |
|---|---|---|---|
| | | $ | $ |
| Material | – Price | | 18,675.00 |
| | – Usage | 6,187.50 | |
| Labour | – Rate | 0 | |
| | – Efficiency | | 13,600.00 |
| | | 6,187.50 | 32,275.00 |
| | | | 26,087.50 |
| Actual contribution | | | 195,500.00 |

**Workings**

**Planning variances**

(i) **Material**
= (Standard material cost) – (Revised standard material cost)
Price = (2,850 × (4 + 0.5) × $20) – (2,850 × (4 + 0.5) ×
$16.50)
= $256,500 – $211,612.50
= $44,887.50 F
Usage = (2,850 × 4 × $20) – (2,850 × 4.5 × $20)
= $228,000 – $256,500
= $28,500 A

(ii) **Labour rate**

(1) Weather bonus

= (2,850 × 6 × $7) – (2,850 × 6 × $6.50)
= $119,700 – $111,150
= $8,550 (F)

(2) Alternative material difficulties

= (2,850 × 6 × $6.50) – (2,850 × 6 × $8)
= $111,150 – $136,800
= $25,650 A

∴ Revised unit contribution is as follows.

|  | $ | $ |
|---|---|---|
| Selling price |  | 200.00 |
| Direct material: 4.5 × $16.50 | 74.25 |  |
| Direct labour: 6 × $8 | 48.00 |  |
|  |  | (122.25) |
| Contribution |  | 77.75 |

**Operational variances**

(i) **Material**

Price = (12,450 × $16.50) – (12,450 × $18)
= $205,425 – $224,100
= $18,675 A

Usage = (2,850 × 4.50 × $16.50) – (12,450 × $16.50)
= $211,612.5 – $205,425
= $6,187.5 F

(ii) **Labour**

Rate = 0

Efficiency = (2,850 × 6 × $8) – (18,800 × $8)
= $136,800 – $150,400
= $13,600 A

(c) The analysis of variances in part (b) makes it possible to separate those variances which are non-controllable (the planning variances) from the variances which are controllable by the individual managers (the operational variances).

In this case the change in type of material used was unavoidable. Similarly, the change in weather conditions could not have been anticipated. The cost implications of these changes are reflected in the planning variances. Management's attention should be focused primarily on the operational variances.

In particular, why did the firm pay $18 per kg for material when this was expected to cost $16.50?

The operational material usage variance indicates that less material was used than expected – this could be due to the workers spending longer working with the material (as evidenced by the adverse efficiency variance).

## Test your understanding 10

A performance reporting and management control system depends on both reliable planning and control over operating activities.

Some planning variances might be caused by factors that could not have been foreseen in advance. However, some planning variances might be caused by weaknesses in the planning process. If so, they can be significant and indicate the need for better planning procedures in the future.

## Test your understanding 11

Standard costing is most suited to organisations whose activities consist of a series of common or repetitive operations. Typically, mass production manufacturing operations are indicative of its area of application. It is also possible to envisage operations within the service sector to which standard costing may apply, though this may not be with the same degree of accuracy of standards which apply in manufacturing. For example, hotels and restaurants often use standard recipes for preparing food, so dealing with conference attendance can be like a mass production environment. Similarly, banks will have common processes for dealing with customer transactions, processing cheques, etc. It is possible therefore that the principles of standard costing may be extended to service industries.

In modern manufacturing and service businesses, continuous improvement and cost reduction are topical. In order to remain competitive it is essential that businesses address the cost levels of their various operations. To do this they have to deal with the costing of operations. But the drive to 'cost down' may mean in some cases that standards do not apply for long before a redesign or improvement renders them out of date. In such a setting an alternative to the use of standard costs is to compare actual costs with those of the previous operating period. We have seen above that a standard costing system has a variety of purposes. It is for management to judge their various reasons for employing standard costing and, consequently, whether their aims of continuous improvement and cost reduction render the system redundant.

## Test your understanding 12

A is the correct answer.

Greater participation by staff in standard setting is likely to slow down the process of agreeing values.

**Test your understanding 13**

In a rapidly-changing environment it may be necessary to:

- continually revise standards to reflect up-to-date prices and methods of working

- frequently introduce new products or customise existing products.

This will involve frequent changes to standards and may mean that it is:

- difficult to set meaningful standards for the measurement of performance

- too time consuming to encourage participation in the setting of standards.

It will be difficult to use standards effectively for planning and control and it may not be possible to use standards effectively to motivate staff.

# Performance measurement and control

## Chapter learning objectives

Upon completion of this chapter you will be able to:

- describe, calculate from given data, and interpret financial performance indicators (FPIs) for profitability, in both manufacturing and service businesses, and suggest methods for improving these measures

- describe, calculate from given data, and interpret FPIs for liquidity in both manufacturing and service businesses, and suggest methods for improving these measures

- describe, calculate from given data, and interpret FPIs for risk in both manufacturing and service businesses, and suggest methods for improving these measures

- describe, calculate from given data and interpret non-financial performance indicators (NFPIs) in both manufacturing and service businesses, and suggest methods for improving the performance indicated

- explain, using non-numerical examples, the causes of, and problems created by, short-termism and financial manipulation of results, and suggest methods to encourage a long-term view

- describe the main behavioural aspects of performance management

- explain the need to allow for external considerations in performance management, in general, with particular reference to:

  - stakeholders

  - market conditions

  - allowance for competitors

- describe ways in which external considerations could be allowed for in performance management, in general, and interpret performance in the light of external considerations

- using simple non-numerical examples, explain and interpret the balanced scorecard and its elements

- using simple non-numerical examples, explain and interpret the building block model proposed by Fitzgerald and Moon

- describe, using simple non-numerical examples, the difficulties of target setting in qualitative areas.

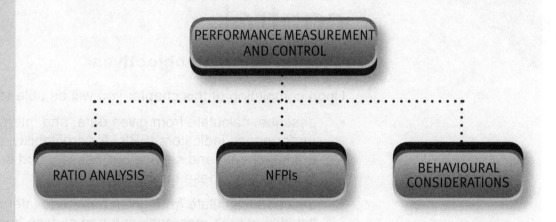

## 1    Ratio analysis

A key aspect of performance measurement is ratio analysis. Specific ratios are discussed below but some general considerations need to be taken into account with all ratio analysis:

- Many ratios use figures at a particular point in time and thus may not be representative of the position throughout a period. For example, seasonal trade or large one-off items may make year-end figures uncharacteristic.

- Ratios are of little use in isolation. Comparitors can include:

  - budgets, for control purposes

  - last year's figures to identify trends

  - competitors' results and/or industry averages to assess performance.

- Ratios can be manipulated by management. A well known example of 'window dressing' is to issue spurious invoices before the year end and then issue credit notes just after.

- As with variances, ratios indicate areas for further investigation, rather than giving a definitive answer for management.

## 1.1 Measuring profitability

The main ratio to measure profitability in an organisation is return on capital employed (ROCE), which can then be sub-analysed into

- Net profit margin – if ROCE indicates poor performance then the net margin would indicate if it is due to low margin or poor overhead control and further ratios can be calculated to investigate.

- Asset turnover – if this indicates poor performance then fixed asset utilisation and working capital management may be further examined.

$$ROCE = \frac{\text{Net profit}}{\text{Capital employed}} \times 100$$

Where capital employed = equity + long-term debt

ROCE = net profit margin × asset turnover

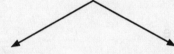

$$\text{Net profit margin} = \frac{\text{Net profit}}{\text{Turnover}} \times 100$$

Net profit margin can be investigated by finding:

$$\text{Gross profit margin} = \frac{\text{Gross profit}}{\text{Turnover}} \times 100$$

and

$$\text{Operating ratios} = \frac{\text{Various expenses}}{\text{Turnover}} \times 100$$

$$\text{Asset turnover} = \frac{\text{Turnover}}{\text{Capital employed}} \times 100$$

Asset turnover can be investigated by finding:

$$\frac{\text{Turnover}}{\text{Fixed assets}} \quad \text{and} \quad \frac{\text{Turnover}}{\text{Net current assets}}$$

## Illustration 1 – Performance measurement

Below are the financial statements for T for the years ended 30 June 20X5 and 20X6:

**Income statements**

|  | 20X5 $000 | 20X6 $000 |
| --- | --- | --- |
| Revenue | 150,000 | 180,000 |
| Cost of sales | (60,000) | (65,000) |
| Gross profit | 90,000 | 115,000 |
| Operating expenses | (28,500) | (39,900) |
| Profit from operations | 61,500 | 75,100 |
| Finance costs | (10,000) | (12,000) |
| Profit before tax | 51,500 | 63,100 |
| Tax | (13,600) | (17,300) |
| Net profit | 37,900 | 45,800 |

Dividends of $25m were paid to shareholders in each year.

**Balance sheets**

|  | 2005 | 2006 |
|---|---|---|
|  | $'000 | $'000 |
| Property, plant and equipment | 190,000 | 266,200 |
|  |  |  |
| Current assets |  |  |
| Inventory | 12,000 | 15,000 |
| Receivables | 37,500 | 49,300 |
| Bank | 500 | – |
|  | 240,000 | 330,500 |
|  |  |  |
| Share capital | 10,000 | 12,000 |
| Share premium | 4,000 | 5,000 |
| Revaluation reserve | – | 30,000 |
| Retained earnings | 78,900 | 99,700 |
|  | 92,900 | 146,700 |
| Non-current liabilities |  |  |
| Loan | 125,000 | 150,000 |
|  |  |  |
| Current liabilities |  |  |
| Trade payables | 10,600 | 11,700 |
| Overdraft | – | 9,100 |
| Taxation | 11,500 | 13,000 |
|  | 240,000 | 330,500 |

## PROFITABILITY

**Required:**

(a) For each of the two years, calculate the following ratios for T:

|  |  | 2005 | 2006 |
|---|---|---|---|
| Gross profit margin | $\dfrac{\text{Gross profit}}{\text{Revenue}}$ |  |  |
| Operating profit margin | $\dfrac{\text{Operating profit}}{\text{Revenue}}$ |  |  |
| Net profit margin | $\dfrac{\text{Net profit}}{\text{Revenue}}$ |  |  |
| ROCE | $\dfrac{\text{Operating profit}}{\text{Capital employed}}$ |  |  |
| Asset utilisation | $\dfrac{\text{Revenue}}{\text{Capital employed}}$ |  |  |

(b) Suggest reasons why T's ratios have changed.

**Solution**

**(a)**

| | | 2005 | 2006 |
|---|---|---|---|
| Gross profit margin | $\dfrac{\text{Gross profit}}{\text{Revenue}}$ | 90/150 = 60% | 115/180 = 63.9% |
| Operating profit margin | $\dfrac{\text{Operating profit}}{\text{Revenue}}$ | 61.5/150 = 41% | 75.1/180 = 41.7% |
| Net profit margin | $\dfrac{\text{Net profit}}{\text{Revenue}}$ | 37.9/150 = 25.3% | 45.8/150 = 25.4% |
| ROCE | $\dfrac{\text{Operating profit}}{\text{Capital employed}}$ | 61.5/(92.9+125) = 28.2% | 75.1/(146.7+150) = 25.3% |
| Asset utilisation | $\dfrac{\text{Revenue}}{\text{Capital employed}}$ | 150/(92.9+125) = 0.69 times | 180/(146.7+150) = 0.61 times |

**(b)** Possible reasons why T's ratios have changed:

Gross profit margin increased:

- increase in sales due to increasing volume sold and so economies of scale result in lower costs per unit sold

- increase in sales price per unit

- changes in product mix.

Operating profit margin unchanged:

- increase in expenses such as advertising to boost revenue

- increased depreciation charges following acquisitions of net current assets (NCAs)

- poor control of costs since revenue increased by 20% but operating expenses increased by 40%.

Net profit margin unchanged:

- Increase in finance costs in line with increase in revenue. Increased borrowing to fund expansion has resulted in increased finance costs.

ROCE and asset utilisation have fallen:

- no change in operating profit margin and so fall is due to fall in asset utilisation

- revaluation of NCAs will reduce asset utilisation (and ROCE) but not a 'real' deterioration in efficiency

- significant increase in NCAs during year. If acquired near year end, will not have generated returns as yet.

### Test your understanding 1

Companies X and Y are both involved in retailing.

Relevant information for the year ended 30 September 20X5 was as follows:

|  | X | Y |
|---|---|---|
|  | $000 | $000 |
| Sales revenue | 50,000 | 200,000 |
| Profit before tax | 10,000 | 10,000 |
| Capital employed | 50,000 | 50,000 |

**Prepare the following ratios for both companies and comment on the results:**

**(a) ROCE**

**(b) profit margin**

**(c) asset turnover.**

## 1.3 Measuring liquidity

Working capital management is a major part of the F9 syllabus and you can thus expect it to feature only briefly within F5 questions. However, the F5 syllabus does not specify which ratios are required so the 'full package' of liquidity ratios are given below for completeness. Liquidity is the ability of an organisation to pay its debts when they fall due. There are two main measures of liquidity:

- the current ratio

- the quick (or acid test) ratio

which can be sub-analysed into their working capital components.

$$\text{Current ratio} = \frac{\text{Current assets (CAs)}}{\text{Current liabilities}}$$

$$\text{Quick ratio (acid test ratio)} = \frac{\text{Quick assets (CAs} - \text{Stock)}}{\text{Current liabilities}}$$

$$\text{Holding period of raw materials} = \frac{\text{Average value of raw materials}}{\text{Purchases}} \times 365$$

$$\text{Work-in-progress (WIP) period} = \frac{\text{Average value of WIP}}{\text{Cost of sales}} \times 365$$

$$\text{Finished goods period} = \frac{\text{Average value of finished goods}}{\text{Cost of sales}} \times 365$$

$$\text{Debtor (receivables) period} = \frac{\text{Average debtors (receivables)}}{\text{Sales}} \times 365$$

$$\text{Creditor (payables) period} = \frac{\text{Average creditors (payables)}}{\text{Purchases}} \times 365$$

- These ratios could be found using year-end figures or average figures.
- In some divisionalised companies some of these liquidity ratios are less important since the assets are managed centrally.
- Comparison would be made with group standards, other divisions, other periods and other firms in the same business.

## Illustration 2 – Performance measurement

(a) For each of the two years, calculate the following ratios for T:

|  |  | 2005 | 2006 |
|---|---|---|---|
| Current ratio | $\dfrac{\text{CAs}}{\text{Current liabilities}}$ |  |  |
| Quick ratio | $\dfrac{\text{(CAs – Inventory)}}{\text{Current liabilities}}$ |  |  |
| Inventory holding period | $\dfrac{\text{Inventory}}{\text{Cost of sales}} \times 365$ |  |  |
| Receivables collection period | $\dfrac{\text{Receivables}}{\text{Revenue}} \times 365$ |  |  |
| Payables payment period | $\dfrac{\text{Trade payables}}{\text{Cost of sales}} \times 365$ |  |  |

(b) Suggest reasons why T's ratios have changed:

**Liquidity**

|  |  | 2005 | 2006 |
|---|---|---|---|
| Current ratio | $\dfrac{\text{CAs}}{\text{Current liabilities}}$ | 50,000/22,100 = 2.3:1 | 64,300/33,800 = 1.9:1 |
| Quick ratio | $\dfrac{\text{(CAs – Inventory)}}{\text{Current liabilities}}$ | 38,000/22,100 = 1.7:1 | 49,300/33,800 = 1.5:1 |
| Inventory holding period | $\dfrac{\text{Inventory}}{\text{Cost of sales}} \times 365$ | 12,000/60,000 x 365 = 73 days | 15,000/65,000 x 365 = 84 days |
| Receivables collection period | $\dfrac{\text{Receivables}}{\text{Revenue}} \times 365$ | 37,500/150,000 x 365 =91 days | 49,300/180,000 x 365 = 100 |
| Payables payment period | $\dfrac{\text{Trade payables}}{\text{Cost of sales}} \times 365$ | 10,600/60,000 x 365 = 65 days | 111,700/65,000 x 365 = 68 days |

Possible reasons why T's ratios have changed:

Inventory holding period increased:

- build-up of inventory levels as a result of increased capacity following expansion of non-current assets

- increasing inventory levels in response to increased demand for product.

Receivables collection period increased:

- deliberate policy to attract customers

- poor credit control procedures.

Payables payment period largely unchanged.

Overall liquidity situation deteriorated:

- Current and quick ratios have both fallen but not yet at levels that give cause for concern. However, T is showing signs of liquidity issues with significant overdraft at year end. This is partially due to increasing inventory-holding and receivables-collection periods but suppliers being paid more or less as quickly as last year. It appears that the increase in non-current assets has also been partially funded via the overdraft.

### Test your understanding 2

**Calculate the liquidity and working capital ratios for P for the year ended 31 December 20X7.**

|  | $m |
|---|---|
| Sales revenue | 1,867.5 |
| Gross profit | 489.3 |
| Inventory | 147.9 |
| Trade receivables | 393.4 |
| Trade payables | 275.1 |
| Cash | 53.8 |
| Short-term investments | 6.2 |
| Other current liabilities | 284.3 |

## 1.4  Measuring risk

There are many different measures of risk that you will meet in your studies. Conventional ratio analysis looks mainly at financial gearing – if the firm has excessive debt then the need to pay interest before dividends will increase the risks faced by shareholders if profits fall. Typical ratios include the following:

Financial gearing $= \dfrac{\text{Debt}}{\text{Equity}} \times 100\%$

Financial gearing $= \dfrac{\text{Debt}}{\text{Debt + Equity}} \times 100\%$

Interest cover $= \dfrac{\text{Profit before interest and tax (PBIT)}}{\text{Interest charges}}$

Dividend cover $= \dfrac{\text{Net profit}}{\text{Dividends}}$

A further measure of risk is operating gearing. This looks at whether operating costs are fixed or variable and indicates how changes in contribution will affect profit. There are two measures commonly used.

Operating gearing $= \dfrac{\text{Fixed costs}}{\text{Variable costs}}$

Operating gearing or leverage $= \dfrac{\text{Contribution}}{\text{PBIT}}$

---

**Illustration 3 – Performance measurement**

(a) For each of the two years, calculate the following ratios for T:

|  |  | 2005 | 2006 |
|---|---|---|---|
| Gearing | $\dfrac{\text{Debt}}{\text{Debt + Equity*}}$ |  |  |
| Gearing (alternative) | $\dfrac{\text{Debt}}{\text{Equity}}$ |  |  |
| Interest cover | $\dfrac{\text{PBIT}}{\text{Finance costs}}$ |  |  |
| Dividend cover | $\dfrac{\text{Net profit}}{\text{Dividends}}$ |  |  |

*(Debt + Equity) = (Long-term loans + Equity) = (Capital employed)

(b) Suggest reasons why T's ratios have changed:

|  |  | 2005 | 2006 |
|---|---|---|---|
| Gearing | $\dfrac{\text{Debt}}{\text{Debt + Equity*}}$ | 125/(125+92.9) = 57.4% | 150/(150+146.7) =50.5% |

---

| Gearing (alternative) | $\dfrac{\text{Debt}}{\text{Equity}}$ | 125/92.9 = 134.6% | 150/146.7 = 102.2% |
|---|---|---|---|
| Interest cover | $\dfrac{\text{PBIT}}{\text{Finance costs}}$ | 61.5/10 = 6.15 times | 75.1/12 = 6.26 times |
| Dividend cover | $\dfrac{\text{Net profit}}{\text{Dividends}}$ | 37.9/25 = 1.5 times | 45.8/25 = 1.8 times |

Gearing fallen:

- primarily due to revaluation of NCAs. Without revaluation, gearing in line with previous year

- increase in loan, but also an increase in equity financing

- additional finance used to increase NCAs and on other measures to expand company, e.g. increased advertising expenditure

- gearing ratio appears quite high, but interest cover also high and so not an immediate cause for concern.

Dividend cover is adequate.

As well as measuring risk, you may be asked to comment how identified risks might affect performance measures.

### Test your understanding 3

**An internet retailer is concerned about the risk of hackers disabling their website. Comment on how this could affect gross margins and ROCE.**

### Test your understanding 4

You are employed in the small business section of a medium-sized bank. Some time ago the bank provided a local manufacturing company, F, with an overdraft facility of $3,000,000. This limit was reached on 30 September 20X4 but was increased then to $5,000,000.

Your section head has just received the half-yearly financial statements of F for the period to 30 September 20X5. Having read these statements, your section head is extremely concerned as to the performance of the company over the last year and is considering recommending the termination of the overdraft facility. Before making any further decision, your section head wishes to have a second opinion. Accordingly, he leaves a file of information concerning F on your desk and requires a report recommending the best course of action.

Information contained in the file:

**Item 1:** Income statements:

|  | Six months to 30 September 20X5 | Six months to 31 March 20X5 |
|---|---|---|
|  | $000 | $000 |
| Sales | 10,000 | 11,000 |
| Cost of sales | (5,000) | (5,500) |
| Gross profit | 5,000 | 5,500 |
| Other operating expenses | (5,000) | (4,500) |
| Operating profit | – | 1,000 |
| Interest payable | (1,000) | (900) |
| Profit/(loss) before tax | (1,000) | 100 |
| Tax estimate | – | – |
| Profit/(loss) after tax | (1,000) | 100 |

**Item 2:** Balance sheets at 30 September

|  | 20X5 | | 20X4 | |
|---|---|---|---|---|
|  | $000 | $000 | $000 | $000 |
| Non-current assets: |  |  |  |  |
| property | 5,000 |  | 5,200 |  |
| plant | 3,500 |  | 3,000 |  |
|  |  | 8,500 |  | 8,200 |
| Current assets: |  |  |  |  |
| inventories | 3,000 |  | 2,600 |  |
| receivables | 5,000 |  | 4,600 |  |
| cash in hand | 80 |  | 80 |  |
|  | 8,080 |  | 7,280 |  |
| Current liabilities: |  |  |  |  |
| trade payables | 2,600 |  | 2,600 |  |
| bank overdraft | 5,000 |  | 3,000 |  |
|  | 7,600 |  | 5,600 |  |
| NCAs |  | 480 |  | 1,680 |
| 12% loan notes (secured against the property) |  | (4,800) |  | (4,800) |
|  |  | 4,180 |  | 5,080 |
| Share capital ($1 shares) |  | 4,000 |  | 4,000 |
| Retained earnings |  | 180 |  | 1,080 |
|  |  | 4,180 |  | 5,080 |

**Item 3:** Estimated realisable values of the assets of F at 30 September 20X5, based on a 'forced sale' scenario:

|  | $000 |
|---|---|
| Property | 5,000 |
| Plant | 1,000 |
| Inventories | 800 |
| Receivables | 2,500 |
|  | 9,300 |

(a) **Using the items contained in the file, write a report to your section head which contains an appraisal of the performance and financial position of F and considers the implications for the bank of calling in the overdraft.**

(b) **Produce a short appendix to the report you have compiled in (a). This should summarise the limitations of the information available to you as a basis for making a recommendation as to the wisdom or otherwise of calling in the overdraft.**

# 2 Non-financial performance indicators (NFPIs)

## 2.1 Critical success factors and key performance indicators

- A firm's success usually involves focussing on a small number of critical areas where they must win. These critical success factors (CSFs) vary from business to business but could include, e.g.

    - Having a wide range of products that people want.

    - Brand name.

    - Low prices.

    - Quick delivery.

    - Customer satisfaction.

- Most of these are best assessed using non-financial performance indicators. Financial performance appraisal often reveals the ultimate effect of operational factors and decisions but non-financial indicators are needed to monitor causes.

- CSFs need to be translated into key performance indicators (KPIs). These are what we can measure and set targets on – in order to achieve the CSFs identified. For example, customer satisfaction could be measured using the following:

    - Customer repurchase rate.

    - % cancellation rate within 7 days.

    - % of sales returns due to problems.

- Again, many KPIs are non-financial.

## Test your understanding 5

**An internet retailer has identified having an effective website as one of its CSFs. Suggest some corresponding KPIs.**

## Illustration 4 – Performance measurement

BAA (the former state-owned British Airports Authority) uses regular customer surveys for measuring customer perceptions of a wide variety of service quality attributes, including, the cleanliness of its facilities, the helpfulness of its staff and the ease of finding one's way around the airport. Public correspondence is also analysed in detail, and comment cards are available in the terminals so that passengers can comment voluntarily on service levels received. Duty terminal managers also sample the services and goods offered by outlets in the terminals, assessing them from a customer perspective.

They check the cleanliness and condition of service facilities and complete detailed checklists, which are submitted daily to senior terminal managers. The company has also a wealth of internal monitoring systems that record equipment faults and failures, and report equipment and staff availability. These systems are supported by the terminal managers who circulate the terminals on a full-time basis, helping customers as necessary, reporting any equipment faults observed and making routine assessments of the level of service provided by BAA and its concessionaires.

Examples of service quality measures and mechanisms at BAA plc are shown below:

| Quality | Measures | Mechanisms |
|---|---|---|
| Access | walking distance/ease of finding way around | surveys/ operational data |
| Aesthetics | staff appearance/airport appearance/quality of catering | surveys/inspection |
| Availability | equipment availability | internal fault monitors |
| Cleanliness | environment and equipment | surveys/inspection |
| Comfort | crowdedness | surveys/inspection |
| Communication | information clarity/clarity of labelling and pricing | surveys/inspection |
| Competence | staff efficiency | management inspection |
| Courtesy | courtesy of staff | surveys/inspection |
| Friendliness | staff attitude | surveys/inspection |

| Reliability | equipment faults | surveys/inspection |
|---|---|---|
| Responsiveness | staff responsiveness | surveys/inspection |
| Security | efficiency of security checks/ number of urgent safety reports | surveys/internal data |

## 2.2 The balanced scorecard

**Kaplan and Norton** developed an approach to performance measurement with the idea that the business develops a comprehensive framework for translating a company's strategic objectives into a coherent set of goals and performance measures. The goals and measures should be clear and limited in number.

A balanced scorecard for a company would be constructed by considering four perspectives:

Financial — how do we create value for our shareholders?

Customer — what is it about us that customers value?

Internal — what processes must we excel at to achieve our financial and customer objectives?

Innovation and learning — how can we continue to improve and create future value?

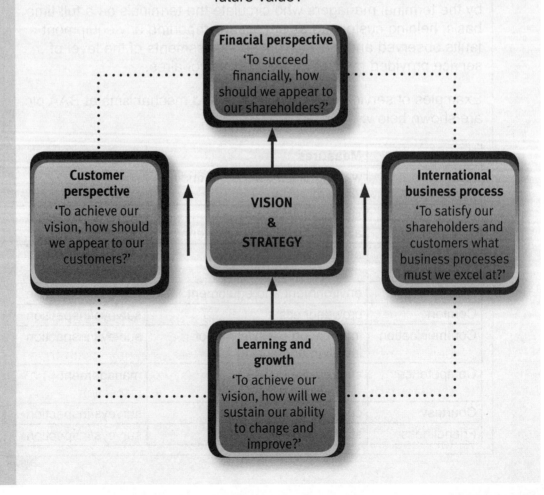

Within each of these categories a company should seek to identify a series of **critical success factors** and **key performance indicators**.

Illustration 5 – Approaches to performance measurement

Some general examples of CSFs/KPIs within a balanced scorecard framework

| Perspective | CSF | KPI |
|---|---|---|
| Financial | Cost reduction | Benchmark costs versus competitors |
| | Asset utilisation | ROI |
| | Growth | Percentage of income from new customers |
| | Risk management | Sales order book |
| Customer | Price | Benchmark prices versus competitors |
| | Quality | Defect rate |
| | Time | Delivery lead times |
| Internal | Operational process | Cycle time |
| | After-sales process | Rectification time |
| | Employees | Staff turnover |
| Innovation and learning | Internal learning | Suggestions implemented |
| | Innovation | Percentage of income from new products |

**Note:** the ultimate measure of corporate performance (for quoted companies) is the share price.

Illustration 6 – Approaches to performance measurement

One example reported in management literature of how the balanced scorecard might be applied is the US case of Analog Devices (a semi conductor manufacturer) in the preparation of its five-year strategic plan for 1988-1992.

Analog Devices had as its main corporate objective:

'Achieving our goals for growth, profits, market share and quality creates the environment and economic means to satisfy the needs of our employees, stockholders, customers and others associated with the firm. Our success depends on people who understand the interdependence and congruence of their personal goals with those of the company and who are thus motivated to contribute towards the achievement of those goals.'

Three basic strategic objectives identified by the company were market leadership, sales growth and profitability.

The company adopted targets as follows:

Customer perspective

- Percentage of orders delivered on time. A target was set for the five-year period to increase the percentage of on-time deliveries from 85% to at least 99.8%.

- Outgoing defect levels. The target was to reduce the number of defects in product items delivered to customers from 500, to fewer than 10, per month.

- Order lead time. A target was set to reduce the time between receiving a customer order to delivery from 10, to less than 3, weeks.

Internal perspective

- Manufacturing cycle time. To reduce this from 15 weeks to 4-5 weeks over the five-year planning period.

- Defective items in production. To reduce defects in production from 5,000, to fewer than 10, per month.

Learning and innovation perspective

- Having products rated 'number one' by at least 50% of customers, based on their attitudes to whether the company was making the right products, performance, price, reliability, quality, delivery, lead time, customer support, responsiveness, willingness to co-operate and willingness to form partnerships.

- The number of new products introduced to the market.

- Sales revenue from new products.

- The new product sales ratio. This was the percentage of total sales achieved by products introduced to the market within the previous six quarters.

- Average annual revenues for new products in their third year.

- Reducing the average time to bring new product ideas to the market.

Financial targets were set for revenue, revenue growth, profit and return on assets. But the idea was that the financial targets would flow from achieving the other targets stated above.

Analog Devices sought to adopt financial and non-financial performance measures within a single system, in which the various targets were consistent with each other and were in no way incompatible.

## Benefits of the balanced scorecard:

- It provides external as well as internal information.
- It focuses on factors, including non-financial ones, which will enable a company to succeed.

## Problems with the balanced scorecard:

- Selection of measures.
- Obtaining information.
- Information overload.
- Conflict between measures.

### Test your understanding 6

**A company has identified the following CSFs. Suggest suitable KPIs for each factor.**

**Customer perspective**

| CSFs | KPIs |
| --- | --- |
| new products | |
| responsive service | |
| preferred supplier | |
| partnership ventures | |

**Internal perspective**

| CSFs | KPIs |
| --- | --- |
| manufacturing excellence | |
| design productivity | |
| new product development | |

**Learning and growth perspective**

| CSFs | KPIs |
| --- | --- |
| time to market | |
| product focus | |
| manufacturing learning | |
| technology leadership | |

**Financial perspective**

| CSFs | KPIs |
| --- | --- |
| survival | |
| success | |
| prosperity | |

## 2.3 The building block model

**Fitzgerald et al** adopted a framework for the design and analysis of performance management systems. They based their analysis on three building blocks:

- Dimensions – sources of CSFs.

- Standards – KPIs.

- Rewards – the incentives given to managers who achieve standards.

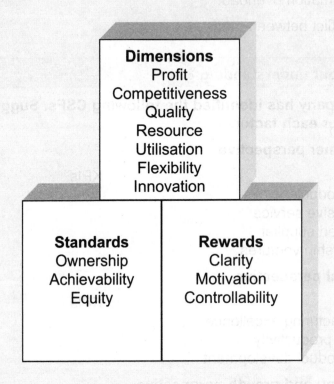

**Dimensions**
Profit
Competitiveness
Quality
Resource
Utilisation
Flexibility
Innovation

**Standards**
Ownership
Achievability
Equity

**Rewards**
Clarity
Motivation
Controllability

### Dimensions

Dimensions are critical success factors for the business and suitable measures must be developed to measure each performance dimension.

| Performance Dimension | Measures |
|---|---|
| Competitive performance. | Market share.<br>Sales growth.<br>Customer base. |
| Financial performance. | Profitability.<br>Liquidity.<br>Capital structure.<br>Market ratios. |

| Quality of service. | Reliability.<br>Responsiveness.<br>Aesthetics.<br>Tidiness.<br>Communication.<br>Competence. |
|---|---|
| Flexibility. | Volume flexibility.<br>Delivery speed.<br>Specification of service. |
| Resource utilisation. | Productivity.<br>Efficiency. |
| Innovation. | Ability to innovate.<br>Performance of the innovations. |

### Standards

To ensure success it is vital that employees view standards as achievable, fair and take ownership of them.

### Rewards

To ensure that employees are motivated to meet standards, targets need to be clear and linked to controllable factors.

### Test your understanding 7

Explain why it is important to:

(i) consider ownership, achievability and equity when setting standards.

(ii) consider clarity, motivation and controllability when setting rewards.

### Test your understanding 8

Using the six dimensions of Fitzgerald suggest some KPIs for a national car dealership network.

## 3 Behavioural and external considerations

### 3.1 The problem of short-termism

Performance measures are used to monitor the progress of divisions and business units and may also be used to measure the performance of managers. Achievement of target FPIs may be linked to a reward system in order to motivate managers to improve performance. To be useful reward systems must:

- link reward to effort

- give regular feedback.

This usually means that reward systems are based on the achievement of short-term, measurable targets agreed with the manager.

However, targets must be selected and interpreted carefully as they can lead to:

- short-termism

- manipulation of financial results.

### Illustration 7 – Behavioural and external considerations

A company may measure the performance of managers on the basis of a target ROCE. This may lead to the following undesirable behaviour:

- Managers may focus on generating short-term profit at the expense of long-term profit. For example, managers may reduce expenditure on training, research and development and maintenance.

- The ROCE will improve if the capital employed figure falls. Managers may therefore be reluctant to invest in new assets.

- Year-end results may be manipulated to improve ROCE. For example, managers may delay payments to creditors or stock purchases.

- Managers may focus their attention on financial performance and neglect non financial performance such as quality and customer service. This may improve profit in the short-term but lead to a long-term decline in profitability.

### Test your understanding 9

**Suggest methods of overcoming the problems of short-termism and manipulation of results and encouraging a long-term view.**

## 3.2 Behavioural issues

The purpose of performance measurement is to control and motivate the organisation to improve performance. Care must be taken when designing a performance measurement system to avoid dysfunctional behaviour and demotivation.

Measures designed to assess the performance of a division or its manager should:

- provide incentives to promote performance as a division with overall company objectives – goal congruence

- only incorporate factors for which the manager (division) can be held responsible (accountable) – motivation

- recognise both financial and non-financial aspects of performance

- recognise longer-term, as well as short-term, objectives.

Potential problems with inappropriate measures:

- manipulation of information provided by managers

- demotivation and stress-related conflict between a manager, his subordinates and his superiors

- excessive concern for control of short-term costs, possibly at the expense of longer-term profitability.

### Illustration 8 – Behavioural and external considerations

A conference centre has a newly-appointed (unqualified) management accountant who has sent the following report to the supervisor of the restaurant. Prior to the receipt of this report the restaurant supervisor has been congratulating herself on a good start to the year, with a substantial increase in the use of the restaurant.

| | |
|---|---|
| **To:** | Restaurant supervisor |
| **From:** | Management accountant |
| **Subject:** | Performance report |
| **Date:** | 5 April |

As part of the campaign to improve efficiency within the conference centre, quarterly budgets have been prepared for each department.

I attach a performance report for your department for the three months to the end of March, showing all discrepancies between budgeted and actual expenditure. ('A' indicates an adverse variance and 'F' a favourable variance.)

| | Budget $ | Actual $ | Discrepancy $ | |
|---|---|---|---|---|
| Food and other consumables | 97,500 | 111,540 | 14,040 | A |
| Labour – hourly paid | 15,000 | 16,500 | 1,500 | A |
| – supervisor | 3,750 | 3,700 | 50 | F |
| Power | 8,500 | 9,250 | 750 | A |
| Breakages | 1,000 | 800 | 200 | F |
| Allocated overheads | 21,000 | 24,000 | 3,000 | A |
| | 146,750 | 165,790 | 19,040 | A |
| No. of meals served | 32,500 | 39,000 | 6,500 | F |

You have apparently incurred costs, which exceed the budget by $19,040.

Please explain this to me at the meeting of the management committee on 15 April.

**Required:**

Discuss the various possible effects on the restaurant supervisor's behaviour caused by receipt of this report.

**Solution**

The possible effects have been considered under the various factors affecting motivation.

• The way in which the targets were communicated to and understood by the supervisor.

• If a target is to have any influence on performance the recipient must be aware of its existence and feel committed to achieving it. From the wording of the memo, it would seem likely that until she received the performance report the restaurant supervisor was unaware of the budget.

Furthermore, the reaction of the supervisor to the memo comparing the department's performance to a previously-unheard-of budget is likely to be defensive and rebellious. With no knowledge as to how the budget was calculated, the supervisor is very likely to devote time and energy to attacking the 'unfair budget'. How can management hope to obtain commitment by issuing budgets 'from on high', with no scope for consultation or explanation with those responsible for fulfilling the budget?

• Does the supervisor feel able to achieve the target?

Is she being held responsible for costs that she is unable to control?

Has the budget been properly prepared?

If a target is to act as a motivator the recipients must feel that they are able to reach the target by their own efforts. Clearly the supervisor is not in a position to influence the level of allocated overheads, which is presumably determined by the amount paid for such things as rent, rates and administrative salaries, and the chosen method of allocation to the departments. Thus the inclusion of such costs in the performance report will demotivate the supervisor.

She can hardly be held responsible for the fact that her own salary differs from the budget. Indeed becoming aware that she has been paid less than anticipated is likely to alienate her from the senior management.

Finally, the variances have been calculated by comparing the original budget with actual costs. The original budget is based on an anticipated usage of the restaurant of 32,500 meals. In fact, 39,000 meals have been served. If the explanation of variances is to be meaningful it should have been based on a comparison of actual costs with flexed budget. (This has been done in the suggested redraft of the performance report.)

- Is the supervisor being offered rewards for achieving the target?

The memo with the report is very brief, concentrating on the fact that costs have been above budget, with no mention of the fact that the restaurant has served more meals than was anticipated.

There is no indication that the supervisor is to be rewarded in any way for her efforts to increase the use of the restaurant, and the summons to explain the 'excessive' costs at a formal meeting seems almost threatening. This is likely to demotivate the supervisor. She will feel that the successful aspects of the restaurant's operation are being ignored while the less successful are being unfairly highlighted.

- Is the target of the right degree of difficulty?

As discussed above, the target costs communicated to the supervisor in the performance report are unrealistic because they have been left at the level of the original budget and have not been flexed to take account of the greater use made of the restaurant. Unrealistic budgets are bound to demotivate. Indeed, rather than working to reach the target, management is likely to expend time and effort criticising the target as unfair.

- Is the supervisor the sort of person who reacts well to targets?

As a final consideration it is important to remember that even the most perfect responsibility accounting system will fail if the managers of the responsibility centres are the sort of people who find any target frightening and thus demotivating. Although there are such people, evidence supports the view that most managers are motivated by well-designed, clearly understood targets.

**Test your understanding 10**

**Redraft the performance report given in the above illustration and memorandum in a way which, in your opinion, would make them more effective management tools.**

### 3.3 External considerations

Performance measures provide useful information to management which aid in the control of the business. They need to be considered in the context of the environment external to the business to gain a full understanding of how the business has performed and to develop actions which should be taken to improve performance. External considerations which are particularly important are:

- stakeholders
- market conditions
- competitors.

**Stakeholders**

Stakeholders include:

- shareholders
- employees
- loan providers
- government
- community
- customers
- environment.

Stakeholders will have different objectives and companies may deal with this by having a range of performance measures. Performance required by different stakeholders may conflict, and therefore the company may adopt an approach of satisfactory performance in each area rather than optimising profit at the expense of other objectives.

**Give examples of measures/factors that specific stakeholders, e.g. shareholders, employees, management, community, customers and government, will use to assess the success of the company and give three examples of how these may conflict.**

**Test your understanding 12**

Selected bi-annual data from NW's accounts are provided below relating to its first six years of operation as a private sector concern. Also shown, for comparison, is the proforma data as included in the privatisation documents. The proforma accounts are notional accounts prepared to show the operating and financial performance of the company in its last year under public ownership as if it had applied private sector accounting conventions. They also incorporate a dividend payment based on the dividend policy declared in the prospectus.

The activities of privatised utilities are scrutinised by a regulatory body, which restricts the extent to which prices can be increased. The demand for water in the area served by NW has risen over time at a steady 2% pa , largely reflecting demographic trends.

**Key financial and operating data for year ending 31 December ($m)**

|  | 20X1 (proforma) | 20X3 (actual) | 20X5 (actual) | 20X7 (actual) |
|---|---|---|---|---|
| Turnover | 450 | 480 | 540 | 620 |
| Operating profit | 26 | 35 | 55 | 75 |
| Taxation | 5 | 6 | 8 | 10 |
| Profit after tax | 21 | 29 | 47 | 65 |
| Dividends | 7 | 10 | 15 | 20 |
| Total assets | 100 | 119 | 151 | 191 |
|  |  |  |  |  |
| Capital expenditure | 20 | 30 | 60 | 75 |
| Wage bill | 100 | 98 | 90 | 86 |
| Directors' emoluments | 0.8 | 2.0 | 2.3 | 3.0 |
| Employees (number) | 12,000 | 11,800 | 10,500 | 10,000 |
| P/E ratio (average) | – | 7.0 | 8.0 | 7.5 |
| Retail price index (RPI) | 100 | 102 | 105 | 109 |

**Using the data provided, assess the extent to which NW has met the interests of the following groups of stakeholders in its first six years as a privatised enterprise. If relevant, suggest what other data would be helpful in forming a more balanced view.**

(i) **Shareholders**

(ii) **Consumers**

(iii) **Workforce**

(iv) **Government, through NW's contribution to the achievement of macroeconomic policies of price stability and economic growth.**

## Chapter summary

**PERFORMANCE MEASUREMENT AND CONTROL**

**RATIO ANALYSIS**

**NFPIs**

**BEHAVIOURAL AND EXTERNAL CONSIDERATIONS**

- Profitability – ROCE, asset turnover, gross/ net profit margin
- Liquidity – current and acid test ratios
- Risk – operational and financial gearing, dividend and interest cover.

- Balanced scorecard
  - customer
  - internal
  - learning and growth
  - financial
- Building block
  - dimensions
  - standards
  - rewards.

- Short-termism
- Manipulation of results
- Participation in target setting
- Achievability of targets
- Stakeholders
- Market conditions and competitors.

## Test your understanding answers

### Test your understanding 1

| | X | Y |
|---|---|---|
| ROCE | $\dfrac{10{,}000}{50{,}000} \times 100\%$ | $\dfrac{10{,}000}{50{,}000} \times 100\%$ |
| | = 20% | = 20% |
| Profit margin | $\dfrac{10{,}000}{50{,}000} \times 100\%$ | $\dfrac{10{,}000}{200{,}000} \times 100\%$ |
| | = 20% | = 5% |
| Asset turnover | $\dfrac{10{,}000}{50{,}000}$ | $\dfrac{200{,}000}{50{,}000}$ |
| | = 1 | = 4 |

The ROCE for both companies is the same. X has a higher profit margin, whilst Y shows a more efficient use of assets. This indicates that there may be a trade-off between profit margin and asset turnover.

### Test your understanding 2

| | | |
|---|---|---|
| Current ratio | $\dfrac{147.9 + 393.4 + 53.8 + 6.2}{275.1 + 284.3}$ | $= \dfrac{601.3}{559.4}$ |
| | | = 1.07 |
| Quick ratio | $\dfrac{601.3 - 147.9}{559.4}$ | = 0.81 |
| Receivables payment period | $\dfrac{393.4}{1{,}867.5} \times 365$ | = 77 days |
| Inventory turnover period | $\dfrac{147.9}{1{,}867.5 - 489.3} \times 365$ | = 39 days |
| Payables payment period | $\dfrac{275.1}{1{,}867.5 - 489.3} \times 365$ | = 73 days |

## Test your understanding 3

The main problem with website downtime will be lost sales. This could affect margins and ROCE as follows:

**Gross margin**

You could argue that gross margins will be unaffected as the largest element of cost of sales for an internet retailer will be the purchase price of the goods. A lost sale will also result in avoided purchase costs.

**Note:** the presence of fixed costs within cost of sales will see margins increase if volume falls.

**ROCE**

Lost sales will inevitably result in lower profit yet leave capital employed unchanged. Thus ROCE would fall as a result of website downtime.

## Test your understanding 4

### REPORT

**To:**       Section head
**From:**     Bank accountant
**Subject:**  F
**Date:**     22 November 20X5

(a)  The performance of F appears to have deteriorated in the six months to 30 September 20X5. Sales and cost of sales have both fallen by 9%, so that the gross profit percentage of 50% has been maintained. However, operating expenses have increased, so that total operating costs equal operating income. There is no longer any cover for interest payments. The interest charge has also increased, following the increase in the overdraft facility.

Despite this deterioration in performance, non-current assets and working capital have increased. The additional $2 million provided by the bank (an increase in overdraft of 66%) appears to have been used to finance the purchase of plant at a cost of approximately $500,000 (the figure represents the change shown by the balance sheet and is net of depreciation). The additional depreciation has probably contributed to the increase in operating expenses.

The retained loss for the year is $900,000 but the actual cash outflow from operating activities is much greater than this. A rough calculation is given below:

|  | $000 |
|---|---|
| Loss | 900 |
| Less depreciation (buildings only) | (200) |
| Increase in inventories | 400 |
| Increase in receivables | 400 |
|  | 1,500 |

The company's financial position has deteriorated during the year. At 30 September 20X5 it had a current ratio of 1.06 :1 and a quick ratio of 0.67:1 (compared with 1.3:1 and 0.83:1 at 30 September 20X4). The company is likely to experience severe liquidity problems in the near future.

The company's gearing also gives cause for concern. The company is very dependent upon finance from outside the business. The most recent balance sheet shows a debt to equity ratio of 2.97:1 and gearing of 53%. Interest on the loan notes amounts to $576,000 annually. At current activity levels, this means that there is very little profit available for distribution or investment and very little interest cover. The loan notes are barely covered by the property on which they are secured.

The combination of adverse cash flow, increase in non-current assets and working capital and fall in profits seems to suggest bad management. However, it is impossible to reach a firm conclusion without further information.

The withdrawal of the overdraft facility would result in the liquidation of the company. It is estimated that the assets would realise $9,300,000. The loan note holders would be repaid their $4,800,000 in full, leaving a balance of $4,500,000 for the other creditors. This does not cover the $7,600,000 owed to the bank and the other creditors. Assuming that all unsecured creditors would rank equally, the bank would receive 59c in the dollar or $2,950,000. The bank would make a loss of $2,050,000.

These calculations show that the bank is facing considerable risk. If the overdraft facility is to be continued, the bank should consider renegotiating the terms in order to take account of this risk.

(b) **Appendix**

Only limited information is available as a basis for making this decision.

One major shortcoming of conventional financial statements is that they are based on historical information. They give a good indication of the financial position at 30 September 20X5, but some time has already elapsed since that date. During that time the position could have changed dramatically. For example, the company could have won substantial new business, or receivables could have been realised, or inventory could have been sold. Financial statements are only of limited use in predicting the future of a company.

To make an informed decision, the bank would need information about several other factors which are not reflected in the financial statements. The velocity of circulation of working capital, the quality of the company's management and its ability to attract new business will all be crucial in determining whether or not F survives. For example, the decision to invest in additional plant and to increase inventory levels might have been taken as a result of several new orders. The bank would also need to assess the willingness of the loan note holders and other creditors to continue to support the company. For example, there is no information as to how soon the loan notes will become repayable or as to the means by which the company intends to repay the loan.

## Test your understanding 5

KPIs could include:

- number of visitors to website ('hits')
- average length of visit
- % of hits that result in sales
- average sales value per customer
- % down time.

**Test your understanding 6**

| CSFs | KPIs |
|------|------|
| new products | percentage of sales from new products |
| responsive service | percentage on-time delivery (as defined by customer) |
| preferred supplier | customer ranking |
| partnership ventures | number of co-operative operations |

**Internal perspective**

| CSFs | KPIs |
|------|------|
| manufacturing excellence | production cycle time, unit cost |
| design productivity | engineering and material efficiency |
| new product development | introduction times, actual versus plan |

**Learning and growth perspective**

| CSFs | KPIs |
|------|------|
| time to market | introduction times, actual v competition |
| product focus | percentage of products giving 80% of sales |
| manufacturing learning | process time to maturity |
| technology leadership | time to develop next generation products |

**Financial perspective**

| CSFs | KPIs |
|------|------|
| survival | cash flow |
| success | quarterly sales growth and operating income |
| prosperity | increase in market share and ROE |

**Test your understanding 7**

(i) Managers who participate in the setting of standards are more likely to accept and be motivated by the standards than managers on whom standards are imposed. An achievable standard is a better motivator than an unachievable one – although research has been undertaken into how much 'stretch' ought to be built into budgets. When setting standards across an organisation, care should be undertaken to ensure that all managers have equally-challenging standards. Achieving equity in this last regard may be difficult when measures used for different managers and business sectors within an organisation may be very different in character to one another.

(ii) Consideration of rewards involves use of concepts including 'clarity', 'motivation' and 'controllability'. Goal clarity contributes to motivation. For example, a standard of 'achieving 4 product innovations per year' might be a more effective motivator than 'giving a high profile to product innovation'. The actual means of motivation may involve performance-related salary bonuses, an assessment scheme point score or access to promotion channels. Managers will be better motivated if they actually control the factors contributing to achievement of the measures and standards on which their rewards are based.

**Test your understanding 8**

| Dimension | Measures |
|---|---|
| Financial performance. | • Profit per dealer.<br>• Average margins.<br>• Average discount agreed as a % of displayed list price. |
| Competitive performance. | • Local market share (e.g. look at new car registrations by postcode).<br>• National market share (e.g. from published market research data). |
| Quality of service. | • 'Mystery shopper data', i.e. outside consultants visit or ring dealerships posing as customers.<br>• Post-sale satisfaction surveys of customers. |

| Flexibility. | • Post-sale satisfaction surveys of customers to highlight whether they felt sales staff were flexible in getting different vehicle specifications, etc. |
|---|---|
| Resource utilisation. | • Sales per employee.<br><br>• Sales per square metre of available floor space.<br><br>• Average length of time a second hand car (e.g. taken as part-exchange) remains unsold. |
| Innovation. | • Central inspection by senior staff could enable a subjective assessment of local innovation to be made. |

### Test your understanding 9

- Rewards may be linked to a wider variety of performance measures including some non-financial measures.

- Capital investment decisions may be reviewed centrally and judged on the basis of net present value (NPV).

- Managers may be rewarded according to the overall performance of the company rather than their own responsibility centre. This may help goal congruence but may not be motivating if poorly- performing managers are rewarded in the same way as managers who are performing well.

### Test your understanding 10

**To:** Restaurant supervisor
**From:** Management accountant
**Subject:** Performance report
**Date:** 5 April

I enclose a performance report for your department for the three months to the end of March. The aim of this report is to aid in the efficient use of resources by providing information as to which costs differ from their expected level (the original budget figures) and why.

The original budget figures were based on last year's costs. I would like to meet you next Tuesday to discuss whether these figures are sensible targets for this year. I have tried to make the budget more realistic by adjusting the costs upward to reflect the increased use of the restaurant (the flexed budget figures). I would welcome any ideas you have as to:

other adjustments that are necessary to the figures in this report and

how the budgets should be established for future periods.

| | Original budget | Flexed budget | Actual | Variance flexed budget to actual |
|---|---|---|---|---|
| No. of meals served | 32,500 | 39,000 | 39,000 | |
| | $ | $ | $ | $ |
| Controllable costs | | | | |
| Food and other consumables | 97,500 | 117,000 | 111,540 | 5,460 F |
| Labour – hourly paid | 15,000 | 18,000 | 16,500 | 1,500 F |
| Power | 8,500 | 10,200 | 9,250 | 950 F |
| Breakages | 1,000 | 1,200 | 800 | 400 F |
| | 122,000 | 146,400 | 138,090 | 8,310 F |
| Allocated costs – overheads | 21,000 | 21,000 | 24,000 | 3,000 A |
| | 143,000 | 167,400 | 162,090 | 5,310 F |

F = favourable variance    A = adverse variance

The restaurant is evidently being well-managed, with many more meals served than in the same period last year, whilst costs have risen by a small proportion. Following our discussion on Tuesday, the performance report, with any agreed amendments, will be reviewed at the meeting of the management committee on 15 April; please ensure you attend to participate in the discussion and explain the reasons for the variances.

## Test your understanding 11

### Shareholders

- Share price.
- Earnings per share.
- Dividend per share (gross dividend).

### Employees

Earnings in relation to:

- RPI
- general earnings
- similar industrial sectors.

Job security determined by:

- growth
- total complement.

### Management

Remuneration in terms of:

- salary
- share options
- status in terms of turnover and profile of the company
- security in terms of vulnerability to takeover.

### Community

Social costs and benefits in terms of:

- salary
- employment
- pollution
- congestion.

### Customer

- Price
- Quality
- Service.

## Government

- Taxation.

- Inflation.

- Exports (imports).

- Employment.

- Training.

Stakeholder objectives may conflict in many ways. Examples include.

- Management remuneration may conflict with shareholders requirement for profit (EPS and dividends per share).

- The government and community objective of employment may conflict with the shareholders' requirement of increased profitability by modern computerised methods.

- Customer requirement of quality may conflict with the managers' bonus scheme based on short-term profit.

## Market conditions and competitors

In a very competitive market a high performing company may achieve lower levels of profitability compared to an average company in a less competitive market. Performance measures should be compared against:

- targets which take into consideration the competitive conditions in the market

- previous years' performance

- other competitors in the same market where this is possible

- external benchmarks such as the cost of borrowing.

### Test your understanding 12

## Shareholders

Shareholders will want returns in the form of dividends and share price growth. By following policies to promote these requirements NW will maximise shareholder wealth.

The dividend has risen from a proforma 7c in 20X1 to 20c in 20X7. This represents growth of approximately 186% over the period. EPS has grown at a similar rate and the pay-out ratio has remained steady at round about one-third. This policy suggests that dividends are closely linked to profits, and the pay-out ratio should be compared with the rest of the industry.

PAT has increased from 21 in 20X1 to 65 in 20X7, and increase of 210%. Since inflation is only 9% for the period, it would suggest that the needs of the shareholders have been met.

## Consumers

Consumers will be interested in prices, which whilst no longer government defined will be laid down by the regulator (e.g. OFWAT).

We have information about the volume of the market (growing at 2 % pa) and can therefore measure the price rises by removing the volume growth from turnover.

|  | 20X1 | 20X3 | 20X5 | 20X7 |
|---|---|---|---|---|
| Turnover | $450m | $480m | $540m | $620m |
|  |  | $\times \dfrac{1}{1.02^2}$ | $\times \dfrac{1}{1.02^4}$ | $\times \dfrac{1}{1.02^6}$ |
| Turnover in 20X1 volume | 450 | 461 | 498 | 550 |

We can see that after taking out the growth, prices have risen at approximately 3.4% pa, which is above the rate of inflation for the period (1.4%).

Whether or not this is justified depends on factors such as where the money has been spent. Has it gone into capital expenditure (improving the supplies or preventing leaks) or has it been used to increase dividends?

## Workforce

The workforce has fallen by 2,000 from its 12,000 level in 20X1. Whilst it is possible that Cleevemoor was overstaffed, shedding over 15% of the workforce will have affected morale.

Average wages have risen from $8,333 to $8,600 over the period, a rise of just over 3% for the period. Had the workforce enjoyed pay rises in line with inflation they could have expected to earn $9,083 in 20X7. This means they are actually worse off in real terms. Without more information (e.g. skills mix of labour force, full/part-time employees) it is hard to comment, but the increased profitability of NW does not appear to have been passed on to them.

At the same time, the directors' emoluments have nearly quadrupled. We could again do with more information such as the number of directors involved. Part of the increase will be to bring fees in line with the private sector and part of it could be linked in with the share price. However, their fees as a percentage of the whole wage bill have risen from 0.8% to 3.4% over the period.

The figures probably will not include other perks such as share options.

The directors may increasingly find themselves having to justify 'fat cat' salaries.

## Government

## Price stability

Prices have risen by 38% in absolute, and 22% in real, terms which will not be in line with price stability.

Wages have been held down to less than the headline RPI, but at the same time directors' emoluments have risen sharply.

## Economic growth

Efficiency is difficult to measure without more details, but we could calculate various ratios such as ROCE or net margin to measure the situation. Both have shown improvement over the period.

|  | **20X1** | **20X3** | **20X5** | **20X7** |
|---|---|---|---|---|
| Net margin | 5.8% | 7.2% | 10.2% | 12.1% |

Capital expenditure has risen by 275% over the period, which combined with the multiplier effect would be expected to generate a knock-on growth elsewhere in the economy.

# Divisional performance measurement and transfer pricing

**Chapter learning objectives**

Upon completion of this chapter you will be able to:

- explain the meaning of, and calculate from supplied data, return on investment (ROI) in the context of divisional performance appraisal

- discuss the shortcomings and benefits of using ROI for divisional performance appraisal

- explain the meaning of, and calculate from supplied data, residual income (RI) in the context of divisional performance appraisal

- discuss the shortcomings and benefits of using RI for divisional performance appraisal

- compare divisional performance using supplied data and recognise the problems that can arise from the comparison

- explain, using simple numerical examples, the basis for setting a transfer price using variable cost

- explain, using simple numerical examples, the basis for setting a transfer price using full cost

- explain, using simple numerical examples, how transfer prices can distort the performance assessment of divisions and decisions made, including dysfunctional decision making

- explain, using simple numerical examples, the principles behind allowing for intermediate markets.

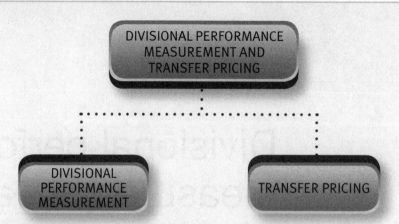

# 1 Divisional performance measurement

## 1.1 Key considerations

When assessing divisional performance it is vital that the measures used match the type of division:

| Type of division | Description | Typical measures |
|---|---|---|
| Cost centre. | • Division incurs costs but has no revenue stream. | • Total cost.<br>• Cost variances.<br>• Cost per unit and other cost ratios.<br>• NFPIs related to quality, productivity, efficiency, etc. |
| Profit centre. | • Division has both costs and revenue.<br>• Manager does not have the authority to alter the level of investment in the division. | All of the above PLUS:<br>• Sales.<br>• Profit.<br>• Sales variances.<br>• Margins.<br>• Market share.<br>• Working capital ratios (depending on the division concerned).<br>• NFPIs related to customer satisfaction. |
| Investment centre. | • Division has both costs and revenue.<br>• Manager does have the authority to invest in new assets or dispose of existing ones. | All of the above PLUS:<br>• ROI.<br>• RI.<br><br>These are discussed in more detail below. |

For each of these care must be taken to assess managers on controllable factors only. So for example, the manager of a cost centre should only be assessed on controllable costs.

## 1.2 ROI

Return on investment (ROI) = $\dfrac{\text{Controllable profit}}{\text{Capital employed}} \times 100\%$

- Controllable profit is usually taken after depreciation but before tax.

- Capital employed includes both non-current assets and working capital.

- Non-current assets might be valued at cost, net replacement cost or net book value (NBV). The value of assets employed could be either an average value for the period as a whole or a value as at the end of the period. An average value for the period is preferable.

### Illustration 1 – Divisional performance measurement

An investment centre has reported a profit of $28,000. It has the following assets and liabilities:

|  | $ | $ |
|---|---|---|
| Non-current assets (at NBV) |  | 100,000 |
| Inventory | 20,000 |  |
| Trade receivables | 30,000 |  |
|  | 50,000 |  |
| Trade payables | 8,000 |  |
|  |  | 42,000 |
|  |  | 142,000 |

- ROI might be measured as: $28,000/$142,000 = 19.7%.

- However, suppose that the centre manager has no responsibility for debt collection. In this situation, it could be argued that the centre manager is not responsible for trade receivables, and the centre's CE should be $112,000. If this assumption is used, ROI would be $28,000/$112,000 = 25.0%.

### Test your understanding 1

Division A of Babbage Group had investments at the year end of $56 million. These include the cost of a new equipment item costing $3 million that was acquired two weeks before the end of the year. This equipment was paid for by the central treasury department of Babbage, and is recorded in the accounts as an inter-company loan.

> The profit of division A for the year was $7 million before deducting head office recharges of $800,000.
>
> **What is the most appropriate measure of ROI for Division A for the year?**

### 1.3 Evaluation of ROI as a performance measure

ROI is a popular measure for divisional performance but has some serious failings which must be considered when interpreting results.

**Advantages**

- It is widely used and accepted.

- As a relative measure it enables comparisons to be made with divisions or companies of different sizes.

- It can be broken down into secondary ratios for more detailed analysis.

**Disadvantages**

- It may lead to dysfunctional decision making, e.g. a division with a current ROI of 30% would not wish to accept a project offering an ROI of 25%, as this would dilute its current figure.

- Different accounting policies can confuse comparisons (e.g. depreciation policy).

- ROI increases with age of asset if NBVs are used, thus giving managers an incentive to hang on to possibly inefficient, obsolescent machines.

- It may encourage the manipulation of profit and CE figures to improve results.

### Illustration 2 – Divisional performance measurement

For the past few years, an investment centre has been making annual profits of $60,000 on average capital employed of $400,000 (NBV as at the end of each year). This performance is expected to continue unless a decision is taken to invest in Project X. Project X would cost $100,000 and have a life of four years. It would make the following additions to the annual cash profits of the division:

| Year | $ |
|---|---|
| 1 | 10,000 |
| 2 | 30,000 |
| 3 | 60,000 |
| 4 | 60,000 |

Based on the firm's current hurdle rate of 12%, the project gives a NPV of $13,682 and so should be accepted. The investment centre manager, however, might evaluate the investment on the basis of how it might affect the centre's reported performance in the short-term, say over the next two years.

Depreciation of Project X assets will be $25,000 each year.

| Year | Profit/loss from Project X $ | Year-end CE Project X $ | Divisional profit $ | Divisional CE $ | ROCE |
|---|---|---|---|---|---|
| Current | – | – | 60,000 | 400,000 | 15.0% |
| 1 | (15,000) | 75,000 | 45,000 | 475,000 | 9.5% |
| 2 | 5,000 | 50,000 | 65,000 | 450,000 | 14.4% |
| 3 | 35,000 | 25,000 | 95,000 | 425,000 | 22.4% |
| 4 | 35,000 | 0 | 95,000 | 400,000 | 23.8% |

The investment centre manager is unlikely to undertake Project X because ROI over the next two years would be reduced. The project would make a loss in Year 1 (negative ROI) and in Year 2 the project's ROI is only 10% (5,000/50,000), which is lower than the ROI for the rest of the investment centre.

### Test your understanding 2

Nielsen Ltd has two divisions with the following information:

|  | Division A $ | Division B $ |
|---|---|---|
| Profit | 90,000 | 10,000 |
| CE | 300,000 | 100,000 |
|  |  |  |
| ROCE | 30% | 10% |

Division A has been offered a project costing $100,000 and giving returns of $20,000. Division B has been offered a project costing $100,000 and giving returns of $12,000. The company's cost of capital is 15%. Divisional performance is judged on ROCE and the ROCE-related bonus is sufficiently high to influence the managers' behaviour.

(a) **What decisions will be made by management if they act in the best interests of their division (and in the best interests of their bonus)?**

(b) **What should the managers do if they act in the best interests of the company as a whole?**

### 1.4 Residual income (RI)

RI is a measure of the profitability of an investment centre after deducting a notional or imputed interest cost. This interest cost is a notional charge for the cost of the capital invested in the division.

RI = Accounting profit – Notional interest on capital

- Accounting profit is calculated in the same way as for ROI.

- Notional interest on capital = the CE in the division multiplied by a notional cost of capital or interest rate.

- The selected cost of capital could be the company's average cost of funds (cost of capital). However, other interest rates might be selected, such as the current cost of borrowing, or a target ROI.

### Illustration 3 – Divisional performance measurement

An investment centre has net assets of $800,000, and made profits before interest of $160,000. The notional cost of capital is 12%.

If performance is measured by RI, the RI for the period is:

|  | $ |
| --- | --- |
| Profit before interest | 160,000 |
| Notional interest (12% × $800,000) | 96,000 |
| RI | 64,000 |

Investment centre managers who make investment decisions on the basis of short-term performance will want to undertake any investments that add to RI.

### Test your understanding 3

An investment centre expects to make a profit of $100,000 next year, and to have CE of $630,000. An opportunity exists to invest in new equipment costing $140,000. The equipment would have a three-year life and would have a residual value of $20,000 at the end of Year 3. The investment would increase the annual cash profits of the investment centre by $56,000. The investment centre's performance is measured by residual income, with notional interest charged at 10% on the mid-year value of net assets.

**Calculate the RI in the first year if the investment is undertaken.**

## 1.5 Evaluation of RI as a performance measure

Compared to using ROI as a measure of performance, RI has several advantages and disadvantages:

### Advantages

- It encourages investment centre managers to make new investments if they add to RI. A new investment might add to RI but reduce ROI. In such a situation, measuring performance by RI would reduce the probability of dysfunctional behaviour.

- Making a specific charge for interest helps to make investment centre managers more aware of the cost of the assets under their control.

- The notional interest charge might be a reasonably good measure of the economic cost of the capital employed in the investment centre. (In contrast ROI has no real significance in financial or economic terms.)

### Disadvantages

- It does not facilitate comparisons between divisions.

- It does not relate the size of a division's profit to the assets employed in order to obtain that profit.

- It is based on accounting measures of profit and CE which may be subject to manipulation.

### Illustration 4 – Divisional performance measurement

An investment centre has net assets of $800,000, and made profits before interest of $160,000. The notional cost of capital is 12%.

An opportunity has arisen to invest in a new project costing $100,000. The project would have a four-year life, and would make cash profits of $40,000 each year.

**Required:**

(a) What would be the average ROI with and without the investment? Would the investment centre manager wish to undertake the investment if performance is judged on ROI in Year 1?

(b) What would be the average annual RI with and without the investment? Would the investment centre manager wish to undertake the investment if performance is judged on RI in Year 1?

To calculate ROI and RI, use the value for CE as at the start of Year 1.

**Solution**

(a) ROI

It is assumed that depreciation is charged on a straight-line basis at $25,000 each year, so that the increase in annual profit with the investment will be $15,000 ($40,000 – $25,000).

|  | Without the investment | With the investment |
|---|---|---|
| Profit | $160,000 | $175,000 |
| Capital employed | $800,000 | $900,000 |
| ROI | 20.0% | 19.4% |

ROI would be lower; therefore the centre manager will not want to make the investment.

(b) RI

|  | Without the investment $ |  | With the investment $ |
|---|---|---|---|
| Profit | 160,000 |  | 175,000 |
| Notional interest | ($800,000 × 12%) 96,000 | ($900,000 × 12%) | 108,000 |
| RI | 64,000 |  | 67,000 |

The investment centre manager will want to undertake the investment because it will increase RI. (This is because the accounting return on the new investment is 15% in Year 1 (= $15,000/$100,000) which is higher than the notional cost of interest.)

**Test your understanding 4**

Two divisions of a company are considering new investments.

|  | Division X | Division Y |
|---|---|---|
| Net assets | $1,000,000 | $1,000,000 |
| Current divisional profit | $250,000 | $120,000 |
|  |  |  |
| Investment in project | $100,000 | $100,000 |
| Projected project profit | $20,000 | $15,000 |
|  |  |  |
| Company's required ROI |  | 18% |

**Assess the projects using both ROI and RI.**

## 1.6 Comparing divisional performance

Divisional performance can be compared in many ways. ROI and RI are common methods but other methods could be used.

- Variance analysis – is a standard means of monitoring and controlling performance. Care must be taken in identifying the controllability of, and responsibility for, each variance.

- Ratio analysis – there are several profitability and liquidity measures that can be applied to divisional performance reports.

- Other management ratios – under this heading would come contribution per key factor and sales per employee or square foot as well as industry specific ratios such as transport costs per mile, brewing costs per barrel, overheads per chargeable hour, etc. The role of NFPIs is often key here.

- Other information – such as staff turnover, market share, new customers gained, innovative products or services developed.

### Test your understanding 5

**Comment on the problems that may be involved in comparing divisional performance.**

## 2 Transfer pricing

### 2.1 Introduction

A transfer price is the price at which goods or services are transferred from one division to another within the same organisation. The transfer price represents 'revenue per unit' to the profit centre 'selling' the good or service and 'cost per unit' to the profit centre 'buying' the good or service.

Transfer pricing is purely an internal bookkeeping exercise, which does not affect the overall profitability of the organisation in the majority of circumstances, but allows the performance of each division to be evaluated on the basis of profit. If set correctly, it can also motivate divisional managers to improve performance. However, a poorly set transfer price can result in sub-optimal decisions thus reducing overall firm profitability.

### Illustration 5 – Transfer pricing

Division A makes components, all of which are transferred to division B for use in making the firm's major product. At present there is no system of transfer pricing.

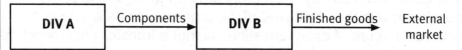

Comment on the current system with respect to the following areas:

(a) Division A's performance appraisal.
(b) Division B's performance appraisal.
(c) Division B's decision making.

**Solution**

(a) Division A has no external revenue so there is no problem treating it as a cost centre and assessing performance accordingly.
The lack of a transfer price does not cause issues for A.

(b) Division B has revenue and costs so should be treated as either a profit centre or an investment centre. Either way, profit will be a key measure of performance.

- Under the current system division B effectively receives the components for free, thus making it appear to be more profitable than it deserves.

- Also division B is not being held responsible for all factors under its control. For example, suppose employees in B wasted some components due to carelessness – this will result in more costs for A to make additional components but there is no adverse impact on B's profit.

- A transfer price should make B's profit more realistic and ensure better cost control.

Note: If, however, division A were to acquire external revenue streams
(e.g. selling components to other firms), then it would also have to be treated as a profit centre. To determine a fair profit for division A the firm would have to introduce a transfer price so A has the cost of components made for B and some corresponding revenue.

(c) The lack of transfer price means that B is not taking into account all of the company's costs when making decisions. For example:

- the price of the final product may be set too low

- new products may be developed that are not commercially viable.

## 2.2 Objectives of a transfer pricing system

- Goal congruence

The decisions made by each profit centre manager should be consistent with the objectives of the organisation as a whole. A common feature of exam questions is that a transfer price is set that does result in sub-optimal behaviour.

- Performance measurement

The performance of each division should be capable of being assessed and a good transfer price would enable each centre to be evaluated on the basis of profit.

- Autonomy

The system used to set transfer prices should seek to maintain the autonomy of profit centre managers. If autonomy is maintained, managers tend to be more highly motivated but sub-optimal decisions may be made.

- Minimising the global tax liability

When a divisionalised company operates entirely within one tax regime the transfer pricing policy will have a minimal impact on the corporate tax bill. However multinational companies can and do use their transfer pricing policies to move profits around the world and thereby minimise their global tax liabilities.

- Recording the movement of goods and services.

In practice, an extremely important function of the transfer pricing system is simply to assist in recording the movement of goods and services.

- A fair allocation of profits between divisions.

Most of the advantages claimed for divisionalisation are behavioural. Insofar as transfer pricing has a material effect on divisional profit it is essential that managers perceive the allocation of corporate profit as being fair if the motivational benefits are to be retained.

A number of these objectives can conflict with each other, and prove difficult to achieve in practice. It is highly unlikely that any one method would meet all the firm's requirements in all circumstances; the best that can be hoped for is a reasonable compromise.

### Test your understanding 6

Division A makes components, all of which are transferred to division B for use in making the firm's major products.

The company is considering introducing a new product that will require a new component. The following data has been estimated for the new product:

- Variable cost of a new component in division A = $10.

- Variable cost of making new product in division B = $27 (excluding any transfer price).

- Final selling price = $50.

Division A currently has spare capacity and fixed costs are not expected to rise as a result of the new product.

(a) **Is the new product worth making from the company perspective?**

(b) **Division A has suggested a transfer price of $25. Comment.**

(c) **Division B has suggested a transfer price of $5. Comment**

## 2.3 Theoretical transfer pricing

### The general rule

The transfer price should be set at marginal cost plus opportunity cost.

This general rule has certain implications.

- When there is a perfectly competitive market for the intermediate product the transfer price should be set at market price. The market price represents marginal cost + opportunity cost.

- When there is surplus capacity in the producing division transfer price should be set at marginal cost as there is no opportunity cost.

- When there are production constraints in the producing division the transfer price should be set at marginal cost + the opportunity cost of using resources to produce for the internal market rather than the next best alternative.

### Illustration 6 – Transfer pricing

Division A of the Robin Group makes a product A22, which it sells externally and to another division in the Robin Group, Division B. Division B uses product A22 as a component in product B46, which it sells externally. There is a perfect external market for both A22 and B46.

Costs and sales prices are as follows:

|  | Division A Product A22 | Division B Product B46 |
|---|---|---|
| Variable production cost | $12 per unit | |
| Further variable costs | | $15 per unit |
| Fixed costs | $200,000 | $300,000 |
| Sales price | $20 per unit | $45 per unit |

Division A can either sell product A22 externally for $20 or transfer the product internally to Division B. Unless the transfer price is $20 or more, Division A will prefer to sell externally, in order to maximise its profit.

Division B can either buy product A22 from external suppliers at $20, or buy internally from Division A. If the transfer price exceeds $20, Division B will prefer to buy externally, in order to minimise its costs and so maximise its profit.

Conclusions:

- The only transfer price at which Division A and Division B will be willing to trade with each other is $20, the external market price.

- At a transfer price of $20, each division would produce and sell up to its capacity. Each division would maximise its profit by making and selling as much as possible, and the total company profit would be maximised. Goal congruence would be achieved.

- In both Divisions A and B, the manager should be motivated to make and sell as much as possible, and to keep costs under control, in order to maximise profit.

- This price would probably be negotiated freely between the managers of Divisions A and B, without head office interference.

- The performance of each profit centre would be measured on a fair basis.

- If company policy is to encourage inter-divisional sales unless there is a good commercial reason for selling or buying externally, the two divisions should trade internally up to the output capacity of the lower-capacity division.

Another way of stating the ideal transfer price is:

|  | $ |
|---|---|
| Marginal cost in Division A | 12 |
| Opportunity cost: contribution foregone from external sale by transferring a unit to Division B: ($20 – $12) | 8 |
| Ideal transfer price (= market price) | 20 |

It can be seen that, in these circumstances, setting the transfer price as the market price satisfies all of the objectives of a transfer pricing system outlined above.

## Test your understanding 7

A company has two profit centres, Centre A and Centre B. Centre A supplies Centre B with a part-finished product. Centre B completes the production and sells the finished units in the market at $35 per unit.

Budgeted data for the year:

|  | Division A | Division B |
|---|---|---|
| Number of units transferred/sold | 10,000 | 10,000 |
|  | $ per unit | $ per unit |
| Materials costs | 8 | 2 |
| Other variable costs | 2 | 3 |
| Annual fixed costs | $60,000 | $30,000 |

> **Calculate the budgeted annual profit of each profit centre and the organisation as a whole if the transfer price for components supplied by Division A to Division B is:**
>
> **(a)  $20.**
>
> **(b)  $25.**
>
> **(c)  Explain why it is necessary to set a transfer price.**
>
> **(d)  If Division A can sell the part-finished components to external customers at $23 per unit, explain why this is the optimum transfer price.**

## 2.4  Practical transfer pricing

In the real word transfer prices are set using the following techniques:

- Market prices.
- Production cost (either variable or full, possibly with a mark-up).
- Negotiation.

### Market Prices

If there is a market price available then this is often seen as the optimum transfer price as all managers concerned with it view it as fair. However, there are many situations when it would be difficult to agree a market price.

### Problems with market-based transfer prices

- There may be no intermediate market price. The product or service might not be readily available on the open market (an example might be a partly-completed car being transferred from one division to another).

- The market price might not be independent. This would occur if the transferring division was in the position of a monopolist both within the company and in the outside market.

- Difficulty in agreeing a source of market prices. Debates will occur over the size, quality, timing and location of internal transfers compared with a range of published prices.

- The need to adjust prices for different volumes. Prices quoted may well not relate to the levels of transfers that are likely to take place. In the same way, the extent of reductions due to saved selling costs will be difficult to estimate.

- Published prices may be fictitious. This is a variation on the previous problem but is typified by those products for which it is customary for a seller to publish a price, then the buyer to negotiate a lower figure.

## Cost based transfer prices

If there is no market price then the transfer price is based on cost. It is generally argued that any transfer price based on cost should be based on standard cost rather than actual cost. A transfer cost based on actual cost would give the transferring division no incentive to control costs as any cost overrun could simply be passed to the buying division.

### Illustration 7 – Transfer pricing

Archer Group has two divisions, Division X and Division Y. Division X manufactures a component X8 which is transferred to Division Y. Division Y uses component X8 to make a finished product Y14, which it sells for $20. There is no external market for component X8.

Costs are as follows:

|  | Division X Component X8 | Division Y Product Y14 |
|---|---|---|
| Variable production cost | $5 per unit | $3 per unit* |
| Annual fixed costs | $40,000 | $80,000 |

* Excluding the cost of transferred units of X8.

The budgeted output and sales for Product Y14 is 20,000 units. One unit of component X8 goes into the manufacture of one unit of Y14.

The profit of the company as a whole will be maximised if Divisions X and Y produce up to their capacity, or to the maximum volume of sales demand. For each extra unit sold, the marginal revenue is $20 and the marginal cost is $8 ($5 + $3); therefore the additional contribution is $12 for each extra unit of Y14 made and sold.

Since there is no external market for component X8, the transfer price will be cost-based. 'Cost' might be marginal cost or full cost. The transfer price might also include a mark-up on cost to allow a profit to Division X.

### The maximum transfer price that the buying division will pay

Division Y has a marginal cost of $3 per unit, and earns revenue of $20 for each unit sold. In theory, Division Y should therefore be prepared to pay up to $17 ($20 – $3) for each unit of X8.

It could be argued, however, that Division Y would not want to sell Product Y14 at all if it made a loss. Division Y might therefore want to cover its fixed costs as well as its variable costs. Fixed costs in Division Y, given a budget of 20,000 units, are $4 per unit. The total cost in Division Y is $7 ($3 + $4). On this basis, the maximum transfer price that Division Y should be willing to pay is $13 ($20 – $7).

### Transfer price = marginal cost

The short-term opportunity cost to Division X of transferring units of X8 to Division Y is the marginal cost of production, $5.

At a transfer price of $5, Division X would be expected to sell as many units of X8 to Division Y as Division Y would like to buy.

However, although marginal cost represents the opportunity cost to Division X of transferring units of X8, it is not an ideal transfer price.

- At a transfer price of $5, Division X would make $0 contribution from each unit transferred. The Division would therefore make a loss of $40,000 (its fixed costs).

- This transfer price would not motivate the manager of Division X to maximise output.

- It is unlikely that the manager of Division X would be prepared to negotiate this price with Division Y, and a decision to set the transfer price at $5 would probably have to be made by head office.

- If Division X is set up as a profit centre, a transfer price at marginal cost would not provide a fair way of measuring and assessing the division's performance.

### Transfer price = marginal cost plus

If the transfer price is set at marginal cost plus a mark-up for contribution, the manager of Division X would be motivated to maximise output, because this would maximise contribution and profit (or minimise the loss).

As indicated earlier, Division Y would want to buy as much as possible from Division X provided that the transfer price is no higher than $17, or possibly $13.

If a transfer price is set at marginal cost plus a mark-up for contribution, the 'ideal' range of prices lies anywhere between $5 and $17. The size of the mark-up would be a matter for negotiation. Presumably, the transfer price that is eventually agreed would be either:

- imposed by head office, or

- agreed by negotiation between the divisional managers, with the more powerful or skilful negotiator getting the better deal on the price.

## Test your understanding 8

A company operates two divisions, Able and Baker. Able manufactures two products, X and Y. Product X is sold to external customers for $42 per unit. The only outlet for product Y is Baker.

Baker supplies an external market and can obtain its semi-finished supplies (product Y) from either Able or an external source. Baker currently has the opportunity to purchase product Y from an external supplier for $38 per unit. The capacity of division Able is measured in units of output, irrespective of whether product X, Y or a combination of both are being manufactured. The associated product costs are as follows:

|  | X $ | Y $ |
|---|---|---|
| Variable costs per unit | 32 | 35 |
| Fixed overheads per unit | 5 | 5 |
| Total unit costs | 37 | 40 |

**Using the above information, advise on the determination of an appropriate transfer price for the sale of product Y from division Able to division Baker under the following conditions:**

**(i) when division Able has spare capacity and limited external demand for product X**

**(ii) when division Able is operating at full capacity with unsatisfied external demand for product X.**

## Illustration 8 – Transfer pricing

Continuing the Archer example in illustration 7:

Discuss the implications of setting the transfer cost at full cost plus.

### Solution

There is an argument that the opportunity cost of transfer, in the absence of an intermediate market, is full cost.

This assumes that, if the selling division decided against making any transfers at all, it would save all costs, both marginal and fixed costs, by shutting down.

In the above example, the full cost for Division X of making component X8 is $7 ($5 variable plus $2 fixed).

At this price, Division X would want to sell as many units as possible to Division Y, and Division Y would buy as many units as it could, subject to the limit on capacity or sales demand.

However, although full cost represents the long-term opportunity cost to Division X of transferring units of X8, it is not an ideal transfer price.

- At a transfer price of $7, Division X would make $0 profit from each unit transferred. If output and sales are less than the budget of 20,000, Division X would make a loss due to the under-absorbed fixed overhead. If output and sales are more than the budget of 20,000, Division X would make a profit due to the over-absorbed fixed overhead. The only ways in which Division X could make a profit are therefore:

  - to hope that sales demand exceeds the budgeted volume, and/or

  - reduce its variable costs and fixed cost expenditures.

- It is unlikely that the manager of Division X would be prepared to negotiate this price with Division Y, and a decision to set the transfer price at $7 would probably have to be made by head office.

- If Division X is set up as a profit centre, a transfer price at full cost would not provide a fair way of measuring and assessing the division's performance.

### Transfer price = full cost plus

If the transfer price is set at full cost plus a mark-up for profit, the manager of Division X would be motivated to maximise output, because this would maximise the division's profit.

As indicated earlier, Division Y would want to buy as much as possible from Division X provided that the transfer price is no higher than $13.

If a transfer price is set at full cost plus a mark-up for profit, the 'ideal' range of prices lies anywhere between $7 and $13. The size of the mark-up would be a matter for negotiation. Presumably, the transfer price that is eventually agreed would be either:

- imposed by head office, or

- agreed by negotiation between the divisional managers, with the more powerful or skilful negotiator getting the better deal on the price.

## Test your understanding 9

Manuco Ltd has been offered supplies of special ingredient Z at a transfer price of $15 per kg by Helpco Ltd, which is part of the same group of companies. Helpco Ltd processes and sells special ingredient Z to customers external to the group at $15 per kg. Helpco Ltd bases its transfer price on total cost plus 25% profit mark-up. Total cost has been estimated as 75% variable and 25% fixed.

**Discuss the transfer prices at which Helpco Ltd should offer to transfer special ingredient Z to Manuco Ltd in order that group profit maximising decisions may be taken on financial grounds in each of the following situations:**

**(i)   Helpco Ltd has an external market for all its production of special ingredient Z at a selling price of $15 per kg. Internal transfers to Manuco Ltd would enable $1.50 per kg of variable packing cost to be avoided.**

**(ii)  Conditions are as per (i) but Helpco Ltd has production capacity for 3,000kg of special ingredient Z for which no external market is available.**

**(iii) Conditions are as per (ii) but Helpco Ltd has an alternative use for some of its spare production capacity. This alternative use is equivalent to 2,000kg of special ingredient Z and would earn a contribution of $6,000.**

## 2.5  Transfer pricing and dysfunctional decision making

A transfer price based on an absorbed total cost can lead to dysfunctional behaviour in the buying division. This is because, although the total cost is made up of fixed and variable cost elements relating to the supplying division, the transfer price per unit is regarded by the receiving division manager as variable.

The receiving division manager, making decisions for his own area of responsibility and thinking primarily of optimising the profits of his own division, treats the transfer price as a variable item in the analysis. The danger is that in situations where the receiving division has spare production capacity, the manager may make the decision not to accept business at a lower selling price than usual, because it would apparently not make a profit or even a contribution for that division. However, for the company as a whole, the special price does exceed the variable costs and in the short-term it would be worth while to accept the business.

The solution to this problem may be to:

- set transfer prices at variable cost but this is unlikely to be acceptable to the selling division

- adopt two-part pricing.

The transfer price is marginal cost, but in addition a fixed sum is paid pa or per period to the supplying division to go at least part of the way towards covering its fixed costs and possibly even to generate a profit.

### Test your understanding 10

Kwaree Inc, producing a range of minerals, is organised into two trading groups – one group handles wholesale business and the other deals with sales to retailers.

One of its products is a moulding clay. The wholesale group extracts the clay and sells it to external wholesale customers as well as to the retail group. The production capacity is 2,000 tonnes per month, but at present sales are limited to 1,000 tonnes wholesale and 600 tonnes retail.

The transfer price agreed is $180 per tonne, in line with the existing external wholesale trade price.

The retail group produces 100 bags of refined clay from each tonne of moulding clay, which it sells at $4 per bag. It would sell a further 40,000 bags if the retail trade price were reduced to $3.20 per bag.

Other data relevant to the operation:

|  | Wholesale group | Retail group |
| --- | --- | --- |
| Variable cost per tonne | $70 | $60 |
| Fixed cost per month | $100,000 | $40,000 |

**You are required to prepare estimated profit statements for the current month for each group and for Kwaree Inc as a whole when producing at:**

**(a) 80% capacity**

**(b) 100% capacity, utilising the extra sales to supply the retail trade.**

**Comment on your results.**

## Chapter summary

```
┌─────────────────────────────┐
│   DIVISIONAL PERFORMANCE     │
│      MEASUREMENT AND         │
│      TRANSFER PRICING        │
└─────────────────────────────┘
```

```
┌──────────────────┐          ┌──────────────────┐
│   DIVISIONAL      │          │    TRANSFER       │
│   PERFORMANCE     │          │    PRICING        │
│   MEASUREMENT     │          │                   │
└──────────────────┘          └──────────────────┘
```

- ROI = EBIT/CE ×
  100%
- RI = EBIT – notional
  interest
- Notional interest =
  CE × cost of capital
- Dysfunctional
  behaviour
  – conflict with
    NPV in the
    short-term
  – manipulation of
    profit/CE
- Alternative
  performance
  measures:
  variances, ratios,
  non-quantitative
  measures.

- Objectives
- General rule =
  variable cost +
  opportunity cost
- Market prices
- Cost based
  – variable cost
  – full cost
- Dysfunctional
  behaviour.

# Test your understanding answers

## Test your understanding 1

Since the new equipment was bought just two weeks before the year end, the most appropriate figure for capital employed is $53 million, not $56 million.

The figure for profit should be the controllable profit of $7 million.

ROI = $7 million/$53 million = 13.2%

## Test your understanding 2

(a)

|  | Division A $000 | Division B $000 |
|---|---|---|
| **Old ROCE** |  |  |
| Profit | 90 | 10 |
| CE | 300 | 100 |
| Old ROCE | 30% | 10% |
| **New ROCE** |  |  |
| Profit | 90 + 20 | 10 + 12 |
| CE | 300 + 100 | 100 + 100 |
| New ROCE | 27.5% | 11% |
| Will manager want to accept project? | No | Yes |

The manager of Division A will not want to accept the project as it lowers her ROCE from 30% to 27.5%. The manager of Division B will like the new project as it will increase their ROCE from 10% to 11%. Although the 11% is bad, it is better than before.

(b) Looking at the whole situation from the group point of view, we are in the ridiculous position that the group has been offered two projects, both costing $100,000. One project gives a profit of $20,000 and the other $12,000. Left to their own devices then the managers would end up accepting the project giving only $12,000. This is because ROCE is a defective decision-making method and does not guarantee that the correct decision will be made.

## Test your understanding 3

Additional annual depreciation = $(140,000 – 20,000)/3 years = $40,000.

Additional annual profit = $56,000 – $40,000 = $16,000.

Additional capital employed (mid-Year 1 NBV) = $140,000 – 50% of $40,000 = $120,000.

|  |  | $ |
|---|---|---|
| Profit | ($100,000 + $16,000) | 116,000 |
| Notional interest | (10% × $(630,000 + 120,000)) | 75,000 |
| RI |  | 41,000 |

## Test your understanding 4

Consider divisional performance:

**Without project**

|  | Division X | Division Y |
|---|---|---|
| Divisional ROI | 25% | 12% |
| Divisional RI ($) | + 70,000 | – 60,000 |
| **With project** |  |  |
| Investment ($) | 1,100,000 | 1,100,000 |
| Profit ($) | 270,000 | 135,000 |
| ROI | 24.5% | 12.3% |
| RI ($) | 72,000 | – 63,000 |
| **Project in isolation** |  |  |
| ROI | 20% | 15% |
| RI ($) | + 2,000 | – 3,000 |

Based on ROI, Division X will reject its project as it dilutes its existing ROI of 25%. This is the wrong decision from the company perspective as the project ROI of 20% beats the company hurdle of 18%.

Likewise Division Y will accept its project, which should be rejected as it fails to hit the company target.

In each case there is a conflict between the company and divisional viewpoints.

RI does not have this problem as we simply add the project RI to the divisional figures.

## Test your understanding 5

Problems may include:

- Divisions may operate in different environments. A division earning a ROI of 10% when the industry average is 7% may be considered to be performing better than a division earning a ROI of 12% when the industry average is 15%.

- The transfer pricing policy may distort divisional performance.

- Divisions may have assets of different ages. A division earning a high ROI may do so because assets are old and fully depreciated. This may give a poor indication of future potential performance.

- There may be difficulties comparing divisions with different accounting policies (e.g. depreciation).

- Evaluating performance on the basis of a few indicators may lead to manipulation of data. A wider range of indicators may be preferable which include non-financial measures. It may be difficult to find non-financial indicators which can easily be compared if divisions operate in different environments.

## Test your understanding 6

(a) Fixed costs are unchanged, so the product can be assessed in the short term by looking at contribution per unit.

Contribution per unit for the company = 50 – (10+27) = $13.

This is positive, so the new product should be made.

(b) With a TP of $25, division B will assess the contribution made by the new product as

Contribution per unit for B = 50 – 27(own costs) – 25(paid to A) = -$2.

This is negative, so B will reject the proposal.

The high transfer price has resulted in a sub-optimal decision by division B.

(c) With a TP of $5, division A will assess the contribution made by the new product as

Contribution per unit for A = 5 – 10 = -$5.

This is negative, so A will reject the proposal.

The low transfer price has resulted in a sub-optimal decision by division A.

**Note:**

The product generates contribution of $13. The transfer price splits this between the two divisions. For goal congruence, both divisions should see themselves earning positive contribution and would thus accept the proposal.

- From B's perspective the TP must be less than $23 to accept the product.

- From A's perspective the TP must be greater than $10 to accept the product.

- Goal congruence could thus be achieved by setting a transfer price of, say, $15 for components.

## Test your understanding 7

(a) If the transfer price is $20.

|  | Division A | Division B | Company as a whole |
|---|---|---|---|
|  | $000 | $000 | $000 |
| External sales | 0 | 350 | 350 |
| Inter-divisional transfers | 200 | 0 | 0 |
|  | 200 | 350 | 350 |
| **Costs** |  |  |  |
| Inter-divisional transfers | 0 | 200 | 0 |
| Other material costs | 80 | 20 | 100 |
| Other variable costs | 20 | 30 | 50 |
| Fixed costs | 60 | 30 | 90 |
| Total costs | 160 | 280 | 240 |
| **Profit** | 40 | 70 | 110 |

(b) If the transfer price is $25.

|  | Division A | Division B | Company as a whole |
|---|---|---|---|
|  | $000 | $000 | $000 |
| External sales | 0 | 350 | 350 |
| Inter-divisional transfers | 250 | 0 | 0 |
|  | 250 | 350 | 350 |

| Costs | | | |
|---|---|---|---|
| Inter-divisional transfers | 0 | 250 | 0 |
| Other material costs | 80 | 20 | 100 |
| Other variable costs | 20 | 30 | 50 |
| Fixed costs | 60 | 30 | 90 |
| Total costs | 160 | 330 | 240 |
| | | | |
| Profit | 90 | 20 | 110 |

Conclusions

- The choice of transfer price does not affect the profit of the organisation as a whole, provided that there is agreement on the quantity of transfers.

- However, the choice of transfer price affects the profitability of the individual profit centres.

(c) It is necessary to set a transfer price because if the part-finished product was transferred at no cost Division A would earn no income. The purpose of setting up a divisional structure in an organisation is to allow operating units autonomy to improve performance. With no income division A would make no profit and would effectively become a cost centre.

(d) If Division A can sell the part-finished product in the external market any transfer price below this level would have to be imposed by head office. This would remove divisional autonomy and affect managerial motivation. An external market price is fair for the purposes of performance evaluation and will result in goal congruence. Division B may argue that certain savings can be made by trading internally rather than externally. For example, there may be savings in packaging costs and in after-sales service. An adjusted market price may therefore be agreed.

### Test your understanding 8

(i) The transfer price should be set between $35 and $38. Able has spare capacity, therefore the marginal costs to the group of Able making a unit is $35. If the price is set above $38, Baker will be encouraged to buy outside the group, decreasing group profit by $3 per unit.

(ii) If Able supplies Baker with a unit of Y, it will cost $35 and they (both Able and the group) will lose $10 contribution from X. So long as the bought-in external price of Y to Baker is less than $45, Baker should buy from that external source. The transfer price should therefore be set at $45.

## Test your understanding 9

The general rule of transfer pricing to assist in profit maximising decisions is to set transfer price equal to marginal cost plus net opportunity cost to the group.

If we apply this rule to the three situations given we have:

(i)   Since Helpco Ltd has an external market, which is the opportunity foregone, the relevant transfer price would be the external selling price of $15 per kg. This will be adjusted to allow for the $1.50 per kg avoided on internal transfers due to packing costs not required.

The transfer price should be $15 – $1.50 = $13.50 per kg.

(ii)  In this situation Helpco has no alternative opportunity for 3,000kg of its special ingredient Z. It should, therefore, offer to transfer this quantity at marginal cost. This is variable cost less packing costs avoided = $9 – $1.50 = $7.50 per kg.

(Note: Total cost = $15 × 80% = $12, Variable cost = $12 × 75% = $9.)

The remaining amount of special ingredient Z should be offered to Manuco Ltd at the adjusted selling price of $13.50 per kg as in (i) above.

(iii) Helpco Ltd has an alternative use for some of its production capacity, which will yield a contribution equivalent to $3 per kg of special ingredient Z ($6,000/2,000kg). The balance of its square capacity (1,000kg) has no opportunity cost and should still be offered at marginal cost.

Helpco Ltd should offer to transfer:

2,000kg at $7.50 + $3 = $10.50 per kg; 1,000kg at $7.50per kg (= MC); and the balance of requirements at $13.50 per kg.

## Test your understanding 10

(a) Wholesale group at 80% capacity

Estimated profit statement for the current month

Transfer price: $180 per tonne

Wholesale group operating at 80% capacity.

|  | Wholesale group $000 | Retail group $000 | Kwaree Ltd $000 |
|---|---|---|---|
| Sales outside the company: |  |  |  |
| 1,000 tonnes @ $180/tonne | 180 |  | 180 |
| 60,000 bags @ $4/bag |  | 240 | 240 |
| Internal transfer of 600 tonnes | 108 | (108) | Nil |
| Less: Costs: |  |  |  |
| Variable |  |  |  |
| 1,600 tonnes @ $70/tonne | (112) |  | (112) |
| 600 tonnes @ $60/tonne |  | (36) | (36) |
| Fixed | (100) | (40) | (140) |
| Profit | 76 | 56 | 132 |

(b) Wholesale group at 100% capacity

Estimated profit statement for the current month

Transfer price: $180 per tonne

Wholesale group operating at 100% capacity.

|  | Wholesale group $000 | Retail group $000 | Kwaree Inc $000 |
|---|---|---|---|
| Sales outside the company: |  |  |  |
| 1,000 tonnes @ $180/tonne | 180 |  | 180 |
| 100,000 bags @ $3.20/bag |  | 320 | 320 |
| Internal transfer of 1,000 tonnes | 180 | (180) | Nil |
| Less: Costs: |  |  |  |
| Variable |  |  |  |
| 2,000 tonnes @ $70/tonne | (140) |  | (140) |
| 1,000 tonnes @ $60/tonne |  | (60) | (60) |
| Fixed | (100) | (40) | (140) |
| Profit | 120 | 40 | 160 |

If it is assumed that the group (divisional) managers of Kwaree Inc are being measured in terms of the profitability of their divisions, then the effect on divisional profits of utilising the spare capacity in the wholesale group can be summarised as follows:

| | Profits in Wholesale group $000 | Profits in Retail group $000 | Profits in Kwaree Inc $000 |
|---|---|---|---|
| 80% capacity | (76) | (56) | (132) |
| 100% capacity | 120 | 40 | 160 |
| Increase/(decrease) | 44 | (16) | 28 |

As a result of utilising spare capacity, the profits of Kwaree would increase by $28,000. However, the wholesale group profits would increase by $44,000, whereas the manager of the retail group would see his division's profits fall by $16,000.

This fall is caused by the reduction in the selling price per bag of the moulding clay, affecting all the sales of the retail group and not only the additional sales. The manager of the retail group, acting independently, is unlikely to accept a decision to increase his production and sales if, as a result, the profit on which he is assessed is likely to decline. The action which he sees to be most beneficial for the retail group, for which he is responsible, is not the action which is in the best interests of the whole company. This is an example of sub-optimisation. Ideally the transfer price should be such that the profits of wholesale and retail groups and the company would all increase as a result of moving from the 80% to 100% capacity.

A transfer price must be adopted which will encourage the higher level of transfer to take place – since Kwaree Inc then makes an additional $28,000 profit. At the moment it will not occur since the retail group can see its profits fall. The only way to encourage the retail group to increase its purchases from the wholesale group is to reduce the transfer price.

**Note:** it is not sufficient to simply determine a new transfer price at which the retail group's profit at full capacity is higher than that at 80% under the old transfer price. Once a price is set, the manager of the retail group will pick the operating level that gives him maximum profit. Thus the new transfer price must ensure that the profits operating at 100% capacity exceed those when operating at 80% capacity under the new transfer price.

# Performance measurement in not-for-profit organisations

## Chapter learning objectives

Upon completion of this chapter you will be able to:

- comment on the problems, with particular reference to not-for-profit organisations and the public sector, of having non-quantifiable objectives in performance management

- describe how performance could be measured in not-for-profit organisations

- comment on the problems, using simple examples, of having multiple objectives in not-for-profit organisations and the public sector

- describe, in outline, value for money (VFM) as a public sector objective.

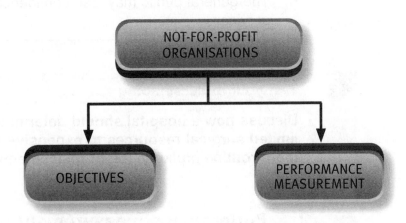

# 1 The problem of non-quantifiable objectives

The not-for-profit sector incorporates a diverse range of operations including national government, local government, charities, executive agencies, trusts and so on. The critical thing about such operations is that they are not motivated by a desire to maximise profit.

Many, if not all, of the benefits arising from expenditure by these bodies are non-quantifiable (certainly not in monetary terms, e.g. social welfare). The same can be true of costs. So any cost/benefit analysis is necessarily quite judgemental, i.e. social benefits versus social costs as well as financial benefits versus financial costs. The danger is that if benefits cannot be quantified, then they might be ignored.

Another problem is that these organisations often do not generate revenue but simply have a fixed budget for spending within which they have to keep (i.e. a capital rationing problem). Value for money ('VFM') is often quoted as an objective here but it does not get round the problem of measuring 'value'.

## Illustration 1 – The problem of non-quantifiable objectives

A hospital might use a cheaper cleaning firm because of difficulties evaluating how well the cleaning is being done. This may create problems in many areas:

- It may indirectly lead to the spread of infection which is costly to eliminate.

- Nursing staff may become demotivated as they are unable to carry out their own work effectively.

- The general public may lose confidence in the quality of the service.

## Test your understanding 1

**Discuss how a hospital should determine whether to allocate limited surgical resources to expensive organ transplants or to more routine hip/knee joint replacements.**

# 2 Performance measurement in not-for-profit organisations

Not-for-profit organisations may have some non-quantifiable objectives but that fact does not exempt them from the need to plan and control their activities.

**Illustration 2 – Performance measurement in not-for-profit organisations**

Education is an example of a non-profit making organisation whose objectives include the provision of a VFM service.

The costs of the service must be compared with budgets but other performance indicators may be used in total for the establishment and within each faculty/department. These measures include:

Overall:

- numbers of students
- amount of research funding received
- proportion of successful students (by grade)
- quality of teaching – as measured by student and inspector assessments
- number of publications by staff.

Faculty:

- cost per student
- cost per examination pass
- staff/student ratios
- students per class
- number of teaching hours per member of staff
- availability of learning resources, e.g. personal computer (PC) per student ratio
- number of library books per student
- average age of library books.

387

**Test your understanding 2**

St Alice's Hospice is a charity which collects funds and donations and utilises these in the care of terminally ill patients. The governing body has set the manager three performance objectives for the three months to 30 June 20X7:

- to achieve a level of donations of $150,000

- to keep administration costs to no more than 8% of donations

- to achieve 80% of respite care requested from the community.

Actual results were as follows:

|  | April | May | June |
|---|---|---|---|
| Donations($) | 35,000 | 65,000 | 55,000 |
| Administration costs ($) | 2,450 | 5,850 | 4,400 |
| Respite care requests (days) | 560 | 570 | 600 |
| Respite care provided (days) | 392 | 430 | 510 |

**Prepare a statement to assist the manager in evaluating performance against objectives and comment on performance.**

# 3 The problem of multiple objectives

Multiple stakeholders in not-for-profit organisations give rise to multiple objectives so there is a need to prioritise/compromise.

Objectives may:

- be difficult to define

- change as a result of the political process

- be achievable in different ways.

**Expandable text**

A further consideration is that the distinction between objectives and ways of achieving these is often misunderstood. For example, one public objective is 'to contain crime within reasonable limits'. One means of achieving that objective is to have police officers patrolling the streets on foot. In fact, police foot patrols are a very inefficient method of containing crime. The use of video surveillance cameras and police response units using fast cars is much more cost effective.

**Illustration 3 –The problem of multiple objects**

A museum may have the following objectives:

- Educating the public.

- Research.

- Preservation and restoration.

One possible conflict here could arise if the decision to charge an entry fee were considered. This would raise funds for research but discourage potential visitors.

**Test your understanding 3**

**Describe the different groups of stakeholders in an international famine relief charity. Explain how the charity may have conflicting objectives and the impact this may have on the effective operation of the organisation.**

## 4 Value for money (VFM)

A common method of assessing public sector performance is to assess VFM. VFM comprises three elements:

- economy

- efficiency

- effectiveness.

Economy – an input measure. Are the resources used the cheapest possible for the quality required.

Efficiency – here we link inputs with outputs. Is the maximum output being achieved from the resources used?

Effectiveness – an output measure looking at whether objectives are being met.

**Illustration 4 – The problem of multiple objects**

Many UK local authorities in the 1970s were judged to be making an inefficient use of the resources available to them. They undertook most of their activities (e.g. council house maintenance, road repairs, maintenance of parks and gardens, etc.) using large numbers of direct council employees. It was often found that the use of obsolete equipment and inefficient working practices (strict job demarcation was widespread) resulted in the operation involving excessive costs.

Financial management initiatives in the 1980s required local authorities to put much of their activities 'out to tender'. Private contractors submit bids in order to undertake programmes of work for the local authorities. If councils retain a direct works department, then that department has to bid in competition with private contractors for most available work.

### Test your understanding 4

A local authority may have 'maintaining an acceptable quality of life for elderly residents' as one of its objectives. It has several means by which it may achieve this objective, including:

- providing 'meals on wheels' (Social Services Department)

- providing a mobile library (Libraries Department)

- maintaining access to and facilities in local parks (Parks Department)

- providing police support to the elderly at home (Police Department)

- providing nursing homes (Housing Department).

**Explain how the local authority would determine whether the service was effective in providing VFM.**

# Chapter summary

```
                    ┌─────────────────────┐
                    │   NOT-FOR-PROFIT     │
                    │    ORGANISATIONS     │
                    └─────────────────────┘
                              ┊
              ┌───────────────┴───────────────┐
        ┌──────────────┐              ┌──────────────────┐
        │  OBJECTIVES  │              │   PERFORMANCE    │
        │              │              │   MEASUREMENT    │
        └──────────────┘              └──────────────────┘
              ┊                              ┊
```

- Non-quantifiable (social costs versus social benefits)
- Multiple
- Subject to political change
- Achievable in different ways.

- Use of performance indicators
- VFM
  - economy
  - efficiency
  - effectiveness.

## Test your understanding answers

### Test your understanding 1

A hospital may have many specific quantifiable objectives such as a minimum waiting time for treatment but may also have non-quantifiable objectives such as improving general healthcare in the area.

The question of deciding priority between different kinds of treatment cannot simply be determined by comparing measurable cost data as there would be many social costs/benefits to consider. By carrying out expensive transplant surgery this may directly benefit relatively few patients but would be life-saving. It might improve knowledge of surgical techniques and life-threatening conditions which could be used to detect and prevent illness in the future. Hip/knee replacements may give mobility to many people who would otherwise be totally reliant on carers.

It may be impossible for a hospital to decide priorities on financial grounds.

### Test your understanding 2

| For 3 months ending 30 June | Total | Objective |
|---|---|---|
| Donations | $155,000 | $150,000 |

| | April | May | June |
|---|---|---|---|
| Administration costs as a % of donations | 7% | 9% | 8% |
| Target | 8% | 8% | 8% |
| Respite care provided | 70% | 75.4% | 85% |
| Target | 80% | 80% | 80% |

Total donations received have exceeded the target for the period. There is no discernable trend and it is possible that there were special fund-raising activities in May which generated greater income. Administration costs have been within the target of 8% in April and June but exceeded the target in May. More information is needed to establish why this occurred. There has been a steady improvement in the level of respite care provided and in June the target was exceeded.

## Test your understanding 3

The stakeholders will include donors, people needing aid, voluntary staff, paid staff, the governments of the countries granting and receiving aid.

There may be conflicting objectives. Donors and people needing aid will want all of the funds to be spent on famine relief. Management staff may require a percentage of the funds to be spent on administration and promotion in order to safeguard the long-term future of the charity.

Donors may have their own views on how donations should be spent which conflict with management staff.

The charity may wish to distribute aid according to perceived need. Governments in receiving countries may have political reasons for distorting information relating to need.

These conflicts may make it difficult to set clear objectives on which all stakeholders agree.

## Test your understanding 4

All of these departmental activities contribute to achievement of the objective. The problem is to find the optimum combination of spending for each of the departments.

- Many elderly people continue to live in their own homes, but are just on the threshold of requiring accommodation in a nursing home. A small cutback in spending in one area (e.g. the withdrawal of a mobile library) may push a lot of elderly people over that threshold. There is then an enormous demand for extra spending by the Housing Department. Nursing home accommodation is an expensive last resort in caring for the elderly.

- An occasional visit by a care worker or a police officer may enable many elderly people to stay in their own homes for much longer than would otherwise be the case.

The key to effectiveness is in finding an optimum pattern of spending to achieve a given objective.

# Questions

## Chapter 1

**Q** **Question 1: Dumbbell Co (ABC)**

Dumbbell Co makes two types of high quality dumbbell – the light (L) and the heavy (H).

Details of the two products are as follows:

|  | L | H |
|---|---|---|
| Budgeted production volume (units) | 10,000 | 5,000 |
| Direct material cost per unit | $8 | $16 |
| Direct labour hours per unit | 1.5 | 1.0 |
| Machine hours per unit | 2 | 3 |

Direct labour costs $8 per hour and labour hours for the period are budgeted at 20,000.

Machine hours for the period are budgeted at 25,000.

Production overheads are estimated at $260,000. An analysis of the production overheads establishes that this cost arises in relation to four activities in the following proportions and has the following associated volumes:

| | Proportion of production overhead costs | Activity Volumes L | H | Total | |
|---|---|---|---|---|---|
| Order handling | 24% | 167 | 83 | 250 | (No of orders processed) |
| Set ups | 38% | 40 | 90 | 130 | (No of set ups) |
| Materials handling | 18% | 67 | 33 | 100 | (No of movements of materials) |
| Quality control | 20% | 287 | 193 | 480 | (No of inspections) |
| | 100% | | | | |

**Required**

(a) Calculate the cost per unit for each product using traditional methods, absorbing overheads on the basis of labour hours.

(b) Calculate the cost per unit using ABC principles.

(c) Drawing upon the information from Dumbbell Co to illustrate your answer, explain why the use of ABC often produces costs that are different to those calculated under more traditional methods.

## Chapter 2

### Question 1: Quarko Co

Quarko Co manufactures two products, Xerxes and Yoraths. No inventories are held.

The following data relates to the budget for each unit of product.

|  | Xerxes | Yorath |
| --- | --- | --- |
| Budgeted sales price | $51 | $36 |
| Direct material costs | $3 | $4 |
| Machining department time | 4 hours | 2 hours |
| Finishing department time | 30 minutes | 30 minutes |
| Variable overheads | $5 | $6 |
| Expected weekly demand (units) | 100 | 100 |

Fixed costs are $13,000 per quarter. Direct materials are known to be in short supply, with only $600 worth being available to purchase each week.

There are currently twelve people working in the machining department (paid $6 per hour) and two in the finishing department (paid $8 per hour). Due to the specialised nature of the work involved in each area, skills are not transferable between the departments. All employees work a 40-hour week.

Assume that there are twelve weeks in the three month period.

### Requirements

(a) Calculate the shortfall (in hours) in each department if production were to reach the expected demand levels at the budgeted selling prices.

(b) Calculate the optimum production plan per week if the company aims to maximise profits, and indicate the budgeted profit for the three month period.

(c) Calculate how much Quarko would be willing to pay for more machining hours.

## Chapter 3

### Question 1: Car Components Inc

Car Components Inc ('CCI') manufactures and sells brake and suspension components used in the car industry. Some components are sold through garages and motor factors to the public but the bulk are sold direct to car manufacturers. In particular, CCI has provided components for many years to Victor Motors, its largest client, who takes 40% of CCI's output. Pricing has always been based on full production cost plus 25%.

Intense competition within the car industry has seen CCI's market share decline and last year it only operated at 70% capacity. CCI's clients have not been immune to industry pressure either and recently Victor Motors was bought out by a multinational manufacturer. The new owners have decided that the component contract would now be put out to tender each year and have made it clear that price, while not the only consideration, would be a major factor in deciding on the preferred supplier.

The management accountant of CCI has put together the following cost schedule for the CCI contract for the next year:

|  |  | $000 |
|---|---|---|
| Materials | Note 1 | 5,000 |
| Labour | Note 2 | 2,000 |
| Variable overheads |  | 1,000 |
| Fixed overheads | Note 3 | 2,000 |
|  |  | **10,000** |

Note 1: There is currently $500,000 of materials inventory. If not used on Victor Motors components this would be sold at a loss of $100,000.

Note 2: Victor Motors components are highly specialised. If the contract was lost, then all of the current staff making Victor components would have to be made redundant. Redundancy costs re estimated to be $500,000 now or $600,000 in one year's time.

Note 3: Fixed overheads consist of unavoidable company wide costs and depreciation. If the contract is lost then machinery would be sold for $600,000 now or $450,000 in one year.

**Required**

(a) Calculate the incremental cost of completing the Victor Motors contract for one more year and suggest a minimum tender price.

(b) Discuss the factors that must be taken into consideration when bidding for the Victor contract.

### Chapter 4

**Q** **Question 1: Access Inc**

Access Inc makes electrically-driven disability scooters aimed at elderly and/or disabled customers. At present wheels and tyres are bought from external suppliers but all other parts are manufactured in-house. The scooters have a strong reputation due mainly to innovative designs, special power units that can be recharged at home and seats that enable easy access for a wide range of disabilities. Access Inc also sells power units to other firms.

Current monthly costs are as follows.

| | Seating Department $ | Power unit Department $ |
|---|---|---|
| Costs | | |
| Direct materials | 9,300 | 4,140 |
| Direct labour | 12,600 | 9,450 |
| Apportioned overheads | 26,700 | 17,200 |
| | 48,600 | 30,790 |
| Production level | 60 units | 90 units |

Note: The power unit department currently produces 90 units a month – 60 being used in Access' own scooters, and 30 being sold externally at $376 each.

A new order has been won to supply an additional 10 scooters per month. However, the directors are considering how best to meet the additional demand:

- Sufficient capacity exists for the company to increase its monthly production to 70 scooters, except that making an extra 10 seating assemblies would require reallocation of labour and other resources from the power unit to the seating department. This would cut power unit output by 20 units per month.

- The alternative course would be to buy 10 seating assemblies from an outside supplier and fit the 10 power units from the present production of 90 units. The cheapest quote for seating assemblies is $610 per assembly.

**Required**

(a) Show whether Access should make or buy the extra seats, stating any assumptions made

**(10 marks)**

(b) Comment on the relevance of the apportioned overhead cost figures to your recommendation.

**(2 marks)**

**(12 marks)**

## Chapter 5

Q **Question 1: Product Tom**

Product 'Tom' is a highly perishable commodity which can be sold on the retail market for $20 per case or for animal food @ $1 per case. Tom costs $10 per case from the wholesale market and is only suitable for sale at the retail market for up to 24 hours after purchase.

Orders for 'Tom' must be placed in advance each day.

Amanda, a market stall owner, has kept the following records of sales of the Tom over the past 50 days.

| Daily sales | Days sold |
|---|---|
| 10 | 15 |
| 20 | 25 |
| 30 | 10 |

**Required:**

(a) Prepare a summary that shows the forecast net margin earned by Amanda for each possible outcome.

(b) On the basis of maximising expected value, advise Amanda.

(c) On the basis of using the maximin and maximax criteria, advise Amanda.

(d) Use minimax regret to advise Amanda.

## Chapter 6

### Q Question 1: Budget behaviour

For many organisations in both the private and public sectors the annual budget is the basis of much internal management information. When preparing and using budgets, however, management and the accountant must be aware of their behavioural implications.

**Required:**

(a) Briefly discuss four purposes of budgets.

**(8 marks)**

(b) Explain the behavioural factors which should be borne in mind and the difficulties of applying them in the process of budgeting and budgetary control.
**(12 marks)**

**(Total: 20 marks)**

## Chapter 7

### Q Question 1: Zero based budgeting

(a) Explain why Zero Based Budgeting might be a useful tool to employ to ensure that budgetary requirements are kept up to date.

**(4 marks)**

(b) Describe the steps needed to be undertaken in order to implement a Zero Based Budgeting system in respect of:

– the questioning of why expenditure needs to be incurred

– how a decision is made as to which activities should be provided with a budget, and

- what questions should be asked when budgeted activities need to be ranked to allocate scarce resources.

**(8 marks)**

(c) Critically assess the use of Zero Based Budgeting as a tool that might be used to motivate employees.

**(6 marks)**

(d) Explain the advantages of encouraging employee participation in budget setting.

**(7 marks)**

**(Total: 25 marks)**

## Chapter 8

**Q** **Question 1: Fashion Co**

Fashion Co, a manufacturer of fashion garments, is investigating whether or not to accept a retailer's order for 100,000 winter coats which will be codenamed Winners.

The following information is available in relation to Winners:

1 The 100,000 garments will be manufactured in batches of 1000 garments. Fashion Co has been offered a price of $50,000 for each batch of 1000 garments supplied to the retailer.

2 New machinery costing $250,000 will have to be purchased for this contract and it is estimated that this machinery will have a value of $25,000 at the end of the contract.

3 A 75% learning curve will apply for the first 60 batches of Winners after which a steady state production time will apply. The labour time per batch after the first 60 batches will therefore be equal to the time for the 60th batch. The cost of the first batch was measured at $15,000. This was for 1500 hours at $10 per hour.

4 Variable overhead will be 30% of the direct labour cost.

5 Given the above learning effect for labour, direct material will be $10,000 per batch for the first ten batches, $7,500 per batch for the next ten and $6,000 per batch thereafter.

6 A new warehouse will have to be rented for three months to store Winners at a cost of $5000 per month

Fashion Co is seeking to achieve a net profit equal to 80% of the sales revenue arising from the manufacture and sale of Winners.

**Required**

a) Prepare detailed calculations to show whether the targeted 80% net profit margin will be achieved.

**(12 marks)**

(b) Calculate what length of time the second batch will take if the actual rate of learning is

(i) 70%

(ii) 80%

**(5 marks)**

(c) Suggest specific steps that Fashion Co could take to improve the net margin calculated above.

**(8 marks)**

## Chapter 9 - Standard costing and basic variances

**Q** **Question 1: Satelite Navigation Systems**

S Inc installs complex satellite navigation systems in cars, at a very large national depot. The standard cost of an installation is shown below. The budgeted volume is 1,000 units installed each month. The operations manager is responsible for three departments, namely: purchasing, fitting and quality control. S Inc purchases navigation systems and other equipment from different suppliers, and most items are imported. The fitting of different systems takes differing lengths of time, but the differences are not more than 25% from the average, so a standard labour time is applied.

Standard cost of installation of one navigation system

|  | $ | Quantity | Price ($) |
|---|---|---|---|
| Materials | 400 | 1 unit | 400 |
| Labour | 320 | 20 hours | 16 |
| Variable overheads | 140 | 20 hours | 7 |
| Fixed overheads | 300 | 20 hours | 15 |
| | | | |
| Total standard cost | 1,160 | | |

The operations department has gathered the following information over the last few months. There are significant difficulties in retaining skilled staff. Many have left for similar but better paid jobs and as a result there is a high labour turnover. Exchange rates have moved and commentators have argued that this will make exports cheaper, but S Inc has no exports and has not benefited. Some of the fitters have complained that one large batch of systems did not have the correct adapters and would not fit certain cars, but this was not apparent until fitting was attempted. Rent, rates, insurance and computing facilities have risen in price noticeably.

The financial results for September to December are shown below.

## Operating statement for S Inc for September to December

|  | September $ | October $ | November $ | December $ | 4 months $ |
|---|---|---|---|---|---|
| Standard cost of actual output | 1,276,000 | 1,276,000 | 1,102,000 | 1,044,000 | 4,698,000 |
| **Variances materials** | | | | | |
| Price | 5,505 F | 3,354 F | 9,520 A | 10,340 A | 11,0 A |
| Usage | 400 A | 7,200 A | 800 A | 16,000 A | 24,400 A |
| **Labour** | | | | | |
| Rate | 4,200 A | 5,500 A | 23,100 A | 24,000 A | 56,800 A |
| Efficiency | 16,000 F | 0 | 32,000 A | 32,000 A | 48,000 A |
| **Variable overheads** | | | | | |
| Expenditure | 7,000 A | 2,000 A | 2,000 F | 0 | 7,000 A |
| Efficiency | 7,000 F | 0 | 14,000 A | 14,000 A | 21,000 A |
| **Fixed overheads** | | | | | |
| Expenditure | 5,000 A | 10,000 A | 20,000 A | 20,000 A | 55,000 A |
| Volume | 30,000 F | 30,000 F | 15,000 A | 30,000 A | 15,000 F |
| Actual costs | 1,234,095 | 1,267,346 | 1,214,420 | 1,190,340 | 4,906,201 |

A = adverse variance      F = favourable variance

### Required

(a) Prepare a report to the operations manager of S Inc commenting on the performance of the company for the four months to 31 December. State probable causes for the key issues you have included in your report and state the further information that would be helpful in assessing the performance of the company.

(15 marks)

(b) Prepare a percentage variance chart for material usage and material price for the four-month period. Explain how this could be used to decide whether or not to investigate the variances.

(10 marks)

(Total: 25 marks)

## Q Question 2: Malcolm Reynolds

Malcolm Reynolds makes and sells a single product, Product Q, with the following standard specification for materials:

|  | Quantity kg | Price per kg $ |
|---|---|---|
| Direct material X | 12 | 40 |
| Direct material Y | 8 | 32 |

It takes 20 direct labour hours to produce one unit with a standard direct labour cost of $10 per hour.

The annual sales/production budget is 2,400 units evenly spread throughout the year. The standard selling price was $1,250 per unit.

The budgeted production overhead, all fixed, is $288,000 and expenditure is expected to occur evenly over the year, which the company divides into 12 calendar months. Absorption is based on direct labour hours.

For the month of October the following actual information is provided.

|  | $ | $ |
|---|---|---|
| Sales (220 units) |  | 264,000 |
| Cost of sales |  |  |
| Direct materials used | 159,000 |  |
| Direct wages | 45,400 |  |
| Fixed production overhead | 23,000 |  |
|  |  | 227,400 |
| Gross profit |  | 36,600 |
| Administration costs | 13,000 |  |
| Selling and distribution costs | 8,000 |  |
|  |  | 21,000 |
| Net profit |  | $15,600 |

Costs of opening inventory, for each material, were at the same price per kilogram as the purchases made during the month but there had been changes in the materials inventory levels, viz.:

|  | 1 October kg | 30 October kg |
|---|---|---|
| Material X | 680 | 1,180 |
| Material Y | 450 | 350 |

Material X purchases were 3,000 kg at $42 each.

Material Y purchases were 1,700 kg at $30 each

The number of direct labour hours worked was 4,600 and the total wages incurred $45,400.

Work-in-progress and finished goods inventories may be assumed to be the same at the beginning and end of October

**Required:**

(a) to present a standard product cost for one unit of product Q showing the standard selling price and standard gross profit per unit

**(3 marks)**

(b) to calculate appropriate variances for the materials, labour, fixed production overhead and sales, noting that it is company policy to calculate material price variances at time of issue to production (i.e. based on usage not purchases)and that the firm does not calculate mix and yield variances

**(12 marks)**

(c) to present a statement for management reconciling the budgeted gross profit with the actual gross profit

**(5 marks)**

**(20 marks)**

## Chapter 10

### Question 1: Paint Mixers Inc

Paint Mixers Inc manufactures and sells a range of paints, including a high performance green paint that will attach to any surface without flaking or peeling.

The purchasing manager is responsible for buying the three ingredients (blue paint, yellow paint and a specialist bonding agent) that are used to make green paint whilst the production manager is responsible for mixing the paints and the volume and quality of green paint that is produced. Both the purchasing manager and the production manager joined the company on January 1st in the current year.

The standard ingredients of the green paint mix are as follows:

|  |  |  | $ |
|---|---|---|---|
| 2 litres blue paint | @ $2.5 per litre | = | 5.0 |
| 7 litres yellow paint | @ $3.0 per litre | = | 21.0 |
| 1 litre bonding agent | @ $10.0 per litre | = | 10.0 |
| Total cost to produce 9 litres of green paint | | = | 36.0 |
| Standard cost of one litre of green paint | | = | 4.0 |

The Managing Director wishes to compare the performance of the purchasing manager and the production manager during their first three months at the company. The Sales Director has commented that sales are significantly up and appear to be on a rising trend, customers being very happy with the quality of the paint they have purchased in the first quarter of the year.

The Finance Director has produced the table below showing the variance results for the first three months of the year.

**Table 1**
F = Favourable    A = Adverse

|  | $ | $ | $ |
|---|---|---|---|
|  | January | February | March |
| Material Price variance | 3000 (A) | 2000 (A) | 1000 (A) |
| Material Mix variance | 2000 (A) | 750 (A) | 100 (F) |
| Material Yield variance | 4000 (A) | 2000 (A) | 50 (F) |
| Total variance | 9000 (A) | 4750 (A) | 850 (A) |

Production activity levels throughout the period varied little and the standard monthly material total cost was approximately $20,000

**Required**

1   Using the information in Table 1:

(i) Explain the significance of the three variances above (the price, mix and yield variances) and assess the extent to which each variance is controllable by the purchasing manager and the production manager.

**(6 marks)**

(ii)  Compare the performance of the purchasing manager and the production manager taking into account the cost variance results and the comments of the sales director.

**(10 marks)**

2   The Finance Director has provided the following data in relation to April's production of 5000 litres of green paint.

**Purchases in April**

| 1000 | litres blue paint | @ $2.6 per litre | = | $2,600 |
|---|---|---|---|---|
| 4000 | litres yellow paint | @ $3.1 per litre | = | $12,400 |
| 500 | litres bonding agent | @ $9.9 per litre | = | $4,950 |
| 5500 | litres |  |  | $19,950 |

**Required**

Calculate the material price, mix and yield variances for April.

**(9 marks)**

**(25 marks)**

## Chapter 11

**Q**

### Question 1: Success Services Co

The following information relates to Success Services Co, a provider of productivity-improving software to small and medium sized businesses.

The company was founded by and is wholly owned by David Speed. David Speed was MD of the business until the end of last year when he handed over control to his son, Michael Speed. Michael has an MBA and at the start of the current year introduced a number of initiatives aimed at giving greater authority and incentives to middle management.

You have been provided with financial information relating to the company in Appendix1. In Appendix 2 you have been provided with non-financial information which is based on the balanced scorecard format.

| Appendix 1: Financial information | Current year | Previous year |
|---|---|---|
| Turnover ($'000) | 4,900 | 3,400 |
| Net profit | 987 | 850 |
| Interest cover | 3x | 5x |
| Average trade receivables days (industry average 40 days) | 42 | 30 |

**Appendix 2: Balanced Scorecard (Extract)**

| Customer perspective | Current year | Previous year |
|---|---|---|
| Number of customers | 910 | 620 |
| % of sales from new software products | 24% | 15% |
| % on time installation of software products | 47% | 65% |
| Average value of software sales | 4180 | 5300 |
| % customers who complained | 4.5% | 1.5% |

| Internal perspective | Current year | Previous year |
|---|---|---|
| Number of new software products launched | 2 | 0 |
| % of tenders for new business won | 38% | 24% |

| Learning and growth perspective | Current year | Previous year |
|---|---|---|
| Average annual no. of lines of code written by each programmer | 4,800 | 4200 |
| Average no. of bugs per 1000 lines of code | 64 | 48 |
| % staff who have completed software development course | 10% | 18% |
| Employee retention rate | 75% | 90% |

**Required**

(a) Using the information in Appendix 1 only, comment on the financial performance of the company (briefly consider growth, profitability, gearing and credit management)

(8 marks)

(b) Explain why non financial information such as that shown in appendix 2 is likely to give a more reliable indication of the likely future prosperity of the company than the financial information given in Appendix 1.

(5 marks)

(c) Using the data from Appendix 2 comment on the performance of the business. Include separate comments on the three perspectives, customer, internal and learning and growth, and provide a concluding comment on the overall performance of the business.

(12 marks)

## Chapter 12

**Q** **Question 1: KDS**

KDS is an engineering company which is organised for management purposes in the form of several autonomous divisions. The performance of each division is currently measured by calculation of its return on investment (ROI). KDS's existing accounting policy is to calculate ROI by dividing the net assets of each division at the end of the year into the operating profit generated by the division during the year. Cash is excluded from net assets since all divisions share a bank account controlled by KDS's head office. Depreciation is on a straight-line basis.

The divisional management teams are paid a performance-related bonus conditional upon achievement of a 15% ROI target. On 20 December 20X5 the divisional managers were provided with performance forecasts for 20X5 which included the following:

| Forecast | Net assets at 31 December 20X5 | 20X5 operating profit | ROI |
|---|---|---|---|
| | $ | $ | |
| Division K | 4,400,000 | 649,000 | 14.75% |
| Division D | 480,000 | 120,000 | 25.00% |

Subsequently, the manager of Division K invited members of her management team to offer advice. The responses she received included the following:

- From the divisional administrator:

  'We can achieve our 20X5 target by deferring payment of a $90,000 trade debt payable on 20 December until 1 January. I should add that we will thereby immediately incur a $2,000 late payment penalty.'

- From the works manager:

  'We should replace a number of our oldest machine tools (which have nil book value) at a cost of $320,000. The new equipment will have a life of eight years and generate cost savings of $76,000 per year. The new equipment can be on site and operational by 31 December 20X5.'

- From the financial controller:

  'The existing method of performance appraisal is unfair. We should ask head office to adopt residual income (RI) as the key performance indicator, using the company's average 12% cost of money for a finance charge.'

**Requirements:**

(a) Compare and appraise the proposals of the divisional administrator and the works manager, having regard to the achievement of the ROI performance target in 20X5 and to any longer term factors you think relevant.

**(12 marks)**

(b) Explain the extent to which you agree or disagree with the financial controller's proposal.

**(8 marks)**

(c) Explain how non-financial performance measures could be used to assess the performance of divisions K and D.

**(5 marks)**

**(Total: 25 marks)**

## Chapter 13

**Q**  **Question 1: Not-for-profit organisations**

**Required:**

(a) Discuss how costing information and principles may be applied in a not-for-profit organisation in the following areas:

(i) the selection of cost units;

(ii) the use of performance measures to measure output and quality;

(iii) the comparison of planned and actual performance.

**(10 marks)**

(b) Discuss the key features of zero-based budgeting and explain how it may be applied in a not-for-profit organisation.

**(8 marks)**

(c) Briefly discuss how activity-based budgeting might be introduced into a manufacturing organisation and the advantages that might arise from the use of activity-based budgeting in such an organisation.

**(7 marks)**

**(Total: 25 marks)**

# Answers

## Chapter 1

**A**   **Answer 1: Dumbbell Co (ABC)**

(a) Traditional cost per unit

|  | Product L | Product H |
|---|---|---|
| Direct materials | 8 | 16 |
| Direct labour | 12 | 8 |
| Total direct costs | 20 | 24 |
| Production overhead ($13 per labour hour) | 19.5 | 13 |
| Total production cost / unit | 39.50 | 37.00 |

(Amounts in $)

(b) ABC cost per unit
   (i) Cost per driver

| Overhead type | Cost driver | % | Total overhead $ | Driver activity volume | Cost per driver |
|---|---|---|---|---|---|
| Order handling | No orders processed | 24 | 62,400 | 250 | 249.6 |
| Set ups | No. set ups | 38 | 98,800 | 130 | 760 |
| Materials handling | Material movements | 18 | 46,800 | 100 | 468 |
| Quality control | No inspections | 20 | 52,000 | 480 | 108.33... |
|  |  | 100 | 260,000 |  |  |

ii) Overheads by product and costs per unit

| Type of overhead | Cost per driver | Product L | | Product H | |
|---|---|---|---|---|---|
|  |  | Activity | Cost | Activity | Cost |
| Order handling | 249.6 | 167 | 41,683.20 | 83 | 20,716.80 |
| Set ups | 760 | 40 | 30,400.00 | 90 | 68,400.00 |
| Materials handling | 468 | 67 | 31,356.00 | 33 | 15,444.00 |
| Inspections | 108.33... | 287 | 31,091.66 | 193 | 20,908.34 |
|  |  |  | 134,530.86 |  | 125,469.14 |
|  |  |  |  |  |  |
| Units produced |  |  | 10,000 |  | 5,000 |
| **Cost per unit** |  |  | **$13.45** |  | **$25.09** |

| | Product L<br>$ | Product H<br>$ |
|---|---|---|
| Direct costs – see (a) above | 20.00 | 24.00 |
| Overheads – see (b) (ii) above | 13.45 | 25.09 |
| | 33.45 | 49.09 |

(c) The overhead costs calculated for Dumbbell Co under traditional costing and ABC are as follows:

| | Product | |
|---|---|---|
| | L | H |
| Volume | 10,000 | 5,000 |
| Traditionally calculated overheads | 19.50 | 13.00 |
| ABC overheads | 13.45 | 25.09 |

The move to Activity Based Costing has resulted in a substantial increase in the overhead costs of Product H whilst the overhead cost of Product L has fallen.

This reflects the views of proponents of ABC who argue that it takes into account the volume of work required to make different products. We can see that Product H, whilst having a lower labour content than Product L (and therefore attracts a modest overhead via a labour hour based recovery rate), requires disproportionate amounts of set up and inspection activity per 1000 units, relative to Product L. The use of ABC ensures that this relatively heavy usage of resources is reflected in the overhead costs.

If we look at the number of activities per 1000 units produced as shown in the table below we see that:

- Product H requires substantially more set ups and inspections than Product L per 1000 units

- The order handling and materials handling costs for the two products however are very similar on a per unit basis – highlighting the significance of the set up and inspection costs which drive up the costs of Product H.

- These greater volumes of set up and inspection activity result in Product H's unit costs more than doubling whilst L's has fallen

| | Order<br>handling | Set ups | Materials<br>Handling | Inspections |
|---|---|---|---|---|
| Product L | 16.7 | 4 | 6.7 | 28.7 |
| Product H | 16.6 | 18 | 6.6 | 38.6 |

# Chapter 2

## Answer 1: Quarko Co

### (a) Department shortfall

|  | Machining | Finishing |
|---|---|---|
| Hours available per week | 40 × 12 = 480 | 40 × 2 = 80 |
| Hours required for production | | |
| Xerxes | 100 × 4 | 100 × 0.5 |
| Yorath | 100 × 2 | 100 × 0.5 |
|  | = 600 | = 100 |
| Shortfall | 120 hours | 20 hours |

### (b) Optimum production plan

Let  $x$  =  number of units of Xerxes produced each week

$y$  =  number of units of Yoraths produced each week

$C$  =  total contribution per week

Contribution per unit is as follows.

|  |  | Xerxes $ | Yorath $ |
|---|---|---|---|
| Selling price |  | 51 | 36 |
| Less : | Variable costs | | |
|  | Direct material | (3) | (4) |
|  | Machining cost | (24) | (12) |
|  | Finishing cost | (4) | (4) |
|  | Variable overheads | (5) | (6) |
| Contribution per unit |  | 15 | 10 |

The objective function is to maximise

$$C = 15x + 10y$$

subject to constraints of

| (1) | Materials | $3x + 4x$ | $\leq$ | 600 |
|---|---|---|---|---|
| (2) | Machining time | $4x + 2y$ | $\leq$ | 480 |
| (3) | Finishing time | $0.5x + 0.5y$ | $\leq$ | 80 |
|  | Non-negativity | $x \geq 0,$ | $y \geq$ | 0 |

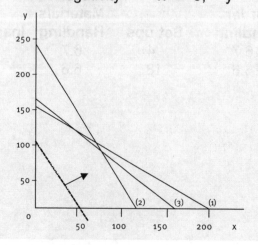

The optimum point is where (2) and (3) cross.

Thus simultaneously

solving $\quad 4x + 2y \quad = 480$

and $\quad 0.5x + 0.5y \quad = 80$

gives

$x = 80$ and $y = 80$

Therefore the optimum production plan is to manufacture 80 of both.

This gives a budgeted profit as follows.

Contribution per week $= (15 \times 80) + (10 \times 80)$

$= \$2,000$

Contribution for period $= \$2,000 \times 12$

$= \$24,000$

Budgeted profit $= \$(24,000 - 13,000)$

$= \$11,000$

## (c) Obtaining extra machining hours

Suppose one extra hour of machining time was available each week.

The optimal solution would now be found at the intersection of

$4x + 2y \quad = 481$

and $\quad 0.5x + 0.5y \quad = 80$

Solving these simultaneously gives $x = 80\frac{1}{2}$ and $y = 79\frac{1}{2}$ and a total contribution of

$C = (15 \times 80\frac{1}{2}) + (10 \times 79\frac{1}{2}) = \$2002.50$

This is an increase of $2.50 over the existing optimal solution. Quarko would thus be willing to pay a premium of $2.50 over the normal cost ($6 per hour) for extra machining hours or $8.50 an hour.

## Chapter 3

### Answer 1: Car Components Inc

(a) Relevant costs are as follows:

|  |  | $000 |
|---|---|---|
| Materials | W1 | 4,500 |
| Labour | W2 | 2,100 |
| Variable overheads |  | 1,000 |
| Fixed overheads | W3 | 150 |
|  |  | **7,750** |

The minimum tender price is thus $7,750,000

(b) The following considerations should be taken into account when putting together a tender:

### Costs

- A calculation of the extra costs involved in continuing the contract is shown in part (a) and would tend to indicate that the minimum price that could be offered is $7,750,000. At this price, however, CCI will not make any contribution to its profit.

- The calculation was based on the estimates provided but any change in these could lead to losses on the contract if this minimum price was quoted.

- The original pricing policy of cost plus 25% allowed CCI a large margin, which may have encouraged the company to ignore possible production inefficiencies.

### Customers

- It is likely, however, that in order to secure this price in the past CCI will have had to reveal its costs to Victor Motors. This will have given the customer considerable power over CCI and is therefore a disadvantage of such a policy.

- However, the specialist nature of Victor Components would suggest that there may be quality issues and other teething problems if Victor awarded the contract to a new supplier.

- CCI has enjoyed a long business relationship with Victor and it is important that it continues to stay on good terms with the Victor management as they are likely to have a major impact on the awarding of the contract. They may also be able to advise on the likely price level of the successful bid

- CCI also needs to find out from Victor management how likely it is that the contract will actually be awarded to different companies each year, or whether there is a strong possibility that the initial successful bid will keep the contract for some time. The incremental costs in part (a) have been based on one year only.

- If CCI were to lose the contract, it may have an impact on its reputation in the car industry and a consequent loss of business from other sources.

### Competition

- It will be important to know what other component manufacturers are likely to be involved in the tender. CCI must try to identify possible rivals and then estimate the general nature of such competitors' costs and therefore possible tender levels.

- Other firms are also likely to have spare capacity, so may bid on the basis of variable rather than full cost. However, competitors may have to commit to significant investment in new machinery and retooling to be able to make Victor's specialist components.

**Other factors**

- Victor currently accounts for 40% of CCI's output. Should the contract be lost CCI would result in operating at only 42% capacity (70 × 60%). It is questionable whether CCI would remain a viable operation under such circumstances.

## Chapter 4

**A**

### Answer 1: Access Inc

**(a) Buy v Make**

| | $ |
|---|---:|
| **The buy alternative** | |
| Cost of bought-in seats: 10 × $610 | 6,100 |
| | ——— |
| | 6,100 |
| | ——— |

**The make alternative**

| | $ |
|---|---:|
| Sales of power units forgone: 20 × $376 | 7,520 |
| Cost savings of making fewer batteries: | |
| $\dfrac{(4,149 + 9,450)}{90} \times 20$ | (3,020) |
| Increase in cost of making seats: | |
| $\dfrac{(9,300 + 12,000)}{60} \times 10$ | 3,650 |
| | ——— |
| | 8,150 |
| | ——— |

**Note**: In either case, 10 external sales of power units will be lost as these are now used internally. You could have included the cost of these lost sales in both of the above calculations. It is quicker to recognise they are a common cash flow and hence not relevant to the decision.

On the basis of the information given the required seats should be bought in rather than made.

The following assumptions have been made:

- The external supplier can produce seats of the same quality as Access Inc.

- Customers will not view bought-in seats as inferior.

- Dependence on an external supplier of extra seating assemblies does not lead to difficulty in maintaining sales volume in the future.

- None of the apportioned overheads are incremental – see answer to part (b) below.

- The average variable costs of production calculated above are constant over the relevant range of output, i.e. no economies of scale or learning effects result from the increased production.

- No goodwill is lost by the reduction in sales of power units to the existing external clients.

- No additional transport costs are encountered.

- Demand will be maintained at the increased level

**(b) Relevance of overhead cost figures**

In the short run apportioned overhead costs are not relevant to the decision, on the assumption that they are all fixed and not variable. Therefore the decision is not affected by their apportionment.

However, in the long run all costs become relevant and, given the relatively high fixed cost/unit charge to the seating department, the decision may need further consideration

## Chapter 5

**A**

### Answer 1: Product Tom

(a)

| Outcome<br>- Demand | Probability | 10 Cases<br>€ | Action<br>- Order<br>20 Cases<br>€ | 30 Cases<br>€ |
|---|---|---|---|---|
| 10 cases | 0.3 | 100 | 10 | (80) |
| 20 cases | 0.5 | 100 | 200 | 110 |
| 30 cases | 0.2 | 100 | 200 | 300 |

(b)

| | | | | |
|---|---|---|---|---|
| Expected<br>net margin | | 100 | 143 | 91 |

If Amanda wishes to maximise E.V. she should order 20 cases per day

(c)

| | | | | |
|---|---|---|---|---|
| Maximin –<br>worst outcomes | | 100 | 10 | (80) |

Amanda should order 10 cases/day

| | | | | |
|---|---|---|---|---|
| Maximax –<br>best outcomes | | 100 | 200 | 300 |

Amanda should order 30 cases/day

(d)     Table of regrets

| Demand | Order 10 | 20 | 30 |
|---|---|---|---|
| | € | € | € |
| 10 | 0 | 90 | 180 |
| 20 | 100 | 0 | 90 |
| 30 | 200 | 100 | 0 |
| Maximum regret | 200 | 100 | 180 |

Amanda should order 20 cases/day

## Chapter 6

**A**   **Answer 1: Budget behaviour**

(a)   An answer should cover four purposes from the six provided below.

**Planning**

The budget is a major short-term planning device placing the overall direction of the company into a quarterly, monthly and, perhaps, weekly focus. It ensures that managers have thought ahead about how they will utilise resources to achieve company policy in their area.

**Control**

Once a budget is formulated a regular reporting system can be established so that the extent to which plans are, or are not, being met can be established. Some form of management by exception can be established so that deviations from plans are identified and reactions to the deviation developed if desirable.

**Co-ordination**

As organisations grow the various departments benefit from the co-ordination effect of the budget. In this role budgets ensure that no one department is out of line with the action of others. They may also hold in check anyone who is inclined to pursue his or her own desires rather than corporate objectives.

**Communication**

The construction of the budget can be a powerful aid to defining or clarifying the lines of horizontal or vertical communication within the enterprise. Managers should have a clearer idea of what their responsibilities are, what is expected of them, and are likely to work better with others to achieve it.

**Performance evaluation**

When budgets are 'tailored' to a department or manager they become useful tools for evaluating how the manager or department is performing. If sales targets are met or satisfactory service provided within reasonable spending limits then bonus or promotion prospects are enhanced.

### Motivation

The value of a budget is enhanced still further if it not only states expectations but motivates managers to strive towards those expectations. This is more likely achieved if a manager has had some involvement in the budget construction, understands its implications and agrees it is fair and controllable by him/her.

(b) If budgetary control is to be successful, attention must be paid to behavioural aspects, i.e. the effect of the system on people in the organisation and vice versa. The following are some of the points which should be borne in mind:

### Budget difficulty

It is generally agreed that the existence of some form of target or expected outcome is a greater motivation than no target at all. The establishment of a target, however, raises the question of the degree of difficulty or challenge of the target. If the performance standard is set too high or too low then sub-optimal performance could be the result. The degree of budget difficulty is not easy to establish. It is influenced by the nature of the task, the organisational culture and personality factors. Some people respond positively to a difficult target others, if challenged, tend to withdraw their commitment.

### Budgets and performance evaluation

The emphasis on achievement of budget targets can be increased, but also the potential for dysfunctional behaviour, if the budget is subsequently used to evaluate performance. This evaluation is frequently associated with specific rewards such as remuneration increases or improved promotion prospects. In such cases it is likely that individuals will concentrate on those items which are measured and rewarded neglecting aspects on which no measurement exists. This may result in some aspects of the job receiving inadequate attention because they are not covered by goals or targets due to the complexity of the situation or the difficulty of measurement.

### Managerial style

The use of budgets in evaluation and control is also influenced by the way they are used by the superior. Different management styles of budget use have been observed, for example:

**Budget constrained** – placing considerable emphasis on meeting budget targets

**Profit conscious** – where a balanced view is taken between budget targets, long-term goals and general effectiveness

**Non-accounting** – where accounting data is seen as relatively unimportant in the evaluation of subordinates.

The style is suggested to influence, in some cases, the superior/ subordinate relationship, the degree of stress and tension involved and the likelihood of budget attainment. The style adopted and its implications are affected by the environment in which management is taking place. For example, the degree of interdependency between areas of responsibility, the uncertainty of the environment and the extent to which individuals feel they influence results are all factors to consider in relation to the management style adopted and its outcomes.

## Participation

It is often suggested that participation in the budget process and discussion over how results are to be measured has benefits in terms of budget attitude and performance. Views on this point are varied however, and the personality of the individuals participating, the nature of the task (narrowly defined or flexible) and the organisation structure influence the success of participation. But a budget when carefully and appropriately established can extract a better performance from the budgetee than one in which these considerations are ignored.

## Bias

Budgetees who are involved in the process from which the budget standards are set are more likely to accept them as legitimate. However, they may also be tempted to seize the opportunity to manipulate the desired performance standard in their favour. That is, they may make the performance easier to achieve and hence be able to satisfy personal goals rather than organisational goals. This is referred to as incorporating 'slack' into the budget. In this context there may be a relationship between the degree of emphasis placed on the budget and the tendency of the budgetee to bias the budget content or circumvent its control.

Any organisational planning and control system has multiple objectives but primary amongst these is encouraging staff to take organisationally desirable actions. It is never possible to predict with certainty the outcomes of all behavioural interaction however it is better to be aware of the various possible behavioural implications than to be ignorant of them.

## Chapter 7

### Answer 1: Zero based budgeting

**Note:** this answer is longer than required in the exam but gives an indication of the potential scope of an answer.

**Introduction**

(a) Zero Based Budgeting (ZBB) is a method of budgeting that re-examines, at each budgeting exercise, whether the budgeted activity is to be funded at any level. Hence, the budgeting exercise begins at a **zero or nil cost base**. It is a device that is particularly useful when an organisation is unsure if its costs are at the most efficient levels. Most efficient costs are not the same as minimum levels, since very low costs might impinge on service or product quality. The purpose of ZBB is to overcome inefficient forms of budgeting that might lead to **slack practices**, which consume more resources than the most effective and efficient organisations face.

(b) There are a series of steps that would ordinarily be taken in order to implement an effective ZBB system.

#### The questioning of why expenditure needs to be incurred

The development of a questioning attitude to activities that incur costs is the first step to ensuring that costs are kept to most efficient levels. It is important to recall that ZBB, in the short term, can only change costs over which the organisation has short-term control. Longer-term, or period costs, can only be changed over a longer horizon. Taxes and other regulatory costs cannot be the focus of ZBB because they are difficult to influence.

Thus ZBB can be immediately effective where costs can be related to identifiable activities. The questions that might emerge in such situations are as follows:

Can costs associated with an activity be isolated? If costs cannot be identified to a particular activity to a degree that provides management with confidence that they can change the costs then there is little point in applying ZBB techniques to the cost.

An even more basic question is to ask how important the activity is to the business and what, if the costs can be identified, is the total cost saving that might result should the activity be stopped. In this respect, it is important to identify effects on costs elsewhere in the business. If the activity to be stopped absorbed fixed costs, then the fixed costs will have to be re-apportioned without absorption to the activity that is to be stopped. Moreover, there may be joint costs such that stopping one activity may have an uncertain effect on joint costs incurred with another activity.

Is the activity in question the cheapest way of providing the service or contribution to production? Thus, it is important not to ask simply if the costs relating to the activity are the most efficient, but are there alternatives that might reduce costs still further and still maintain a given level of service or production.

A more fundamental question about conducting ZBB processes is whether the benefits of employing ZBB outweigh the costs. It is important to appreciate that conducting a ZBB exercise is not a costless process if, as will inevitably be the case, management time is consumed.

### How a decision is made as to which activities should be provided with a budget?

Budgeted activities should be capable of being monitored and controlled. If an activity is recognised as a budget centre, and is going to be subject to a ZBB process, then it is important that management undertake the task of monitoring costs in relation to activity and taking corrective action when appropriate. Thus, if an activity consumes resources and is capable of being monitored and controlled then it should be provided with a budget. This will then make the activity subject to ZBB processes.

'Decision packages' are sometimes referred to in the context of ZBB and activities. These relate to how activities can be described when thinking about how ZBB can be used to judge an activity. There are two types of decision activity:

1   **Mutually exclusive decisions**: When ZBB assessments are made of an activity, alternative courses of action are sometimes benchmarked against existing activities. A choice is then made over which activity might be the preferable course of action. The preferred choice will involve budgeted information, but may also involve other factors such as product quality and service level provision.

2   **Incremental decisions**: ZBB assessments are often related to the level of activity within a budget centre. Thus, there will be a minimum level of activity that provides the essential level of product or service. This is often referred to as the **'base' activity**. Further levels of activity are then incremental and, subject to correctly identifying and isolating the variable costs related to an activity, ZBB assessments can be made separately of both the base and the incremental activities. This division might then provide management with an understanding of the degree of flexibility the organisation has.

### What questions should be asked when budgeted activities need to be ranked to allocate scarce resources?

The allocation of scarce resources is a key management task. Scarce resources will have to be allocated to the activities of a business in terms of providing appropriate labour and materials, along with any other costs related to an activity. Whilst ZBB is most often applied to support activities the technique can also be applied to a production process.

Some sorting of **ranking** will have to be applied in order to determine which activities are funded by a budget against those that are not. The key question for budgeting purposes relates to:

1 defining the appropriate decision package (as described above)

2 the importance of the activity in relation to the organisation in terms of:

   – support for the organisation's objective (for example, maximising shareholder wealth)

   – support for other service or product activities

3 how the ranking system is to be used:

   – are all activities to be funded above a certain rank, or

   – is there a scaling of funds allocated against funds requested as determined by the rank, or

   – is there a combination of methods?

Essentially, a judgement has to be made by management of the benefit of the activity to the organisation. Theoretically, this is best achieved by determining deprival value. In practice, deprival values are difficult tools and some level of arbitrary judgement has to take place in which non-financial factors might play a significant role.

(c) **Critical assessment of the use of Zero Based Budgeting as a tool that might be used to motivate employees**

The motivation of employees is one of the most difficult tasks facing management since the problems are complex and not always referable to financial performance indicators. To the extent that employees are not responsive to financial performance indicators then ZBB is going to be less effective as a device to motivate employees.

The problem of employee motivation is one of achieving goal congruence with the organisational objectives. ZBB can be useful in this respect as a method of tackling the problem of incentivising employees to achieve targeted performance when a clear understanding of the activities and their related decision packages is essential for the management tasks of monitoring and controlling an activity.

**In this respect ZBB has the following advantages**

1 It ensures that only forward looking objectives are addressed. This limits the potential for historical abuses in budget-setting to be established. Employees can be set targets that are consistent with the future objectives of the organisation.

2 Building 'budget slack' is minimised because, in principle, the entire costs of an activity are reviewed at each budget-setting stage. Employees are then set realistic targets that relate to activity levels that are the most efficient.

3   Managers are made to understand, as part of the ZBB process, the activity itself. This reduces tension between those who decide (management) and those who have to implement manager decisions. Claims that management do not really understand the nature of an activity are thus reduced.

4   ZBB encourages flexibility in employees since they know that, potentially, activities may be stopped. Flexibility induces goal consistency by enabling incentive schemes to reflect activity. In other words, employees are more likely to be responsive to management directives if they are aware and trust that the budget setting process encourages and supports payments that are responsive to flexibility.

(d)   **The advantages of encouraging employee participation in budget-setting**

Generally, participative budget-setting will result in:

1   An informed budget-setting process, such that management are aware of the detail of budgeted activities as provided by the people who work daily within the budgeted activity.

2   Avoiding the criticism that budgets are unrealistic.

3   Reducing the adverse effects of budget imposition when difficult management decisions have to be made (e.g. staff reduction).

4   Employees become aware and more involved in the management activities of the organisations. To the extent that they become more aware, then a greater understanding of the needs of the organisation as a whole is reached.

5   Co-ordination within an activity might be improved. If activities are jointly budgeted, or are part of the same process, then co-ordination between activities might be improved.

6   Budgetary slack may be reduced as management become more aware of the operational activities within an activity.

7   Achievable budgets are more likely to be set.

8   When budgets are not met management are more likely to have a deeper knowledge of the operational issues involved.

9   There is less risk that budgets will be undermined by subordinates.

## Chapter 8

**A**   **Answer 1: Fashion Co**

(a)

|  |  | $ | $ |
|---|---|---|---|
|  | 100 batches |  |  |
| Sales | @ $50,000 |  | 5,000,000 |
| Costs: |  |  |  |
| Direct materials | W1 | 655,000 |  |
| Direct labour | W2 | 229,460 |  |
| Variable overhead | W3 | 68,838 |  |
| Rent |  | 15,000 |  |
| Depreciation |  | 225,000 |  |
|  |  |  | (1,193,298) |
| Net profit |  |  | 3,806,702 |
| Net margin |  |  | 76.13% |

The targeted net profit margin of 80% of sales will not be achieved.

**Workings**

(1)   Direct materials

|  | $ |
|---|---|
| First 10 @ $10,000 | 100,000 |
| Second 10 @ $7,500 | 75,000 |
| Remaining 80 @ $6,000 | 480,000 |
| Total | 655,000 |

(2)   Direct labour

All batches after the first 60 will take the same time as the 60th batch. To calculate the time for the 60th batch we need to take the time of 59 batches from the time of 60 batches.

In the learning curve formula $b = \log r / \log 2 = \log 0.75 / \log 2 = -0.415$

| 60 batches | 59 batches |
|---|---|
| Cumulative average time per batch $y = ax^b$ <br> $y = 1{,}500 \times 60^{-0.415}$ <br> $y = 274.3$ hours per batch | Cumulative average time per batch $y = ax^b$ <br> $y = 1{,}500 \times 59^{-0.415}$ <br> $y = 276.2$ hours per batch |
| Total time for 60 batches <br> $= 274.3 \times 60$ <br> $= 16{,}458.0$ hours | Total time for 59 batches <br> $= 276.2 \times 59$ <br> $= 16{,}295.8$ hours |

Time to make the 60th batch = 16,458.0 – 16,295.8 = 162.2hours

Total time for the 100 batches = 16,458 + (162.2 × 40) = 22,946 hours.

Total cost of the first 100 batches = 22,946 × $10 per hour = $229,460

(3)  Variable overhead is 30% of direct labour = 30% × 229,460 = $68,838

(b)  The learning rate measures the relationship between the average time taken between two points when production doubles. Since we:

- can work out the average rate for the two batches by X the time of the first batch by the learning factor

- can then work out the total time taken for the two batches by doubling the average rate

- know the time of **first** batch (1500 hours) we can then calculate the time of the **second** batch by simply deducting the time of the first batch from the average rate.

70%

| | |
|---|---|
| Time for first batch | 1500 |
| Average time taken for two batches @ 70% 1500 × 0.7 | 1050 |
| Therefore total time for two batches 2 × 1050 | 2100 |
| Therefore time taken for second batch (2100 – 1500) | 600 |

80%

| | |
|---|---|
| Time for first batch | 1500 |
| Average time taken for two batches @ 80% 1500 × 0.8 | 1200 |
| Therefore total time for two batches 2 × 1050 | 2400 |
| Therefore time taken for second batch (2400 – 1500) | 900 |

**Note**: The 70% learning rate produces a lower average time (1050 hours) than the 80% learning rate (1200 hours) and hence is the faster learning rate of the two.

(c)  Steps that could be taken to improve the net profit margin include:

- Negotiate a higher price with the retailer. The ability of Fashion Co to negotiate a higher price will depend upon a number of factors including its reputation for quality and delivery and the ease with which the retailer could find alternative suppliers that can deliver garments of the required quality and quantity by the required delivery date.

- Reduce the labour cost by identifying a simpler and faster production method that does not affect the quality or appearance of the finished garment.

- Increase the learning rate. This may be possible via a review of the training procedures and the recruitment of more highly skilled staff. Both these approaches however are likely to involve additional time and costs in the short term.

- Explore the possibility of outsourcing the production to another manufacturer in a lower cost area. This is a major step that would require careful evaluation but it has the substantial attraction - in addition to the possibility of reducing production costs – of eliminating depreciation costs of $225,000 since Fashion Co would no longer have to purchase machinery to satisfy this order.

- Explore the use of substitute materials that would not prejudice the quality or appearance of the garment. Any changes would have to be discussed and agreed with the retailer.

- Investigate ways to reduce the level of variable overhead

- Seek to deliver production direct to the retailer and thereby avoid the storage costs of $15,000.

# Chapter 9

## Answer 1: Satelite Navigation Systems

(a) **Report**

| | |
|---|---|
| **To** | Operations Manager |
| **From** | Management Accountant |
| **Date** | May 2005 |
| **Subject** | Performance of S Inc for four months to 31 December |

### Production and sales

Production and sales were 1,100 units in September and October, 950 units in November and 900 units in December. There has thus been a marked decline over the four-month period. This good performance in the first two months and poor performance in the latter two months may be due to a seasonal variation. If this is the case, it would be good for the budget to reflect the expected seasonal variation, rather than just being a flat 1,000 units per month.

Tutorial note: The output was calculated by taking the standard cost of actual output and dividing by the standard cost per system, i.e. $1,276,000/$1,160 = 1,100 units, $1,102,000/$1,160 = 950 units and $1,044,000/$1,160 = 900 units.

### Materials

The material price variance was favourable for the first two months, and then very adverse for November and December. This was possibly due to the exchange rate movement if the systems are imported. The effect of the exchange rate variations should be quantified. Any remaining adverse variances may be due to inefficient purchasing by the purchasing manager. It should be investigated as to whether there are alternative suppliers for the systems.

The material usage variance was adverse in every month, but was particularly bad in October and even worse in December. In October the variance was $7,200 A and as the material cost was $400 per unit, this meant that an extra $7,200/$400 = 18 units were used on a production of 1,100 units. In December, the variance was $16,000/$400 = 40 extra units on production of 900 units. This variance could possibly be due to the large batch of systems which did not have the correct adaptors. The variance needs careful investigation in order to find out where the excess units were used, which systems and which teams of fitters were involved.

## Labour

The labour rate variance was adverse in September and October and substantially adverse in November and December. Expressing the variances as percentages, for September the standard labour cost was $320 x 1,100 units = $352,000 and thus the variance was $4,200 A/$352,000 = 1.1% A. In November the variance was $5,500 A/$352,000 = 1.6% A. These minor variances could be explained by more overtime than expected being worked, especially as production was high in the first two months. Then things were much worse in the latter two months, for November the variance was $23,100 A/($320 per unit x 950 units) = 7.6% A and in December the variance was $24,000 A/($320 per unit x 900 units) = 8.3%. These substantial variances are almost certainly due to higher wage rates being offered in order to retain staff and lower the labour turnover. It would be very useful to have information on the number of staff leaving the business. Overtime is unlikely to be the cause for the variances in November and December as production was lower than budget.

The labour efficiency variance was $16,000 favourable in September ($16,000/$352,000 = 4.5% F), zero in October and $32,000 adverse in November and December ($32,000 A/$320 per unit x 950 units) = 10.5% A, and $32,000 A/$320 per unit x 900 units) = 11.1% A). It would be expected that some of this variance was due to the large batch of systems which did not have the correct adaptors. This problem was not apparent until fitting was attempted, thus involving the fitters in extra work. If this were the case then we would expect the labour efficiency variance to tie up with the material usage variance, but it does not. We are also told that there is a fluctuation of ± 25% in the fitting times, so even the substantial variances for November and December fall within this range and thus might not represent inefficiency, but simply the fitting of a higher proportion of more labour intensive systems.

It would be useful to have information on the standard times for different systems and the numbers of the different systems, instead of treating all systems alike. The high labour turnover also means that experienced workers are leaving and that new workers are constantly having to be trained. The efficiency of the new workers would be poor to start off with.

## Variable overheads

The variable overhead efficiency variance is based on labour hours and thus simply moves in line with the labour efficiency variance.

The expenditure variance was $7,000 A in September, improved to $2,000 A in October and then $2,000 F in November. It was zero in December. For this variance to have any meaning it must be sub-analysed into its different components in order to determine which ones are being overspent and which ones underspent.

Taking the variable overheads as a whole, the variance gets worse as production levels fall, perhaps indicating that the variable overheads are not entirely variable but may include a fixed element.

## Fixed overheads

The fixed overhead volume variance simply reflects the better than expected production in the first two months and the worse than expected production in the latter two months. The fixed overhead volume variance has no significance as it does not represent a cash flow (if we make more or fewer units than expected then the fixed overheads do not change), but is simply a mathematical device to reconcile budgeted profit with actual profit in an absorption costing system.

The fixed overhead expenditure variance is $5,000 A, $10,000 A, $20,000 A and $20,000 A over the four months and thus shows a worsening pattern, but again in order to understand where things are going wrong we need to sub-analyse the fixed overhead into their different components. We have been told that rent, rates insurance and computing costs have risen in price noticeably; these costs may be regarded as uncontrollable. Managers' attention should be devoted to investigating the controllable costs and reducing any overspend.

## Conclusion

Overall the actual cost was 4.4% worse than expected (($4,906,201 − $4,698,000)/$4,698,000). Whilst this variance might not be regarded as significant, the individual variances in many cases are much bigger and should be investigated. There is a marked decline in performance in November and December. It is important that the individual variances are investigated and their causes understood so that future performance improves.

(b)

| | September $ | October $ | November $ | December $ |
|---|---|---|---|---|
| Standard cost of actual output | 1,276,000 | 1,276,000 | 1,102,000 | 1,044,000 |
| Standard cost per unit | 1,160 | 1,160 | 1,160 | 1,160 |
| Actual units of output | 1,100 | 1,100 | 950 | 900 |
| Standard material usage (x $400) | 440,000 | 440,000 | 380,000 | 360,000 |
| Price % variance | 1.25 F | 0.76 F | 2.51 A | 2.87 A |
| Usage % variance | 0.09 A | 1.6 A | 0.21 A | 4.4 A |

**Percentage variance chart for September to December**

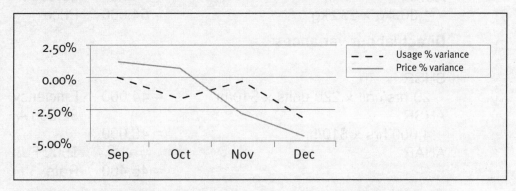

The percentage variance chart can be used to monitor the trend of variances. Significant variances may be identified by setting a control limit. If variances exceed the control limit then action is taken. Alternatively variances which show a worrying trend, such as the material usage variance for S limited, may be investigated before the variance exceeds the control limit.

**Answer 2: Malcolm Reynolds**

(a) **Standard product cost**

| | $ | $ |
|---|---|---|
| Standard selling price | | 1,250 |
| Material X 12 kg @ $40/kg | 480 | |
| Material Y 8 kg @ $32/kg | 256 | |
| Direct labour 20 hrs @ $10/hr | 200 | |
| Production overhead (W1) | 120 | |
| | | 1,056 |
| Standard gross profit | | 194 |

### Material X variances

|  |  | $ |  |
|---|---|---|---|
| SQSP | | | Usage |
| 12 kg/unit × 220 units × $40/kg | = | 105,600 | $5,600 F |
| AQSP | | | |
| 2,500 kg (W2) × $40/kg | = | 100,000 | |
| AQAP | | | $5,000 A |
| 2,500 kg × $42/kg | = | 105,000 | Price |

### Material Y variances

|  |  | $ |  |
|---|---|---|---|
| SQSP | | | Usage |
| 8 kg/unit × 220 units × $32/kg | = | 56,320 | $1,280 A |
| AQSP | | | |
| 1,800 kg (W2) × $32/kg | = | 57,600 | |
| AQAP | | | $3,600 F |
| 1,800kg × $30/kg | = | 54,000 | Price |

### Direct labour variances

|  |  | $ |  |
|---|---|---|---|
| SHSR | | | Efficiency |
| 20 hrs/unit × 220 units × $10/hr | = | 44,000 | $2,000 A |
| AHSR | | | |
| 4,600 hrs × $10/hr | = | 46,000 | |
| AHAR | | | $600 F |
| | = | 45,400 | Rate |

### Fixed Overhead Expenditure variance

|  | $ |
|---|---|
| Budgeted Cost (W3) | 24,000 |
| Actual Cost | 23,000 |
| | ——— |
| | 1,000 F |
| | ——— |

### Fixed Overhead Volume variance
Units

|  | |
|---|---|
| Budgeted output (2,400 units p.a. ÷ 12 months) | 200 |
| Actual output | 220 |
| | ——— |
| | 20 F |
| × Std Fixed Overhead Cost per unit | x120 |
| | $2,400 F |

### Sales price variance

|  | $ |
|---|---|
| Std selling price | 1,250 |
| Actual selling price ($264,000/220 units) | 1,200 |
| | 50 A |
| × Actual no of units sold | × 220 |
| | $11,000 A |

**Selling volume profit variance**

| Units | |
|---|---:|
| Budgeted sales | 200 |
| Actual sales | 220 |
| | 20 F |
| x Std profit per unit | × 194 |
| | $3,880 F |

(c) **Operating Statement**

| | $ | $ | $ |
|---|---:|---:|---:|
| Budgeted gross profit (W4) | | | 38,800 |
| Sales volume profit variance | | | 3,880 F |
| Standard profit on actual sales | | | 42,680 |
| Sales price variance | | | 11,000 A |
| | | | 31,680 |

| | | | Favourable | Adverse | |
|---|---|---|---:|---:|---:|
| **Cost variances** | | | | | |
| Material X | Usage | | 5,600 | | |
| | Price | | | 5,000 | |
| Material Y | Usage | | | 1,280 | |
| | Price | | 3,600 | | |
| Direct labour | Efficiency | | | 2,000 | |
| | Rate | | 600 | | |
| Fixed Prod | Expenditure | | 1,000 | | |
| overgead | Volume | | 2,400 | | |
| | | | 13,200 | 8,280 | 4,920 F |
| Actual gross profit | | | | | 36,600 |

*Workings*

(W1) Fixed over head per unit = $288,000/2,400 units = $120 per unit

(W2)

| | Material X Kg | Material Y Kg |
|---|---:|---:|
| Op inventory | 680 | 450 |
| + Purchases | 3,000 | 1,700 |
| | 3,680 | 2,150 |
| - Cl inventory | 1,180 | 350 |
| Materials issued/used | 2,500 | 1800 |

(W3) Budgeted fixed overhead per month = $288,000/12 = $24,000

(W4) Budgeted profit = 200 units × $194 = $38,800

## Chapter 10

**A**

### Answer 1: Paint Mixers Inc

1

(i) **Significance and controllability of the variances**

**Material price variance**

This variance indicates whether Paint Mixers Inc has paid more (adverse) or less (favourable) for its materials input than the standard price set for the period. An adverse variance, for example, could be the result of an unexpected increase in raw material prices that has been passed on by their bonding agent suppliers.

Price variances are controllable to the extent that the purchasing manager can periodically review potential sources of supply to ensure that they are sourcing their materials from a competitively priced supplier. With the blue and yellow paints there is likely to be a large number of potential suppliers so purchasing managers should be able to threaten to switch suppliers to get good deals. The company is however in a weaker position in relation to the pricing of bonding agent and may be unable to prevent price rises.

**Material Mix variance**

This variance arises when the ingredients are not mixed in standard proportions and it indicates whether the actual mix is cheaper or costlier than the standard mix. For example, adding more bonding agent (relatively very expensive) and less blue paint (relatively cheap) will increase the cost of the mix. A more expensive mix will produce an adverse variance. The recipe determines the mix and the recipe is determined by the production manager and hence is entirely under the control of the production manager.

**Material yield variance**

A yield variance arises when the output is less or more than the input should have produced and is a measure of the productivity of the manufacturing process. 10 litres of input produces 9 litres of green paint. If more than 9 litres of green paint is produced from the 10 litres input the variance is favourable. A favourable yield variance can be the result of operational efficiency (eg reduced wastage) or a change in the mix.

The production manager controls the production process and is therefore able to manage the yield. In particular, the production manager should be able to ensure that the appropriate quality of materials are used and that wastage is minimized.

(ii) **Performance of the purchasing manager and the production manager**

**Cost efficiency**

The purchasing manager was responsible for a series of significant adverse material price variances in the first three months of the year which averaged approx 10% of the standard monthly spend.

The adverse variances have steadily declined over the three months (from $3000 to $1000) and if this level of progress is maintained a favourable variance will arise in April. We do not know whether the adverse variances were the result of poor purchasing decisions or the inevitable result of, say, increased commodity prices. The steadily improving trend suggests that the purchasing manager is in control of the situation and that he may have inherited a purchasing environment of rising prices that were not fully reflected in the cost standards. The comments of the Sales Director suggest that the purchasing manager has not sacrificed quality in order to achieve this improving position.

The production manager was also responsible, in his first two months, for significant adverse variances - in relation to both the mix of materials used and the yield achieved. His performance in the first month was exceptionally poor – the adverse mix and yield variances of $6,000 equalled approximately 30% of the standard monthly spend.

The production manager controls both the mix and the production process and must bear responsibility for this initial very poor performance. That said, in month three, the production manager has achieved modest favourable mix and yield variances ($100 and $50), maintaining the improving trend that started in month two. His very poor initial performance may, in part, have been the result of an inadequate induction process or could have reflected a conscious attempt to improve the quality of the output by increasing the quality of the mix. It may also be possible that certain customers requested a different shade of green requiring a change in the mix of blue and yellow paint.

Whatever the background, the very poor yield performance in January suggests that his changes to the mix had very unfortunate consequences in terms of productivity.

**Quality**

The managing director will have been concerned in January and February that the increasing sales and customer satisfaction levels reported by the sales director may have been bought at a high price.

The comment of the sales director however that sales continue to rise suggests that the new production manager – after some initial costly experimentation - has managed to identify a new mix that is both cost efficient and very appealing to customers.

**Overall**

There was cause for concern in January and February over the performance of both new appointments.

The performance of the purchasing manager still continues to be of concern but is on an improving trend, which, if maintained, should ensure that costs are brought fully under control.

The production manager, after a very worrying start, appears now to be delivering green paint using a recipe that is both economical and popular with customers.

**2**

**Variance calculations**

**Material Price Variance**

|  | Standard | Actual | Difference | Actual quantity | Variance |
|---|---|---|---|---|---|
| Blue paint | $2.5 | $2.6 | –0.1 | 1000 | 100 (A) |
| Yellow paint | $3.0 | $3.1 | –0.1 | 4000 | 400 (A) |
| Bonding agent | $10.0 | $9.9 | 0.1 | 500 | 50 (F) |
|  |  |  |  |  | 450 (A) |

**Note**

Compare the standard prices with the actual prices and multiply the difference by the actual amounts bought

**Material Mix Variance**

Standard Mix
a. Blue paint:       $5500 \times 0.2 = 1100$ litres
b. Yellow paint:    $5500 \times 0.7 = 3850$ litres
c. Bonding agent   $5500 \times 0.1 = 550$ litres
                              5500

| Actual mix | Difference | Standard price | | Variance |
|---|---|---|---|---|
| 1000 litres | 100 litres @ | $2.5 | = | $250 (F) |
| 4000 litres | 150 litres @ | $3.0 | = | $450 (A) |
| 500 litres | 50 litres @ | $10.0 | = | $500 (F) |
| 5500 |  |  |  | $300 (F) |

**Note**

1.  Calculate the proportions that make up the standard mix. (2 : 7 : 1) = 0.2 / 0.7 / 0.1.

2.  Apply these proportions to the purchases made in April of 5500 litres to give the standard cost of a standard mix.

3.  Compare the results with the actual mix and × the difference by the standard price to give the mix variance.

**Material Yield variance**

5000 − 4950 = 50 litres X $4 per litre = $200 (F)

**Note**

1.  Calculate standard cost of 1 litre of green paint mix ($36 / 9 litres  = $4 per litre)

2.  Calculate conversion factor (converts standard **input** of 10 litres to standard **output** of 9 litres) i.e. 9 / 10 = 0.9.

3.  Calculate the standard output that **should have been achieved** from the material input (5500 litres × 0.9 = 4950 litres)

4.  Compare the **actual** production of 5000 litres with the standard production of 4950 litres they should have achieved and × the difference by the standard price of $4.0 per litre. (5000 − 4950 = 50 litres × $4 per litre = $200 (F)

Actual production was 5000 litres of green paint

The actual production of 5000 litres should have cost 5000 × $4.0 = $20,000

The overall usage variance was therefore $20,000 − $19,950

= $50 (F)

There are three reasons for the favourable $50 variance:

|  |  | $ |  |
|---|---|---|---|
| • | The price variance | 450 | (A) |
| • | The mix variance | 300 | (F) |
| • | The yield variance | 200 | (F) |
|  | Total variance | 50 | (F) |

## Chapter 11

**A**

### Answer 1: Success Services Co

**(a) Financial analysis**

This data prompts a number of comments.

**Turnover**. This is up substantially, an increase over the previous year of 44%. The new MD has clearly had a significant impact. How has this been achieved?

**Profit**. This is also up, by 16%. However, net profits have grown at a much slower rate than sales and this is reflected in the sharply reduced net profit margin of 20.1%, compared with 25% in the previous year. It appears that the increased turnover may have been "bought" via price reductions and lower margins or a combination of lower prices and increased costs – perhaps increased expenditure on marketing and advertising.

**Gearing**. Interest cover was 5X but has fallen to just 3X. If the company has borrowed at a variable rate it is now substantially more vulnerable to interest rate rises.

**Average receivables days** are up by 12 days – indicating reduced efficiency in chasing up outstanding debts and / or the granting of more generous payment terms to encourage prospective customers.

Overall, significant growth is being achieved – but at the expense of margins, interest cover and extended credit. This is a potentially worrying trend.

### (b) Non- financial information

Financial indicators tell us where the company has been – not necessarily where it is going. They are inevitably backward looking. Furthermore, financial indicators are poor at identifying why performance has improved or declined – they show effects but not causes.

Non financial measures, such as those in the Balanced Scorecard, can provide a better guide to future performance since they measure attributes which are essential to the long term success of a business – e.g. customer satisfaction, new product development, product quality, employee satisfaction and training etc.

Customer perspective is aimed at seeing the business through the eyes of its customers. It uses measures that are judged critical to increasing customer satisfaction.

The Internal perspective considers those key internal processes which the business must master if it is to satisfy customers' needs and flourish. It asks what are the core competencies and critical technologies that are essential to securing market leadership.

Innovation and learning focuses on whether the business can continue to develop and deliver value to its customers. It typically includes measures such as speed to market and employee retention rates.

### (c) Performance of the business

### Customer perspective

Customer numbers

The number of customers has increased by nearly 50%. This is a dramatic increase and suggests that there has been a major promotional drive to recruit new customers. The cost of such promotion may account for part of the reduction in the net profit margin. This recruitment drive may have included some form of new customer incentives such as reduced prices for a limited period and may also have included a relaxation of payment terms

## % of sales from new software products

This metric also reflects a substantial increase, of over 50%, and implies that substantially increased resource has been devoted to new product development. This focus on new development may well have increased costs but has the potential to lay the foundations for a sustainable increase in sales.

## % on-time installation of new products

This metric shows a sharp and worrying fall in the proportion of products that are delivered on time, implying that the increased effort and cost expended on promotion and developing new software products may be being compromised by a failure to meet promised delivery dates.

## Average value of software sales

The average value of software sales has fallen by over 20%. The mix of sales may have changed or, perhaps more likely in view of the reduced margin data, there may have been price reductions to increase sales volume.

## % customers who complained

This metric, showing a tripling in the rate of complaints, suggests that there has been a major failure to meet customer requirements. This data should prompt an urgent review of both product development procedures and customer relationships with a view to:

(a) identifying what went wrong and the steps needed to prevent a recurrence of the development / installation problems and

(b) establishing the general level of customer satisfaction and seeking to repair any damaged relationships

## Internal perspective

The launch of two new products – from a zero base in the previous year – suggests that significant effort has gone into new product launches in the current year.

The two products could have been under development for some time or they could have been initiated and launched within the current year. The launch of these new products – if they were not thoroughly tested to ensure they were bug free – could have been a major contributor to the dramatic increase in the level of customer complaints. If it is found that the new products were a significant contributor to customer complaints the procedures for testing and launch of new products will need to be reviewed.

The tender success rate has increased by just over 50%. This could reflect a number of factors such as better understanding of customer requirements which has been successfully translated into product specifications or – much less encouraging - a decision to tender at lower prices or to offer more challenging delivery dates. The latter interpretation appears more likely in the light of the deterioration in service levels suggested by other indicators.

**Learning and growth perspective**

Programmer output has increased sharply – by some 14%. This has been accompanied however by a worrying 33% increase in the number of bugs per 1000 lines of code. Has the company been selling products that were released prematurely – hence the customer complaints?

The 40%+ fall in the number of development staff who have completed a development course and the 16% deterioration in the employee retention rate is also indicative of increased pressure to "get product out of the door".

This perspective suggests that product quality – and customer satisfaction – is taking second place to a sales drive.

Overall, the company appears to have made a major change in direction under its new MD. Priority appears to have been given to short term sales and profit growth at the expense of customers, product quality, staff, margins, interest cover and liquidity.

The financial data shows growth but has some worrying features – margins, gearing and liquidity.

The balanced scorecard data reveals a dramatic deterioration in service quality and customer and staff satisfaction which suggests that the sales and profit growth is likely to be short lived. Urgent action is required by Michael Speed to ensure that much greater emphasis is given to product quality and customer satisfaction – this may mean longer development times and a reduced rate of sales growth but this is a price that is worth paying.

## Chapter 12

**A**  **Answer 1: KDS**

(a) **Divisional administrator's proposal**

**Effect on 20X5 ROI**

It will have been assumed in arriving at the 31/12/X5 net assets that the debt will have been paid. Reversing this assumption has the effect of increasing liabilities and has no effect on assets, as cash is excluded. Thus net assets will be reduced by $90,000 (to $4,310,000).

Whether the $2,000 late payment penalty is accounted for in 20X5 or 20X6 will depend to some extent on the company's accounting policy. The accruals concept would, however, lean towards it being accounted for in 20X5. Thus operating profits would be reduced by $2,000 (to $647,000).

The new ROI would thus be $\frac{647}{4,310}$ x 100 = 15.01%

Thus the target will have been achieved and bonuses paid. This is, of course, no indication of improved performance, but simply an arithmetical anomaly arising as a result of one side of the transaction being ignored in the calculation. In fact, the finance cost of the late payment is extremely high.

**Longer term effects**

There would be no quantifiable long-term effects, although relationships with the supplier may be adversely affected by the late payment.

**The works manager's proposal**

**Effect on 20X5 ROI**

Assuming no depreciation charge in 20X5, net assets would be increased by the cost of the new assets, $320,000 (to $4,720,000), and operating profits would be unaffected.

The new ROI would thus be $\frac{649}{4,720}$ x 100 = 13.75%

This represents a reduction of ROI in the short term.

**Longer term effects**

In 20X6 and beyond, the full impact of the cost savings and depreciation charge would be felt – operating profits would be increased by a net $(76,000 – 40,000) = $36,000. Net assets value will be increased, but the increase will be smaller each year as the asset is depreciated.

In 20X6, the equipment's own ROI would be

$$\frac{36}{(320 - 40)} \text{ x } 100 = 12.86\%$$

This will still not help the division to achieve its target of 15%, although it does exceed the company's cost of capital and thus may be desirable overall.

However, by the end of 20X7, the equipment WDV will be $(320,000 – 80,000) = $240,000, giving a ROI of 15%, exactly on target. As it increases above this level it will help the division to achieve its overall target.

This illustrates one of the major problems with using book values for assets in performance measures – as the assets get older, they appear to give better performance. This can have the effect of deterring managers from replacing assets even though this may be of benefit in the long term through cost savings (as above), increased productivity etc.

(b) Residual income (RI) is an absolute measure of performance, and is arrived at by deducting a notional interest charge at the company's cost of capital on the net assets. Appraising the two divisions' performance forecasts under this method would have the following results:

| | 20X5 operating profit $ | Interest charge (12% net assets) $ | Residual income $ |
|---|---|---|---|
| Division K | 649,000 | 528,000 | 121,000 |
| Division D | 120,000 | 57,600 | 62,400 |

The performance rankings of the two divisions are now apparently reversed. However, the RIs of the two divisions are not directly comparable – whilst Division K has produced nearly twice the level of RI than that of Division D, the net asset base required to do this is over nine times as large. RI cannot be meaningfully used to compare investments of differing sizes, as ROI can.

One could also question the use of the company's average cost of money in computing the notional interest charge. The two divisions have been set a target well above this - this may be because they are considered riskier than average. If 15% had been used in the computation, Division K would have negative RI, whilst Division D has positive RI - reflecting the same information as the ROI, that K is not achieving its target return.

The RI uses the same principles for establishing profit and asset values as the ROI, and thus shares the same problems. As assets get older and their WDV falls, the imputed interest falls and RI rises.

However, RI can be of greater benefit than ROI in management decision making. Management may only feel inclined to undertake new investment if doing so improves their performance measure. For example, Division D currently enjoys a ROI of 25% and its manager may only consider new projects that give a return at least as good as this (although this may depend upon the particular structure of the bonus scheme - a fixed bonus provided the target of 15% is reached may not provoke such an attitude).

However, the RI measure will improve with new investment, i.e. increase, provided the investment's returns are at least covering the rate used in computing the notional interest (12% or 15%). This will ensure that projects that are worthwhile from the company's point of view will also be seen as such by the divisional manager (goal congruence).

In summary, RI has advantages and disadvantages over ROI as a performance measure, and both suffer from common valuation problems. One of these can be used as part of a package of performance indicators – market share, productivity, employee satisfaction, technological advancement, etc – but neither is perfect in isolation.

(c) Financial measures taken in isolation are unlikely to tell the whole story of a division's or company's performance. They must be put into context, taking account of the circumstances in which they were achieved – new products being introduced, market changes, technological changes, competitors' moves, availability of resources, etc.

For example, one might question why the two divisions in KDS are apparently performing at such different levels. Whilst quality of management may well be a contributory factor, it is unlikely to explain a difference of over 10 percentage points in ROI.

The age profile of assets used should be considered, as discussed above. Division K may have recently invested in new machinery, possibly in response to technological advances. Not to do so would put them at a disadvantage over their competitors, and thus is for long-term benefit. The industry of the much smaller Division D may be more static, requiring less asset changes.

Performance relative to the market and competitors should be considered (market share, product leadership, etc) and the degree of innovation achieved. Level of complaints received may also be monitored.

of a manager – labour turnover, staff morale, managers' relationships with both subordinates and superiors. The level of job satisfaction felt by employees at all levels is an important consideration in the plan for achievement of company objectives.

## Chapter 13

**A**    **Answer 1: Not-for-profit organisations**

(a) Not-for-profit (NFP) organisations such as charities deliver services that are usually limited by the resources available to them. It may be possible neither to express their objectives in quantifiable or measurable terms, nor to measure their output in terms of the services they deliver. The financial focus in NFP organisations is therefore placed on the control of costs.

(i) **Selection of cost units**

A cost unit for a NFP organisation is a unit of service for which costs are ascertained. These cost units will be used to assess the efficiency and effectiveness of the organisation. The problem for a NFP organisation is that it may not have easily identifiable cost units, and it may not be possible to identify costs with specific outputs. Once appropriate cost units have been identified, however, they can be used to provide cost control information. Examples of costs units used by an NFP organisation are patients, wards, drug treatment programmes, bed-nights and operations, which are all used by a hospital.

(ii) **The use of performance measures to measure output and quality**

Where output for a NFP organisation can be quantified, targets can be set and performance against these targets can be measured. In a university, for example, targets could be set in terms of the number of students graduating with a first-class degree, the number of students in a tutorial group, and the percentage of students who complete a degree course having started it. Information could easily be gathered to enable an assessment of the University's performance compared to agreed, budgeted or imposed targets.

Measuring performance in terms of quality is not so easy. It may be possible to use a surrogate or substitute performance measure if a quality cannot be directly measured. For example, the efficiency of hospital outpatient treatment could be measured by the average length of the queue for treatment. The quality of a University course could be assessed by a composite weighting of responses to individual student questionnaires.

(iii) **Comparison of planned and actual performance**

It is likely that a NFP organisation will have a budget that details expected levels of income (for example from donations and investments) and expenditure (for example on staff wages, continuing programmes, fixed overheads and planned purchases). The use and application of costing principles and information here is no different than in a profit-making organisation. Planned performance can be compared to actual performance, income and cost variances calculated and investigated, and corrective action taken to remedy under-performance.

Where objectives cannot be specified in terms of quantifiable targets, costing information will serve no purpose and assessment of actual performance with planned performance will need to be undertaken from a more subjective perspective.

(b) Zero-based budgeting requires that activities be re-evaluated as part of the budget process so that each activity, and each level of activity, can justify its consumption of the economic resources available. This is in contrast to incremental budgeting, where the current budget is increased to allow for expected future conditions. Zero-based budgeting prevents the carrying forward of past inefficiencies that can be a feature of incremental budgeting and focuses on activities rather than departments or programmes. Each activity is treated as though it was being undertaken for the first time and is required to justify its inclusion in the budget in terms of the benefit expected to be derived from its adoption.

The first step in zero-based budgeting is the formulation of decision packages. These are documents which identify and describe a given activity or group of activities in detail. The base package represents the minimum level of activity that is consistent with the achievement of organisational objectives. Incremental packages describe higher levels of activity which may be delivered if they are acceptable from a cost-benefit perspective.

Following the formulation of decision packages, they are evaluated by senior management and ranked by decreasing benefit to the budgeting organisation. Resources should then be allocated, theoretically at least, to decision packages in order of decreasing marginal utility until all resources have been allocated.

Advantages claimed for zero-based budgeting are that it eliminates the inefficiencies that can arise with incremental budgeting, that it fosters a questioning attitude towards current activities and that it focuses attention on the need to obtain value for money from the consumption of organisational resources.

Value for money is important in not-for-profit (NFP) organisations, where the profit motive found in the private sector is replaced by the need to derive the maximum benefits from limited resources available. Providers of funds to NFP organisations expect to see their cash being used wisely, with as much as possible being devoted to the achievement of organisational aims. For this reason, NFP organisations emphasise cost control and the need for economy in the selection of resources, efficiency in the consumption of resources and effectiveness in the use of resources to achieve organisational objectives (i.e. value for money).

Zero-based budgeting can therefore be applied in a NFP organisation to analyse its activities and the services it provides into decision packages, with a view to ranking them on a cost-benefit basis relative to organisational aims and objectives. In has been noted that zero-based budgeting can be applied more effectively in service-based rather than manufacturing organisations and so it may be ideally suited to a NFP organisation such as a charity.

(c) Activity-based budgeting (ABB) would need a detailed analysis of costs and cost drivers so as to determine which cost drivers and cost pools were to be used in the activity-based costing system. However, whereas activity-based costing uses activity-based recovery rates to assign costs to cost objects, ABB begins with budgeted cost-objects and works back to the resources needed to achieve the budget.

Once the budgeted activity levels have been determined, the demand for resource-consuming activities is assessed from an organisational perspective. The resources needed to provide for these activities are then assessed and action taken to ensure that these resources are available when needed in the budget period.

The budgeted activity levels are determined in the same way as for conventional budgeting in that a sales budget and a production budget are drawn up. ABB then determines the quantity of activity cost drivers (e.g. number of purchase orders, number of set-ups) needed to support the planned sales and production. Standard cost data would be compiled that included details of the activity cost drivers required to produce a product or number of products.

The resources needed to support the budgeted quantity of activity cost drivers would then be determined (e.g. number of labour hours to process purchase orders, number of maintenance hours needed to complete set-ups). This resource need would then be matched against the available capacity (i.e. number of purchase clerks to process purchase orders) to see whether any capacity adjustment were needed.

One advantage suggested for ABB is that organisational resources are allocated more efficiently due to the detailed cost and activity information obtained by implementing an ABB system. Another advantage of ABB is that it avoids the pitfalls of incremental budgeting due to its detailed assessment of the activities and resources needed to support planned sales and production. In ABB the costs of support activities are not seen as fixed costs to be increased by annual increments, but as depending to a large extent on the planned level of activity.

# Index

KAPLAN PUBLISHING